Government House Square, designed by Halcrow in 1984, as seen from Emiri Diwan (see p. 331). Mahmood AlSawan, who contributed many photographs to this book, was born in Gaza in 1929 and, after working at Saudi Aramco and Shell in Qatar, moved to Dubai in 1962 where he served as secretary for the Trucial States Council. A legal translator by training, AlSawan documented Sharjah and other Gulf cities with his Canon 35mm camera. In 2015, he published a selection of his photographs in *A Tale of Beginnings*. AlSawan died in 2021, the year of this book's publication. Mahmood AlSawan.

JVC

BUILDING SHARJAH

BIRKHÄUSER

Note on images:
This project has been made possible for the most part by the personal archives of residents and former residents of Sharjah as well as those of building-industry experts who once worked in the city. These images therefore do not usually conform to the expectations of professional photography. There has been an editorial decision to maintain these images largely in the state they were found, as a testament to the state of a modern city's historical documentation. Sharjah's landscape has been preserved through the eyes of its builders and users.

Note on transliteration and translation:
In transliterating individuals' names from Arabic, we have used the spelling preferred by that person, wherever possible. For this reason, there are shared family names that are transliterated differently for individual family members. For place names in Sharjah, we have sought to use official English spellings provided by the municipality; otherwise we have chosen commonly found spellings. For titles of publications and productions, we have largely depended on the preferences of the various writers and any transliterated titles already published. We have usually opted for transliterated terms that do not include diacritical marks. In terms of translations from Arabic and other languages, we have followed each writer's preferences.

An erstwhile "Smile, You Are in Sharjah" sign along the Dubai–Sharjah road. Sharjah Municipality, courtesy of Juma Al Majid Center for Culture and Heritage.

ابتسم انت في
YOU ARE IN SHARJAH

With contributions by
Ammar Al Attar
Mohamed Elshahed
Roberto Fabbri
Reem Khorshid
Michael Kubo
Hind Mezaina
Abdulla Saad Moaswes
Mona El Mousfy
Hammad Nasar
Sultan Sooud Al Qassemi
Talal Al-Rashoud
Todd Reisz
Alia Al Sabi
K. V. Shamsudheen
Łukasz Stanek
Suheyla Takesh
Deepak Unnikrishnan

Acquisitions Editor:
David Marold, Birkhäuser Verlag, AUT-Vienna

Content and Production Editors:
Angelika Gaal, Bettina R. Algieri, Birkhäuser Verlag, AUT-Vienna

Proof reading:
Ada St. Laurent, AUT-Vienna

Printing:
Holzhausen, die Buchmarke der Gerin Druck GmbH, AUT-Wolkersdorf

Library of Congress Control Number: 2020948457

Bibliographic information published by the German National Library
The German National Library lists this publication in the Deutsche Nationalbibliografie; detailed bibliographic data are available on the Internet at http://dnb.dnb.de.

ISBN 978-3-0356-2276-8
e-ISBN (PDF) 978-3-0356-2277-5

P.O. Box 44, 4009 Basel, Switzerland
Part of Walter de Gruyter GmbH, Berlin/Boston

www.birkhauser.com

Cover:
Two women leaving the Central Souk. Above them is one of the souk's two pedestrian overpasses. Seen in background is the Crescent Petroleum headquarters, designed by Tony Irving and Gordon Jones, Design Construction Group. Regnault & Partners.

Book's first image:
Ramesh Singh in the offices of Page & Broughton, Dubai, 1970. The following year Singh opened his own practice on Al Arouba Street in Sharjah (p. 432).

Book's final image:
Elevation, building for Sheikha Sheikha Sultan Bin Saqr Al Qasimi and Mariam Abdulrahman Saif, Gulf Consulting Office, 1977. The architecture and engineering firm was the first to be established in Sharjah by Emiratis, Ahmed Al Ghroobti and Ali Al Shamsi. There was scant archival material available to feature the firm's contributions to Sharjah. Whatever could be found included documents filed with the municipality for construction of this landmark building at Al Zahra'a Square. Courtesy of Gulf Consulting Office, Sharjah Municipality.

Editors:
Sultan Sooud Al Qassemi
Todd Reisz

Lead researcher:
Reem Khorshid

Graphic designer:
Farah Fayyad

Photo editor:
Ammar Al Attar

Researchers:
Azza Abou Alam
Noura Al Mahmoud

Copy editor:
Eyad Houssami

Image editing:
Edo Smitshuijzen

Administration:
Ahmad Imran Ahmad Kamal
Asma Faizal

Project made possible by
Barjeel Art Foundation, Sharjah

بارجيل
مؤسسة للفنون
BARJEEL
ART FOUNDATION

Acknowledgements
The *Building Sharjah* team thanks: Abdul Kareem A.R., Salma Al Abdouly, Abdul Khaliq Abdulla, Shadi Abdulsalam, Elias Abou Rjeily, Omar Aboulnaga, John Adams, Shereen El Agamy, Farida El Agamy, Zaidi Tanweer Ahmad, Bruce Aitken, Altug Ajun, Necdet Ajun, Hassan Abdallah Mohamed Akram, Waleed Al Dabal, Manar Alawni, Abdul Sattar AlAzzawi, Badr K. Al Badr, Khalid AlBanna, Nujoom Alghanem, Amna Yousif Saleh AlMasoud AlHemeiri, Asma Ali, Hadi Ali, Fatima Mohamed Al Ali, Khalid Al Ali, Ibrahim Aljarwan, Latifa Saeed Abdullah Alketbi, Ihsan Alkhateeb, Hassan Salem Alkhayyal, Louis Allday, Ahmed Y. Almaazmi, Wedad Saeed AlMashgoni, Faten Saeed AlMashgoni, Dana AlMathkoor, Hatem Mohammad AlMosa, Ahmed Amin Ahmed AlMulla, Rana Almutawa, Mohamed Ibrahim AlNakhi, Saif AlNuaimi, Mariam Alnuaimi, Anas Alomaim, Ahmed Khairi Alomari, Zainulabdeen Ahmed Alomari, Maath Alousi, Sheikh Faisal Saoud AlQassimi, Sheikh Rashid Saqer Alqasimi, Monjed Alqenaei, Mahmood M. AlSawan, Sami Alwash, Mustafa Ismail Alzarooni, Samaj Angolkar, George Arbid, Sulaiman Al-Askari, Bariya Ataya, Manal Ataya, Myrna Ayaad, Prema Babu, Lamia Bahaie, Elisabeth R. Baldwin, Humaid Abdelqadder Al Bannah, Saleh Barakat, Devkishan Bhatia, Damien Brook, Brian Broughton, Rosie Bsheer, Pablo Bueno, Khalaf Bukhatir, Jonathan Burr, Miriam Butti, Melis Cankara, Jean-Paul Cassia, Fahad Chalabi, Fadi Chammas, Susan Clark, Gabriel Colboc, Eric Cooley, Barry Cruse, Adib Dada, Rashed Demas, Farrokh Derakhshani, Dheyaa Younis Dheyaa, Viktor Dimas, Shikha Duggal, Rida Ekhail, Rudi Eller, Rania Fahmy, Basil Al Farhan, Baha Fathi, Arlene Feinberg, Josephine Finzi, Mark Furrer, Ismail Abd el Samei Gaafar, Mohamed Gaber, Patricia Maria Garcia Kilroy, Mohamed Fouad Al Ghanem, Mohammad Obaid Ghubash, Rafia Ghubash, Sultan bin Khalifa Al Habtoor, Samir Abdel Hadi, Ali Abdallah Al Halabi, Michael Hamilton-Clark, Carole Harris, Mark Harris, Taimur Hassan, Osama Hassanien, Hanna Hawa, Jamal Hazbun, Fadi Helal, Nadim Helal, Adina Hempel, Khaldoon Heneidy, Sven Hertner, Alex Hoehe, Amy Howard, Jonathan Hubbard-Ford, Peter Hudson, Mostafa Mohammed Al Husseini, Ali El Ibrashi, Fakhar Ul Islam, Joumana Al Jabri, Peter Jackson, Sabha N. Al Jalili, Turath Jamil, Hazem Jamjoum, Khaled Jamous, Kiran Jathal, Neil Jennings, V Rory Jones, Rafeeq Kallil, Randa Kamal, Reem Kambris, Rania Kataf, Fadi A. Khalaf, Mohammed Parvez Khalidi, Nafees Ahmad Khan, Amer Khansaheb, Abdulaziz Al-Khateeb, Ibrahim Al Khawaja, Hassan Khayal, Omar Kholeif, Naif Khoury, Nina Kler, Sham Kolhatkar, Nick Krebs, Haro Levonian, Alejandro Lopez Palma, Daniel Lowe, Jeremy Lyell, Matthew Maclean, Angus MacNab, Jasser Al Madi, Mohamed Mahran, Marianne Makdisi, Najeeb Maktari, Sheikh Butti Bin Suhail Al Maktoum, Ahmed Al-Mallak, Steve Matthews, Kambar Mahmood Al Mazem, Ahmad Al Mazemi, Mey Al Mazroua, Margaret McCowan, Medina Publishing, Sammi Mesmari, Jack Meusey, Jim Meusey, Samar Mikati, Salwa Mikdadi, Saeed Mitrif, Lubna Mobied, Mohamed Moez, Yasser Momen, Karima Momen, Nagwa Galal Momen, Magdy Galal Momen, Robert Montague, Omar Mujaes, Hana Mujaes, Talal Murad, Abdulla Mohammed Al Murad, Mohammed Abdul Haq Musa, Nadia Mohammed Abdul Haq Musa, Mina Naguib, Bahaa Nahawy, Hala Nassar, Asef Nassef, Asma Nasser, Mohamed Riyas Nellissery, Varouj Nerguizian, Catherine Page, Fiona Page, Hazelle Anne Page, Esra Par, Selena Patton, Per Pedersen, Peichär GmbH & Co., Carlos Perez Martinez, Salem Yousef Al Qaseer, Sheikha Bodour bint Sultan Al Qasimi, Sheikha Jawaher Bint Mohammed Al Qasimi, Sheikh Khalid bin Sultan Al Qasimi, Sheikh Faisal bin Khalid bin Mohamed Al Qasimi, Sheikh Salem Faisal Al Qassimi, Sheikh Saud bin Majid Al Qassimi, Sheikha Hana Hamed Al Qassimi, Abdalla Mohamed Al Quraidi, Abdalla Mohamed Al Quraidi, Radisson Blu Resort–Sharjah, Asseel Al-Ragam, Shamsa Ali Rashed, Guillaume Regnault, Mahmoud Mohamed Riad, Matt Saba, Mohamed M. Sadiyyah, Muhammad Saeed, Rasha Saffarini, Noora Saffarini, Nima Sagharchi, Tarik Salama, Balsam Saleh, SALT Archive, Mohamed Saqr, George Sarkis, Hanan Sayed Worrell, Anna Seaman, Ola Seif, Marah Shaaban, Abdallah Al Shamsi, Sharjah Chamber of Commerce and Industry, Sharjah Public Library, Nadia Simeon, Sue Simpson, Moonmoon Singh, Akram Skaik, Huda Smitshuijzen Abifarés, South and Southeast Asian Video Archive, University of Wisconsin–Madison, Mel Stewart, Karim Sultan, Dina Taha, Abdulrahman Taha, Ahmed Taleb, Noor Tannir, Aysha Taryam, Nitin Tavkar, Omar Thawabeh, Richard Thompson, Charlotte Todd, Saeed Al Tunaiji, Obaid Al Tunaiji, Graham Turner, UAE Federal Competitiveness and Statistics Authority, Guillaume Vannier, Jesús Velasco, Pilar Velasco, Bill Woodburn, Naomi Woods, Diaa Younis, Eissa Yousif, Ismail Al Zarooni.

At Sharjah's Al Ittihad Park, municipal workers maintain gardens planted as part of citywide "beautification" efforts, undated. In background: Al Arouba Street overpass above the "Smile, You Are in Sharjah" hillock. Al Saud Co. Building (p. 183), Sharjah Cinema (p. 201), and SNTTA Building (p. 187) mark the horizon. Khaleej Times Archives.

SIEMENS

Nick Ruehl, director, Sharjah office, Fowler Hanley, Inc. (left), and Bahram Danish, Fowler Hanley's locally based aide for administration, translation, and client relations, at the Novotel construction site in Sharjah's Al Khan district, early 1970s.

While we can name some members of the design and development team, we can only provide a photograph of members of the Novotel construction team, early 1970s. Images: Michael Fowler, Fowler Hanley Inc.

Contents

Featured Projects

Appendices

Map of Sharjah, based on one from the mid- to late-1980s, identifies new and old districts, roundabouts, and famous landmarks. Cast across Sharjah is the clear grid of roadways prescribed in Halcrow's master plan (see p. 62). English translations and other landmarks have been added. Names reflect those in use in the 1980s. Dar Al Khaleej Printing & Publishing.

الشارقة، سنة ١٩٨٠
SHARJAH, CIRCA 1980

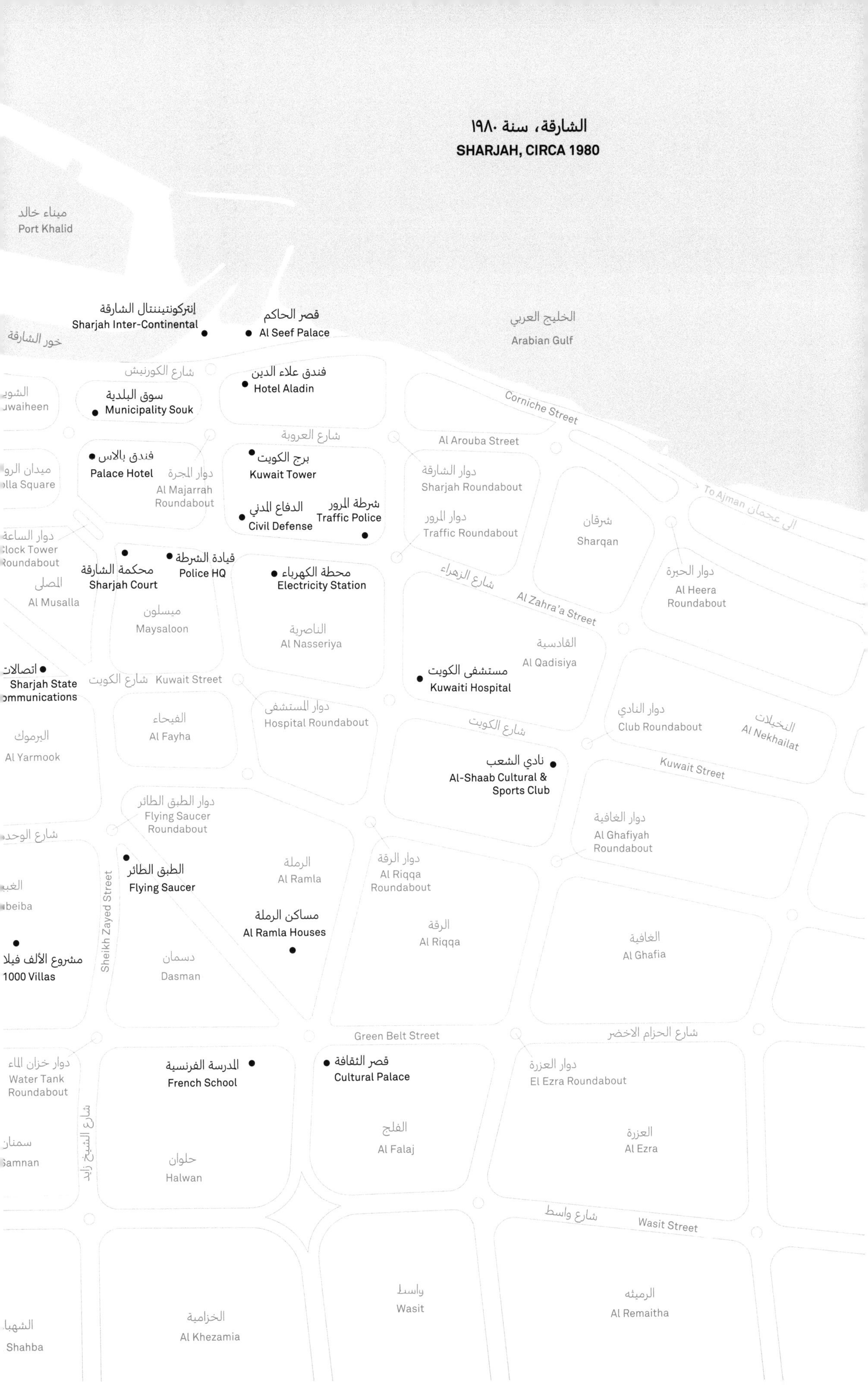

By the time oil wealth seemed imminent in the early 1970s, Sharjah's old city center was being transformed by both a growing municipal government and a private market of local and foreign investors. Old residences like this one—memorable with its enormous wind tower—were replaced with concrete and steel buildings along Sharjah's waterfront. Demolitions preceded the eventual recreation of these districts to recall a past that, during the 1960s and 1970s, could not be forgotten fast enough. Zainal Al Khaja.

Sharjah Fire Department, designed by Egyptian firm Momen Architects & Consulting Engineers, 1975. Momen Architects.

Foreword

Being born and brought up in a city certainly does not make one an expert in its history, which became even clearer to me when we started working on this book. The seven years I spent as an adult with my dad between 1998 and his passing in 2005 exposed me to the older generation of Sharjah's natives, experts in their own right and witnesses to vast and largely undocumented change. We would visit his friends at their offices and majlis gatherings. They would make jokes in honor of those who had already moved on: "Imagine if our late friend were still around and you told him that there are now rooms whose doors close on their own, and when the doors open again, you find yourself in another place!" or "What would so and so say if we told him there are now faucets extending from the wall that, when you turn them slightly, fresh, drinkable water comes out? He'd think we're making it up." Then they would all break out in collective laughter. Many of these bearers of knowledge proved indispensable in creating this book.

As it wasn't until 1974 that Sharjah began to export oil, the city could be considered the last oil boomtown of the Gulf region, presenting a final opportunity for the flow of experts and consultants who had already made their mark, for better or worse, in Sharjah's sister Gulf cities. A slew of architects, engineers, and developers from the world over descended upon Sharjah, applying tested strategies and repeating mistakes. Over the next decade, these confluent forces produced a city ever in search of an identity, vacillating from efficient modernism to vernacular architecture and to sources from elsewhere in the Islamic world. In the tussle among these three tendencies, the city seems willing to revisit the last two categories at the expense of the first.

I recall being astounded, even at the turn of the millennium, at the scope of demolition endured by this city. And while it is impossible to save many of Sharjah's modernist structures, which became painfully evident to me as I tried and failed, due to mounting maintenance costs, to save our own family's building, one could at the very least attempt to preserve their memory, if only for a generation that has not been exposed to these structures. Indeed, they have played a major role in forming the post-oil generation's identity, offering them directional references, landmarks, and above all a sense of belonging to the city.

We didn't set out to write an encyclopedic survey of Sharjah. Rather, this book offers a chance to reconstruct a landscape of a city that, in some ways, no longer exists and parts of which never did.

We sought to capture an era that once seemed enduring but now has proven fleeting. The story many know of Sharjah, like other cities made rich with oil, is that a mere fifty years separate mudbrick houses from today's glass skyscrapers. What existed in the in-between? What structures did people of this land live in after they abandoned *areesh*, or palm frond huts, and mudbrick homes and before the advent of twenty-first-century glass and aluminum towers? Through this book, we attempt to construct a landscape as well as a context to consider these questions and more.

I am proud to have collaborated with my co-editor Todd Reisz in realizing this book. Our book's lead researcher Reem Khorshid was the first recruit to this project. We then approached photographer Ammar Al Attar, whose Sharjah-based photo archive proved essential in obtaining material and documenting the city. Finally, our texts and images came together seamlessly thanks to the skills of graphic designer Farah Fayyad.

Our featured authors provide a great diversity of voices, shedding more light on communities that have not only lived in the city but have also shaped it.

Working on this book in the second decade of the twenty-first century posed challenges just as it offered numerous opportunities. Many buildings we sought to document were already demolished or renovated beyond recognition. Meanwhile, a number of people involved in the city's development have passed away or were unable to communicate with us. Still, we took great advantage of digital technologies such as social media networks to connect with their descendants around the world to obtain photos and biographies. Looking back, it may have been the perfect time to write this book.

The availability, or unavailability, of images and information certainly influenced what we were able to include, promote, or demote. Much of what we were able to find came from family archives, taken by amateur photographers and passed down through generations often with scant information or context. Aerial images—sometimes wobbly and out of focus—were taken from fast moving planes and helicopters; they may tell as much about the building as they do of the person behind the lens. In spite, or perhaps because, of several years of research on Sharjah, I am left with as many questions as answers about the city. These remaining questions have shaped my understanding of the city's modern history. It is my hope that this compendium will afford readers both a greater understanding and a deeper appreciation for this city, which has never fully come to terms with any identity applied to it. If there is a consistent theme in the stories of Sharjah, it is of a city that has given way to economic conditions and political affiliations: from mudbrick architecture, to the faintest advancements under British protectionism, to the Pan-Arab modernity of the 1950s and 1960s, to the oil boom of the 1970s, and finally the Islamic tide of the 1980s. The search for an identity has left behind an urban patchwork: traditional, modern, Islamic, and global all at once. It would be an amazing testament to history, if only it could continue to exist.

Sultan Sooud Al Qassemi
Sharjah
January 6, 2021

Two-story buildings that for a while survived the asphalting of Sharjah's corniche road, one of the first hardened roadways to be lined with streetlights. Once the corniche's souk was displaced, the road was widened according to the Halcrow master plan. John R. Harris Library, courtesy of Mark Harris.

R. B. JEWELLERS
JEWELLERS

Dubai-based photographer Ramesh Shukla arrived in the Trucial States in 1965, when he took his earliest photographs of the coastal cities. His archive is an important documentation of ongoing urban development in Sharjah and other regional cities. For this photo, Shukla climbed to the upper floors of an unattended construction site to capture ongoing construction of Sharjah's Al Wahda Street, 1978. © Ramesh Shukla, Four Seasons Ramesh Gallery.

01

Sultan Sooud
Al Qassemi

THE LONGEST NIGHTS WITH JOY ARE SHORT

The exact year of Nama bint Majid bin Saqr Al Qasimi's birth remains a mystery. She gauges her age not by the passing years, but instead in relation to important events. She was maybe twelve, maybe fourteen, when her father Majid died on a hot summer day in 1958. He was a member of Sharjah's ruling family and had earned a reputation during his life in Sharjah's busy Al Arsa Souk as an adjudicator of disputes. Amidst the shops, people could always recognize him by his *daftar*, or notebook. Later in life, Majid bin Saqr was able to afford the construction of three mudbrick houses, *makhzans*, for his three wives and seven children. One makhzan was in Al Shuwaiheen (also known as Al Sharq), and the other two were close to Sharjah Fort, Al Hisn, in an area known as Fareej Al Shyookh. Majid's main house, constructed in the 1940s just south of Al Hisn on what later became Bank Street, or Al Burj Street, was the largest. For months, contracted laborers, women and men, mixed mud with rocks from the sea before baking the bricks to complete the three makhzans. Majid spent each night in one of the houses, traveling between them on horseback and later by Jeep. Nama was Majid's eldest daughter and recalls that, around the time when he was building the makhzan where she lived, Sharjah's ruler Sultan bin Saqr Al Qasimi II (who reigned from 1924 to 1951) died in London.

Majid's life was cut short by sudden illness. A few days before he passed, he noticed a skin rash, and his fingertips turned greenish. His wife and Nama's mother, Mouza Al Mashghouni (1930–2017), took him to Dubai, where the region's only clinic functioned under the purview of a British doctor named "Macooly."[1] Realizing that his time was nearing its end, he called for Nama and recited to her a famous poem:

فقصارهن مع الهموم طويلة وطوالهن مع السرور قصار
(The shortest nights with sorrow are long ...
And the longest with joy are short.)[2]

Nama's mother Mouza, now widowed, was in her twenties and bereft of a male breadwinner. To provide the family with a livelihood, their first cousin Khalid bin Mohammed Al Qasimi, who would become ruler of Sharjah in 1964, gave them a brand-new Singer sewing machine. Their mudbrick house came to double as a workplace, where they tailored dishdashas and *nafnoofs* (women's dresses, also called *gawan* after the English word "gown"). Mouza, herself illiterate, knew that education was key to her daughters' success. Despite the conservative society's norms, she chose to never marry again and focused instead on sending her daughters to school. In 1960, the family moved to a small new brick house,

02

03

which Mouza had built with her inheritance. The house consisted of four adjacent units under a *liwan*, or colonnaded veranda. Mouza had sketched out the design herself on a piece of paper which she handed to the Iranian contractor named Hussein.

Although Nama cannot confirm the year of her birth, she does know for certain that she was born in winter because her mother gave birth to her in a *khaima*, a tent made of palm tree fronds woven, or "stitched," together as tightly as possible to protect inhabitants from cold winds and rain. Even as late as the mid-twentieth century, concrete and even mudbrick structures were few and far between in Sharjah. The majority of them were inhabited by members of the ruling family, wealthy merchants, and Western officials. Most of the indigenous population lived their winters in *areesh*, also called *barasti*, homes. Rectangular in plan, the areesh summer homes were, like the khaimas, constructed of stitched palm fronds, but the weave held together loosely, letting in not only more air but also snakes and spiders. Nama's family fetched water from the town's well, a long walk away. She recalls having to use her *sheila*, a light garment worn by women over their shoulders, to filter sand and small seashells from the water she collected.

For a teenage girl in 1960s Sharjah, balancing work, study, and life was a challenge. While food and income were in short supply, Nama benefited like many others from the largesse of Kuwait's emir, Abdullah Al Salim Al Sabah. By 1952, he had ordered his government to build schools and send supplies to inhabitants of towns in the lower Arab Gulf. Sharjah's ruler, Sheikh Saqr bin Sultan Al Qasimi, regularly traveled to Kuwait to request aid from the emir, who had visited Sharjah in November 1951. Kuwaiti aid proved instrumental to hundreds of individuals who otherwise would not have had a chance to study. Nama recalls that, as a student, she would receive a *kiswa*, a package of clothing, from the Kuwaiti government. It included two sets of garments, one for the winter and one for the summer, and a pair of shoes. By the mid-1960s, the kiswa also included vitamins, but Nama had graduated by then.

04

In 1953, the Palestinian teacher Kafa Al Sarraj handed out copies of a first-grade lesson book from the Kuwaiti benefactors and asked each student to read aloud from it. Depending on their reading proficiency, students were then separated into grades. As Nama had learned to read and write from her maternal grandfather, Hamad Al Mashghouni (1898–1988), a merchant who studied religion in Qatar and officiated marriages, she recited the text effortlessly and was assigned to a higher grade.[3]

05

Between 1953 and 1964, Nama studied at the Kuwait-funded Fatima Al Zahra School. The school attracted a number of visitors including Abdulaziz Husain (1920–1996), who served as Kuwait's first ambassador to Egypt and later as education minister. He inspected classrooms and assessed the education level of the students. The school occupied a large house owned by the Bin Kamel family not far from Al Hisn, initially accommodating both girls and boys until the latter were moved to Al Qasimiyah School, also funded by Kuwait. To graduate from high school, Nama had to pass final exams administered in Kuwait. The head of the Kuwait Office for Education,

06

Hamad Al Moumin, organized a trip to Kuwait for the Sharjah girls to complete their studies. During that trip, Nama stayed in a girls' dormitory for a few weeks with three other girls from Sharjah: Aisha Sayyar, Aisha Al Qasimi, and Amina Salim Al Hajri.[4] Upon returning to Sharjah, Nama became a teacher at Fatima Al Zahra School, where she taught Arabic, mathematics, religious studies, and science.

Kuwait's presence in the Trucial States would have a further impact on the young teacher. During her last year of high school, a distant cousin landed at Sharjah's airport, returning from his nearly twelve-year stay in Kuwait. Saud bin Khalid (1939–2005) had grown up between Bombay and Kuwait City. Living with his grandmother and younger brother, Saud first studied at Salahuddin School before working as a *myaoumiya*, a daily wage earner, and at a hospital. In 1961, upon hearing that Kuwait planned to open an office in his homeland, he applied for a job. On Wednesday, January 2, 1963, the Kuwait Office was officially inaugurated in Dubai, and twenty-four-year-old Saud bin Khalid became its first treasury secretary, responsible for distributing Kuwait-government salaries to judges, imams, and teachers. At first, Saud lived in the house of his wealthy merchant father, Khalid bin Khalid Al Qasimi (1906–1982), adjacent to Mouza Al Mashghouni's mudbrick home. A first

07

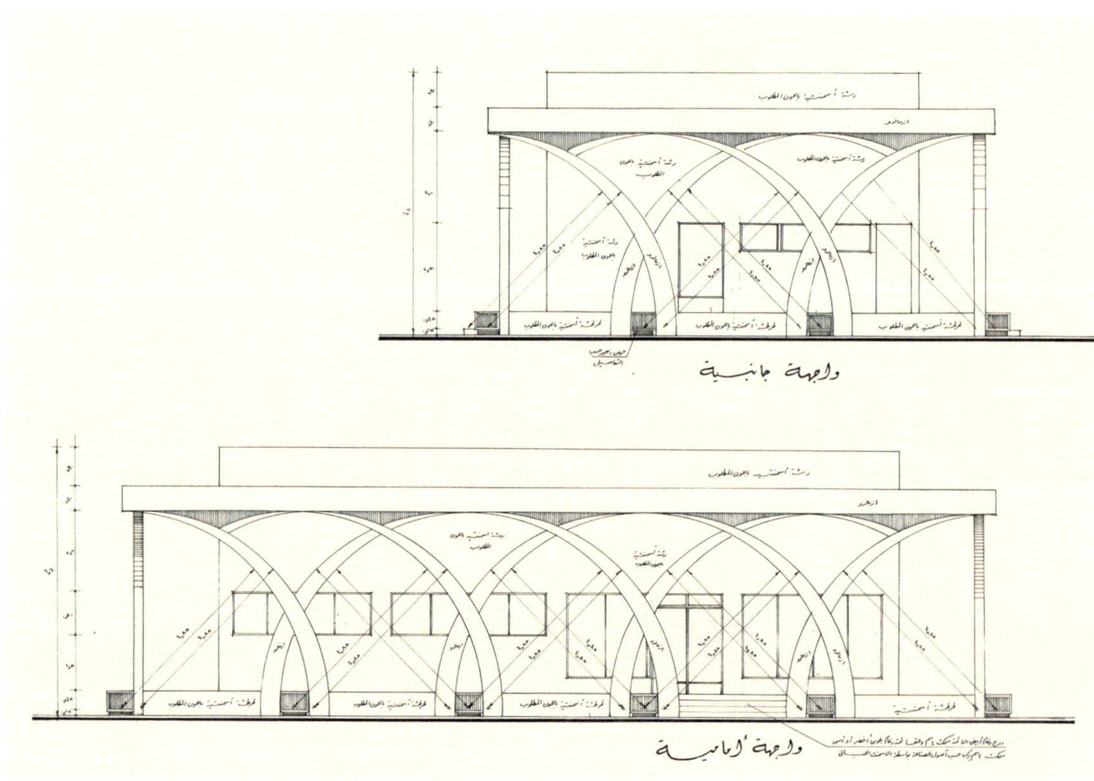

08

09

10

attempt at marriage had faltered when the fiancée's father asked Saud to build a makhzan for his daughter close to his own, a prohibitively costly request for the young clerk. Saud's stepmother Mariam Al Shamsi suggested he marry his half-sister's neighborhood friend, Nama. Saud and Nama married on July 2, 1964. Following the wedding, Khalid bin Khalid offered his son the house's annex, which featured a large *barjeel*, or wind tower, to which Saud added two rooms. Saud and Nama lived there for six years.

In 1970, Saud and Nama asked their close family friend Ismail Al Zarooni, who operated one of Sharjah's few modern construction firms, to build them a house in Sharjah's Al Fayha district based upon a design by the Palestinian engineer Adnan Saffarini.[5] The single-story, two-bedroom house was finished in the summer of 1971 and cost 75,000 dirhams, the equivalent of $15,800. The Fayha house was a significant upgrade from the mudbrick structure in which Nama had grown up. It included a larger garden with a fountain and was situated in a district famous for its tarmac road. Opposite their home was a German colony of engineers working on Sharjah's new port. Next door was the ruler Sheikh Khalid bin Mohammed's diwan.

Saud encouraged his wife to continue working.[6] During Nama's seven-year career as a teacher, from 1964 to 1971, she often earned more than her husband. She had faith in his business acumen, nevertheless, and handed him her entire salary at the end of each month. In 1972, Nama became a member of the Sharjah Women's Association, the first such organization in the country. The association was chaired by Sheikh Khalid bin Mohammed's wife, Noura bint Sultan Al Qasimi, and managed by Aisha Mohamed Al Noman. The Women's Association, registered in 1974, later merged with the federal General Women's Union on August 27, 1975. In 1977, the Women's Association moved to a purpose-built facility.[7] It was there that the seeds of a new organization, the Sharjah Cooperative Society, were sown. Nama, along with forty men and women including her sister and mother, as well as Aisha Mohamed Al Noman and Aisha Ahmed Abdul Rahman, each invested 10,000 dirhams, or $2,500, to start the Sharjah Cooperative Society in March 1977, the first of its kind in the UAE. The co-op's small grocery store operated out of the Maysaloon neighborhood until a store built for the purpose was opened in Al Fayha.[8]

By the late 1970s, Nama and Saud's family had outgrown their two-bedroom home. They now had five children and a sixth on the way. Conny Fernandes, a live-in maid from Goa, joined the household in 1972. For the next half century, she played a major role in raising two generations of the family.

Having quit his Kuwait Office job in 1967, Saud started investing in the construction of shops in Sharjah's expanding souk. He leased the new spaces to the increasing number of expatriates arriving in town to set up new lives. This influx converted into a booming business. Saud's business deals brought him into contact with Ashok Mody, an architect from Bombay who designed the family's new home in Sharjah's Al Ramla district. Mody had just finished work on Al Zahra Hospital and the 1000 Villas project.[9] His design for Saud and Nama's new house was so imposing that the architect nicknamed it "The Citadel." As the house took shape, one of Saud's cousins remarked that the house was "so large that, if invaders came, they would think that it is the ruler's house." Without any adjacent roads, Saud and Nama had to walk over sand from Al Fayha to visit the new construction site. The project was overly ambitious and stood idle for months. It was only after a wild animal entered the Fayha house and bit one of the children that Saud decided to call Sharjah's ruler Sheikh Sultan bin Muhammad to ask for help. The ruler visited the house and donated doors, a Persian carpet, and a framed work of art bearing the word Allah, also suggesting that the master bedroom be expanded by knocking down a wall. Nama hired an Italian woman known as "Um Juliana" to design the interior and the family moved in by 1980.

By this time, Nama had retired from teaching and was playing a major role in her husband's construction business. In the afternoons, she visited construction sites of the buildings and shops that she co-owned with her husband. She used the labor lifts to inspect the room layouts. Bricks would be laid out to outline floorplans, on which she would base her design modifications. In one instance, when Saud was about to buy a plot of land, she brought up the site's major shortcoming—it lay directly under the nearby airport's flight path. Saud took her advice and decided against the purchase.

Perhaps she gained this foresight about the skies in her childhood days, spent in her father's home. Like many other Sharjah residents in the 1960s, Nama sought nocturnal refuge from the summer heat by laying modest mattresses on the rooftop in the hope of catching a breeze. To maintain privacy, a parapet of perforated gypsum tiles, about a meter high, crowned the roof of Nama's small villa. The parapet may have kept peering eyes at bay but did little to contain the rumble of airplanes flying overhead, departing from the nearby Imperial Airways Airport.

It was on this rooftop, one afternoon in early 1964, that a friend took a snapshot of her using a new camera that she had bought for four rupees (or Qatari riyals) at Souk Sager. Nama had climbed up to the roof overlooking Al Hisn's *mushrif* tower, wearing a green polka-dot dress, a pair of earrings, a few golden bracelets on her right wrist, a watch on her left, and the only pendant she owned around her neck. The photograph taken that afternoon captured a moment in Nama's youth before she knew the future that life held for her. It shows Nama smiling, and behind her lies a spare concrete tile featuring a five-pointed star inside a crescent. On that afternoon, Nama was unaware that, in the next few months, her life would take a major turn. As a new ruler assumed power, she would receive a marriage proposal and graduate from school to become one of the first two teachers of Sharjah's modern school curriculum. Ultimately, she would play a vital role in helping educate a generation and propel the city forward into the twenty-first century.

Notes:

1. British medical officer Dr. Desmond McCaully operated Al Maktoum Hospital in Dubai.
2. Translation of poem (author contested) by Labiba Laith.
3. Other Palestinian teachers included Sharifa Al Ba'ba', Laila Al Mazeeni, and Itidal Al Saffarini who taught English. The school's director, also Palestinian, was Muhammad Diyab Al Musa.
4. In order to supplement her family's low income, Nama participated in writing competitions. In the early 1960s, she submitted her work to one such competition sponsored by *Al Arabi* magazine, under the pseudonym of Janet Al Qasimi, and won a considerable sum.
5. For more information on Al Fayha, see Abdulla Saad Moaswes's article, p. 253.
6. In 1967, her third year as a teacher, Nama headed the student delegation to Kuwait for the final exams. Most of the eight or so high school students accompanying her, including her younger sister Mahra, Noura Abdul Rahman Al Midfa, and Aisha Salem Al Hajeri, also became teachers.
7. The Sharjah Women's Association facility was designed by Arab Engineering Bureau.
8. The store was designed by Egyptian architects M. F. Howeedy & Associates.
9. See Al Zahra Hospital, p. 325, and 1000 Villas, p. 351.

11

Images:

01. Nama bint Majid bin Saqr Al Qasimi with her students at Fatima Al Zahra School, 1970. Author, courtesy of Shaikha Nama bint Majid bin Saqr Al Qasimi.
02. Nama (right) and her sisters Mahra and Farida in their areesh house, 1956. Author, courtesy of Shaikha Nama bint Majid bin Saqr Al Qasimi.
03. Areesh houses in Sharjah, 1961. Collection of Mohammed Shamis Al Maazmi, courtesy of Ahmad Al Maazmi.
04. The *liwan* house, 1966. Author, courtesy of Shaikha Nama bint Majid bin Saqr Al Qasimi.
05. Conny Fernandes, Majid bin Saud, and Noura bint Saud in the Fayha house, 1972. Author, courtesy of Shaikha Nama bint Majid bin Saqr Al Qasimi.
06. Students of Fatima Al Zahra School, 1953–54. Nama is second from right, front row. Author, courtesy of Shaikha Nama bint Majid bin Saqr Al Qasimi.
07. Nama (top row, left) during a visit by the Arab League delegation to Fatima Al Zahra School, October 1964. Standing next to her is fellow native Sharjah teacher Amina Salim Al Hajri. Fifty years later, both women were recognized by the UAE government as the first woman Emirati teachers in formal education. To the right of Al Hajri is Egyptian teacher Zainab Al Araby. Third from left in the second row is Layla Al Mazini, recruited with her husband Abdul Moti Morad by the Kuwait Office in 1957. First row (from right): Assistant Secretary General of the Arab League Sayed Nofal, Sharjah Ruler Sheikh Saqr bin Sultan Al Qasimi, Arab League Secretary General Abdul Khalek Hassouna, Ambassador of Saudi Arabia to Kuwait Mohamed Mansour, and Iraqi delegate to the Arab League Mahmoud Ali Daoud. Badr Khalid Al Badr, courtesy of Center for Research and Studies on Kuwait.
08. Front and side elevation of a prototype for the Sharjah Cooperative Society, Consulting Architecture & Civil Engineering Bureau (CAB), undated. CAB.
09. The Ramla house under construction, late 1970s. Architectural Consultants, Ashok Mody.
10. Sharjah Women's Association, late 1970s, Arab Engineering Bureau. Al Azmenah Al Arabiya.
11. Nama photographed by her friend on the roof of the liwan house, 1963. Author, courtesy of Shaikha Nama bint Majid bin Saqr Al Qasimi.

01

Airport Mosque

The Airport Mosque, or Masjid Al Matar, was built along the main road from Sharjah to Dubai, now King Faisal Street, across the tarmac from a BP filling station and adjacent to the runway of Sharjah's earlier airport. After the airport's demolition and move to its current location much further inland, many were left confused by the name left behind with the mosque.

Designed for fewer than 100 worshipers, the prosaically named mosque was commissioned by Sheikh Khalid bin Mohammed Al Qasimi to serve travelers to and from the airport and those en route between Sharjah and Dubai. It is said that the ruler wanted a beautiful building to greet arrivals. The mosque was also referred to as the Bedouin Mosque because, back when no other buildings surrounded it, petitioners would wait there for their appointments with the ruler.[1]

Atop a raised platform, the building was bedizened with many recognizable elements of mosque architecture, all compressed into the building's tiny cubic volume. The building carried two large domes not in proportion with its profile: one a part of the elaborate canopy entrance and another the central element of the roof. The facades were draped in screens, and the roof was finished with a carved wood spirelet on each corner and trimmed with *arayes al samaa*, a decorative parapet. The protruding mihrab had its own pair of scaled-down spirelets while the even more elaborate minaret stood apart on the concrete platform. The architect employed similarly intricate workings on the fence and gates of Sharjah's *musalla al eid*, an open prayer space outside a mosque used during Eid and other occasions.[2]

The building's expressive, traditional ornamentation foreshadowed a preference for embellished details, referred to as Islamic, in the 1980s; its scale made the ornament seem less a social statement than a visual treat amidst tarmac and sand.

02

03

Architect
Mohamed Al Azhari

Contractor
Bin Hadda

Client
Sheikh Khalid bin Mohammed Al Qasimi

Completed
1969

Status
Demolished

1. Michael Tomkinson, *The United Arab Emirates* (Hammamet: Tominkson, 1975).
2. See p. 212.

04

01. Sharjah Airport Mosque, or Masjid Al Matar, on King Faisal Street, undated. H. Brey, Peichär, courtesy of Sharjah Finance Department.
02. Minarets and ornamental detail, from rear elevation including the mihrab. Prem Ratnam, Hemlyn Photography Studio.
03. Sharjah residents watching flight arrivals and departures at the airport, 1960s. The photo was taken by Narain Sawlani, an Indian businessman in the UAE since 1958, during one of his trips to wish traveling friends farewell. Narain R. Sawlani.
04. An aerial photograph captures fenced-in accessory areas for Sharjah's airport. Above, left to right, along the road from Dubai are the Airport Mosque and executions of design prototypes for Shell and British Petroleum filling stations (p. 205 and p. 47). Mahmood AlSawan.

Construction of the British-controlled air base, used for civil and military flights, 1934. Its establishment in Sharjah, as well as its gradual expansion into a vast Royal Air Force camp, was one of Sharjah's first demarcated sites of urban development. The site eventually included a tennis court, sports fields, and a cinema with two to three screenings per week. The fence around the site, prescribed by the ruler, was initially meant to keep British subjects inside it. By 1965, the guest house for overnight layovers had been branded the Fort Hotel, offering air conditioning. Even though its earliest showers spouted saltwater, the vast site still stored more than half of Sharjah's total fresh water supply as late as 1969. Kenneth Mackay, courtesy of HH Private Collection, Mahatta Museum.

تحية
GREETINGS
إلى
TO
الشيخ صقر بن سلطان القاسمي
SHEIKH SAQR BIN SULTAN AL-QASSIMI
حاكم الشارقه وتوابعها
RULER OF SHARJAH
BP
BP
BP
BP

01

02

British Petroleum in Sharjah

01. A BP guard and official welcome guests, including ruler Sheikh Saqr bin Sultan Al Qasimi, to BP compounds, date unknown. © BP plc, courtesy of BP Archive.
02. Sheikh Saqr is welcomed at BP's residential compound. © BP plc, courtesy of BP Archive.
03. Perspective and elevation drawings, BP filling station prototype, 1959. National Archives United Kingdom.

On land wedged in between a silty corner of Sharjah Creek and a cemetery, a site demarcated for early oil explorers became two enclosed compounds of British Petroleum (BP). In May 1952, the oil company signed a lease with Sharjah's ruler for what became known as the "Old BP Depot." In August 1958, another contract was signed, for an annual payment of 15,000 riyals (less than $30,000 today), allowing BP to pursue expansive domestic and infrastructural projects on its leased site.

Inside one compound, the company assembled prefabricated offices and bungalows for employee families, accessorized with thick curtains that, when closed, repelled the bright daylight and achieved an interior with a closer likeness to mid-century British domesticity. The second, larger, compound housed the plants and industrial equipment. Though situated a distance from the center of town, the compounds were not cut off. Quite the contrary, their plant was connected underground to the Layah peninsula by a buried pipe that extended out beneath the seabed to a hook-up for passing oil tankers. It is no coincidence that Sharjah's major port works were later positioned near BP's early marine works. The Sharjah jetty would be built in parallel to the BP pipe. Extending from the jetty was Al Meena Street, or Port Road, that for a while defined Sharjah's commercial and infrastructural axis. In the opposite direction, underground oil lines connected the compound by to the Royal Air Force camp.[1]

BP's presence was not only characterized by the enclosed Western comforts that were accommodated inside the compound walls; it was also dispersed throughout the Trucial States by means of a filling-station prototype. The simple and quickly executed design was modestly reminiscent of the curves and angles associated with European and American car culture. The drawings here were issued for a filling station in Deira, Dubai, dated 1959, but the design was more or less the same for stations in Sharjah, including the one on the future King Faisal Street.

1. See p. 45.

03

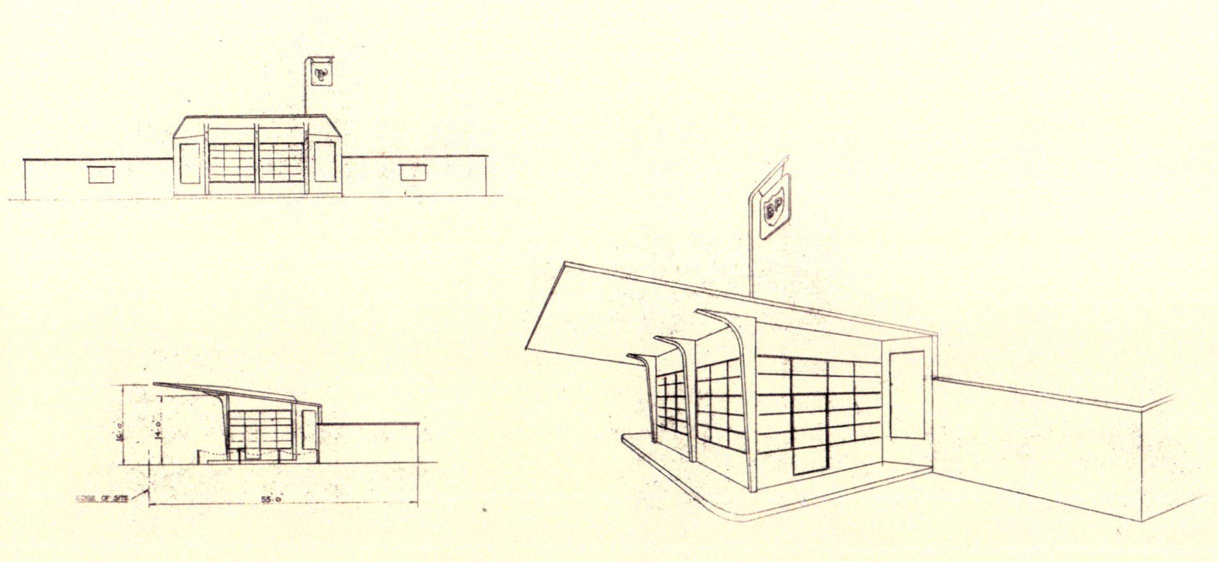

Shelter
Rubbish Tip
Open Air Cinema
Water Tank
Tank
Pylon
Pipe
Ditch
Ruin
Fuel Storage Tanks
Oil Storage Tanks
Tennis Court
Line of Boundary Stones
Aircraft Control Building
Flagstaff
AIRSTRIP

Royal Air Force Camp

On August 1, 1966, the British government made the first annual payment of £100,000 to the ruler of Sharjah for use of a vast tract of land for its expanded military presence. Since 1934, British civil and military officials had been housed in and around the air station (no. 3).[1] The new British-controlled territory would extend north from the air station toward higher land and in the direction of the built-up city. In 1966, the air station site accommodated about 2,700 people, including some British officials but mostly Arab and South Asian staff housed in tents. At the time, Sharjah city's population was estimated at 8,000. Through a later land deal, tent living was relegated to a "modest" new Trucial Oman Scouts site further out. Air conditioning was deemed essential only for British staff at the new Royal Air Force (RAF) camp. The layout was a quick planning solution to the pending loss of a military base in Aden at the end of 1967.

The camp was enclosed with high-security steel fencing. Its interior roads were paved before those outside the fencing. Beyond the exclusivity of its air-conditioned quarters, the RAF camp also enjoyed a private oil pipeline from British Petroleum's storage units on the Sharjah coast, its own supply of electricity, and a secure source of water that at one point accounted for more than half the city's storage capacity. The camp included its own sports fields, and there was an exclusive beach nearby for water recreation. The cinema (no. 60) held screenings two or three times a week. While it is not clear whether the design was the actual one realized, a 400-seat cinema was proposed by the UK-based firm Tripe & Wakeham in 1962.

The building schedule was rapid, until it was called off. In January 1968, the British government announced plans to vacate the Trucial States, leaving the fenced-off city for British officers and staff behind. In preparation for the departure, the compound became an ad-hoc outdoor market. According to the Kuwait-based magazine *Al Arabi*, British officials were selling off scrap metal and auto parts to ease the burden of transferring supplies elsewhere.[2] Abandoned barracks became the first school rooms of Beirut's displaced National College of Choueifat.[3] Other parts were designated for churches (some of them still in what is now Al Halwan district). Except for the original air station, the camp was cleared out, opening the land up for Sharjah's development in the direction of Dubai.

1. See p. 40.
2. See p. 113.
3. See p. 235.

02

03

04

05

06

07

01. Site plan details, stamped April 23, 1968. UK MOD © Crown copyright, courtesy of the British Library.
02. Residential bungalow interior at RAF Camp, undated. Peter Hudson.
03. Travelers approach an RAF "Aden Airways" airplane, undated. Clive E. M. Adams, courtesy of John S. Adams.
04. Sharjah residents greet an arrival. Narain R. Sawlani.
05. South Asian employee of British air base serves British official at bar cafe. Clive E. M. Adams, courtesy of John S. Adams.
06. Passengers' view of air base and control tower, later added, undated. Rahma bin Nasser Al Owais, courtesy of Abdallah Mohamed Al Quraidi.
07. The earliest lease contracts signed by British officials included payment clauses for salaries of local guards, undated. Clive E. M. Adams, courtesy of John S. Adams.

SHARJAH INT
ATIONAL AIRPORT

Sharjah International Airport, King Faisal Street

The decommissioned Royal Air Force compound housed Sharjah's first airport until 1968 when it was moved to new, more civic-minded premises, designed by Sir William Halcrow and Partners. Built almost equidistant between Sharjah's city center and Dubai's Deira district, the blue terminal building served as a landmark for those arriving to join the Gulf's latest oil boom. With green landscaping, designated pick-up areas, and shaded porticoes, Sharjah's second airport signaled an attempt, made in vain, to slow the shifting of air traffic to Dubai's three-year-old airport.

The new terminal stood along the tarmac laid by British forces, now King Faisal Street, for less than a decade. Deemed critical to Sharjah's economy, it was the reason that two of Sharjah's earliest hotels, the Sheba and the Federal, could galvanize a real estate market in the area. Having worked on this building, Halcrow urged the government to select a site for a new and larger airport, arguing that the current location impeded Sharjah's urban expansion in the direction of Dubai.[1]

1. See p. 387.

Architect
Sir William Halcrow & Partners

Client
Government of Sharjah

Completed
1968

Status
Demolished

Kuwaiti and Saudi Arabian flags raised next to Sharjah's flag in front of airport terminal, 1970s. Mahmood AlSawan.

01

Residency Agent House

Starting as early as 1890, the British government hired a succession of Arab residency agents to live in Sharjah and report to the political resident in Bushehr, Iran, and later Bahrain.[1] At least some of these agents occupied a rented courtyard house on Sharjah Creek among the few houses made from coral and stone, parts of which were coated in gypsum and lime mortar. Situated in a central and prominent area of Sharjah, the agent could interact with Sharjah's most powerful families, observe the goings-on at the modest port, and report his "intimate knowledge" to his British superiors.

In 1948, when the British government sought to increase its political presence in the Trucial States, it was decided that a white British officer would replace the resident agent. Soon thereafter, the decades-old agency was deemed inadequate as housing for the new officer. Unlike accommodations at the Royal Air Force camp and the oil-company compound, there was hardly enough electricity to run a light bulb, much less an air-conditioning unit, at the agency. The bathroom was no more than a galvanized iron tub. A visiting expert found the house of "poor construction," which probably just meant it was made from unmanufactured parts. Soon after the expert's report on these deficiencies, the British government decided to move its premises to Dubai. Once vacated by the agency in 1954, the building was renovated into the Seaface Hotel. It remained in operation into the 1970s when the business moved to a three-story building with twenty air-conditioned rooms on Al Arouba Street. The waterside building was soon after demolished.

Status
Demolished

02

03

1. Rosemarie Said Zahlan, *The Origins of the United Arab Emirates: A Political and Social History of the Trucial States* (New York: St. Martin's Press, 1978).

Images:

01. British government car in front of residency along Sharjah Creek, 1947. Images: National Archives United Kingdom.
02. The bathroom consisted of a galvanized iron tub and "bucket closets" to be cleaned by hand.
03. The dining room whose furniture was reportedly borrowed, 1947.

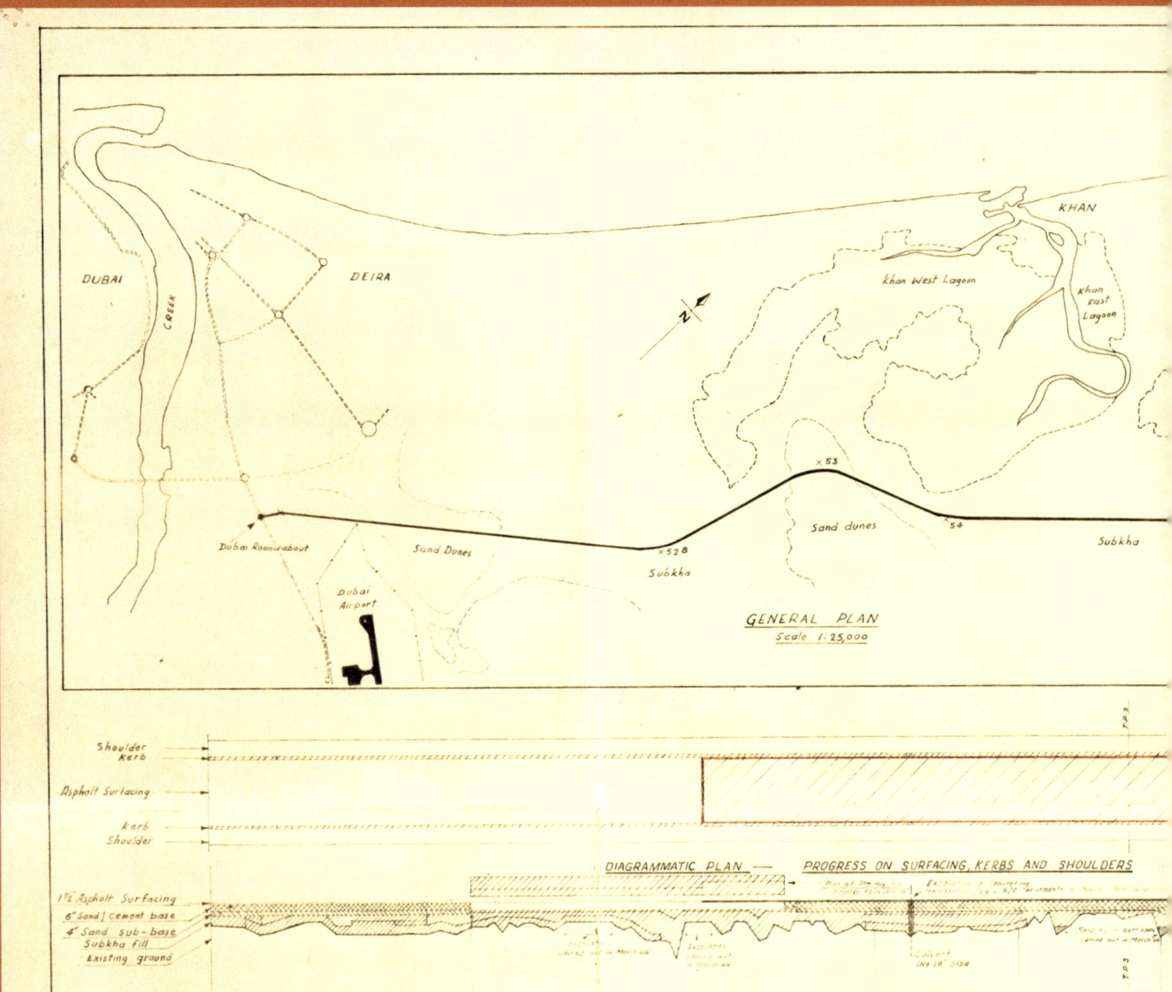

Progress Report, Dubai–Sharjah road, 1966. As early as 1944, the British government mapped how Dubai and Sharjah were connected by a naturally occurring trail of *sabkha*, a crystallized formation hard enough for cars to traverse—that is, until it dissolves in a flash rainstorm. Michael Hamilton-Clark, working for Sir William Halcrow & Partners, created this drawing. It demonstrates how the existing road was transformed by converting the sabkha into lower-level fill, covered with sand and cement layers, and finally capped with an economically thin layer of asphalt. It was from this artery that Sharjah city's first asphalt roads would extend. Connecting Sharjah's center to Dubai's both supported and threatened Sharjah's economic survival; it also foretold an urban convergence undeniable by the late 1970s. Michael Hamilton-Clark.

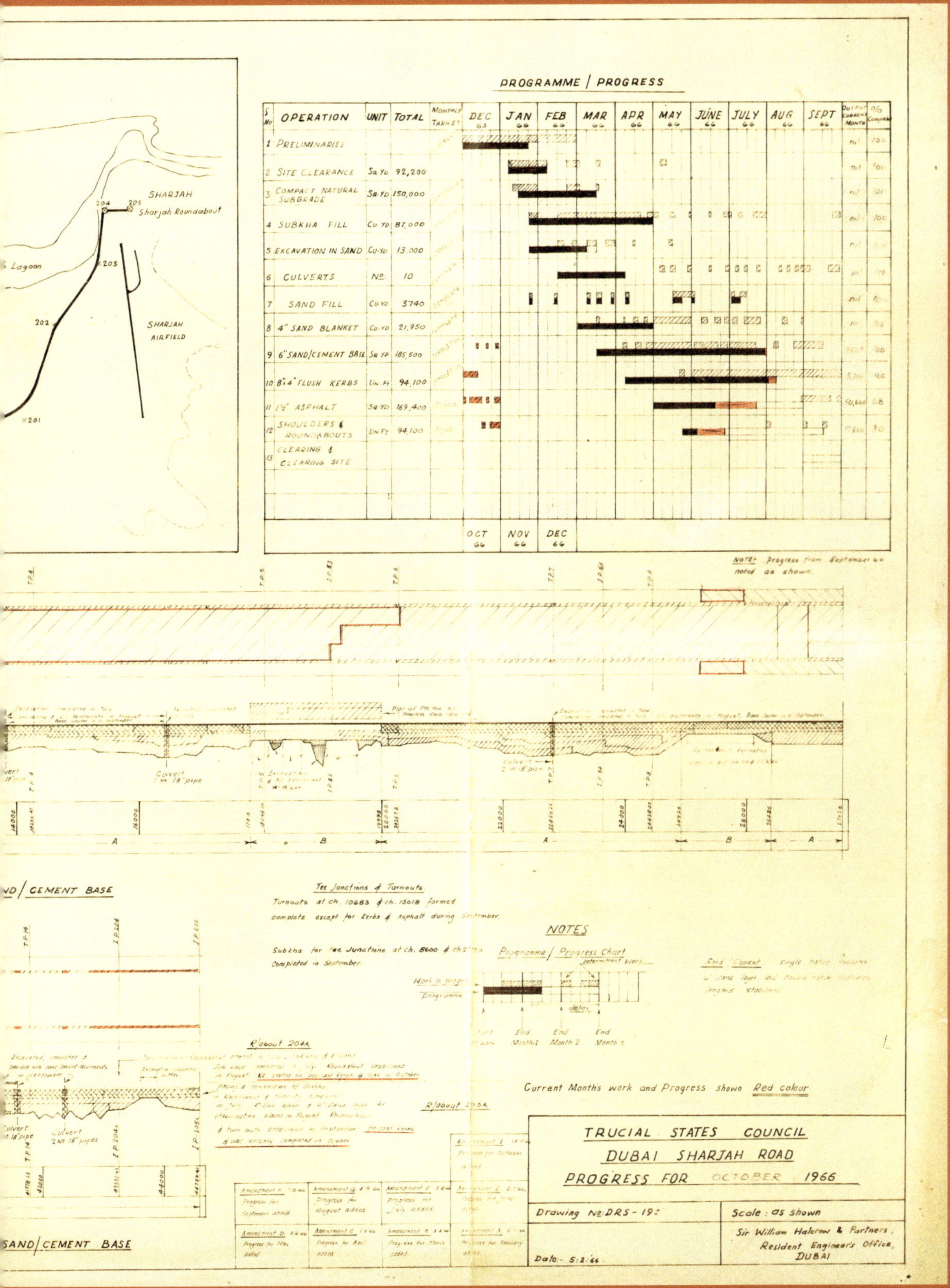
PROGRAMME / PROGRESS
OPERATION
UNIT
TOTAL
MONTHLY TARGET
DEC 65
JAN 66
FEB 66
MAR 66
APR 66
MAY 66
JUNE 66
JULY 66
AUG 66
SEPT 66
1 PRELIMINARIES
2 SITE CLEARANCE Sq.Yd 92,200
3 COMPACT NATURAL SUBGRADE Sq.Yd 150,000
4 SUBKHA FILL Cu.Yd 87,000
5 EXCAVATION IN SAND Cu.Yd 13,000
6 CULVERTS No. 10
7 SAND FILL Cu.Yd 3740
8 4" SAND BLANKET Cu.Yd 21,950
9 6" SAND/CEMENT BASE Sq.Yd 185,500
10 8"x4" FLUSH KERBS Lin.Ft 94,100
11 1½" ASPHALT Sq.Yd 169,400
12 SHOULDERS & ROUNDABOUTS Lin.Ft 94,100
13 CLEARING & CLEARING SITE
OCT 66
NOV 66
DEC 66
SHARJAH
Sharjah Roundabout
Lagoon
SHARJAH AIRFIELD
NOTE: Progress from September 66 noted as shown.
SAND / CEMENT BASE
Tee Junctions & Turnouts
Turnouts at ch. 10683 & ch. 15018 formed complete except for Kerbs & Asphalt during September.
Subkha for Tee Junctions at ch. 8600 & ch. 2... completed in September.
NOTES
Programme / Progress Chart
Work in progress
Programme
delay
End Month 1
End Month 2
End Month 3
R/about 204A
R/about 205A
Current Months work and Progress shown Red colour
TRUCIAL STATES COUNCIL
DUBAI SHARJAH ROAD
PROGRESS FOR OCTOBER 1966
Drawing No. DRS - 19
Scale: as shown
Sir William Halcrow & Partners, Resident Engineer's Office, DUBAI
Date:- 5.2.66
SAND / CEMENT BASE

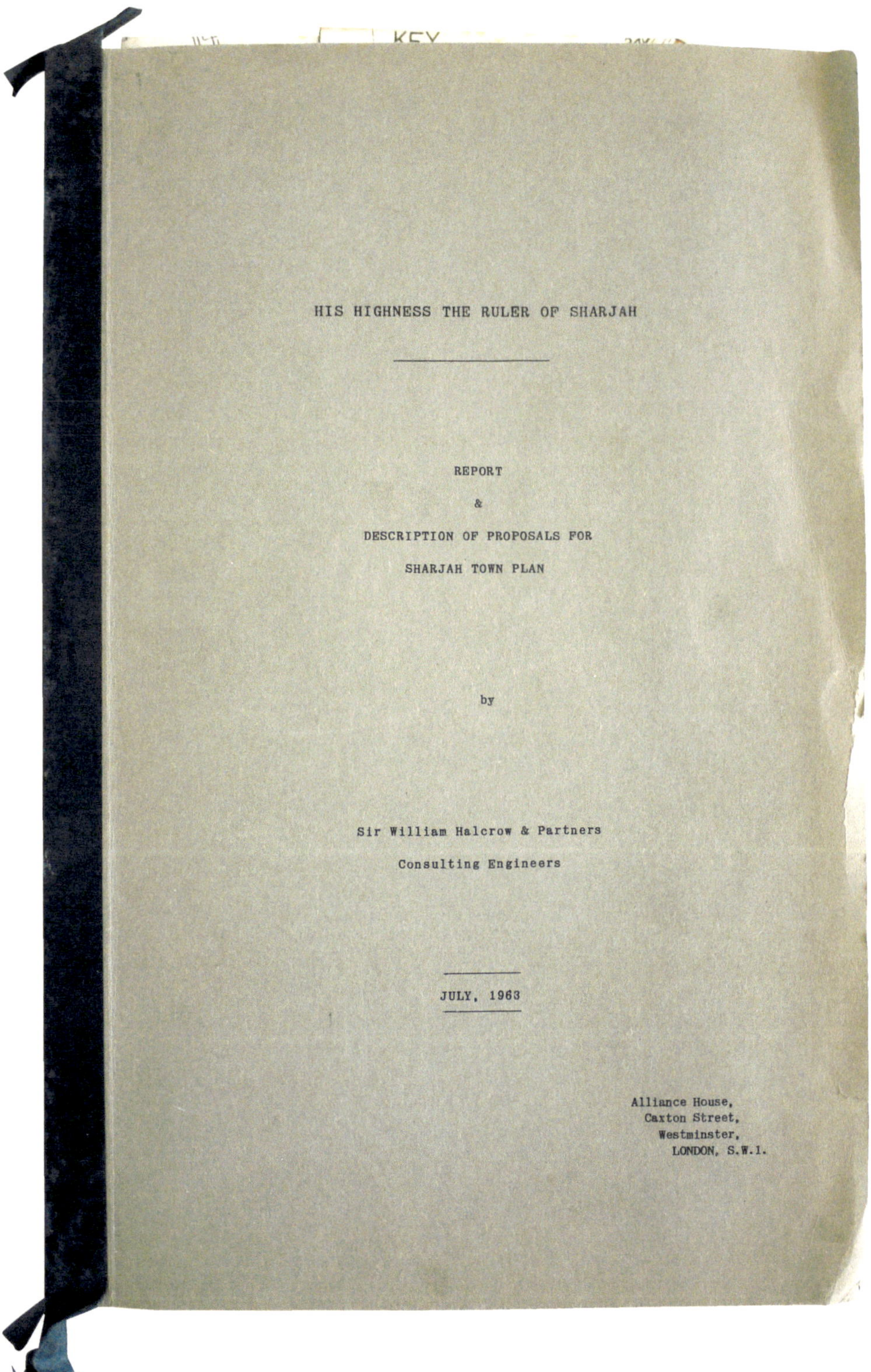

HIS HIGHNESS THE RULER OF SHARJAH

REPORT

&

DESCRIPTION OF PROPOSALS FOR

SHARJAH TOWN PLAN

by

Sir William Halcrow & Partners

Consulting Engineers

JULY, 1963

Alliance House,
Caxton Street,
Westminster,
LONDON, S.W.1.

01

Todd Reisz

WRITING SHARJAH'S LANDSCAPE

Sharjah's twentieth-century history was shaped by those empowered to tell it and by the audience they chose to tell it to. Storytellers crafted plots upon the city's contours—slabbed in concrete, steel, and asphalt. Megatons of imported materials—stirred with local petroleum, water, and sand and assembled by a legion of migrants—hardened into an admixture of architecture and infrastructure, the unyielding evidence of history professed. The power to tell Sharjah's history has been intricately tied to the power to build the city. More than just the setting of a history, Sharjah's built landscape *is* the story. And predominant tellers of that story have been British: first military strategists, then government officials, and later private-sector consultants.

In 1819, British naval officers ransacked Sharjah and the extended coast stretching beyond it. They decimated Sharjah's maritime fleet and, presumably, its harbor. Soon thereafter, their superiors gave the greater coast a name: the Trucial States. Around the same time, an Arab emissary, working out of a house along Sharjah's harbor, started reporting to British officials in Bushehr, Iran.[1] His placement in Sharjah, as opposed to any of the other Trucial States, indicated the city's regional prominence and the need to keep a surveilling eye on it. In the 1930s, nearly a century after destroying Sharjah's seafaring capacity, the British government planted an ad hoc pier on its shore to supply the construction of an inland air base. The air station, as it was called, resulted in both Sharjah's increased prominence and its further subjugation to British oversight.

Just over a decade after the completion of the air station, British officials started to assess nearby Dubai as a more promising location than Sharjah from which to secure impending oil contracts for British companies. By 1950, British officials were using the name *Dubai* as a collective name for two towns—Bur Deira and Bur Dubai—scrambling to dominate a temperamental inland harbor known in English as Dubai Creek. In June 1950, a British official briefly visited Dubai and issued "A Note on the Wealth of Dubai," a five-page report that heralded decades of future reporting about the city, by both British officers and journalists. Without much evidence, a handicap he never admits forthright, he claims that Dubai, fifteen kilometers away from Sharjah, was "destined to become a centre of real importance." There was "a business-like air about the place."[2] There was more "hope" in Dubai.[3] He estimates that the port would survive even without the expectation of oil being fulfilled; and, if oil ever did materialize, it was "urgent" that the British government begin to establish an influential role for itself immediately by addressing the only identified deficiency—the lack of "any administrative progress whatsoever."[4] The report does little more than affirm a decision that had already been taken, namely to move British surveillance from Sharjah to Dubai. There was no mathematical way to measure Dubai's economic landscape against Sharjah's at the time. Any verdict was based on impressions, and impressions are best conveyed in stories. Plans went ahead to build a British government compound in Dubai.

At the end of that summer, the same officer issued a second report that further validated Dubai's prominence, another five-page report, this time titled "Notes on the Finances of Sharjah." It begins, "No detailed picture of Sharjah's economic condition can be drawn because no records are available."[5] Whereas "wealth" in Dubai was corroborated only by impressions, "finances" in Sharjah were deemed untraceable. Like Dubai, Sharjah still operated with a dearth of steel, electricity, clean drinking water, telephones, and steady radio signals. Whereas Dubai's scarcity had signaled resilience, Sharjah's scarcity professed deficiency. Dubai's profit sources had proven no more quantifiable to the official; it was just a matter of how one framed the story. In fact, there were enough known facts available to calculate that documented sources of income actually tallied higher in Sharjah than in Dubai. But impressions outweighed facts. And there was what one could observe on the landscape: compared to Dubai's "bustling port," Sharjah's was often clogged with sandbars, sometimes to the point of being unnavigable. Dubai's own sandbars were overlooked. Sharjah was described as "a sleepy town of two to three thousand inhabitants." Its harbor was "silted beyond recovery," leading to the entire city's "ebb of prosperity," now "stolen" by Dubai. In "striking contrast" to Dubai, "moribund Sharjah" seemed trapped in its own decay.[6]

Sharjah's ruler, Sheikh Saqr bin Sultan Al Qasimi, rejected the British framing of the two cities. His tenacious drive revealed an ingredient absent in the Dubai report: a leader who actively sought to "rescue Sharjah from her decline." He championed the transformative potential of infrastructure—what the report called his interest in "artificial improvement." Saqr endorsed a decades-old plan to create a new coastal harbor for the city, to replace the silty inland creek. Before him, his father Sheikh Sultan bin Saqr Al Qasimi II petitioned the British government to help him find financing for such a solution. The "Notes on Finances" report discerned neither resolution nor initiative in the ruler's pursuits, dismissing them as "wishful optimism." In contrast, again, Dubai was already blessed with "a good harbor," one official observed.[7] The ruler's infrastructure plan was therefore criticized as "grandiose," with another official remarking that any physical improvement to Sharjah would have consequences on Dubai's prosperity. "Nothing," the report boldly concluded, "except the discovery of oil on her territory can rescue Sharjah from her decline."

IMPARTIAL ADVICE

While stationed in Sharjah, British officials thwarted the advancement of their host city. In Dubai, they aimed to galvanize it. Four years after the 1950 reports, they acknowledged that Dubai's harbor also needed "artificial improvement" to escape obscurity. This time, however, the infrastructural proposal was not deemed grandiose but rather correlated to British economic interests. Apparently without alerting local officials, the British Foreign Office commissioned Sir William Halcrow and Partners, a British engineering firm with a portfolio full of government contracts at home and abroad, to design a plan to save Dubai's harbor.

Consultants commonly base claims of objectivity on proclaimed expertise and past experience. They are also aware that paying clients have outcomes they wish to hear; in this case, the British government was the client that had just completed construction of its new compound in Dubai and was already shaping the city into its logistical hub in the region. Halcrow was also tasked with completing a corresponding study of Sharjah's harbor. Again, Dubai's and Sharjah's histories were to be written in contrast. Halcrow personnel visited both harbors in 1954 and delivered two reports in January 1955, one on Dubai—its cover blue, the color of clear skies—and the other on Sharjah—its cover red, the color of cancellation. In their Dubai report, Halcrow engineers made clear the need for the company's continuing services and outlined an engineered solution for the city's harbor. For Sharjah, Halcrow did not consider Sheikh Saqr's proposed shoreline harbor; instead, it focused on Sharjah's silted creek. To repair it, Halcrow estimated a cost nearly three times as high as the proposal to repair Dubai's harbor. Halcrow's assessment affirmed the British narrative of Dubai's ascendancy. One reader of the reports concluded, "Sharjah must face the fact that its present harbour facilities must continue to decline."[8]

02

03

Whereas plans for a new harbor in Sharjah had local political backing, there was no indication that Dubai's de facto leader, Sheikh Rashid bin Saeed Al Maktoum, saw any political value in improving his city's harbor at the time. After issuance of the Halcrow reports, British officials set out to convince him to back the proposal. Instead of offering British funding for the improvements, they urged Rashid to accept an inordinate amount of debt. The high-risk plan, in short, proved successful, thus helping trigger Rashid's esteem for the eye-catching benefits of infrastructural projects—piers, public sanitation systems, asphalt roadways, hospitals, power plants. A common falsehood ensued: that Sheikh Rashid dared to save Dubai Creek while Sheikh Saqr allowed his harbor to flounder. Even the British government propagated the story, as early as 1964, when the Dubai-based political agent James Craig recorded it for the Foreign Office. No one challenged his story. Before long, Craig's revised history was the preface to countless English-language press pieces about Sharjah having "allowed" its harbor to perish.[9]

Halcrow's index of contracts for work on Dubai Creek began in 1958. In Sharjah, rather than conceding to the prescribed doom calculated by Halcrow, Sheikh Saqr canvassed help from other countries (Qatar, West Germany, and Denmark) and went behind the British government's back to approach private British companies (Halcrow and another engineering firm, Costain) in pursuit of the harbor project he believed would revive Sharjah's economy. By seeking assistance elsewhere, Saqr threatened the established British narrative. One British official wrote that they needed to get "this notion out of [Sharjah's] system."[10]

Left to their own assessments, other countries and companies might have determined that Sharjah was a hopeless case, especially in light of the British support for Dubai. To quash any doubts, British officials made their "strong views" known to traveling consultants, emphasizing that Dubai was destined to be the region's port.[11] Abandoned and left to his own devices, Sheikh Saqr reportedly "felt so severely the loss of prestige ... that he felt it necessary to do something immediately." He paid for the construction of a breakwater on the coast—a fragment of his harbor plan—"entirely with his own resources." A British official, surprised, reported of the breakwater's "remarkable effect": Sharjah could again receive light ships.[12]

Sheikh Saqr's persistence was depicted by British papers as irrational and quixotic—and as a thorn in resolute plans. While it may not have been apparent at the time, Saqr had a lasting impact on not only Sharjah's landscape but also Dubai's. An example:

04

05

the portrayal of Sharjah as a forsaken corner of the Arab world in an Arabic-language magazine, likely a 1959 issue of *Al Arabi*, allegedly attracted a wealthy Iraqi sponsor who offered to build a new hospital there. The secured funding was reportedly enough to start work on the building's foundation, but it appears that the hospital was never completed.[13] Still, the possibility, the story, of a future hospital in Sharjah was enough to motivate Dubai's leadership to secure funding for its Al Maktoum Hospital, which had reigned as the region's premier health-care facility for already more than a decade.[14] Dubai's ruler, Sheikh Rashid, recognized by then that the juxtaposition to Sharjah defined Dubai; he also recognized what Sheikh Saqr already knew—the potential of infrastructure to tell a story. Dubai's health-care facility was a signpost of a modern, hygienic city, and something similar to which Sharjah could not yet claim. It was not the last time Saqr's pursuits would provoke ambitions in Dubai.

MASTER PLAN

Saqr's persistence could not bend the narrative woven around Sharjah. Traders based in Sharjah were attracted to Dubai's logistical ease and the smooth new harbor surfaces built by Halcrow. They were lured by Sheikh Rashid's promises of business discounts, land opportunities, and cheap electricity. Once based in Dubai, opportunistic traders were also met with Rashid's censuring of supplying Sharjah too generously. Sharjah's residents were precariously reliant upon Dubai's port, which charged them high tariffs. To pay these fees, they remained reliant upon remittances sent from family members working abroad in the oil fields of Qatar, Bahrain, Kuwait, and Saudi Arabia. There was one arena, however, in which Sharjah was doing better than Dubai: it had cornered the regional gold trade that Kuwait's traders, made rich by oil deals, no longer pursued. To excel in the gold trade, Sharjah's traders used the local airport and, possibly, Saqr's small new harbor to shuttle the gold. Profits made from the trade might very well have given the ruler confidence to consider his next attempt at changing Sharjah's prescribed narrative.

By 1963, when Halcrow had already completed a second contract for Dubai Creek, they were called back to Sharjah. This time, the request came not from the British government but from Sheikh Saqr. A different client requires a change in tone, a new framing of the story. Three years prior, the British government had pushed a town plan upon Sheikh Rashid. Sheikh Saqr instigated one for Sharjah of his own volition. Halcrow returned to the city it had written off and, within four months, produced the *Report and Description of Proposals for Sharjah Town Plan*.

Halcrow still identified Sharjah's deficiencies: residents had trouble finding work; its environs were "relatively barren"; its silted harbor suffered from twenty years of "progressive deterioration"; there was no electricity save for that provided by a few generators; there were no systems for sanitation, waste disposal, and drainage; and the building stock suffered from an "inherent weakness of construction." In 1955, such inauspicious findings had led Halcrow to dismiss Sharjah by delivering an impossible proposal—one that fed with ease into the British government's Dubai narrative. By 1963, Halcrow recast the same ingredients into a new storyline for a new client.

The planners concluded that Sharjah "provides an excellent opportunity." *Opportunity*—in case the client became too complacent—was also outfitted with *threats*: the first, if Sharjah ever became an oil state, it needed to be prepared "in a comprehensive manner" for "rapid expansion"; the second, if Sharjah did not become an oil state, it needed a backup plan to bolster its economy. The setup was that, no matter what happened, Sharjah was faced with a predicament that could be abated only by a comprehensively planned and expanded city. At least now the predicament was framed as surmountable, albeit necessitating additional contracts granted to Halcrow.[15]

Report and Description of Proposals for Sharjah Town Plan includes a section on Sharjah's topography. The British engineers had good reason to examine Sharjah's subsoil, as they had already once underestimated how menacingly volatile the region's shoreline could be. Two years prior, in 1961, when seasonal storms whipped Dubai's new harbor works into a stew of debris and mud—causing lost days of Dubai's sea trade—Halcrow's resident engineer saw firsthand how miscalculations could wreak havoc. The training walls and groins designed by Halcrow caused that year's storms to flood entire areas of Dubai, inundating the palm-frond houses which still sheltered a majority of the city's population, and causing a surge in deaths from influenza and disease. If it hadn't already been obvious before, Dubai was being built at a dangerously low elevation, with a threateningly high water table.

While Halcrow's 1955 reports preferred Dubai's harbor as the more "flourishing," the 1963 town plan found Sharjah to be the more advantageous location for building a modern city. Sharjah, Halcrow engineers concluded, was a coastal town auspiciously protected, geographically and geologically, from just such storms and flooding. In one of the few explicit references to Dubai, the plan reported, "Unlike Dubai which is built almost entirely on the low-lying [sabkha], Sharjah is mainly built on a gently sloping, firm sand ridge."[16] And while drifting sand dunes may have appeared to characterize Sharjah's topography, "The ground is generally firm, only the top 6 inches or so of the surface consisting of loose sand. Below this, the sand is everywhere firmly compacted." Sharjah had the bedrock foundations of a future city.

To take advantage of this auspicious foundation, the Halcrow plan recommended sweeping away what existed above ground and making way for "an immediate redevelopment area." Sharjah's urban fabric was dominated by the palm-frond walls of its *areesh* homes and shops; sturdier houses were made of "roughly shaped coral blocks set in a very weak mortar." "The whole area," according to the plan, was "built haphazardly."[17] Deemed inadequate, Sharjah's housing stock was targeted for a large-scale plan for redevelopment.

The plan proposed casting a web of wide roadways over the existing city and beyond, knotted together by expansive roundabouts. The voids within the web were where the plan imagined "residential areas" cut off from each other by the foretold car traffic. Roads would not just accommodate cars; they would also delineate the new districts. Some of the resulting districts, for example, would be outfitted with communal toilets and ablution spaces, an apparent suggestion that at least one enclosed district would be exclusively for low-income residents. By assembling "blocks of dwelling plots, squares, mosques, and shops," each designated area would be marked by "particular localities" with which residents identified, allowing them "to live in the traditional manner as far as may be desired." While not explicitly organizing the city by its demographics—whether determined by income level, race, or provenance—the confined districts provided a means to segregate the city.

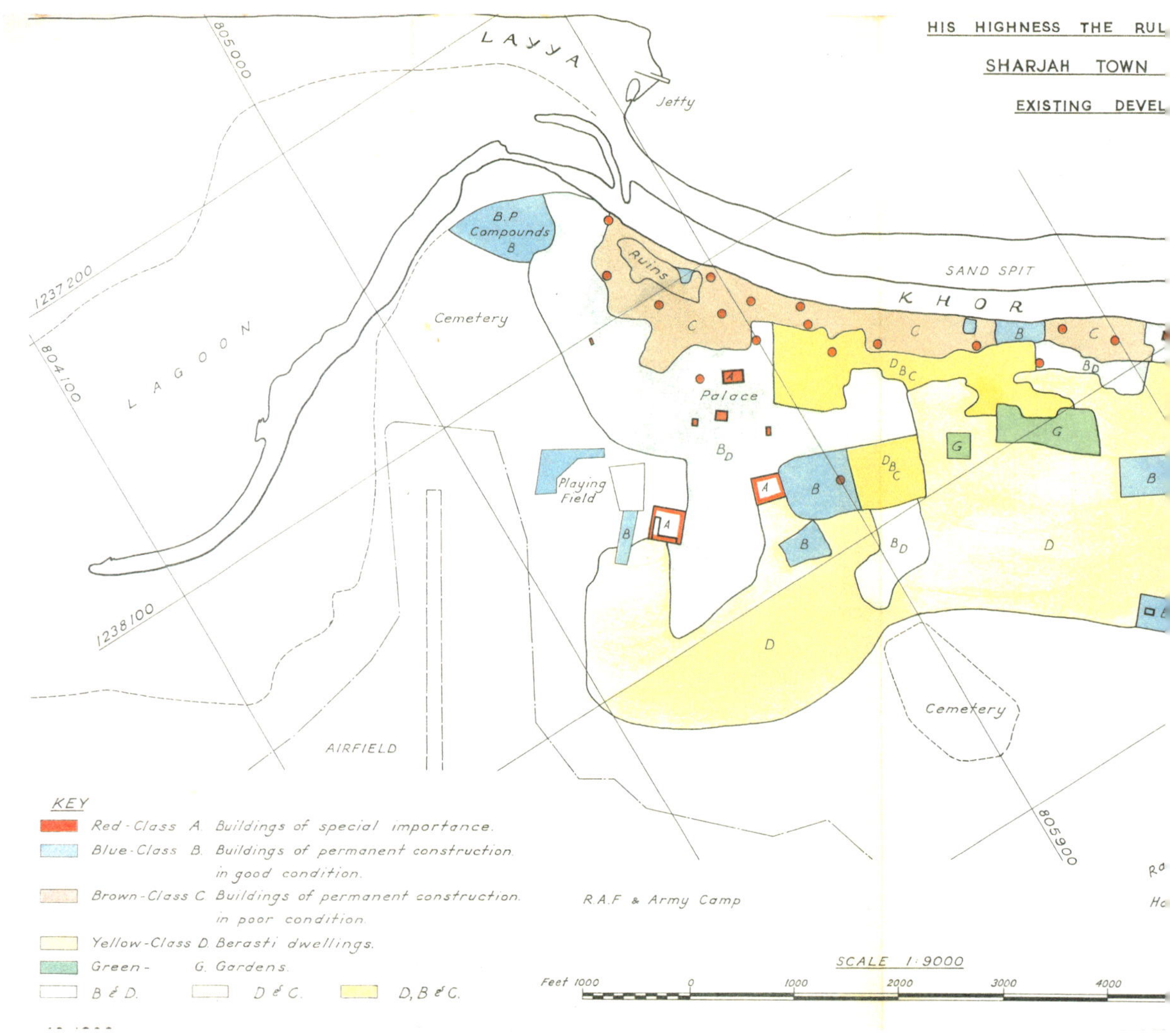

06

There is no apparent set of guiding principles in the plan. One can, however, start a list of proposed development projects that lengthens with each page turned. That list is what makes the plan so relevant to review today. Many of the proposals on that list were eventually realized, often through future Halcrow contracts: a gridded roadway system, vast public "concourses" around the palace and Rolla Tree, a bus depot, a new and enlarged airport outside the city limits, large-scale market halls, and land reclamation around Khalid Lagoon.

The plan also makes an enigmatic suggestion: "There may be other possibilities for the expansion of trade, possibly of a specialized kind where Sharjah could be first in the field. This would require special study." These "possibilities" are not further elucidated, but the reference is probably to a deepwater port, a proposal not unlike the one Sharjah's leader and

traders considered nearly sixty years earlier. The plan does not propose such a harbor, though Saqr's shallow haven appears in drawings, with a proposed jetty. Months after the plan's issuance, Saqr visited Beirut and communicated with West German experts. He was in discussions with two banks, outside the regional monopoly of British Bank of the Middle East, to fund something larger than the jetty inscribed in the plan. The political agency could not keep up with him, reporting that Sharjah's development plans remained "mysterious."[18] In May 1964, the British government and Dubai's ruler Sheikh Rashid caught wind of Saqr's plan for a large, two-berth harbor, likely Halcrow's "specialized" idea. Sharjah's ruler was ready to risk any income source he had on the idea. Dubai's leader was proportionately ruthless in maintaining his ascendancy. "In a burst of characteristic energy and duplicity," Rashid hastily commissioned Halcrow for a nearly $5-million port, with four berths.[19] It seems Halcrow was likely promoting the same idea to both leaders, exploiting a rivalry that British officials had only exacerbated. The result was that Halcrow's profits increased in Dubai at Sharjah's expense. "It was obvious," a British official reported, "that a Dubai deep-water port would kill the Sharjah project stone dead." Sharjah's supposedly "more foolish actions," according to British sources, once again had fueled Dubai's avaricious development.

A SECOND MASTER PLAN

Sharjah's harbor plans were reduced to the jetty Halcrow had drawn in the 1963 plan. Halcrow secured the commission for both Dubai's matchless Port Rashid and Saqr's conciliatory jetty, the first a massive acquisition and the latter a placeholder for possible future contracts. The jetty was connected by an eventual causeway to an onshore point between the British Petroleum compound and the edge of Sharjah's Al Mareija neighborhood. Here, at the terminus of Al Meena Street, the 1963 plan designated a "commercial centre." Along this road, Sharjah was reported to be developing "modern flats" to connect to lines being laid for electricity and running water. For the time being, the road's appendage projecting out to sea was the most visible of Saqr's efforts to harness concrete and steel for reviving Sharjah. He was not around for the jetty's completion. In June 1965, with the finishing details underway in the rising heat of summer, Sheikh Saqr was deposed in a coup.

The British Foreign Office claimed no role in Saqr's removal, a far-fetched assertion according to Pan-Arab media reporting at the time.[20] While news outlets in Cairo and Baghdad presented Saqr as a legitimate

LIST OF ELEMENTS

FIRST STAGE POPULATION 30,000 FINAL 60,000

TOWN CENTRE

PALACE surrounded by public concourse

C.M. CENTRAL MOSQUE new

CIVIC CENTRE containing new majlis, law courts, police station, municipality offices, library, fire station etc. (reservation only)

COMMERCIAL CENTRE containing company offices, main banks, hotels etc. (reservation only)

SPORTS AND RECREATION CENTRE

HIGHER EDUCATION CENTRE

R.T. ROLA TREE

T. ROAD TRANSPORT TERMINUS including garage

M. WHOLESALE OR DISTRIBUTION MARKET

SUQ two stages

SHOPS i.e. larger stores and agencies

HARBOUR

NEW WHARF with open storage area (o.s.a)

AREA for warehouses, workshops, admin., customs etc.

INDUSTRIAL

TWO AREAS for development

LIVING

RESIDENTIAL AREAS (1., 2.) completely new development. pop. 2,500-3,000

NEIGHBOURHOODS including shops, mosques, schools, recreation. Intended that app. 1/3rd. units to have communal toilets.

		POPULATION
FIRST STAGE	'A'	3,500
	'B1, 2'	5,000
	'C'	5,000 (integrated with existing coastal development)
	'D'	5,000
	'E'	5,000
	'F'	3,000
FINAL STAGES	'G'	5,000
	'H'	5,000
	'I'	5,000
	'J''K''L'	15,000 (west of lagoon)

HOSPITAL

AS EXISTING

to DUBAI

Zoning Proposals, Sharjah Town Plan, Sir William Halcrow & Partners, 1963. The plan reveals how zoning was determined largely by laying a grid of wide thoroughfares, called "primary distributors." From 1963, Sharjah's form was determined by idealized traffic patterns. In between proposed roadways (most of which were executed) were designated zones, including a civic sector, education center, and residential neighborhoods, called "precincts." The new jetty (left) was completed in 1965 near BP's compounds and a proposed commercial center to rise along Al Meena Street. Three coastal roundabouts already reveal Halcrow's proposal to reclaim Sharjah Creek. Instead, the narrow waterway was preserved and dredged, and the labeled sand spit was earmarked for expansion into a reclaimed peninsula for the future Port Khalid. The legend's scale has been shifted for legibility. Halcrow/Jacobs. Courtesy of John R. Harris Library.

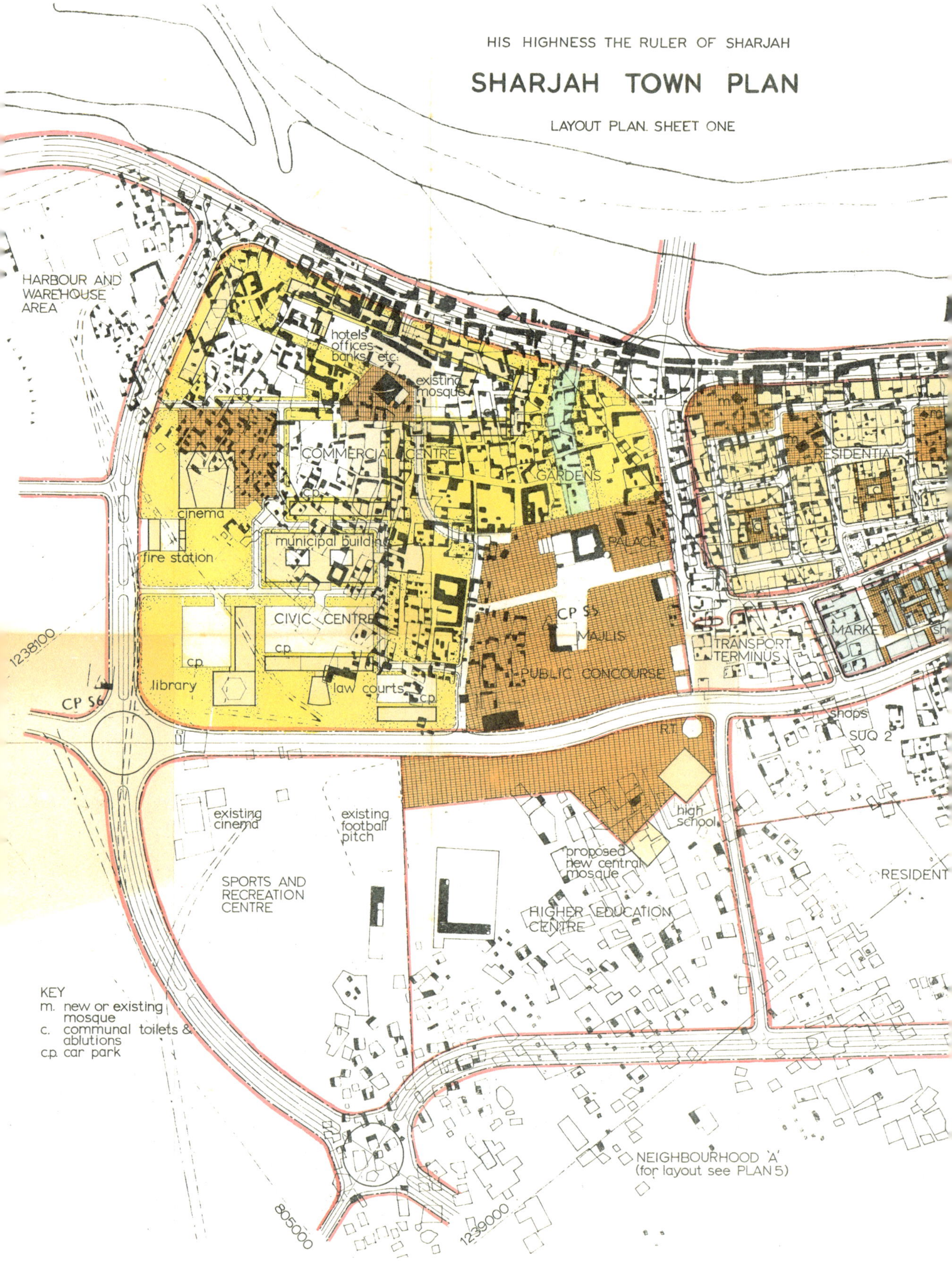

Layout Plan, Sheet One, Sharjah Town Plan, Sir William Halcrow & Partners, 1963. Detail portion of zoning plan reveals how widespread clearance was proposed to make way for “concourses” and “precincts.” Halcrow/Jacobs. Courtesy of John R. Harris Library.

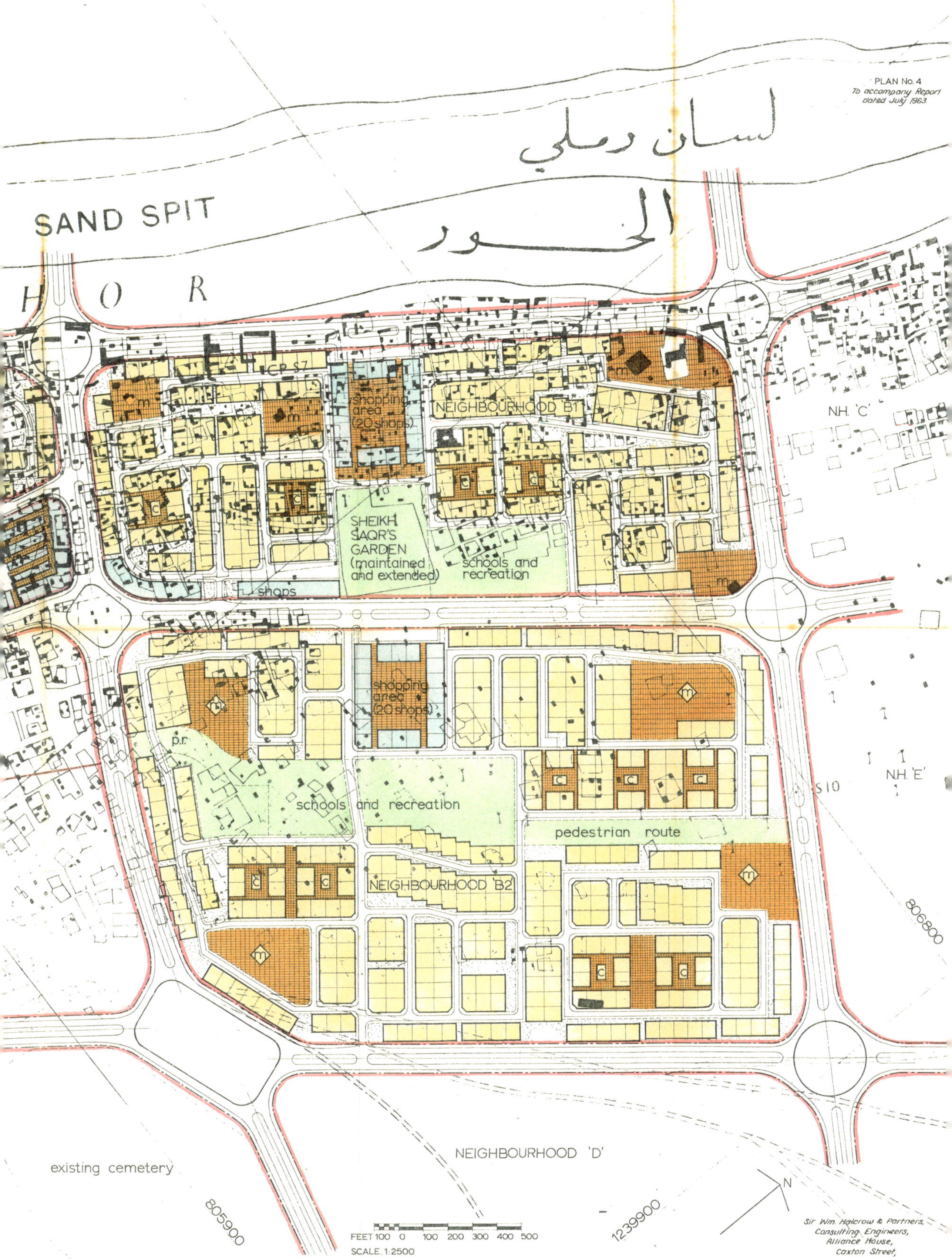
PLAN No. 4
To accompany Report dated July 1963.
لسان رملي
الخور
SAND SPIT
H O R
NEIGHBOURHOOD B1
shopping area (20 shops)
SHEIKH SAQR'S GARDEN (maintained and extended)
schools and recreation
shops
NH. 'C'
shopping area (20 shops)
p.r.
schools and recreation
pedestrian route
NEIGHBOURHOOD B2
S10
N.H. 'E'
806800
NEIGHBOURHOOD 'D'
existing cemetery
805900
1239900
N
FEET 100 0 100 200 300 400 500
SCALE 1:2500
Sir Wm. Halcrow & Partners, Consulting Engineers, Alliance House, Caxton Street,

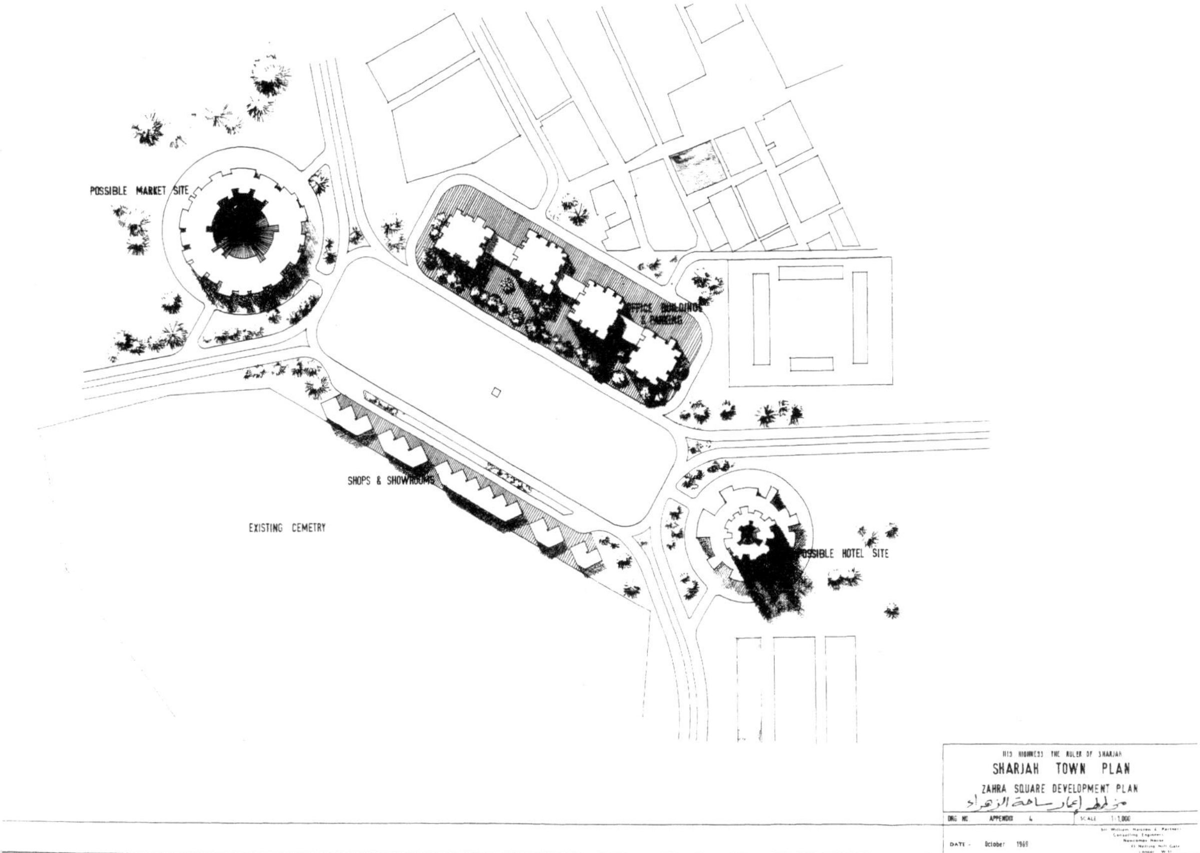

07

ruler in forced exile, other forces rallied to support his cousin and named successor, Sheikh Khalid bin Mohammed Al Qasimi. British officials endorsed the new ruler as "enthusiastic" about pursuing their recommended reforms. From 1966, after a coup that brought him to power, Abu Dhabi's Sheikh Zayed bin Sultan Al Nahyan bolstered Khalid's ascent with cash gifts to fund more development.[21] And while Saqr did not last, his advisors, Sir William Halcrow and Partners, did. Khalid commissioned them to revisit the town plan in 1969. The resulting *Town Planning for the State Capital of Sharjah* report did not define a new era of leadership. Instead, it followed "very closely the recommendations of the 1963 Town Planning Report." To counterbalance the destabilizing coup, the plan was a blueprint for expansion based on continued progress. It speaks confidently of future "stages" and "phases," in which Halcrow would play a major part.[22]

A new asphalt road, completed by means of yet another separate contract for Halcrow, connected Sharjah to Dubai, easing the flow of people and materials from one city to the other. Thereafter, any proposed projects in Sharjah were framed not as a challenge to Dubai's dominance but as part of an expanded field of private-industry contracts.[23] In 1969, when the plan was issued, "Sharjah continued to prosper, for reasons which nobody can quite explain." The jetty, by then in full operation, was active, so much so that its supply of cheap cement threatened Dubai-based merchants' profitable hold on the building staple. "The main streets of Sharjah are wider than those of Dubai, and at night they are better lit. Water and electricity supplies ... are now improving under the hands of British engineers imported and paid for by the government of Sharjah." All of these projects, initiated by the deposed ruler and executed by his hired advisors, were now endorsed by the British government. At this point, the British saw good reason to support Sharjah's expansion, but the rivalry between Sharjah and Dubai had already taken hold: "Sheikh Rashid was trying to strangle Sharjah's port, kill Sharjah truck driving, put Sharjah travel agencies out of business." The observing British official surmised that Sheikh Khalid didn't "want to compete with Dubai, but neither will he accept the status of a suburb." The summer before the plan's issuance, Khalid traveled to London, "not seeking pleasure but talking to businessmen, and returned with a parcel of signed contracts in his pocket."[24] Khalid wasn't more successful because his plans were less "grandiose" than Saqr's; his predecessor had successfully demonstrated that

Sharjah could also be a generator of contracts for British companies. If there was now any British concern about hindering Dubai's development, it was redeemed by the perpetual rivalry that only produced more British-sourced contracts.

Like the previous one, the 1969 town plan refers to designated "residential areas," just more of them. Each of these "precincts," confined by Halcrow's prescribed roadways, was still conceived as a "self-contained element," whose inner growth and changes could be monitored and isolated from other zones. "Each residential area," according to the plan, needed to be "accurately planned and assessed" for its "ultimate population." Beyond this, there is no evidence of any demographical analysis or even a mere observation that Sharjah had a tenuous and fluid population, whose growth was largely determined by unmonitored migration. The plan acknowledges that "it is not possible to determine the rate of growth of the population of Sharjah as there are no available statistics." What is especially strange about this claim is that, in the previous year, Sharjah had taken part in a regional census, an effort that for all practical purposes attempted to provide not only an accurate population count but also more granular data about residents, including their home countries and their employment status in the city. Halcrow makes no mention of having access to the results, but the plan also appears to have no need for them. The census had been pursued to gather a clearer picture of how immigration and population growth were transforming Sharjah. The plan functioned according to different reasoning: that the city is transformed not by its residents but by the deliberate arrangement of property rights, infrastructure, and architecture. Rather than to *respond* to an existing reality, the 1969 plan aimed to *create* one.

Wide new roads, or "primary distributors," provided the figurative and actual guidelines for shaping the city. The plan conceded that Sharjah's unquantified level of vehicle traffic did not yet require a "modern urban road system"; such a system, however, needed to be laid out and reserved for the time when automobile traffic would expect "to enter and leave the town rapidly and to circulate freely."[25] When the plan was issued, the city likely had a mere two kilometers of hardened roads, Halcrow reserved swaths of land large enough to accommodate eight lanes of traffic. These roadways were designed to be void of building frontage and pedestrian access.[26] The plan also proposed that "in the foreseeable future" the city's prosperity would demand a "two-level road system"—not to separate cars from city life but to ensure that the network's intersections did not impede vehicle movement. The city was defined as a conveyor system for cars. Today, one immediately feels the repercussions of this planning when trying to walk from one "self-contained" district to another; the pedestrian's movement is often necessarily illegal.

The 1969 plan paid little attention to the older sections of Sharjah, which had been laid out in "rigid gridiron pattern" but not attentive to the 1963 plan's proposed districts. The proposal had been to flatten the old neighborhoods to make way for vast "concourses" encircling civic centers and shopping complexes; the land was mostly cleared, but it proved unamenable to the planner's pen. Despite the absence of improved roads, or maybe in anticipation of them, the real estate market had surged in these areas, causing the unmanaged razing of the palm-frond complexes and a whirlwind of demolitions of the old coral buildings for private developments.

While the 1963 plan had prized the elevation of this area of Sharjah, the 1969 plan focused on the city's low-lying region, on the water-soaked lands toward Dubai. This was also where larger tracts of land had not yet been apportioned for sale. Deemed "unsuitable for building development," the area around Khalid Lagoon was available for Halcrow's planning proposals and thus for potential contracts. The site was also propitiously adjacent to the Dubai–Sharjah road, recently surfaced with asphalt, situated conveniently in relation to Dubai and to Sharjah's extending road network.[27] Halcrow's plan foresees the indeterminate, marshy land transformed through a tactic that had made the company a profitable part of Dubai's ongoing overhaul: land reclamation. An estimated 4.5-million cubic meters of earth had to be excavated from the temperamental lagoon's floor to create a deep "recreational lake." The gathered earth was then redistributed to raise the area's lowest points and ready them for development. In addition, a new channel was cut through the shoreline to provide a more constant flow of water into the now deep lake. The water levels raised as a result of this massive project could entertain a constant stream of "local craft"—a reference to the wooden ships, which, though still fueling most of Sharjah's sea trade, were held in regard for their aesthetic contribution to lake views.

Halcrow pitched the land reclamation work the same way as in Dubai: project costs would be recouped by "making available large areas of valuable land" for sale to developers. Halcrow's plan brought forth a whole new realm of solid land no one could lay claim to, except for the government that created it. Today, the lagoon is known as Lake Khalid, indeed a recreational lake that has served few purposes other than to absorb

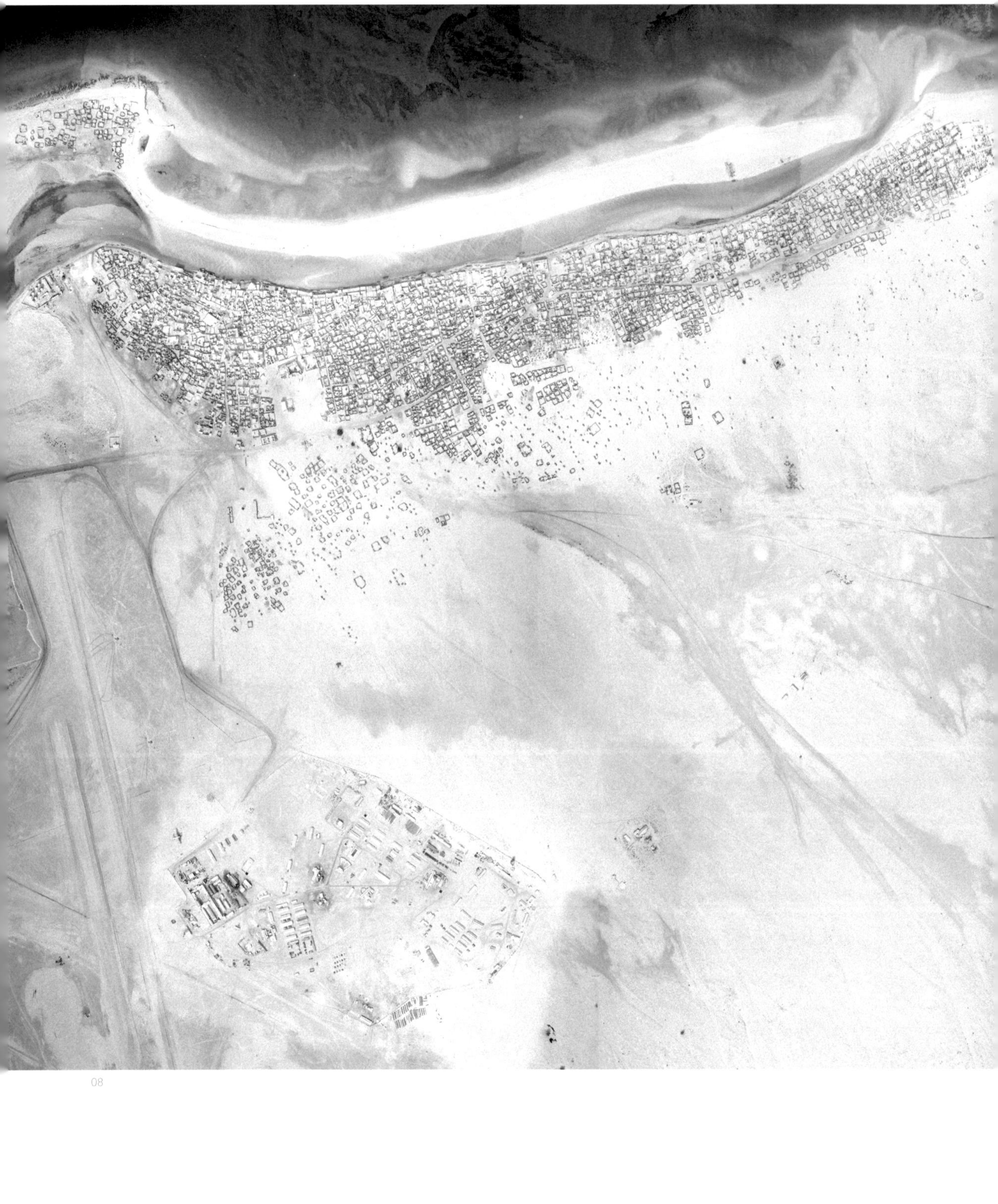

08

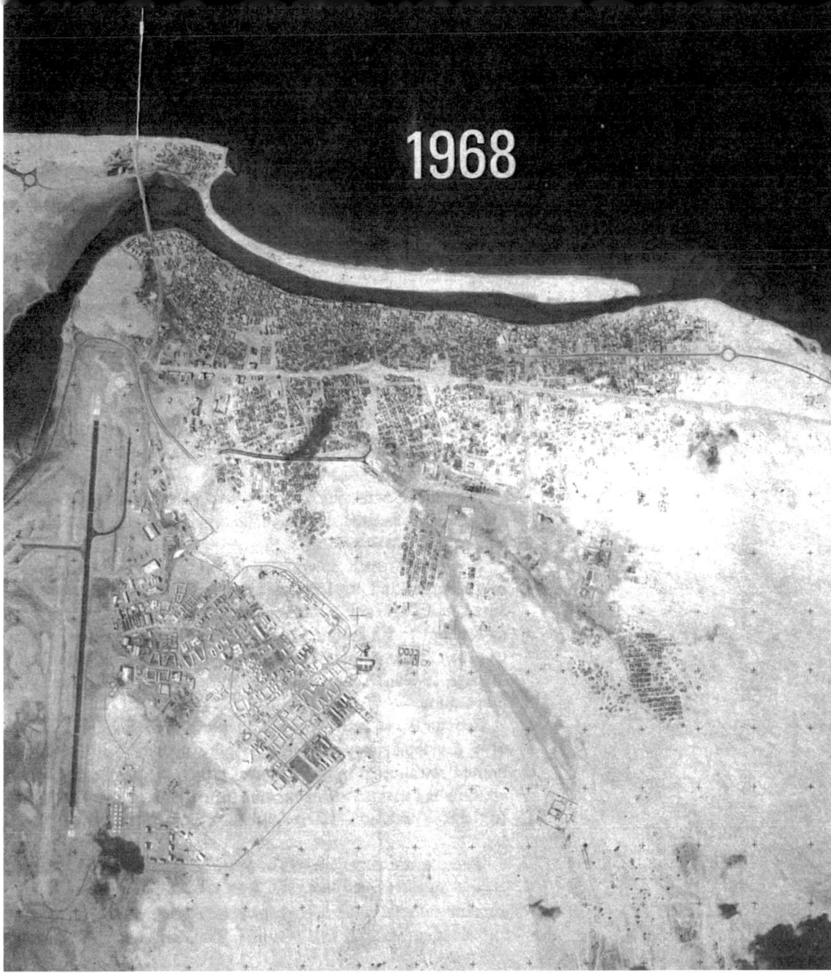

09

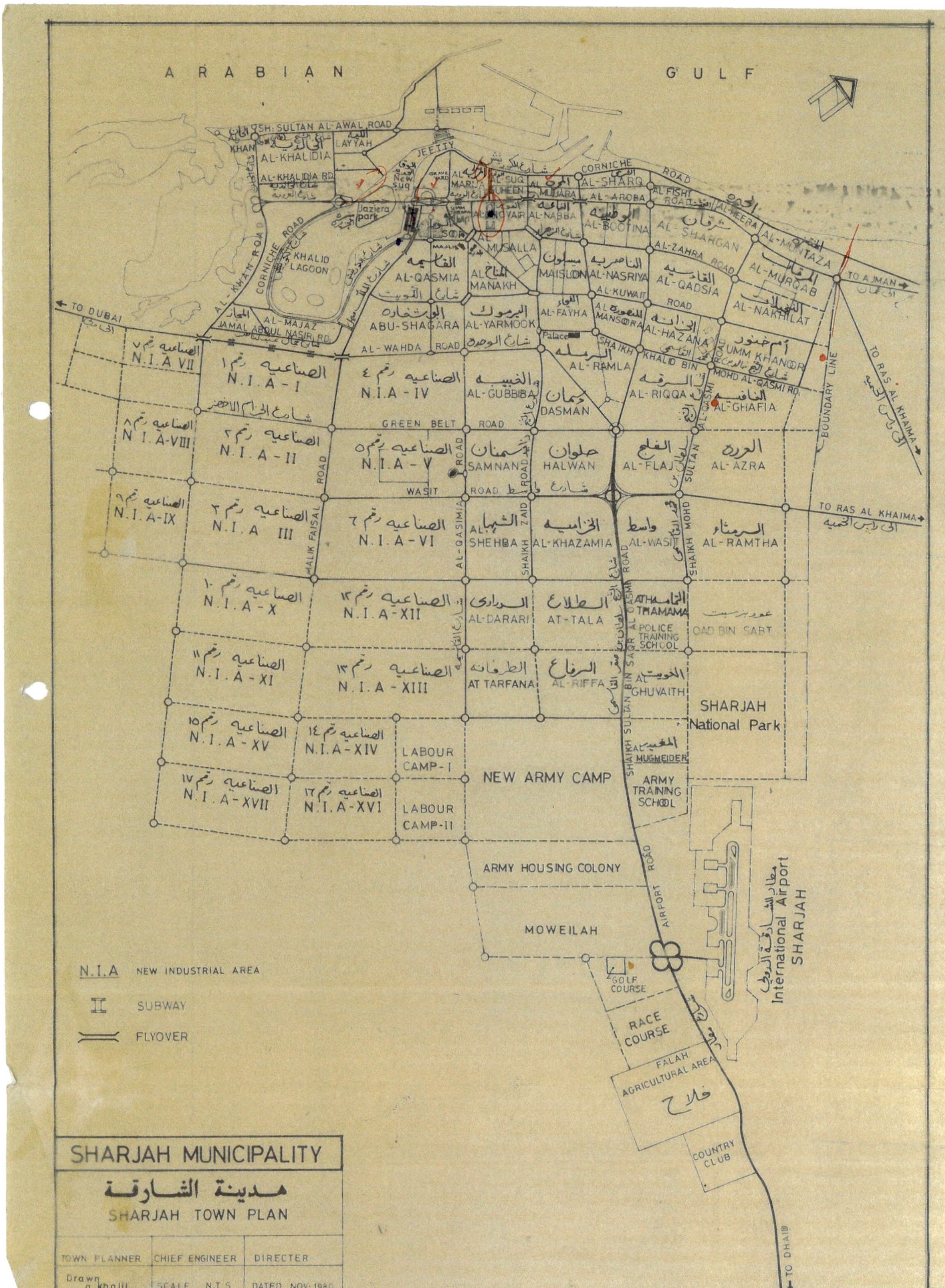

ARABIAN GULF
SH. SULTAN AL-AWAL ROAD
LAYYAH
AL-KHALIDIA
AL-KHALIDIA RD.
JEETTY
CORNICHE ROAD
AL-SHARQ
AL-AROBA
AL-FISHT
AL-HEERA
AL-BOOTINA
AL-SHARGAN
AL-MUNTAZA
AL-NABBA
AL-MUSALLA
AL-ZAHRA ROAD
AL-MURQAB
TO AJMAN
KHALID LAGOON
AL-QASMIA
AL-MANAKH
MAISLON
AL-NASRIYA
AL-QADSIA
AL-KUWAIT ROAD
AL-NAKHILAT
TO DUBAI
AL-MAJAZ
JAMAL ABDUL NASIR RD.
ABU-SHAGARA
AL-YARMOOK
AL-FAYHA
AL MANSOORA
AL-HAZANA
UMM KHANOOR
TO RAS AL KHAIMA
AL-WAHDA ROAD
Palace
AL-RAMLA
SHAIKH KHALID BIN MOHD AL-QASMI RD.
N.I.A VII
N.I.A-I
N.I.A-IV
AL-GUBBIBA
DASMAN
AL-RIQQA
AL-GHAFIA
BOUNDARY LINE
GREEN BELT ROAD
N.I.A-VIII
N.I.A-II
N.I.A-V
SAMNAN
HALWAN
AL-FLAJ
AL-AZRA
WASIT ROAD
TO RAS AL KHAIMA
N.I.A-IX
N.I.A III
N.I.A-VI
AL-SHEHBA
AL-KHAZAMIA
AL-WASIT
AL-RAMTHA
MALIK FAISAL ROAD
AL-QASIMIA ROAD
SHAIKH ZAID ROAD
SHAIKH MOHD SULTAN
N.I.A-X
N.I.A-XII
AL-DARARI
AT-TALA
ATHAMAMA
POLICE TRAINING SCHOOL
OAD BIN SART
N.I.A-XI
N.I.A-XIII
AT TARFANA
AL-RIFFA
AL GHUVAITH
SHARJAH National Park
N.I.A-XV
N.I.A-XIV
LABOUR CAMP-I
NEW ARMY CAMP
AL-MUGHEIDER
ARMY TRAINING SCHOOL
N.I.A-XVII
N.I.A-XVI
LABOUR CAMP-II
SHAIKH SULTAN BIN SAQR AL QASMI ROAD
ARMY HOUSING COLONY
MOWEILAH
AIRPORT ROAD
International Airport SHARJAH
GOLF COURSE
RACE COURSE
FALAH AGRICULTURAL AREA
COUNTRY CLUB
TO DHAID
N.I.A NEW INDUSTRIAL AREA
SUBWAY
FLYOVER
SHARJAH MUNICIPALITY
مدينة الشارقة
SHARJAH TOWN PLAN
TOWN PLANNER
CHIEF ENGINEER
DIRECTER
Drawn a. khalil
SCALE N.T.S
DATED NOV. 1980

10

water runoff and offer waterfront views to real estate.[28] Halcrow envisioned it fringed with beach umbrellas, water skiers, and grassy lawns, a district of pleasure and tranquility rendered by municipal mandate and real estate development—all set against the backdrop of the disarray of the existing Sharjah beyond. Halcrow's proposed roadways kept the lake and its lifestyle sealed off from the rest of the city, just as with the plan's other "enclosed areas."

While municipal administration, education, health care, and public transit are cursorily mentioned, the 1969 plan hardly pondered how residents would live in the city. Besides recreation and unimpeded roads, the report also proposed a coherent approach to bolstering industrial areas in Sharjah, including a district larger than that around Lake Khalid, with origins in the 1963 plan. Set inland from the "primary distributor" that enclosed the lake district, the industrial areas were still "sporadic" in development in 1969 but soon spread, seemingly infinitely, inland. These zones were instrumentalized as part of Sharjah's aspirational economy as a low-cost, business-friendly home to a "light industries" sector. Placed beyond Halcrow's proposed lake district, they were also strategically located on the road leading to Dubai. Sharjah could offer affordable real estate just a short distance from the escalating prices of Dubai. It could house the warehouses and work sheds that supplied industrial services not only to its own urban center but also to Dubai. By 1980, with no small contribution from this area, Sharjah was described as surviving on the "relative cheapness of lands and rents." Its most prevalent commercial sector, auto repair shops, kept the roads drawn by Halcrow well populated.

MORE CHANGE, MORE CONTINUITY

As with the 1963 plan, the 1969 plan was issued toward the end of a ruler's reign. In 1972, Sheikh Khalid was assassinated by his predecessor, Saqr, in the latter's attempt to return to power. Once again, Sharjah faced potential political turmoil, quickly defused by the appointment of Khalid's brother Sheikh Sultan bin Muhammad Al Qasimi as the new ruler. And, once again, Halcrow survived political change through its ability to render transformation on the landscape into a conduit for investments. Halcrow's plans did not so much envision a city as deliver the topography of coordinates, schedules, and measurements necessary for doling out future contracts. Announcement of a new ruler was followed by announcements of a new litany of projects. The city, more than ever, was described in the kilometer counts of water pipes, the price of a new project, and the number of new commercial and residential buildings. To maintain the image of a stable city, Sheikh Sultan eagerly presented more transformation. His ascent in 1972 coincided with the confirmation of pending petroleum wealth. The resulting landscape of identifiable and quantifiable projects—hotels, mosques, office towers, and recreation centers—were both a testament to new wealth and a down payment to attracting more investment from abroad.

In 1974, Sharjah received its first earnings from oil sales, most of which had already been spent. That same year, Sheikh Sultan commissioned Halcrow to determine the site for a new airport, as recommended in both master plans.[29] Halcrow engineers allegedly accompanied the new ruler one day out to the chosen site, over a packed sand road that would soon be surfaced with asphalt to become one of the tendrils connecting the old coastal city to the expensive airport fifteen kilometers inland. The motorcade crossed unbuilt territory, toward which the expanding city could stretch on an array of wide roads, giant roundabouts, and sweeping underpasses, all orchestrated by the attending engineers. A seven-berth port to replace the jetty, sanitary souks, massive greenspaces, and imposing government buildings were situated, like pieces on a board game, on the maps Halcrow maintained. Sharjah, it was reported, was also "bent on becoming a tourist center."[30] The city more than just followed the Halcrow plans; it continued to be defined—through media campaigns, travel brochures, and investment pitches—as a city whose form was shaped by engineers, carved out by infrastructure.

"Our basic approach," according to one short-lived advisor to the ruler, "is that we don't have rules." No rules, but apparently a plan. "Town planning," according to a 1976 *Financial Times* article, "was one of the ruler's main enthusiasms."[31] Planning, though, was divorced from rules because the plan was a business offering, a visualization, a technocratic promise that a seemingly endless desert could be apportioned to stoke a real estate market. A plan to presuppose resourcefulness and therefore deny any spoor of desperation. Sharjah's resources were its delineated land bank, a catalogue of offerings, and rumors of more petroleum wealth to come. A plan with no rules, just opportunity. A matrix of real estate, transforming desert into "a pleasant environment almost from scratch." Sharjah could claim being "the fastest growing state in the Middle East" because it still had so far to grow. The plan was supposed to be self-generative. "Development fed on itself exponentially," according to the *Financial Times*.[32] Change was the only constant, that is in addition to the single British engineering firm that tallied and extolled the possibilities. In 1978, Sharjah residents looked out over a landscape designed for dealmaking, a "near-catastrophe ... because its planners [had] created a state infrastructure and are now searching for an economy to drop into place."[33] In 1984, Halcrow submitted a new master plan—the third for its third ruler-client—that pushed the grid further inland to attach to the new airport.

Sharjah's narrative was no longer driven by a simplistic rivalry between two cities too near to each other. Dubai was once pitched as the free and lawless port, but now Sharjah, the lesser-known and more inchoate city, could be pitched according to the old Dubai playbook. But that did not hinder Dubai. The same year Sharjah announced its new airport, Dubai proclaimed a new city for 500,000 people and another airport. The city at Jebel Ali didn't materialize, but the port city of mega-industry around it did. There was little more of note in the intercity competition, once Dubai's proposals proved impossible to match. Sharjah, at least, was now a city that offered a handshake with autocratic power, without bureaucratic paperwork, to secure a business deal. It was the truer realm of "no taxes and less red tape than elsewhere."[34] By the mid-1970s, the Abu Dhabi–based federal government was paying Sharjah's bills for education, policing, health care, and even road building. This freed up the city's leadership to focus further on defining their city as an investment opportunity. The *Financial Times* observed that Sharjah's "booming economy reflects the economic buoyancy of the UAE." No longer framed as the underdog to Dubai's boomtown, Sharjah bore the mantel of Abu Dhabi's magnanimity and solvency. Abu Dhabi would guarantee the rescheduling of mounting loans. Sharjah was merely the latest chapter in a regional story of cities created "out of the desert" on the premise of oil wealth. In a 1976 *Financial Times* supplement focused on Sharjah, there was at least one prophetic observation about Sharjah and Dubai: "The two cities must eventually merge physically." That merging happened, not only through the entangling of built environments but also in the knots of vehicle traffic, both of which now stretch from Dubai, through Sharjah, and into Ajman, the result being a single indistinguishable conurbation. Without rules, Sharjah's plan has merged into greater ones.

Notes:

1. Rosemarie Said Zahlan, *The Origins of the United Arab Emirates: A Political and Social History of the Trucial States.* (London: Macmillan, 1978), 28.
2. H. J. Evans, "A Note on the Wealth of Dubai," 24 Jun. 1950, The National Archives, United Kingdom (NA), FO 371:82047.
3. Pelly to Secretary of States, 26 Jun. 1950, NA, FO 371:82047.
4. "A Note on the Wealth of Dubai."
5. H. J. Evans, "Notes on the Finances of Sharjah," 12 Aug. 1950, NA, FO 371:82047.
6. Ibid. Note from C. M. Rose, 22 Aug., NA, FO 371:8204. Documented sources of Sharjah income included the following: land rent paid by the British government for air and military compounds, payments from oil prospectors (about a third more than Dubai), and profits from red oxide mining (ibid.).
7. British Residency Bahrain to Principal Secretary of State for Foreign Affairs, 12 Aug. 1950, NA, FO 371:82047.
8. Adams, "Minutes of discussions regarding Halcrow's survey of Dubai and Sharjah Creeks," 28 Jan. 1955, NA, FO 371:114696.
9. Craig to Acting Political Resident, 20 Sep. 1964, NA, FO 371:174711. See also Todd Reisz, "Hardened Edges," in *Showpiece City: How Architecture Made Dubai* (Redwood City: Stanford University Press, 2020).
10. Note, 28 Oct. 1959, NA, FO 371:140143.
11. Griffith to Craig, 5 Dec. 1961, NA, FO 371:157025. By the time construction of Dubai's airport and Port Rashid was underway, Costain was also securing contracts in Dubai.
12. Burrows to Macmillan, 28 Nov. 1955, NA, FO 371:114656.
13. The hospital project seems to have been a fraudulent scheme led by a Swiss huckster. See Head of Chancery, British Embassy, Jedda to H. B. M., Political Agency, Dubai, 14 May 1963, NA, FO 371:168926.
14. See Reisz, "Piecemeal: Al Maktoum Hospital," in *Showpiece City*.
15. Sir William Halcrow & Partners, *Report and Description of Proposals for Sharjah Town Plan*, July 1963.
16. *Sabkha* is a characteristic element of the regional landscape where saline deposits result in hardened surfaces traversable by cars and trucks. Rain or tides, however, cause them to disintegrate into deep, mud-like morass.
17. It is not surprising that Sharjah's most prominent houses were dilapidated, as their inhabitants may have either gone to oil states to earn income or moved their businesses to better-serviced Dubai as early as the 1930s. The plan listed the neighborhoods of Al Mareija, Al Shuwaiheen, and Freej bin Darwish as those needing rebuilding.
18. Craig to Brown, 30 Jun. 1964, NA, FO 371:174713.
19. The port in Dubai would become known as Port Rashid, with an estimated cost that ballooned to $57.5 million by 1969.
20. British government files deny any role in the coup against Sheikh Saqr, though British officials reported that Saqr "flatly refused to reconsider the permission he had given for the opening of an Arab League Office in his State." Before his departure, Saqr had also carried out other important developments, including the initiation of an electric grid scheme and power station, completed jointly by Halcrow and Kennedy & Donkin, whom the British political agency had also brought to Dubai. The original power station was on land currently occupied by City Centre Mall.
21. Sheikh Zayed came to power in Abu Dhabi after a coup in 1966, in which the British government played an explicit role.
22. Sir William Halcrow & Partners, *Town Planning for the State Capital of Sharjah*, 1969.
23. See p. 52.
24. "Dubai and the Northern Trucial States Review of the Year 1969," 30 Dec. 1969, NA, FCO 8:1509.
25. The plan claimed that the amount of roadworks underway precluded any traffic surveys to be completed for the plan.
26. A comprehensive and illustrative plan of Sharjah is absent from the copy of the plan used for this article. The 1963 master plan's roadways, however, are largely drawn as they were eventually laid.
27. The area's marshy condition had been intensified by the infrastructure works that gleaned the hardened sabkha surfaces to create road surfaces for more built-up areas of Sharjah. See Halcrow, *Town Planning for the State Capital of Sharjah*, 27.
28. See the proposed master plan for Khalid Lagoon, p. 157.
29. Halcrow would secure several commissions for the planning and design of the new Sharjah International Airport. See p. 387.
30. "Sharjah Moves Rapidly to Modernize," *The Times* (London), June 19, 1975.
31. Kathleen Bishtawi, "Sharjah V: Environment," *Financial Times*, December 10, 1976.
32. James Buxton, "The Economy: Sharjah," *Financial Times*, June 26, 1976; Michael Tingay, "Sharjah: A New Framework," *Financial Times*, June 26, 1976.
33. "Sharjah: A New Framework."
34. James Buxton, "Sharjah II: Economy," *Financial Times*, December 10, 1976.

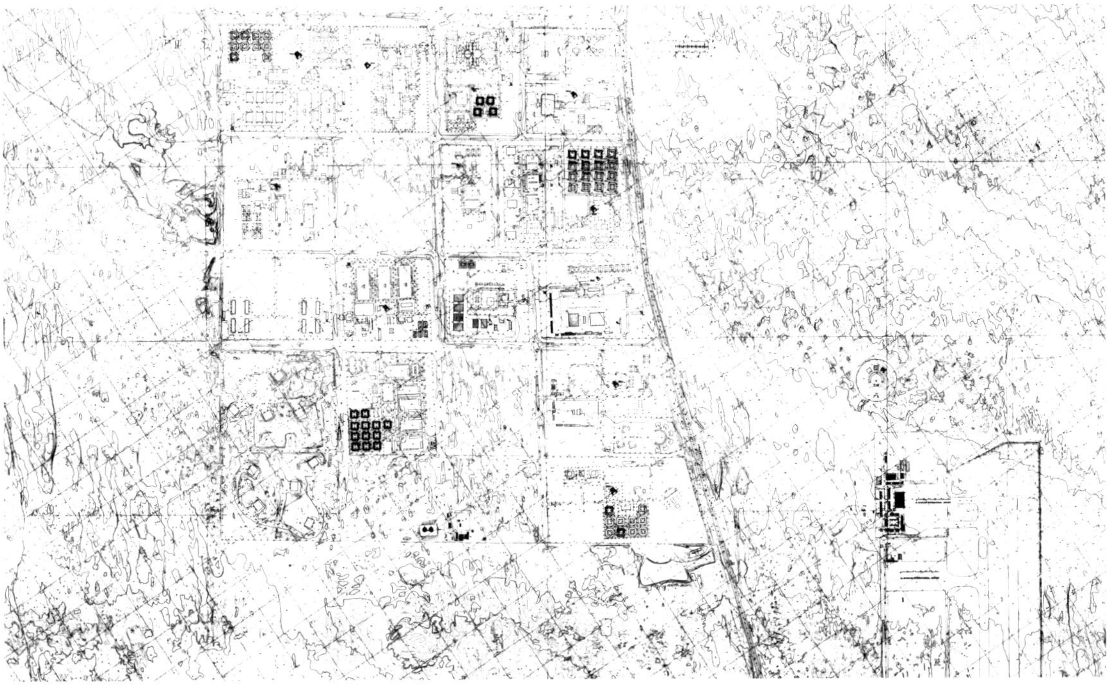

11

Images:

01. *Report and Description of Proposals for Sharjah Town Plan*, cover, Sir William Halcrow & Partners, 1963. Halcrow/ Jacobs. Courtesy of John R. Harris Library.
02. Sharjah ruler Sheikh Saqr bin Sultan Al Qasimi listens to Palestinian teacher Mohammed Abo Foul's explanation of model demonstrating *al yaazra*, a local irrigation technique. Scouts and students of Al Qasimiyah School listen during annual end-of-year exhibition, 1962 or 1963. In center, head of Sharjah courts Sheikh Majid bin Sager with his two sons: Hamad bin Majid peering over his shoulder and Saeed bin Majid to his right. Courtesy of Shaikha Nama bint Majid bin Saqr Al Qasimi.
03. General Plan, Sharjah Town Plan, Sir William Halcrow & Partners, 1963. The drawing was largely based on aerial photograph on p. 72. In Al Layah (top left) one can see an early jetty, likely completed in early 1930s to supply construction materials for British air station, and also the C-shaped shallow harbor Sheikh Saqr had built after British refusal to help rebuild Sharjah's port. Halcrow/Jacobs. Courtesy of John R. Harris Library.
04. Sharjah Port, undated. The 720-meter-long jetty could receive two ships at a time. Contractor, Beton- und Monierbau. MEED.
05. Interior, Sharjah Trade School, British-funded project to train local male students for the intensifying building boom, circa 1960. Students and graduates from the Sharjah program helped construct the trade school in Dubai. Al Arabi.
06. Existing Development, Sharjah Town Plan, Sir William Halcrow & Partners, 1963. The master plan included a color-coded zoning of construction quality. Large swaths of the city, indicated in yellow and brown, were classified as being in poor condition and made up of palm frond buildings and therefore designated for demolition to make way for Halcrow's proposed precincts and roadways. Halcrow/Jacobs. Courtesy of John R. Harris Library.
07. Halcrow's 1969 plan included architectural proposals for Al Zahra'a Square, the oblong open space also known today as Clock Tower Roundabout. In order to accommodate the growing population, the plan proposed shifting the city's commercial center from Al Meena Street further inland to here. For the new center, the Halcrow planners provided the plan's limited architectural proposals, both peculiarly large, round buildings and each at the end of the oblong roundabout, one a "market site" (where Al Zahra Hospital is today) and another a "hotel site." On the longer edges, Halcrow's plan proposed buildings not unlike what stand today—tall office towers and low-rise shops. Halcrow/ Jacobs. Courtesy of Peter Jackson.
08. Aerial of Sharjah city taken in January 1960 by Hunting Aerosurveys as part of contract to photograph Abu Dhabi, Dubai, and Sharjah. Halcrow would base Sharjah's first master plan on this photograph three years later. The existing city was concentrated at the coast. The British-controlled air base, below, can be read as a fenced-in site apart from the rest of the city. National Collection of Aerial Photography, courtesy of Peter Jackson.
09. In the years after Halcrow's issuance of the 1969 plan, the British press also started to chronicle spectacular development in Sharjah, but perhaps not accurately. In a 1970 publication on Sharjah, London-based *Middle East Economic Digest* summed up the early achievements of British industriousness in Sharjah with a pair of before/after aerial photographs: the first, allegedly from 1968—Sharjah portrayed in yet another year of dusty sand trails—and, "exactly a year apart," the second, 1969—a landscape seared by viscous ribbons of tarmac ready to sustain real estate investment. As of late summer 1969, however, Halcrow counted only two tarmac roads in Sharjah, affording good reason to doubt that the after-image was taken in January 1969. A reduction of accuracy, a folding of the timeline, for the sake of a good story further accentuated Sharjah as a city of profitable and malleable landscapes. UK MOD © Crown copyright, courtesy of MEED.
10. The Halcrow plan's guiding principle was a grid of major roadways knitted together by roundabouts. It was replicated as Sharjah expanded inland, reaching beyond Sharjah International Airport, also sited and designed by Halcrow. This drawing, produced by engineers and planners working for the municipality, reveals that Halcrow's plans were by 1980 internalized in the daily operations of ordering new designated sites for development. Dated November 1980, the plan was drafted by Abdul Khalil Shaikh, under the direction of town planner Afzal Ahmed Khan, chief engineer Tanweer Ahmad Zaidi, and director general Obaid Essa Ahmed. Afzal Ahmed Khan, courtesy of Sharjah Municipality.
11. Halcrow's 1984 master plan extended the grid inland toward the new airport. Halcrow/Jacobs, courtesy of Peter Jackson.

The hardening of the road leading from the Dubai–Sharjah road to Al Layah district, as part of Halcrow's road-building contract, 1968. Rahma bin Nasser Al Owais took this photograph from a Gulf Air flight to Bahrain, the first leg of his return to English studies at University of Baghdad. The new asphalt road was part of an infrastructural package to integrate the expanding port into the city of Sharjah. Rahma bin Nasser Al Owais, courtesy of Abdallah Mohamed Al Quraidi.

Workers laying the new asphalt road toward the port in Al Layah, circa 1966. At left, the construction staging site for the port's expansion. Michael Hamilton-Clark took this photograph while working as engineer on Halcrow's road-building contracts in the Trucial States. Michael Hamilton-Clark.

Orient Travel & Touring Agency
وكالة الشرق للسفريات والسياحة
SYRIAN AIR
SABENA
AIR FRANCE
saudia
السعودية
SAUDI ARABIAN AIRLINES
FORMULA 16

FIRST NATIONAL CITY

MONACO

Al Wahda Street, just over a decade after the construction photo on p. 30, 1991. The thoroughfare connected the old center of Sharjah to Dubai. Its mid-rise buildings housed South Asian and Arab (largely Lebanese) newcomers, who made the ground floors into Sharjah's most active commercial strip. Two buildings at left, Khatib & Alami, 1975; building, right, Sharjah Engineering Office, 1974. Dar Al Khaleej Printing & Publishing.

NEW COLD STORES

Arab Bank & British Bank of the Middle East Buildings

Arab Bank

Architect
Consolidated Engineering Company (Khatib & Alami)

Contractors
Darwish Engineering, Consolidated Contractors Company (CCC)

Completed
1968

Status
Demolished

Client
Sheikh Khalid bin Mohammed Al Qasimi

British Bank of the Middle East

Architect
Consolidated Engineering Company (Khatib & Alami)

Contractors
Darwish Engineering

Completed
1972

Status
Existing

Client
Sheikh Khalid bin Mohammed Al Qasimi

Like the kilometers of asphalt, the number of international banks was a commonly referenced indicator of Sharjah's viability in the 1970s and 1980s. Banks, one British magazine noted, embodied "expectations of oil wealth." In September 1970, Sharjah counted ten banks, an increase from four in the mid-1960s. The British Bank of the Middle East, or BBME, was the first to open in February 1953, thanks to coordination with the British government. BBME's first branch in Sharjah was described as a single-story, single-room building in the palm frond–shaded souk. The twenty-year contract signed by BBME and the ruler at the time, Sheikh Saqr bin Sultan Al Qasimi, stipulated that the bank would open at least two mornings every week and would hire Sharjah subjects as "clerical and menial staff if available and found suitable." The bank paid an annual rent of 1,600 riyals, equivalent to about $3,300 or AED 12,000 today.

Around 1967, Sharjah's then ruler, Sheikh Khalid bin Mohammed Al Qasimi, allegedly took an active role in real estate deals that would cultivate Sharjah's reputation in international banking. BBME agreed to partially finance the construction of a five-story block building situated prominently across from Sharjah's Rolla Square. As part of the agreement for what came to be known as the BBME Building, the bank rented the ground-floor retail space with a twenty-five-year lease; the floors above were situated around an open central courtyard and leased as apartments and office space. Sharjah Municipality also occupied some of the upper-floor space.

Before BBME relocated to the Rolla Square location, Amman-based Arab Bank had already opened its Sharjah branch in a three-story building on a neighboring plot. With its two upper floors of residences, the building was one of the city's first modern mixed-use buildings and often advertised as evidence of the city's progress. Following the bank's completion in 1968, more buildings of a similar scale and even larger began to line Al Arouba Street.

Both mixed-use buildings were designed by Consolidated Engineering Company, a Lebanese company that established its Sharjah office after securing the contract for the Arab Bank Building. In a subtle manner, the two buildings shared similar architectural expressions, particularly their use of complex facade screens—often compared to mashrabiya—that unified the facades and provided shading for the interiors. The BBME Building's inner courtyard accommodates open staircases and corridors, which increase air circulation and induce a sense of community. The upper floors are still used as residences today. The attention to the screens and environmental concerns are attributes not often found in the design firm's later work in the UAE. Eventually renamed Khatib & Alami, the company became one of the most prolific architecture firms in the country.

Today, the BBME Building is often affectionately referred to as the Juice World Building, a nod to the building's currently most visible tenant. The Arab Bank Building was demolished in the 1980s, rendered but a vague memory in the city's architectural history.

01. The British Bank of the Middle East Building, from Government Square, Al Arouba Street, 1970s. Reproduced with the permission of HSBC Holdings plc.
02. The Arab Bank, right, just as early streetlights marked Al Arouba Street as the city's primary axis. The BBME Building would rise behind the bank. On the left is a remaining traditional house of coral and stone. Its screened rooftop once provided privacy for sleeping outside in summer, until the arrival of taller buildings. To its right is the Grey Building (see p. 168). Mahmood AlSawan.

01

02

Mothercat Building

On his way to becoming a prominent Lebanese businessman, Emile Bustani returned to Lebanon in 1933 after graduating with a civil engineering degree from Massachusetts Institute of Technology. He soon thereafter founded the Contracting and Trading Company, or CAT, which specialized in constructing roads and oil pipelines throughout the region.

In 1951, Bustani's company merged with the British firm Motherwell Bridge Engineering Company to create the Middle East heavyweight construction company Mothercat LTD. Mothercat was active in the Levant and the Gulf throughout the 1960s and 1970s despite Bustani's sudden death in a plane crash off the coast of Lebanon in 1963.

Following the outbreak of the Lebanese Civil War in 1975, the company's board elected to move its headquarters from Beirut to Sharjah. They commissioned the Cypriot-born and British-educated architect Mesut Cagdas to design the new Mothercat offices on Al Wahda Street, the boom-induced road leading to Dubai.[1] The company remained there throughout the war in Lebanon. Cagdas had previously worked with Mothercat in 1971 on a project to design and construct Al Falaj Hotel in Muscat. Among the projects carried out by Mothercat in Sharjah are the Sharjah–Ras Al Khaimah road and the Sharjah Sports Complex, designed by the British firm RMJM.

An intersection near the company's headquarters was known as Mothercat Roundabout, indicative of the prominence of Mothercat Building in Sharjah.

03

Architect
Mesud Cagdas, Cagdas Associates

Contractor
Mothercat LTD

Client
Mothercat LTD

Completed
1976

Status
Demolished, 2000

1. See p. 78.

01.–02. Mothercat Building on Al Wahda Street, late 1970s. Dr. Naman Al Jalili Archives Collection.
03. Perspective rendering of early proposal for Mothercat Building, as shown in Cagdas Associates' marketing brochure, undated and unnamed, but confirmed after review of municipality documents. Cagdas Associates, courtesy of Dev Bhatia.

01

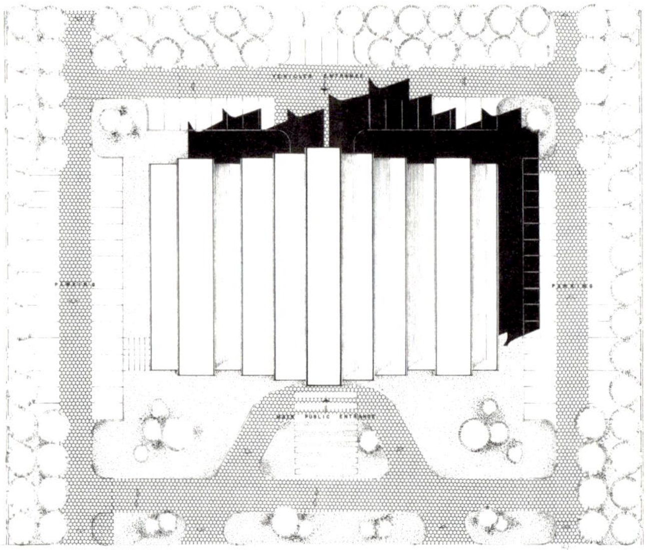

02

Sharjah Post Office

In 1978, a new main post office for Sharjah opened, prominently located on Government House Square. The roof was the most expressive element. Its wing-like, precast sections seemed at once to lift up from and enclose the rest the building. Glazing lining the eaves between the roof and brick walls allowed a cascade of soft daylight into the building's interiors. Today, the post office still stands, but its original design is barely discernible.

The building's initial gestures of a modernist architectural language were somehow realized despite Sharjah's major turn in the late 1970s toward excessive ornamentation, often inspired by Islamic architecture, for new government facilities. The post office survived in its original form until a massive renovation in the early 2000s, which included a complete transformation of the building's outer elevations: its wings were clipped. The result was a massive, monochromatic recladding of the building in patterns and textures, a so-called Islamicization of the building's architecture. A new portico with decorative, structurally superfluous columns was also added to accentuate the new design's aspirations to a classical temperament.

Architect and Engineering Consultant
Dar Al-Handasah, Shair & Partners

Client
Ministry of Public Works and Ministry of Communications

Completed
1978

Status
Significantly renovated

03

04

05

SIDE ELEVATION

PUBLIC ENTRANCE ELEVATION

HANDASAH CONSULTANTS SHAIR AND PARTNERS SHARJAH

07

01. Front elevation along Government House Square. In the background is one of Sharjah Expo's tents (see p. 173), 1980s. Dr. Naman Al Jalili Archives Collection.

02. Site plan as submitted to Sharjah's Ministry of Public Works, 1970s. Dar Al-Handasah, UAE Ministry of Infrastructure Development. Courtesy of Najeeb Maktari.

03.–05. Roof and elevation details, 1980s. Dr. Naman Al Jalili Archives Collection.

06. Side and main entrance elevation drawings as submitted to Sharjah's Ministry of Public Works, 1970s. Dar Al-Handasah, UAE Ministry of Infrastructure Development. Courtesy of Najeeb Maktari.

07. Two roadside snapshots from Government House Square after installation of the fountain designed by Halcrow, late 1980s. In background, left of post office, stands a residential block designed by Adnan Saffarini, completed in 1988. UAE Ministry of Infrastructure Development.

Students and teachers from a local school visit the brick plant for an ongoing construction site not far from Mothercat Roundabout and Sharjah's designated Industrial Area, early 1980s. Other images from this field trip, including the class of girls, appear throughout this book. DAFCO.

HOTEL
POLICE

Sheba Hotel

In 1968, the Yemeni contractor Mohammed Saeed Al Husseiny moved to Sharjah when the British evacuated Aden. Having built his contracting company on British-sourced contracts in Yemen, Al Husseiny hoped to regain his footing in Sharjah by tendering for new road construction projects connecting the city to Ras Al Khaimah. He also saw enough potential in Sharjah to purchase a plot of land near the airport, on what is now King Faisal Street. There, he imagined building a large department store. When the ruler Sheikh Khalid bin Mohammed Al Qasimi heard of his plans, he thought it a lost opportunity. Based on current demand and the site's strategic location near the airport, the ruler argued, the project should be a hotel. The resulting building, whose architect could not be identified, may have been based on drawings for a hotel built in Aden or elsewhere in Yemen.

The eventual hotel comprised two rectangular blocks of concrete bricks, embellished by shading elements. The rooftop shading was wing-like, recalling the nearby airport. The most overwhelming element was made up of slender, precast concrete slabs painted in bright red and gleaming white. The resulting facade bears a striking resemblance to the Sharjah flag.

Contractor
Aden Engineering & Contracting Company

Client
Mohammed Saeed Al Husseiny

Completed
1969

Status
Demolished, 1999

According to *Al Arabi* magazine, the hotel was where arriving entrepreneurs assembled to see and be seen.[1] In addition to its fifty air-conditioned rooms, the hotel housed a swimming pool, a restaurant, two cocktail bars, and a garden casino situated in the atrium between the two adjoining blocks. Interiors were decked out with luxurious, patterned wallpaper and plush upholstery. In 1971, one could enjoy a twin room, graced with red bedspreads and pale magenta curtains, for 100 Qatari riyals (about $20) per night. Downstairs, lobby walls were lined with framed photographs charting the history-in-the-making of Sheba Hotel as the center of Sharjah deal brokering.

According to Al Husseiny, the hotel hosted a twelve-day summit of Trucial States leaders before the union and meetings between the governments of Sharjah and Iran. He also recalled Sharjah leaders holding drawn-out discussions there with representatives of American oil companies for the early oil contracts.

1. See p. 110.

01. Front entrance along King Faisal Street, early 1970s. Images: Collection of Mohammed Saeed Al Husseiny, courtesy of Mostafa Mohammed Al Husseiny.
02. Sharjah's ruler Sheikh Khalid bin Mohammed Al Qasimi with owner Mohammed Saeed Al Husseiny at hotel's opening, 1969.

02

Sharjah Clock Tower

A bygone landmark, once described as the "centrepiece" of Sharjah's nocturnal panorama, was a gift to the city from the Dusseldorf-based company Beton- und Monierbau AG, delivered five years after they secured contracts to design and build the city's expanded port.

After completion of the port's first phase, known as The Jetty, the clock was installed in 1969 at Al Zahra'a Square, which quickly became known as Clock Tower Roundabout, like similar sites in Gulf cities, including the one in Dubai's Deira district.

The structure was a monument, as affirmed in its appearance on the bygone one-AED note and a postage stamp. It became a favorite destination for evening leisure and a backdrop for public festivities, when the structure would sometimes be festooned with colorful lights. The societal role it played accelerated development—the creation of the public space and apportionment of the adjoining land plots—around the oblong Al Zahra'a Square.

The clock tower's base was inspired by flower petals, out of which rose a cylindrical obelisk, bearing a cubic clock, all of this ensconced in a water fountain. The arrival of the clock tower coincided with the ruler's campaign to light Sharjah's streets at night and embellish them with public fountains. He spoke of "fountain therapy." Whenever a news item promoted Sharjah as the "Garden City of the Gulf," it was often accompanied by a photograph of the clock tower's fountain surrounded by colorful flowerbeds.

The campaign to feature more explicit references to Islamic design in Sharjah's public architecture increased in the 1980s, leading to the blue clock tower's replacement with a more compliant design when renovation work on Al Zahra'a Square and its surrounding roadways was carried out.

Architect and Contractor
Beton- und Monierbau AG

Completed
1969

Status
Demolished, 2006. Replaced

03

01. The clock tower at night, photographed by Noor Ali Rashid. Often referred to as the UAE's royal photographer, Rashid was born in what is today Pakistan and eventually became a naturalized citizen of the UAE. His photographic archive bears witness to a nation's history. © The Royal Photographer Noor Ali Rashid. Provided by Noor Ali Rashid Archives.

02. People gather around Al Zahra'a Square—or as most people call it, Clock Tower Roundabout—designated in Halcrow's master plans to be the new center of an expanded Sharjah. While the roundabout never acquired such a role, it did host celebrations and ceremonies throughout the 1970s. The clock tower, manufactured in Sharjah, was often draped with strings of lights during gatherings. Narain R. Sawlani.

03. Sharjah resident Mohammed Shamis Al Maazmi and his friend in front of clock tower, 1980–81. Collection of Mohammed Shamis Al Maazmi, courtesy of Ahmad Al Maazmi.

Córdoba and Granada Buildings, Bank Street

Architect
Juan Paradinas, José Carlos Laredo, Tecnica y Proyectos (TYPSA)

Contractors
Eastern LLC, Kalpataru Limited, Costain International, Arabian Contracting Company (ACC), Gulf General Projects Co.

Completed
1979

Status
Partially demolished

In 1974, Sharjah's ruler Sheikh Sultan bin Muhammad Al Qasimi commissioned the Spanish firm Tecnica y Proyectos, or TYPSA, to design and manage construction of what allegedly aspired to be "a Wall Street in the desert." The project comprised 24 eleven-story buildings on either side of a landscaped boulevard. Burj Al Kubs, the remaining watchtower of the demolished fort, determined the large-scale project's central axis. The buildings' continuous concrete bands conceal partitioned balconies and accentuated the axial perspective. The result was Sharjah's most memorable site of modern architecture, until its pieces, one by one, started to be demolished.

Each building is owned by either the ruler, who according to the architects actively participated in the design process, or a member of the ruling family. Design and construction costs were estimated at AED 138 million, or about $35 million. Around the time of the project's announcement, seventy-nine American and European banks applied to open branches in the city. Recent oil announcements meant that lending opportunities were rampant. The banks to be housed in the lower floors were urged to contribute to the financing of the project's construction, thus shifting the city's banking center from Al Meena Street to the newly named Bank Street, also known as Al Burj Street.

Each row of buildings is named after an Andalusian city—the Córdoba Buildings (southwest) and the Granada Buildings (northeast)—as a nod to the Spanish designers, though they were based in Madrid. For both sets of buildings, apartments with balconies were set above commercial ground floors and mezzanines. Each building also offered communal recreational spaces to residents.

Construction contracts for the first twelve buildings were awarded in 1975 to two companies, Eastern LLC (founded by Abdulrahman Bukhatir) and Bombay-based Kalpataru Limited. All members of the construction team were Indian nationals. Second-phase construction started in 1976 and was concluded by 1979.

Despite the project having delivered some of Sharjah's most recognizable architecture, two of the Córdoba Buildings were demolished in 2016. Plans to demolish the remaining twenty-two buildings have been put on hold, though more demolitions are expected without published redevelopment plans.

02

03

04

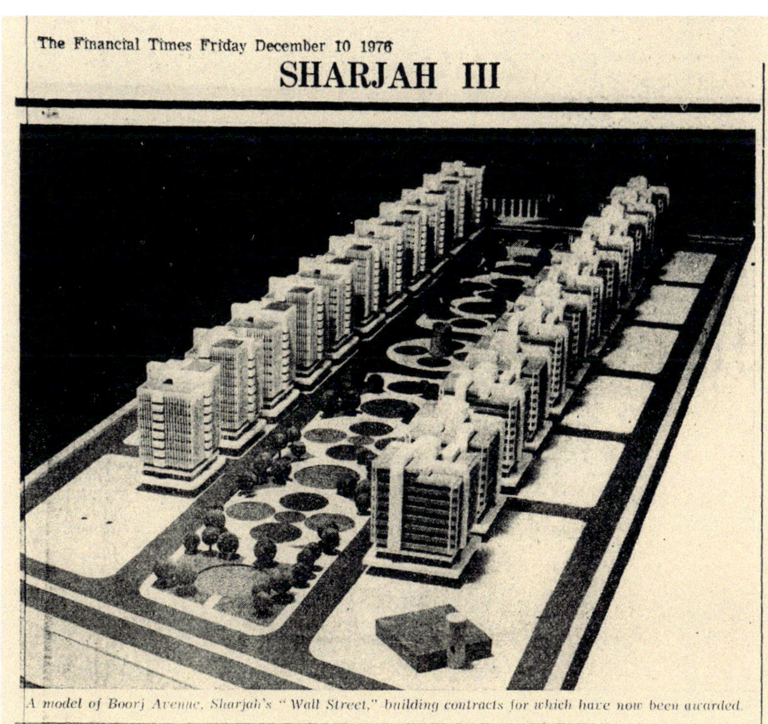

The Financial Times Friday December 10 1976

SHARJAH III

A model of Boorj Avenue, Sharjah's "Wall Street," building contracts for which have now been awarded.

Model of the Bank Street buildings, as featured in the *Financial Times*, reveals how land in between one-way roads was to be landscaped. Formal landscaping design was later replaced with parking lots. The remaining Burj Al Kubs was intended as the axis's centerpiece before plans to reconstruct Sharjah's old fort. Source: Kathleen Bishtawi, *Financial Times*, December 10, 1976, "Sharjah III: Banking." Used under licence from the Financial Times.

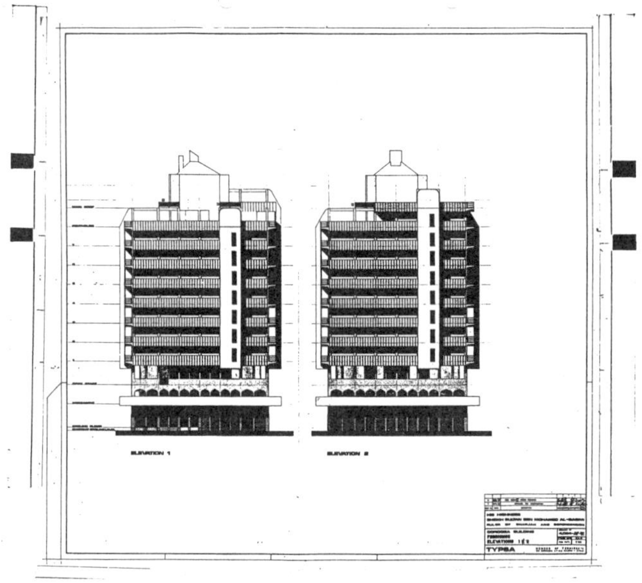

05

06

01. Sharjah's most striking architecture was a boulevard. Featured here are the Granada Buildings on the north side of Bank Street. The photo predates installation of bank branch signage, late 1970s. TYPSA.
02. Jaseera Abobaker, daughter of Sayed Abobaker Mohammed, poses on the roof of Al Saud Co. Building, where she lived and where her father was owner of Al Jasar Supermaket (p. 183). Behind her, left, are the Córdoba Buildings. Collection of Sayed Abobaker Mohammed.
03. The Córdoba Buildings, capped with construction cranes, rise over the first instances of concrete structures in Sharjah. In the foreground are small concrete block buildings and work sheds arising in response to Sharjah's promising economy. Regnault & Partners.
04. The Granada Buildings upon completion, displaying a "blend [of] Islamic architecture with modern technology." Dr. Naman Al Jalili Archives Collection.
05. Elevations, Córdoba Buildings. With no trace of archival drawings of the city's most iconic project in Sharjah, research led to the Madrid offices of the design firm, which provided drawings and archival photographs. TYPSA.
06. The parallel rows of Córdoba and Granada Buildings in direction of Port Khalid, with Rolla Square still under construction in the foreground, circa 1980. TYPSA.

Above: Cover of *Al Arabi* magazine, Issue 156, which included the original article abridged and translated here. The following English captions are translations from the original reporting. Permission to reprint the article provided by *Al Arabi*.

Right: "Smile, You Are in Sharjah." The fountain jets reflect the serenity visible on citizens' faces, despite the mighty transition from Bedouin to modern urban life.

AL ARABI
NOVEMBER 1971

SHARJAH:
SNAPSHOTS OF AN EMIRATE IN THE NASCENT UNION OF THE ARABIAN GULF

Reporting by Salim Zabbal
Photography by Oscar Mitri

An abridged English translation of original text by Karim Traboulsi

The following article is one of several that Kuwait-based *Al Arabi* magazine published on Sharjah and its ongoing development in the 1960s and 1970s. From this series of articles, many people in the Arab world gleaned their first and only impressions of the emirate, largely isolated from the rest of the region until the UAE's independence from the British in 1971. *Al Arabi* enjoyed global distribution, its influence often compared to that of *National Geographic*. What distinguished *Al Arabi* from other Arabic-language publications was the spotlight it shed on often overlooked parts of the Arab world such as the lower Gulf states and Yemen. It was also widely available in Arab capitals such as Beirut and Cairo, offering readers a first glimpse into corners of their own region.

Founded in 1958 by Emir Sheikh Abdullah Al Salim Al Sabah (1895–1965), *Al Arabi* is considered the first major Pan-Arab publication based in the Arab Gulf states, most of which had yet to gain independence from Britain. At the height of the Gamal Abdel Nasser–led movement of Arab Nationalism, *Al Arabi* bore the motto «اعرف وطنك أيها العربي» ("Know your nation, O Arab").

The magazine's dissemination signified that Kuwait's role vis-à-vis its lower Gulf neighbors was not only to offer financial assistance but also to provide support, sometimes moral, in the form of print media in addition to radio and later the establishment of a Kuwait television station outpost in Dubai in 1969.

Lebanese journalist Salim Zabbal (1926–2018) was commissioned to write the pieces on Sharjah, accompanying the images of Cairo-born photojournalist Oscar Mitri (b. 1927), a magazine contributor since 1960.

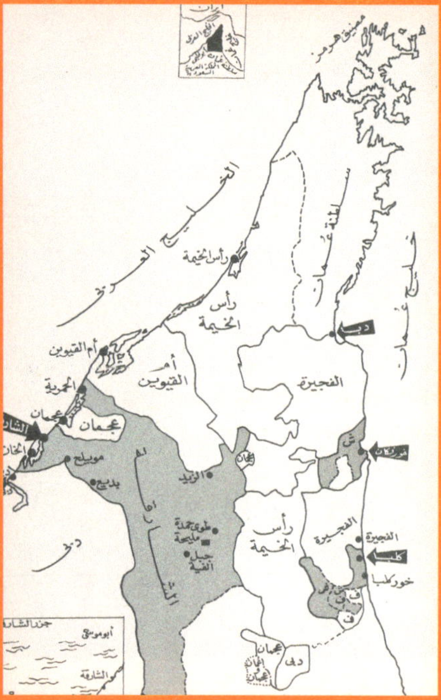

Magnified map of the borders of the emirates of the Coast of Oman before the establishment of the six-emirate union. One will notice the odd, chessboard-like border lines. The shaded part of the map represents the Emirate of Sharjah, divided into four parts, one bordering the Arabian Gulf and three exclaves bordering the Gulf of Oman.

The first map of the United Arab Emirates to be published, consisting of the following emirates: Abu Dhabi, Dubai, Sharjah, Ajman, Umm Al Quwain, and Fujairah. Their total surface area is approximately 31,500 square miles, Abu Dhabi being the largest emirate at 26,000 square miles. The total population (1968 census) is 155,500. The Emirate of Ras Al Khaimah, which may accede to the UAE, has an area of 650 square miles and a population of 24,500. [Ras Al Khaimah joined the UAE in 1972.—Ed.]

A THIRD EXPEDITION

The emirates of the Arabian Gulf are today undergoing a crucial transition. Early next year, the once-everlasting treaties established by Britain with various emirates in 1820 will become void, and British forces will withdraw from their bases in the region, including the massive British base established in Sharjah in 1940.[1]

Sharjah is a land of authenticity and history. It is the home of the Qawasim family, once so mighty that they controlled the mouth of the Arabian Gulf, levying taxes on every ship that crossed the Strait of Hormuz. A few months before the birth of the union, we traveled to Sharjah for our third expedition. We had visited it twice before for issues 20 and 114 of *Al Arabi* magazine, and each time we have found something noteworthy and new.

OUR YOUTH IS OUR REAL WEALTH

When we flew to Sharjah this time, we could not believe our own eyes. Is this the Sharjah we have always known? It was astounding how the people have made a leap from Bedouin to twentieth-century life in one great stride.

But before we recount the tales of our expedition, let us first hear Sheikh Khalid bin Mohammed Al Qasimi, the ruler of Sharjah who works sixteen hours a day, tell us about his country in his own words: "We are very proud of the educational renaissance in our country, our university students, and our students studying in universities abroad, who number around eighty. Those youth are our true wealth and fortune. But promoting education is not enough. It needs to be coupled with a new way of life that suits the new thinking of graduates and intellectuals and to respond to their ambitions and long-term visions. ... They will no longer accept living under roofs made of palm fronds. For this reason, I am building, developing, and planning for the future, not just for today, but also so that future generations do not curse me."

We then left Sheikh Khalid, his grand hopes already coming to fruition, and went out to tour the city. Wide, paved avenues and towering buildings had replaced the old mud houses of yesteryear. We reached the British base by foot. Located at the southwest entrance of Sharjah, the base blocks the city's expansion [toward Dubai].

A SMALL PERMIT

We tried to enter the base and were taken under heavy guard to the chief officer. He welcomed us with an innocent smile, saying: "I don't mind assisting you at all, but you need a small paper, a permit from the British High Commission, to take photographs here."

We left and made our way to meet the British High Commissioner. He was "unavailable," preoccupied with the handover and decommissioning, so we met his assistant who told us, "I will send a telegram to command HQ in Bahrain, but I don't think they will give approval. We have already declined requests from correspondents from *Life* and *Time* magazines to enter the base and take pictures ... so I don't think they will let you ... but call on us again anyway."

The top and bottom pictures are ten years apart. The tree is the same Al Rolla Tree, the most famous tree on the Coast of Oman. People would come with their falcons to rest under its shade. Today, Al Rolla Tree is on the corner of bustling Al Arouba and Al Dhaid Streets. It is no longer an inspiration for poets looking for a muse, but such is the price of progress!

الى اليمين : منذ بضع سنوات، كانت هذه الساحة صحراوية قاحلة ، تحولت الى حديقة عامة غناء ، هي بمثابة الرئة لمدينة الشارقة الحديثة.

الى اليسار : عشر سنوات مضت بين التقاطنا لهاتين الصورتين .. انها نفس الشجرة .. شجرة الدولة ، أشهر شجرة في ساحل عمان .. كان الناس يأتون للاستراحة تحت ظلالها مع صقورهم .. أما اليوم فأصبحت شجرة الدولة تحتل ناصية شارعي العروبة والزيد المزدحمين بحركة المرور الزائدة ..ولم يعد الشعراء يتخذونها مصدر الهام وايحاء..انها سنة التطور ..

For years, this square was barren desert. Now it is a lush public garden and acts as the lung of the modern city of Sharjah. [This was the precursor to Rolla Square, which was sited across from Al Arouba Street seen in background.—Ed.]

AL MUQAWQIS BIN HASSOUN IN SHARJAH!

We went to the Sheba Hotel.[2] It has fifty rooms, all air-conditioned. We paid 100 riyals (10 British pounds) for a twin room with three meals.[3] We sat in the grand lobby and spotted people from all nationalities conversing and divulging their secrets—it is hard to find a secret that people in all the seven emirates do not gossip about! Our sixth sense, so to speak, led us to listen more closely. Diverse groups of people from the four corners of the world were here in Sharjah, whispering and chatting with the locals and discussing all kinds of interesting and even strange topics. Some called for the right to invest in the land parcel of the huge base after the British withdrawal, saying in both English and Arabic, "We are first-class business partners!" and, "Wow, it is really hot in your country. How can you bear this heat? Why don't you leave?"

We also overheard an old man sitting on a large sofa saying, "We will publish a special issue of our magazine covering the whole world, and it will cover Sharjah and immortalize your name, making you more famous than Al Muqawqis bin Hassoun!" But when we asked knowledgeable people about this alleged figure Al Muqawqis bin Hassoun, no one had ever heard of him.

SPECULATION

In the hallway, we heard a man loudly telling the story of his investments in Sharjah. Three years earlier, he said, he had purchased a plot of land in Sharjah at a very cheap price, no more than one riyal per square foot. A while later, he was offered seven riyals for the square foot, but he refused to sell and insisted on ten riyals. As time passed and the buyer vanished, the man was left cursing his luck and his greed.

A so-called "land battle" began in 1969. Arabs from outside Sharjah had been transferring large sums of money in to purchase plots of land in the emirate. Estimates say Arabs bought up to 20 million riyals

خمس سنوات مرت على الشيخ خالد بن محمد
القاسمي وهو يعمل على بناء الشارقة الحديثة:
« المال غير موجود .. ولكننا لا نتجمد وانما
نعمل ونتحرك .. اننا على ثقة تامة من وجود
النفط تحت أراضينا .. ولكننا لا نريد
خسارة الوقت، حتى لا تلعننا الاجيال القادمة»

Sheikh Khalid bin Mohammed Al Qasimi has been working on building a modern city in Sharjah for five years: "The funds are scarce, but we have not stopped working. We are fully confident that there is oil beneath the ground, but we do not want to lose time so that future generations do not curse us!"

worth of land in 1969, totaling an area of 5 million square feet. Land prices in Sharjah have thus risen from an average of one to seven riyals and from 30 to 150 riyals in the city center.

But not all land in Sharjah is for sale. Some land is divided into plots of 10,000 square feet and offered by the ruler for free to Arab citizens who want to develop a commercial, residential, or industrial building in Sharjah.[4] The belief Sharjah's people hold in their Arab identity prompted them to name the main street bisecting their capital Al Arouba, or Arabism, Street.

SMILE, YOU'RE IN SHARJAH!

We left the hotel and headed into Sharjah. Wow! Is this really Sharjah? Neon lights, fancy cars, cinemas, and an illuminated sign reading, "Smile, You Are in Sharjah." And so we smiled, feeling a strange sense of inner peace.

Here, you still feel the presence of authentic Arabs, unchanged by the false promises of modern civilization. "Our doors, our homes, and our chests are open to our kin and loved ones," they say. Indeed, as soon as you sit with a "Sharjawi" and have some *ghawala*, the sweets served before coffee, with bananas, oranges, almonds, Muscat sweets, chocolate, and melon, you will have become their dear friend.

FOUNTAIN THERAPY

We stood admiring a large, great fountain jetting forth water into the sky, the glimmering multicolor lights reflected in the waters. The ruler of Sharjah told us, "I feel delighted when I see people standing and admiring its prancing waters. When I see their faces, I see reassurance and peace. This is why we've built a fountain in every square, as a form of fountain therapy."

الى اليسار: مدفع «الرقاص» الاثرى الذى يرجع تاريخه الى عهد الشيخ صقر بن خالد (١٨٨٣–١٩١٤) كانت طلقاته تصل من الشارقة الى دبي فيهتز لها فأسموه «الرقاص». وهو اليوم قطعة أثرية .

An antique cannon dates back to Sheikh Saqr bin Khalid (1883–1914). From Sharjah, its rounds could reach Dubai. The sound of the blast made the city tremble, thus earning the cannon the nickname "Ar-Raqqas," or "the shaker of things." Today it is a relic of a bygone time.

بدات منذ اكتوبر ١٩٧٠ عملية بيع مخلفات القاعدة
البريطانية ، استعدادا لجلاء القوات البريطانية
في نهاية عام ١٩٧١ عن منطقة الخليج .. وترى هنا
بعض الضباط البريطانيين يتتبعون العملية ..

الى اليمين : مدينة الاشباح..
هكذا تحولت القاعدة البريطاني
بعد أن تركتها القوات العسكري
البريطانية .. وفي الصور
العليا اثنان من الضباط
يقومان بوضع المخلفات
استعدادا لبيعها لاهالي المنطق
.. ونتيجة لعمليات البيـ
هبطت أسعار الشاحنات مـ
١٠ آلاف ريال الى أربعة آلاف

A city of ghosts. This is what became of the British base after the withdrawal of British armed forces. Above, two officers lay out scrap for sale to the locals. As a result of this fire sale, prices of trucks went down from 10,000 to 4,000 [Qatari] riyals.

Since October 1970, scrap at the British camp has been sold in preparation for the withdrawal of British forces from the Gulf region at the end of 1971. Here, we see British officers overseeing sales.

التعليم للجميع .. وفى المساء تفتح المدارس ابوابها ثانية لمن فاتهم سن
التعليم ، وترى هنا حارس المدرسة القاسمية : عيسى عثمان ، يستمع
الى الاستاذ فهد ابراهيم جلال من بعثة البحرين ، وهو يقرأ له ما كتبه

Education is for everyone. In the evening, schools reopen for adults who missed out on a formal education.

We left the fountain and went to explore Al Arouba Street. When we visited Sharjah for the first time, it was a dirt road no more than fifteen feet wide. Today, it is a paved modern road 120 feet wide, crisscrossed by cars in both directions and straddled by streetlights installed here in 1968, turning night into day.

MISPLACED REMORSE

Some feel remorse for the bygone days when camels and falcons roamed free in Sharjah: "The splendor of the past will never return," they say, "We all knew each other then because we were small in number. Today, we are a large and diverse society." (The splendor of the past may have also meant the right to fisticuffs without the threat of police intervention!)

This may carry some truth. No doubt, the Bedouin society had enjoyed things like familiarity, stability, pride, and chivalry as well as a steady life in the shade of old tents. But at the same time, it was a society that lived at the mercy of nature; a rogue storm could easily uproot it, flash floods could easily displace it, and a dry spell could easily decimate it.

WE ARE PLANNING FOR THE NEXT FIFTY YEARS

Aware that Sharjah had entered a new era of development, Sheikh Khalid engaged the services of an international planning consultancy. Large-scale planning was launched for both old and new districts, and work was moved from blueprints to the streets. By 1969, Sharjah was a huge construction site. The first phase concluded with the development of long, paved roads lined with streetlights. Then, buildings went up, some ten stories high, ushering in the Sharjah of tomorrow.

Speaking to *Al Arabi*, the municipal expert Mr. Mukhtar Al Toum said, "We are planning for the next fifty years. Our plan envisages 120,000 people living in the city of Sharjah alone." He continued, "Although its revenues increased from 300,000 riyals in 1966 to around 2 million riyals last year, Sharjah Municipality has found itself unable to cover the cost of projects and infrastructure development; however, the deficit is being covered by the country's ruler."

SHIFTING SANDS DEVASTATE SHARJAH'S CENTER

The city of Sharjah is located on a *khor*, a small inlet, like many cities of the Omani coast. This khor was once the main artery for its prosperity and lucrative commerce. However, Sharjah lost its position when the natural pearl trade collapsed in 1930 following the invention of synthetic pearls. However, Sharjah's real tragedy struck when shifting sands blocked the entrance of the khor to ships and boats. Starting in 1950, many ideas for projects to reopen the khor were put forth, but nothing happened until 1968 when the ruler of Sharjah Khalid bin Mohammed Al Qasimi signed an agreement with an international company to resurrect the khor.

Work began in a frenzy. People had built huts over the sands that blocked the khor, and they had to be compensated and evacuated. The contractor immediately began removing tens of thousands of tons of piled sand and blasting hard rocks; then, they launched concrete and steel works to build piers for the ships. After two years of round-the-clock work, Khor Al Sharjah finally opened last month (October 1971). This was just the first phase of the plan to revive Khor Al Sharjah, and it cost £1 million.

THE STORY OF OIL

People have been talking about oil in Sharjah for fifty years, making it a charged and emotional subject. Interestingly, almost everyone in Sharjah firmly believes there is oil beneath their feet. In 1968, new companies entered the fray with much publicity and began to talk about advanced modern techniques and machinery to explore and find oil by the end of 1971.

LARGEST MAINTENANCE YARD IN THE REGION

A day before we were set to leave, permission came from the High Commission in Bahrain for us to photograph the sale of British army scrap, and thus we entered the base. It was an entire city for 5,000 people and contained 1,200 homes, all air-conditioned. It had its own power plant, with an output double that of the Sharjah and Dubai plants combined, plus 300 telephone lines. It had huge water tanks, a fifty-bed hospital to treat all kinds of diseases, and an elegant club with a swimming pool, restaurants, and playgrounds. All this alongside the massive airstrip, a radar working round the clock, and a modern maintenance workshop for all kinds of planes with equipment worth more than £6 million pounds.

BROTHERHOOD OF THE GULF PEOPLE

When Sharjah's government started naming streets, Kuwait was at the forefront (for source material). The ruler of Sharjah told us, "This is an acknowledgement of Kuwait's great efforts in the region. Kuwait has played an honorable role in our country: it laid down the foundations of our education system and has and continues to help build our health care system."

We went to meet with Sheikh Badr Muhammad Ahmad Al Sabah, head of the Kuwait Office in the emirates, to ask him about Kuwait's role in the region. He invited us to lunch at his elegant home and served us a delicious meal, yet we left hungrier than when we came—at least for information, as Sheikh Badr only told us, "We are here among brothers ... the brotherhood of the Gulf people in every sense of the word, and what goes on between brothers is private and not for publication."

SEVEN THOUSAND LEGAL CASES EACH YEAR

What is remarkable in Sharjah is that it is developing despite the near absence of material resources: "True, oil has not been discovered in our country yet, but we are not sitting idle. We are preparing for the age of oil, when it gushes forth from the ground."

Based on the principle of participatory governance, the ruler established twelve government departments with various fields of responsibility. Some of these departments—such as the land registry and survey department, the municipality, the education department, and the justice department—have begun to produce astounding results. In the past, the ruler would hear and adjudicate complaints in his majlis, but today, there is a comprehensive judiciary in Sharjah that includes Islamic courts, civilian courts, an appellate court, and five judges. In 1970, they heard more than 7,000 cases.

A WAY OF LIFE TRANSFORMED

We envision this ruler as a great sculptor of a masterpiece, an entire city. He gave it everything he has, pouring his love, labor, and sacrifice into his work. We saw him work from morning to evening, trying to get the most possible from the least available. On Friday, when people go to rest, Sheikh Khalid opens his doors to meet them and talk to them in his open shura council.

What is happening today in Sharjah is truly unique. The odds for success are high and will overcome the potential for stagnation. Yet the change underway is not just taking place in buildings and streets. It is taking place in people, their purpose, their direction, and their ways of life. This change will make Sharjah the crown jewel of the nascent state of the United Arab Emirates.

٢٠٩٢ طالبة يتلقين تعليمهن في مدارس الشارقة .. وتقوم بمهمة تعليمهن
١١٦ معلمة ، منهن ١١ فتاة من الشارقة نفسها ٥ تخرجن كأول دفعة
من معهد المعلمات وخمس يدرسن وهن حاصلات على الثانوية العامة .

Two thousand and ninety-two female students are enrolled in Sharjah's schools. They are taught by 116 female teachers, including eleven young women from Sharjah, who had graduated as the first class of the Women Teachers' Academy, and five teachers who only hold secondary school diplomas.

Editors' Notes:

1. Construction of a British air base began in 1932 (see p. 40). The British departure began in December 1971.
2. See p. 93.
3. At the time, Sharjah recognized the Qatari riyal as local currency.
4. See "Land, Houses, and Homes: A Palestinian History of Al Fayha," p. 253.

النظام الاجتماعى في الشارقة يمر بمرحلة تبديل جذرى .. فانتشار التعليم من ناحية ، وانفتاح البلاد من ناحية أخرى ، جعلا الافكار الجديدة تدخل الى هذا المجتمع الذي كانت العصبيات العائلية ، والتكتلات القبلية ، هى السائدة والمسيطرة فيه ..

وعلى هاتين الصفحتين ترى في الصورة اليمنى قاعة الطعام في فندق سبأ وقد امتلأت بعائلات المدرسين والمدرسات ، والعاملين الاجانب في البلاد .. والصور الثلاث الاخرى تبين القديم والجديد فى شوارع الشارقة .. وبينهما فتيات المدارس مرتديات الزى الرسمى المحتشم ..

The social system in Sharjah is undergoing radical change. The propagation of education and the country's opening up to the world have brought in new ideas to this society, once dominated by family and tribal traditions.

On the right, we see the grand restaurant at the Sheba Hotel, teeming with male and female teachers and foreign workers. The other three images contrast old and new snapshots of life in the streets of Sharjah and schoolgirls in their modest uniforms.

One of Sharjah Municipality's first beautification projects was known as Government Square. Opposite the wall on the right was Sharjah Fort, which housed the ruler's majlis until its demolition. To the left is Al Arouba Street, on the other side of which would be designated Rolla Square. The road perpendicular to Al Arouba would become part of Bank Street. Mahmood AlSawan.

01

02

Rolla Square Monument

At over 36,000 square meters, Rolla Square is among the most prominent of public squares in Sharjah, or the UAE for that matter. It owes its origin to a massive banyan tree (*Ficus benghalensis*), named the Rolla Tree, that is said to have survived for some 150 years until 1978 when it allegedly "fell." It had witnessed Sharjah's development over the course of two centuries, since before the arrival of British forces in 1820 to their departure in 1971 and then the feverish first few years of post-oil development.

Sharjah's Rolla Tree was more than an old tree. It was both a meeting point and a sanctuary from the sun and heat. Its shade hosted wedding ceremonies and national celebrations. Sheikh Sultan bin Saqr Al Qasimi I, Sharjah's ruler from 1814 to 1866, is said to have imported the tree from the Indian subcontinent. Toward the end of its life, the tree was 15 meters tall and its crown was 30 meters wide.

In 1979, Spanish sculptor Carlos Marinas, who had come to Sharjah at the invitation of Hotel Aladin's architect Ramzi Shaker, was asked by the emirate's ruler, Sheikh Sultan bin Muhammad Al Qasimi, to design a fitting memorial for the much-loved tree. The design included a bronze, tree-like sculpture housed in a triangular, concrete structure pointing toward the sky. Marinas asserts that the final design was achieved through a collaboration with the ruler, resulting in what some say resembles the latter's signature. The tree's bronze branches were victims of their own success, breaking off as a result of visitors' perching upon and swinging from them, much to the chagrin of the designer.

In 2012, after a first attempt to reconstruct the monument out of fiberglass, Marinas delivered a new monument, this time made of reinforced concrete and with the profile of a tree cut out from its center. The tree, now represented only by a void, offers no more branches to swing from.

Design
Carlos Marinas with Sheikh Sultan bin Muhammad Al Qasimi

Contractor
Contractors Group International

Completed
1979

Status
Existing, replaced

03

01. Residents gather and children play around the Rolla Tree monument constructed as part of Rolla Square, September 1983. The original sculpture included the bronze depiction of the deceased tree. © Gulf News, Dubai.
02. The original banyan tree was situated opposite Government Square and the old Sharjah Fort. Ahmed Abdulrahim Al Mulla, courtesy of Wafa Ahmed Al Mulla.
03. A Sharjah resident poses on steps leading to the original monument. Prem Ratnam, Hemlyn Photography Studio.

A family poses across the street from Government Square. Behind them is Al Arouba Street, which runs along the front of Sharjah Fort. Before its demolition, the fort was extended by a four-story tower, which housed an office for police and a ground-floor garage. Behind the new tower is the older Burj Al Kubs, which is the only part of the fort that survived demolition. To the left, along Al Arouba Street, is another watchtower, built, according to the architect, with more aesthetic than practical purpose. Both new towers were designed by Syrian architect Mohamed Al Azhari and built by Consolidated Contractors Company, 1970. Rudi Eller.

Dubai-based newspaper *Al Bayan* reported on cyclists competing in the Arab Youth Cycling Championship as they pass Sharjah's Central Souk, 1983. Al Bayan.

77

Central Souk

Text by
Suheyla Takesh

Sharjah's central market, commonly referred to as the Blue Souk, the Islamic Souk, and sometimes the Gold Souk, is one of the city's most recognizable landmarks. Designed by the architects of Michael Lyell Associates, the complex opened on December 2, 1978. Imagined by its British designers as a modern rendition of a traditional Arab or Islamic marketplace, the idiosyncratic structure was intended to compensate for the loss of the souk in the district of Al Mareija, displaced as a result of Bank Street's build-out. The new market's cost, estimated at $30 million when it was near completion, constituted a considerable investment in view of the government's "acute shortage of liquidity" in April 1978 and its mounting debt, reported to total somewhere between $600 million and $1 billion in January 1982.[1]

The project was a prominent component of the city's ongoing urban transformation intended to boost the local tourism industry. It was designed to host 600 shops and provide 400 parking spaces. Attracting customers, however, proved to be a challenge. The souk reportedly had "everything except people."[2] The new market lacked the organic configuration and chaotic allure of a traditional marketplace. At the same time, its layout, particularly on the upper level, made it a challenge to navigate through the marketplace. In 1981, the municipality installed escalators in a bid to lure visitors to the neglected upper levels.

The souk complex comprises eight vaulted buildings, or "pavilions," arranged in two parallel rows, with a road between them for car traffic. According to the architect's correspondence, the two parallel parts—at the advice of Sharjah's ruler—were to be connected by sixteen elevated pedestrian walkways inspired by Florence's Ponte Vecchio. After construction had commenced, however, a decision was made to reduce this number to two, requiring demolition of some finished bridges.

In an effort to encapsulate regional building aesthetics and promote the ambiance of a traditional souk, the market's design brings together a highly eclectic mix of elements commonly associated with Islamic architecture, including barrel vaults, rounded arches, blue ceramic tiles, latticework screens, and decorative geometric patterns. The building's roof is punctuated with twenty *barajeel*, or wind towers, an architectural feature adopted in the Gulf region to catch and channel air currents into the interior of a building. While the towers were designed as a functional ventilation system, they were eventually superseded by mechanical air-conditioning units. The labored and ahistorical fusion of multiple regional aesthetics and styles into the market's overall concept—although intended to represent a broadly "Islamic" character—resulted in a hybrid structure of unrelated genealogies. The *London Times* architecture correspondent Charles McKean went so far as to suggest that the building's hybridity resulted from a lack of a local "fixed culture" to guide designers, indicating that architectural projects like this one embodied aspirations in architecture to fix and stabilize an otherwise fluid culture.

The Central Souk, still lauded as one of Sharjah's most photographed buildings, continues to attract tourists with its unique interpretation of regional architectural style. An image of the building is also featured on the UAE five-dirham banknote.

Architect
Michael Lyell Associates, Associated Continental Architects

Structural Engineer
White Young & Partners

Contractor
Joannou & Paraskevaides (Overseas) Limited

Client
Sheikh Sultan bin Muhammad Al Qasimi

Completed
1978

Status
Existing, modified

1. "New Sharjah Souk," *Middle East Construction*, April 1976. "Dubai Shopping Centre," *Concrete*, June 1978. Jim Antoniou, "Sharjah Souk," *Middle East Construction*, August 1978. M.T., "Sharjah: A New Framework," *Financial Times*, June 26, 1978.
2. Celia May, "Sajaa Field Signals Success For Sharjah," *Middle East Economic Digest* (London), January 1, 1982.

02

03

04

05

06

07

08

Images:

01. Wind-tunnel tests at Bristol University's Aeronautical Department purportedly helped design the souk's wind towers, or *barajeel*, provide natural ventilation (with some mechanical assistance). Their function was later fully replaced by air conditioning. Mahmood AlSawan.
02. An early model of the souk (by Thorp Modelmakers) reveals that more gold and colored surfaces were once planned. The final design was featured in *Architecture in Islamic Countries*, published as part of the second Venice Biennale of Architecture, 1981–82, curated by Paolo Portoghesi. Mentioned alongside projects by Hassan Fathy, Kamran Diba, Mohamed Makiya, and Frei Otto, the souk was associated with ongoing interpretations of Islamic design. ® ATOM Ltd, courtesy of RIBA Collections.
03. Sharjah resident Mohammed Shamis Al Maazmi and friend outside Central Souk, 1981. Collection of Mohammed Shamis Al Maazmi, courtesy of Ahmad Al Maazmi.
04. Interior walkway before installation of escalators and sealing of interiors for air conditioning. Dr. Naman Al Jalili Archives Collection.
05. Exterior view of the souk's barrel roof and *barjeel*. Fabian Leidig.
06. Two women leaving the Central Souk. Above them is one of the two pedestrian overpasses. Seen in the background is Crescent Petroleum headquarters, Tony Irving and Gordon Jones of Design Construction Group, 1974. Regnault & Partners.
07. Naturally ventilated interior walkway. Fabian Leidig.
08. Early design rendering. Tony Peters and John Knight developed the conceptual design for Michael Lyell Associates. According to Knight, Sharjah's ruler "produced a 'thumbnail' sketch" at the start of the project and requested that "the design should, if practicable, incorporate local architectural features." Michael Lyell Associates, Tony Peters, and John Knight.

01

Suheyla Takesh

PERFORMING MODERNITY AT THE CENTRAL SOUK

On Friday, April 19, 1985, outside Sharjah's Central Souk, nine bundles of red, orange, and blue cloth—each sized to fit in the palm of one's hand—were laid out in a grid on the terrazzo pavement. Each bundle contained a small rock, wrapped like a cherished object. Two sculptures atop white plinths stood in attendance. From a certain angle, the yellow one, no more than fifty centimeters in height, resembled the stacked vertebrae of a camel's spine. The white-and-gray piece was a more nebulous formation, its shape obscured in the old photographs. The assembly was complemented by a number of paintings leaned against the souk's outer wall. The paintings showed abstract shapes, amorphous drops of paint, and stylized drawings of hands. Two of the largest comprised black-and-white geometric patterns, reminiscent of oversized boards for games like chess. These paintings were displayed either flat on the floor or slightly raised off the ground using plastic water bottles. The collection of objects cannot be called a composition because there was no apparent order; it was more an anomaly in a public space. The coincidental audience, mostly Friday worshippers coming from a neighboring mosque, was intrigued and bewildered.

"If there is meaning, it is not art," was a principle that guided much of Emirati artist Hassan Sharif's work, including this display at the footsteps of one of Sharjah's most recognizable modern landmarks.[1] The unannounced exhibition was carried out not only by Sharif but also by two other members of the Aqwas collective, Nujoom Alghanem and Khalid Albudoor. The three artists were intellectually drawn to one another in the early 1980s: they shared an interest in experimental art forms and an appreciation for the work of pioneering international modernists, pivotal in expanding what constitutes plastic arts. These artists included Marcel Duchamp, Wassily Kandinsky, and Paul Klee. Alghanem and Albudoor both had a background in journalism prior to meeting Sharif and shared an affinity for language as a creative medium. They worked on developing experimental, avant-garde methods of free verse, frustrating the Emirates Writers Union, whose other members pursued more conventional approaches. While their interest beyond orthodox literary forms reached back to the late 1970s, Alghanem and Albudoor say their fascination with performance art was sparked by Hassan Sharif after he returned to the UAE from London's Byam Shaw School of Art in 1984.

Today, Alghanem and Albudoor share a studio in Dubai in a refurbished pool house across from their residence. Surrounded by art supplies, books, and numerous works in progress, they recall their younger years as artists over tea and an array of sweet treats. Alghanem pulls up photographs on her telephone while Albudoor brings in an old scrapbook filled with diary entries, sketches, and newspaper clippings. They recall that, upon his return from London, Sharif brought with him a book of essays on various schools of performance art, titled *Performance: Live Art, 1909 to the Present* by Roselee Goldberg, a 1979 anthology of texts on the Futurists, Russian avant-gardists, Bauhaus, Dadaists, Surrealists, and artists active in Europe and the United States. The worn copy, which Sharif signed and gave to their daughter Fatima in 2015, contains his numerous marginal notes and in-text annotations. It also includes scribbled translations of several curious English-language terms into Arabic, such as *polemical art*, *austerity*, *intima*, *predatory* (misspelled *predactory*), *corpse* (misspelled *corse*), *slot*, and *trash*. Alghanem claims that exposure to the Dada movement in particular was significant for them because they related to its rejection of structure and logic and its accentuation of nonsense, irrationality, and chance through various mediums of expression.[2]

In 1985, Sharif, Alghanem, Albudoor, and Yousif Khalil—a mutual friend and writer involved in theater who had established a local cinema circle—came together to form the Aqwas collective.[3] Operating out of Sharif's atelier in Sharjah's Al Mareija district, the short-lived collective became known for launching the experimental Arabic-language journal *Silsilat Al Ramad* (The Ashes Series). The journal's contributors submitted original content, including abstract illustrations and experimental poetry, and *Silsilat Al Ramad* also published prose, concentrating on artistic practice rather than on theory and critique. The publication's free and idiosyncratic format eschewed conventional modes of writing, composition, and graphic design. In one mischievous, playful gesture, the creators inserted a stick of chewing gum into each of the first issue's twenty Xeroxed copies "to add some sweetness to [the public's] reading experience."[4] The quirky format and seemingly bizarre content, however, quickly resulted in state authorities' demanding that the Aqwas collective obtain official authorization to distribute their publication. In an effort to circumvent this formality, the collective (which had become a trio after Yousif Khalil's departure) staged a public exhibition and performance as an alternative way to release the second issue. Sharjah's Central Souk was the chosen stage.

Often referred to as the Islamic Souk, or the Blue Souk, its buildings were, for some, a vibrant embodiment of regionalism in the larger plan for the city of Sharjah and had become a well-known marker in the urban landscape.[5] As a location for their intervention, Alghanem recalls, the Central Souk was selected for its "cultural significance." The shopping complex, opened in December 1978, was conceived as a modern rendition of a traditional souk, at least according to its British designers. The result of the collaborative effort between the firms Michael Lyell Associates and White Young and Partners brought together a notably eclectic and disparate mix of elements commonly associated with Islamic architecture. This broad fusion included features like rounded arches, latticework screens, twenty sculptural wind towers dotting the vaulted roof, inscriptions of Arabic calligraphy, and blue decorative tiles on the building's exterior. The contrived amalgamation and ahistorical interpretation of multiple regional aesthetics and styles, however, resulted in a distinctly hybrid outcome that also prompted comparisons to London's Crystal Palace or a Victorian railway station.

The construction of the Central Souk was but one component in the city's ongoing urban transformation. It was conceived as a replacement for the old market once situated along the coastline in Al Mareija and displaced by the construction of Sharjah's Bank Street.[6] The new souk materialized as an illustrious manifestation of an Arabian fantasy while also responding to the more pragmatic concerns of providing a public marketplace, attracting tourists, and stimulating the city's economy. By staging their performance in this space, the Aqwas collective created a curious dichotomy between the building's carefully choreographed visual identity, achieved through the conscious manipulation of traditional forms, and the collective's own declared rejection of traditional forms in their work as artists and writers. While the Central Souk relied on architectural configurations from the past in an attempt to convey an Arab or Islamic character, members of the Aqwas collective sought to break free from conventional structures in literature and art, opting instead for amorphous free verse, "number poems," and an improvised exhibition of seemingly found objects.

The deliberate forethought that distinguished the Central Souk design echoed in many ways the prevailing ideas of Sharjah's first master plan created by Sir William Halcrow and Partners in 1963. Setting out to fashion a city that was modern, rational, and efficient, the master plan proposed a calculated set of practical constraints for how the city would be experienced. Similarly, the designers of the Central Souk relied on an orchestrated set of attributes to guide and inform a modern interpretation of a historic souk. The Aqwas collective's intention to deliberately create "nonsense"—to use Hassan Sharif's word—in their art, therefore, diverged starkly from the central idea of the 1963 master plan for the city, which took it upon itself to inject *sense* into Sharjah's urban domain. And at the footsteps of the souk, the artists juxtaposed their performance with the building's calculated assemblage of token architectural elements from across the region.

Using the building as a backdrop against which to stage their presentation, Aqwas wittily brought a number of diametrically opposed notions into close proximity. They confronted the structured with the open-ended, the rationalized with the nonsensical, the empirical with the seemingly absurd. Did the city's increasing regularity—architectural and otherwise—prompt an artistic response that was, conversely, devoid of express purpose? The collective's actions can be read not only as an effort driven by the need for artistic expression but also as a reflection of human experience in response to installed systems of order.

In 1985, the year of the Central Souk performance, many large-scale projects, begun in the 1970s when oil reserves were confirmed, were either completed or nearing completion. The artists—consciously or not—were responding to institutionalized control, progressively more palpable in their environments. While the souk may have been designed as a calculated embodiment of regionalism in the larger plan for the city of Sharjah, its use as a stage for extemporaneous artistic interventions challenged reigning structures of order and premeditation.

"The city fosters art and is art; the city creates the theater and is the theater," was the critic Lewis Mumford's answer to his own 1937 article titled "What is a City?"[7] The 1985 performance by the Aqwas collective brings Mumford's words to mind. The Central Souk can be thought of both as "fostering" an avant-garde art performance because it "creates the theater" and as embodying artistic qualities itself, such as a pursuit of harmony, order, and compositional congruity. It seems, however, that Mumford and the Aqwas collective held divergent notions of art. While Sharif maintained that art should be nonsense, "a game, not to be taken seriously," both architecture in general and the Central Souk in particular are entrenched in purpose and intentionality.[8] It is often through planning, structural rigor, and mathematical precision that aesthetic and conceptual qualities of architecture come into existence, and while chance and speculation may at times be integral to architectural thought, it seems like neither Sharjah's master plan for a modern city nor the design of the Central Souk relied on them in their conception. Both imagined human experience as regulated and choreographed, which is why the Aqwas collective's intervention appeared so impromptu and unscripted in comparison.

Modernity is often framed as development driven by administrative, organizational, and rationalist processes. In Sharjah's case, the performance of modernity was inextricably tied both to a reinterpretation of tradition—carried out in a thoughtful or at times discernibly ahistorical manner—and to a consolidation of national identity in the early decades following Sharjah's incorporation into the United Arab Emirates. A collective identity formed through the expression and celebration of local heritage as well as of Arab, Gulf, and Islamic motifs in architecture and urban spaces. Thus, the Central Souk performance conveyed representations of modernity and the nation on the same stage, eliciting an ever-evolving set of responses.

In his discussion of national identity and its construction, cultural geographer Tim Edensor addresses the use of symbolic sites as stages for

02

03

performing various aspects of national character. These sites, by virtue of their physical or symbolic boundedness, are organized—or "stage managed" —to regulate which acts or actors belong and which do not. While behaviors on these sites may sometimes be spatially guided like in a museum, convention may also be upheld through didactic forms of instruction (for example, warning signs or informational announcements) or through institutionalized regulation (for example, bureaucratic procedures for official permits or deployment of force).[9] If one can imagine the Central Souk as a bounded "symbolic site" or stage, where Arabness and commerce are performed, it then becomes evident how the Aqwas collective's intervention unsettled the norms of behavior that actors on this platform were expected to maintain. The artist trio, unsurprisingly, was interrupted by a security guard shortly after the performance began, who—in an act of "stage managing"—asked to see their license from the municipality. It goes without saying that they didn't have one.

The 1985 event at the Central Souk was not the only instance of performance art set against Sharjah's urban fabric. Hassan Sharif staged a number of performative acts by himself, as did Nujoom Alghanem and Khaled Albudoor, either as a duo or with other collaborators, including Naji Al Hayy, though these other interventions were not well documented. The artists selected sites for these performances strategically, taking into consideration the architectural, cultural, or social significance of each context in the city of Sharjah. These locations included Al Ittihad Park adjacent to the Central Souk, Al Majaz Park on Corniche Street, and a cemetery. Though the planned performance at the cemetery —an effort to "entertain the dead," as Nujoom Alghanem humorously put it—never came to fruition because the artists failed to secure formal permission from the city's municipality. Resistance on the part of official institutions in authorizing these interventions was not the only challenge. The public, too, was often bewildered and confused by the seemingly random and peculiar acts. While performing at Al Majaz Park dressed as clowns, for example, the artists were attacked by a group of children and forced to leave the site.

Sharjah's modernity in the 1980s was interpreted and negotiated by artists in idiosyncratic ways that often defied institutional frameworks and the sequential processes they entailed. "We felt that people here just wanted to *gradually* go to the next level while we were ready to *jump*. They thought that in order for one to 'grow' one would have to do this or that. We were past that, in a way, because we already had something going on," Nujoom Alghanem said in a 2017 interview.[10] These artists, sensitive to the UAE's ongoing systematic modernization, were ambitious in their choice of performance art as a medium. The performance at the Central Souk, while not intended to provoke per se, did nevertheless raise questions about ascribed meaning and accepted artistic forms. It also called attention to how the country's increasingly structured modern institutions often constricted—consciously or not—the parameters of artistic experimentation. At the time of its execution, the eccentric performance as well as the short-lived *Silsilat Al Ramad* triggered little beyond a general denouncement by peers and critics. The collective's collaborative work from this period, however, became pivotal to ways in which conceptual art critically approached a scripted and controlled modernity as a reality, a dynamic stage of unforeseen circumstances, unplanned leaps, spontaneous urban developments, and improvised quotidian practices.

Notes:

1. Christiana de Marchi, "Interview – Hassan Sharif," in *But We Cannot See Them: Tracing a UAE Art Community, 1988–2008*, ed. Maya Allison (Edinburgh: Akkadia Press, 2017), 263.
2. Conversation with the artists, June 2019, Dubai.
3. Aqwas translates to "arches" in English.
4. Rand Abdul Jabbar, Uns Kattan, and Hammad Nasar, "A Dialogue between Rhythm and Form," in *Rock, Paper, Scissors: Positions in Play*, ed. H. Nasar, (Abu Dhabi and Milan: National Pavilion United Arab Emirates, La Biennale di Venezia, and Mousse Publishing, 2017), 165.
5. See the Central Souk, p. 131.
6. See Bank Street project, p. 103.
7. Lewis Mumford, "What is a City?" in *The City Reader*, eds. Richard T. LeGates and Frederic Stout, 5th ed. (London: Routledge, 2011), 91–95.
8. Excerpt from Khalid Albudoor's diary, which he kept in the 1980s.
9. Tim Edensor, "Performing National Identity," in *National Identity, Popular Culture and Everyday Life* (London: Bloomsbury Publishing, 2016), 69–70.
10. "A Dialogue between Rhythm and Form," 165.

04

Images:

01. Friday afternoon shoppers stroll in front of Sharjah's Central Souk as the Aqwas collective stages an impromptu art exhibition at the footsteps of the building, April 19, 1985. Images: Hassan Sharif © Sharjah Art Foundation Archive Collection. Courtesy of Nujoom Alghanem.
02. Souk customers observe rocks wrapped in fabric and laid out in front of the building. Originally arranged in a grid, the rocks were soon kicked out of position by passersby and children who used them for play, April 19, 1985.
03. Men in both traditional and Western-style clothing inspect peculiar paintings leaned against the souk's ornamented walls, April 19, 1985.
04. A man and boy in *kandooras* continue their shopping during the Aqwas collective installation, April 19, 1985.

01

Vegetable Souk

When Sharjah's old, palm frond–covered souk along the corniche road faced demolition in the late 1970s, new premises were planned. There were 4,000 applications for the 186 new shops, with priority given to the old souk's shopkeepers. The limited slots were additionally reserved for "UAE subjects with income above a certain limit." In the new complex, architecture met the modern hygiene standards set by Sharjah Municipality's health department. A shopkeeper interviewed at the time of the opening praised the new "semblance of order." Regarding the shops that did not make their way to the new premises, one lucky shop owner predicted that their regular customers would shift to the new site because the old shops "reeked with overflowing drains."

The 4,000-square-meter vegetable market was housed in an arc-shaped building, trimmed with precast arched facade panels to express a "distinct sense of Islamic architecture." A central arcade, double-loaded with shops, extended through the building as a circulation spine. The adjacent meat market included a public abattoir.

Halcrow's design provided space for coiffured green landscapes, and the complex included new separated facilities for each of the vegetable, meat, and fish markets. The entire complex counted 710 parking spaces and was located adjacent to a new bus station. A local paper reported that the complex was designed "on the lines of the ruler's sketches of Spanish architecture." Mel Stewart, Halcrow's chief representative in Sharjah at the time, claims that he sent initial sketches created together with the ruler Sheikh Sultan bin Muhammad Al Qasimi to architects and engineers at the company's London offices, from which the final designs were completed.

Adjacent Al Arouba Street, raised around the same time to alleviate traffic congestion, cut the new markets off from the Central Souk, another recently completed project intended to reshape Sharjah's commercial dynamics. Part of the vegetable souk is currently slated for demolition.

Architect
Halcrow International Partnership

Contractor
Arabian Contracting Company

Client
Government of Sharjah

Completed
1981

Status
Disused, scheduled for partial demolition

Images:

01. The vegetable souk was designed to provide a "much-required and long-felt healthy, clean, and excellent atmosphere," and "to bring all shopping into one area." Prem Ratnam, Hemlyn Photography Studio.
02. Interior scenes at the vegetable souk, mid-1980s. Carole Harris.
03. Workers complete final details on the vegetable souk, November 1980. Khaleej Times Archives.

02

03

K.M. BROTHERS

Kuwait Tower

By the mid-1970s, several Kuwaiti businessmen were focusing upon Sharjah as a real-estate opportunity. Much like his compatriots Mubarak Al-Hassawi and Mohamed Al-Bahar, Abdulmajeed Behbehani was working with a Kuwait-based consulting firm when he developed his Sharjah project, Kuwait Tower, with seventy-two spacious apartments over three floors of commercial space. With unrivalled views of the Gulf shoreline, pod-like balconies defined the tower's prominent elevations. The curved corner accentuated the design's use of precast concrete units to create efficient yet enviable residences. For over thirty years, Kuwait Tower remained one of Sharjah's most iconic buildings.

Following the 1990 Iraqi invasion of Kuwait, tens of thousands of Kuwaiti refugees fled to neighboring Arab Gulf states. According to the building owner's nephew, Kuwaiti refugees, including the Behbehanis' own family members, were offered free accommodation in Kuwait Tower. It was during this time that the building suffered its first fire.

At 5:30 p.m. on Tuesday, July 6, 2010, Kuwait Tower suffered an even more debilitating fire: flames broke out on the second floor and quickly spread throughout the building. Local news sources reported that fire brigades from Abu Dhabi, Dubai, Ajman, and Umm Al Quwain helped Sharjah firefighters extinguish the fire by morning. Sharjah's seventh major fire that year exposed the widespread use of antiquated construction techniques and marked a turning point for the emirate toward stricter building regulations. The tragedy's capture on mobile phones contributed to an undeniable spectacle online.

A decade after the devastating fire, Kuwait Tower has been neither restored nor demolished and instead stands in testament to both its fragility and resilience.

Architect
Arab Consultants

Client
Abdul Jalil Sayed Hassan Behbehani, Abdulmajeed Sayed Hasan Behbehani

Completed
1976

Status
Disused

Exterior view of Kuwait Tower, built along Al Sharq Street in Sharjah's Al Butaina district, late 1970s. Dr. Naman Al Jalili Archives Collection.

National
BITION
SHARJAH WORLD TRADE & EXPO CENTRE
مركز الشارقة للتجارة و المعارض العالمية

Qasimia Tower

Architect
Jafar Tukan & Partners

Contractor
Allied Contracting, Sogex Contracting & Trading Company

Client
Hammad Hassan Al Harazeen

Completed
1977

Status
Significantly renovated

In ongoing appraisals of the UAE's architectural history, it is often recalled that the Palestinian-Jordanian architect Jafar Tukan designed a kindergarten prototype for the country together with his partner George Rais. Often overlooked is Tukan's design for a nine-story, mixed-used tower in Sharjah's Al Soor district, completed in 1977, a few years after the delivery of the school prototype. Upon its completion, the tower rose defiantly among other sand-covered plots, waiting for the arrival of neighbors. Today, its renovated appearance can be dismissed as non-descript among other residential towers that went up in response to Sharjah's building boom.

Photographs of its original state are rare, but they make clear that Tukan's design was a restrained and sophisticated answer to the ongoing profit-driven housing boom. The architect produced a design that folded the apartments inward, with compressed window openings and articulated concrete columns that expressed the apartments' configurations. The ground floor and mezzanine level were programmed for commercial use and offices, with apartments above. Upper-floor fenestration was covered during the day with delicate metal louvers, no longer present. Originally proposed as a fifteen-story building, Sharjah Municipality approved only nine stories, which today accommodate offices.

The tower was once an elegant, earth-toned deployment of solids and voids. Its front facade has been clad in the tinted glass and aluminum paneling that plagues many of Sharjah's original reinforced concrete buildings. The result is a powerful example of market-driven overhaul vanquishing potential modern architectural heritage.

02

01. Exterior view of Qasimia Tower, also called the Hammad Hassan Al Harazeen Building, as seen from Al Arouba Street overpass. The photograph shows the building's exterior shading devices before they were removed. The incomplete Al Ittihad Park is in the foreground. United Colour Film, Ajman, courtesy of Abdulla Al Murad.
02. Mr. and Mrs. Babu, along with their family, lived in an apartment for thirty-eight years in Al Saud Co. Building. Their balcony faced toward Qasimia Tower. To the right of the tower is an early Sharjah Expo site. Further to the right, King Faisal Mosque is under construction, 1980s. Prema Babu.

01

Sharjah Gate Development

Sharjah Gate Development

Architect
Professional Group Australia

Client
Sheikh Sultan bin Muhammad Al Qasimi

Status
Unbuilt

Sandgate Low-Rise Housing

Architect
Professional Group Australia

Contractors
Nitco-Miller Limited

Client
Sheikh Sultan bin Muhammad Al Qasimi

Completed
1978

Status
Existing

Sandgate High-Rise Lagoon Apartments

Architect
Professional Group Australia

Contractors
Contractors Group International

Client
Sheikh Sultan bin Muhammad Al Qasimi

Completed
1978

Status
Disused

In 1972, Australia's Department of Overseas Trade organized a trade mission, wanting to find work for Australian consultants in the Gulf region's development boom. One of the companies it hoped to promote for the region's building market was Professional Group Australia, or PGA, a consortium of various consultants headed up by director Ivor Lloyd. The mission achieved quick success: by the following year, PGA had finished a ten-story residential building in Sharjah and calculated there was enough work to open an office there.

At the same time that the consortium secured the development of the seaside Garden City Villas in Sharjah's Al Khan district, they were also working on a potentially transformative, large-scale development project called the Sandgate Development.[1] Sited on Sharjah Creek on land that includes the present-day Radisson Blu Resort (formerly Inter-Continental Hotel), the proposed high-end waterfront project was commissioned by Sharjah's ruler as a residential and shopping district containing 325 apartments and spreading across seven precincts. The development plan, however, was never realized. Instead, two prototype residential buildings from the proposal were executed at two other sites in Sharjah.

One of those instances was the Sandgate Low-Rise Buildings in the Abu Shagara district. Walled in later to create a gated compound primarily serving the expatriate personnel of Sharjah TV, the project is made up of three blocks oriented north to protect balconies from direct sun exposure. Each block offered flexibility by making the units adjustable in size, providing between one and five bedrooms. Units could be single, split, or double level, depending on residents' requirements. PGA's consideration of flexible units was a smart acknowledgement of the capricious demographics of Sharjah at the time. The project comprises two- and three-story vertical units with outdoor communal and semi-public spaces, including a playground. Even though it was a mere fraction of a larger and more lucrative proposal, PGA intended the residential project to be a prototype for mid-rise development "providing the density necessary to be financially viable." However, no others were built.

The second prototype was a pair of identical apartment blocks known as High-Rise Lagoon Apartments in Al Majaz district with views of Khalid Lagoon. The project was intended as a housing compound for the staff families of Sharjah's Water and Electricity Department. Later, the apartments were occupied by single men, living there dormitory style. The project comprises two seven- and eight-story residential buildings on a large rectangular plot of land, perhaps originally intended to be landscaped. The buildings' northern elevations bear formal similarities with the low-rise prototype. When they were built, the towers' expressive forms could be seen from many vantage points throughout the city, thanks to the unbuilt plots of Sharjah's Al Majaz district. Now, the towers are tucked among the district's tall glass towers. In 2018, they were evacuated and marked for demolition, but spared by a demolition stay. No new use for the buildings has been announced.

1. See p. 415.

02

03

04

05

01. Sandgate low-rise housing complex during construction, Abu Shagara district, late 1970s. Professional Group Australia (PGA).
02. Sandgate high-rise lagoon apartments, Al Majaz district, late 1970s. Dr. Naman Al Jalili Archives Collection.
03. Aerial rendering of proposed Sharjah Gate Development along Sharjah Creek, unbuilt. PGA.
04. Sandgate high-rise lagoon apartments, 1978. PGA.
05. Sandgate low-rise housing complex, 1978. PGA.

Town planner Afzal Ahmad Khan, under direction of Sharjah Municipality's chief engineer Tanweer Ahmad Zaidi, designed this waterfront proposal. Working as a draftsman after office hours, another municipal worker Mohammed Ishaq prepared the final drawing. All three municipal workers credited their municipal jobs to recruiting efforts pursued by British municipal officials in Pakistan in the mid-1970s. Courtesy of Sharjah Municipality.

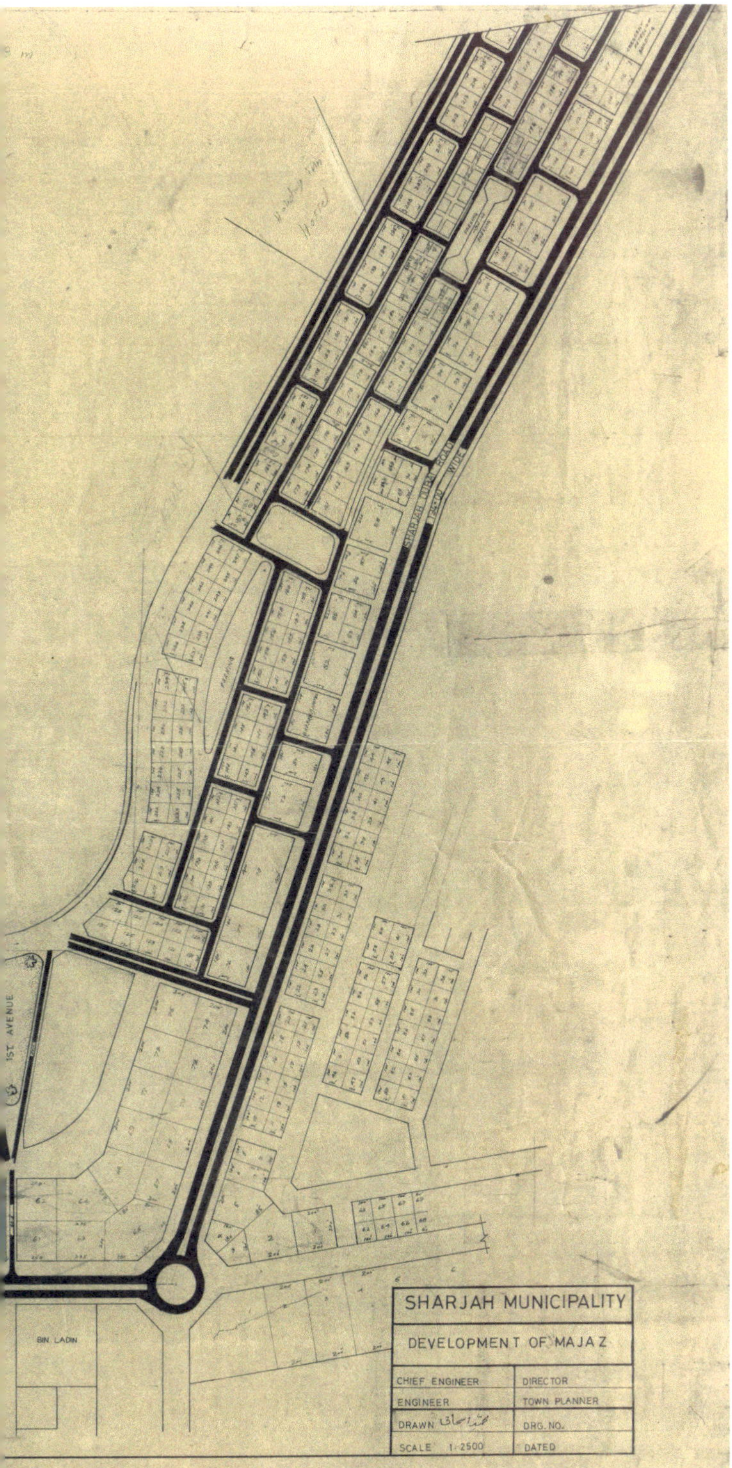

Khalid Lagoon Master Plan

Working off Halcrow's proposal to transform Khalid Lagoon into lakeside resorts and suburbs, Sharjah Municipality officials produced this profit-fueled plan. Beginning about halfway down the northern coastline (right), curved and slanted lines maximize waterfront views. Conspicuous trapezoidal city blocks begin on the lagoon's eastern edge (below) and wrap around the southern coast, alternating with triangular wedges of open space. Greenery and fountains were proposed for the wedged "avenues," but aside from creating unobstructed view corridors to the water for as many properties as possible, these no-build plots do not contribute much in the way of public amenities.

Halcrow produced the 1969 master plan with more than a decade's experience creating waterfront property in Dubai, where land reclamation created a cheap supply of land for great potential gains during a financial frenzy. Sharjah's 1969 master plan reimagined Khalid Lagoon transformed by the frenzy into a waterfront idyll.

The sawtooth plan was never realized: More land was added on the northern edge to make way for the Marbella Club and Holiday Inn (notated on this drawing). The entire eastern edge of the lagoon became Al Majaz Park, perhaps when Sharjah's real estate market was floundering in the mid-1980s. Other drawings suggest that Halcrow's reclamation contracts couldn't lift the land of the coastline high enough to make it suitable for construction. Land along Gamal Abdel Nasser Street (the wide road on the eastern edge connecting the two roundabouts) was lined with apartment blocks—an architectural wall shielding waterfront residents from the dusty industrial area inland.

Urban Planner
Afzal Ahmed Khan, Tanweer Ahmad Zaidi, Sharjah Municipality

Client
Sharjah Municipality

Completed
1978

Status
Not realized

Above: Foreground left, Holiday Inn designed by David Firmin & Partners; center, Marbella Club by Peter Hudson & Partners. Both were built on reclaimed land along Khalid Lagoon, according to the Halcrow plan. In the background, Central Souk under construction on what was formerly a waterfront site. In front of the souk are tents for construction workers. Dr. Naman Al Jalili Archives Collection.

Left: Professional Group Australia's high-rise lagoon apartments overlooked the reclamation work that converted Khalid Lagoon into Lake Khalid. Dar Al Khaleej Printing & Publishing.

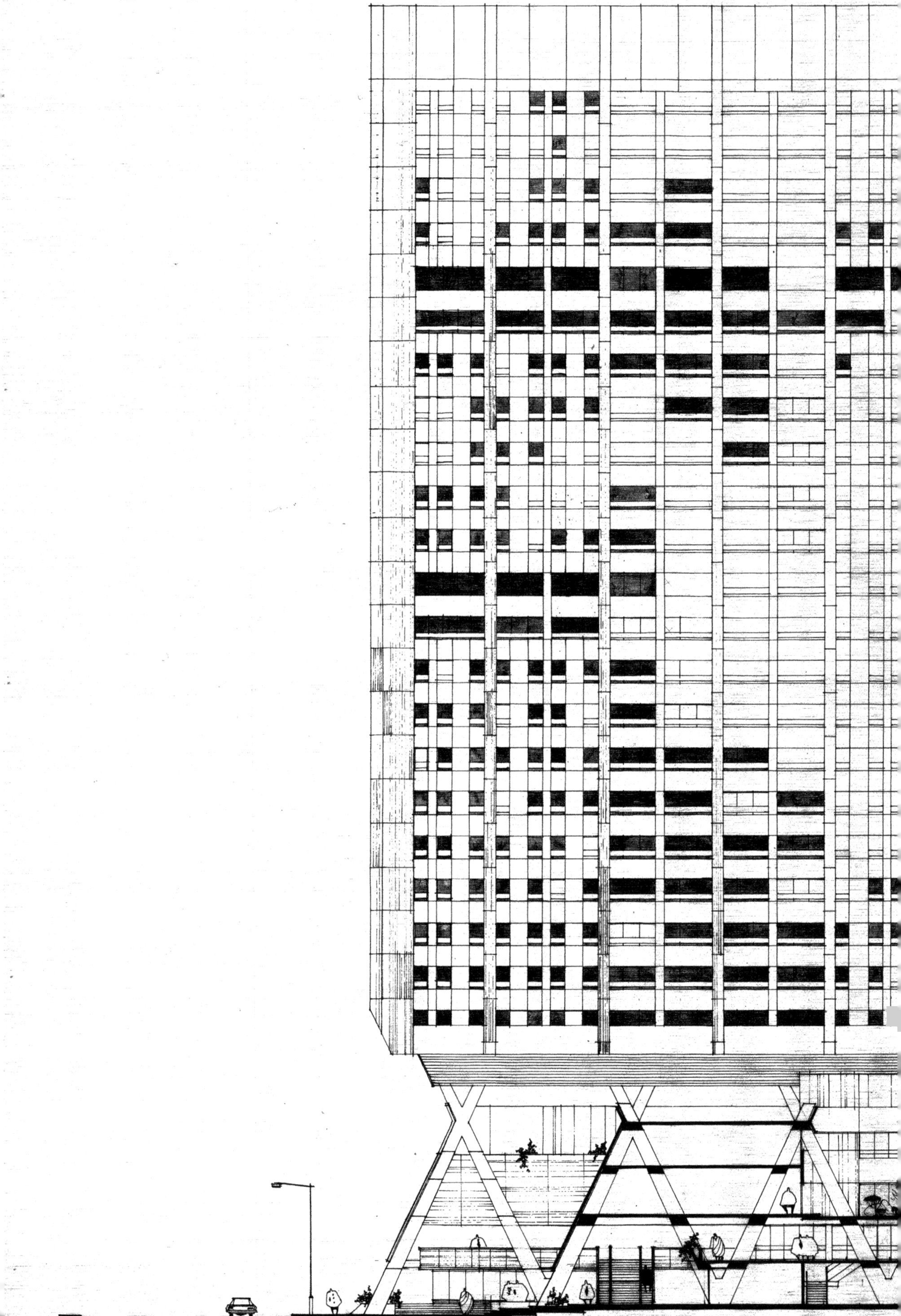

section C-C 1 20

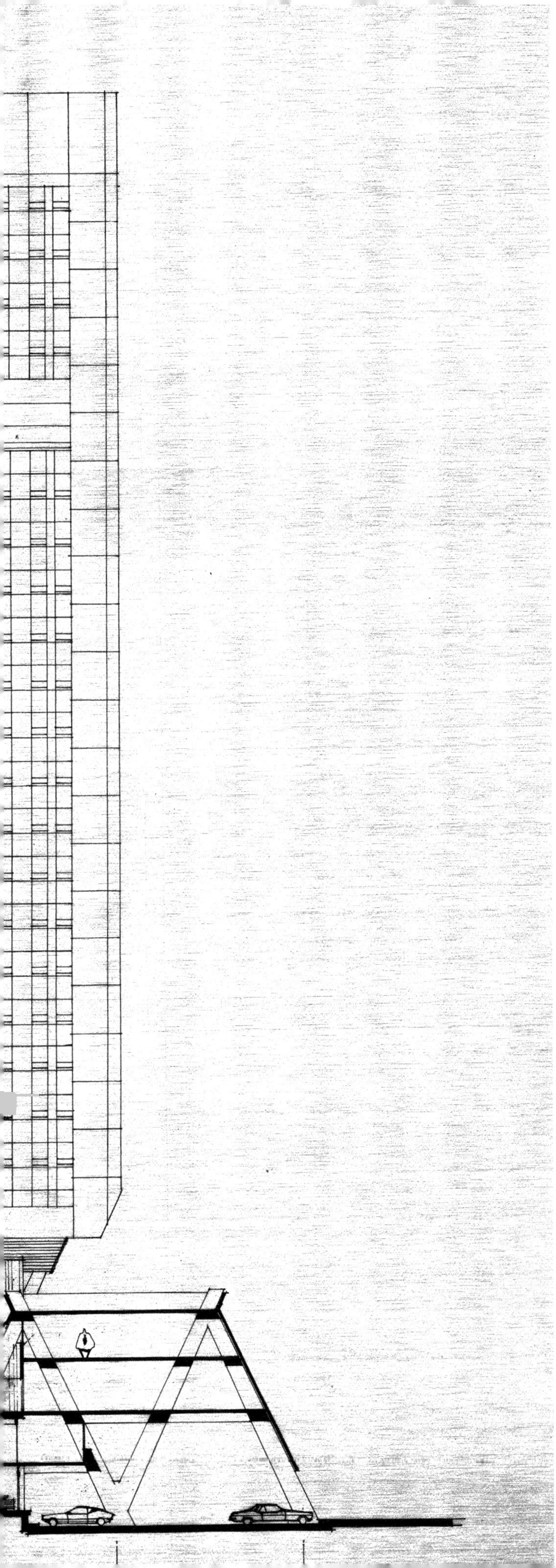

Bin Laden–Amoudi Center

In the mid-1970s, Cairo-based Riad Architecture produced schematic drawings for a lively, mixed-use tower in Sharjah. During that time, Riad Architecture often produced initial designs for Arab Engineering Bureau (AEB), a firm active in Sharjah's urban development. A significant example of their collaboration is the Hassan & Hussein Al Fardan Building on Al Zahra'a Square.[1]

This unbuilt project, labeled the Bin Laden–Amoudi Center, was situated on Sharjah's waterfront, likely along what was to become known as Buhaira Corniche around Lake Khalid. The tower was the largest, most ambitious project proposed by the collaboration. Exactly who the clients were remains unconfirmed, but the center's name indicates two Yemeni-Saudi families who participated in Saudi Arabia's urban development, the former known for the Saudi Binladin Group, which may have been the project's proposed contractor. Representatives of these families possibly consulted with AEB on an investment option in Sharjah that was never realized.

The base's expressive structure houses a parking garage, restaurants, offices, a shopping center, a hotel, and—on its roof—gardens and a swimming pool. The tower offered spacious apartments, including floors of duplex "villas." It was to be topped with a panoramic restaurant. Though large in scale for the time, the 23-story project's mixed-use program is a common development scenario on Buhaira Corniche and elsewhere in Sharjah today.

1. See p. 414.

Architect
Riad Architecture

Architect of Record
Arab Engineering Bureau

Proposed
1975

Status
Unbuilt

Tower elevation and base, 1975. Riad Architecture.

Lake Khalid Tower, background right, as seen from Lake Khalid during Open Polka Sailing Regatta, undated. © Gulf News, Dubai.

Lake Khalid Tower

After the kindergarten prototype for the UAE government, Beirut-based Rais and Tukan Architects completed a second project in Sharjah, this time a mixed-use commercial property on what was becoming the city's most exclusive waterfront strip, eventually known as Buhaira Corniche.

The property's developer was Dubai-based businessman Sultan bin Khalifa Al Habtoor. He first encountered architect Jafar Tukan during his time as undersecretary at the UAE Ministry of Public Works (1972–1974), which had overseen the kindergarten prototype.[1]

Erected on a site surrounded by vacant lots, the building offered its residents views in all directions. Each unit was also assured views toward what was still known as Khalid Lagoon. Eventually, the Halcrow plans artificially bound the limits of the water, leading to a change in name to the more urbane Lake Khalid.

Initially, the building proposal came with its own custom-designed street lampposts and offered residents new amenities, including a service elevator and garbage chute. At thirteen stories, it was one of the tallest towers in Sharjah. From the tower's opening until 1982, the Arab Cultural Club occupied the 800-square-meter penthouse, prior to its official registration and relocation to a purpose-built compound across the street. The club hosted various Pan-Arab cultural events, including art exhibitions and poetry recitals, and also commemorations of the Arab states' national days, military victories, and the Nakba.

1. See p. 243.

Architect
Rais & Tukan Architects

Contractor
Marwan Engineering & Construction Enterprise

Client
Sultan bin Khalifa Al Habtoor

Completed
1979

Status
Existing

Above: A typical juice bar in Sharjah, early 1980s.

Right: A dry-goods shop from the disappearing souk along Sharjah Creek, early 1980s. Images: Peter Hudson.

مؤسسة علي جمعه لبيع العلف
ALI JUMMA FODDER SUPPLY EST.
TEL 350055 P.O.BOX 25 SHJ.

01

Reem Khorshid

UNRAVELED: MAKING *BUILDING SHARJAH*

In 1974, when an oil company's announcement framed Sharjah as a prosperous city for architects, three university friends came to the city to set up an architectural practice. After graduating from the School of Planning and Architecture Delhi in 1967, Kanwal Krishan Duggal, Harbhajan Singh Vedi, and Karnail Singh Kler had gone separate ways—Dubai, Kuwait, and the United States—until the Gulf boom brought them to Sharjah's Al Arouba Street, where they opened a practice together. By then, roving cranes and earth movers defined Sharjah's skyline. Scenes of prodigious construction vigor were featured in photographs, newspapers, and magazine articles previewing the city's future. It was no surprise that the small office found work opportunities in this swirl of activity. It was, however, a shocking loss when one of the friends, Duggal, died in a car accident in 1985, an incident from which the business partnership never recovered.

When we first began the research for this book, Gulf Design Group seemed like just another nondescript office name stamped on drawings filed long ago with the Sharjah Municipality. It wasn't until we stumbled on filings at the Delhi High Court in the late 1980s that we were able to trace the story of short-lived Gulf Design Group. Published proceedings led us to the daughter of the only surviving founder, Karnail Kler. Only because there had been over three decades of litigation could we trace this architectural legacy.[1]

For dozens of architectural practices and building-industry professionals like the partners of Gulf Design Group, Sharjah was a work opportunity. Oil-industry companies and banks, taking advantage of Sharjah's discount properties and regulation rates, commissioned foreign architects to construct headquarters in the UAE's third-largest oil city. Architects from all over the world performed on the city's stage, before their stories were lost in the rubble in preparation for the next round of development.

A leading challenge we faced was access to archival materials, as we were sometimes unsure if they even existed. In pursuing an exhaustive investigation of Sharjah's architectural and urban legacy, we were confronted with the convoluted nature of archival practices in the Arab world, with constant uncertainties about preservation, cataloguing, authorship, and ownership. We faced recurring questions about the term "modernism," specifically in the context of Sharjah. Aware of a critical need for authoritative architectural and urban research studies of the Arab world's cities—very much a motivation behind *Building Sharjah*—we encountered many archives within the region still waiting to be viewed, collected, treated, or preserved in the midst of a charged political climate that threatens tangible and intangible histories. Even searches at London's British Library led us to microfilms and folios viewed for the first time since being filed. The difficulty of research has itself become a theme of this book.

Another search for the archive brought us to the work of Naman Al Jalili, a project manager for the United Nations' aid program dedicated to the UAE's Ministry of Public Works and Housing. Accumulated

SHARJAH ARCHITECTS

Ziki Homsi. Architect Town Planner.
Adnan Abu Shaar. Architect.
P. O. Box: 284 Tel: 8218
SHARJAH - Arabian Gulf

مكتب الشارقة الهندسي
المهندس المعماري ومهندس المدن زكي الحمصي
والمهندس المعماري عدنان ابوشعر
ص . ب : ٢٨٤ هاتف : ٨٢١٨
الشارقة ـ الخليج العربي

Date .... التاريخ ١٠/٦/١٩٧٠

عقد اتفاق

الفريق الأول المالك : السيدة سلمى حارب
الفريق الثاني المقاول : السيد عبدالقادر [illegible]

لقد تم الاتفاق بين الفريقين على أن يقوم الفريق الثاني بتنفيذ بناء طابق أرضي والمؤلف من دكاكين ومطبخ ودرج وذلك حسب المخططات والمواصفات المقدمة من قبل المهندس المشرف . ويتم هدم غرفة ووضع عامود وجسر أرضي .

١ ـ يتم تنفيذ الطابق الأرضي حسب الاتفاق المسبق وذلك بسعر أربعون ألف ريال [illegible]
٢ ـ إن مدة تنفيذ العمل هي [illegible] وذلك اعتباراً من ١٠/٦/١٩٧٠ وحتى تاريخ [illegible]
٣ ـ إن كل يوم تأخير عن تسليم البناء المذكور بالوقت المحدد له يدفع الفريق الثاني للفريق الأول مائة ريال [illegible]
٤ ـ إن أعمال البلوك العادي والمفرغ يجب أن تكون حسب المخططات وحسب تعليمات المهندس المشرف .
٥ ـ إن أعمال [illegible] يجب أن [illegible] وحسب تعليمات المهندس المشرف وأن [illegible] جميع أعمال الباطون [illegible]
٦ ـ إن أعمال الدهان يجب أن [illegible] [illegible] ثلاثة [illegible]
٧ ـ إن جميع [illegible] يجب [illegible] وحسب تعليمات المهندس المشرف
٨ ـ يجب أن تكون الأبواب من [illegible] وحسب رأي المهندس المشرف .
٩ ـ يجب تنفيذ [illegible] حسب المخطط المقدم وحسب تعليمات المهندس المشرف
١٠ ـ إن جميع [illegible] وجميع [illegible] وحسب تعليمات المهندس المشرف .
١١ ـ يجب وضع [illegible] من الخلف على طول البناء بارتفاع ثلاثة أقدام على [illegible]
١٢ ـ يدفع الفريق الأول للفريق الثاني الدفعة الأولى فور توقيع العقد عشرة آلاف ريال [illegible]
١٣ ـ يدفع الفريق الأول للفريق الثاني باقي الدفعات حسب اتفاق الفريقين

وبناء على ذلك فقد تم الاتفاق

الفريق الثاني الفريق الأول

02

during his time in the UAE, from 1977 to 1982, his archive ended up in the basement of an abandoned house in Baghdad. These artifacts included at least fifty documentary photographs of the UAE's modern buildings, many of which we would not have otherwise found. Coming across Al Jalili's archive raised many unanswered questions about the making of the photography collection. Was he paid by the United Nations to document the UAE's newest structures? Or was he just another architect curious about his surroundings? And what were the criteria for choosing which buildings to photograph, and not to photograph?

A local contractor first told us about Adnan Abu Shaar. A Syrian architect, Abu Shaar established an office in Sharjah in the late 1960s with yet another forgettable name, the Sharjah Architects Office. Office letterhead dated 1970 revealed that Abu Shaar had partnered with town planner and architect Ziki Homsi, best known for the design of the Deira Clock Tower. Arriving in Sharjah in 1966, Abu Shaar designed mostly houses and the two-to-three-story, mixed-use buildings prevalent in the Trucial States at the time. The architect's name came up in conversations with several other practitioners active in Sharjah in the 1960s. No one, however, could point us to one of his buildings. They were either forgotten or demolished. Our original source recounted that Abu Shaar left Sharjah in 1972 as a result of non-work-related allegations—an incomplete narrative that bespeaks to the difficulty of finding out more about him. We returned to our files and found that we had drawings from 1969 of a two-story building designed by his office. It had been demolished, but through this project, his work started to reappear.

We sought more information about him in Damascus. "I actually walked the streets of Damascus and asked around," said research contributor Rania Kataf about how she tracked down Abu Shaar's second cousin. It took Kataf numerous phone calls with extended family members to finally find the architect's son, Fawaz. The family informed her that Abu Shaar had died in 1974.

The family had compiled a comprehensive portfolio about the architect, although they knew little of his career. Flipping through documents Kataf had scanned, we stopped at a black-and-white photograph of the architect posing with a pipe in front of a model of a four-story building. In a serendipitous encounter with another photograph from another collection, we confirmed that this was a model of a completed building on Al Arouba Street in Sharjah, its curved balcony identical to that of the model. Fragments of a forgotten past were coming together, piece by piece.

03

BUILDING SHARJAH

To make *Building Sharjah*, we had to unravel the city. We relied on traditional methods of investigation: site visits and interviews with architects, engineers, planners, contractors, practitioners, photographers, and residents. Whatever archives we could access provided indispensable details: we pored over master plans, aerial photographs, architectural and working drawings, and periodicals. Corporate portfolios, brochures, legal documents, and contracts illustrated the professional setting of Sharjah, especially around the 1980s. We investigated multimedia, including film footage, microfilms, and advertisements bearing evidence of Sharjah's evanescing modern identity. Some projects designed by international firms were fairly well documented, albeit scattered across the world in public and architectural libraries, national archives, and architects' private files. In Beirut's Hazmiyeh suburb, for example, the Choueifat school's in-house architect kept his photographs of the Sharjah campus construction in his personal collection. In Amman, a design studio preserved piles of publications pertaining to Jafar Tukan's work, including his project portfolios.

04

Without systematically organized archives of architectural and urban documentation, we were left with the task of outlining the old skyline of Sharjah by comparing photographs. Architectural drawings provided insight into the construction technologies implemented and into the names of some of the participants. We looked for Sharjah in people: architects, builders, locals, residents, tourists, and their survivors. We sought people beyond Sharjah: Dubai, Kuwait, London, Sydney, Scotland, Oslo, Paris, Karachi, Mumbai, Delhi, Kerala, Cairo, Beirut, and Minnesota. The stories we collected are complemented with personal documents and family photographs, the totality of which shapes this publication. We also relied on social media to make several contacts, with a network of friends and acquaintances connecting us to those who knew part of the story we didn't know yet.

After four years of collecting material about Sharjah's urban history, our database encompasses more than 300 projects, including existing, demolished, and unbuilt schemes. The documentation on buildings, whether or not still standing, inspired manifold imaginings of how this new environment was being constructed. Some cityscape photographs reveal plans for Sharjah's entry onto the global stage, leading us to question: what ends was design serving?

Building Sharjah has been an expansive, collaborative effort—just look at our acknowledgments section!—by the researchers, architects, practitioners, and writers who helped define the book's scope as going beyond architecture and urbanism. By accounting for the skills and expertise gathered to build a city, *Building Sharjah* is an account of the optimism that Sharjah once possessed. It illustrates the efforts and contributions of architects, builders, developers, and investors in shaping the cityscape. This book, along with the project's database and archives, proposes a concerted contribution to what we hope will be a lasting conversation about how architecture shapes cultural identity.

1. Gulf Design Group's most memorable work in Sharjah is what is today known as the Choithrams Building (see p. 341).

05

06

Images:

01. The three founders of Gulf Design Group at a Sharjah construction site: from left K. K. Duggal with his wife Veena Duggal, H. S. Vedi, and K. S. Kler, 1970. Collection of Kanwal Krishan Duggal, courtesy of Shikha Duggal.
02. A contract agreement for construction of a residential building signed by three parties: the client, local Sharjah woman Salma Sarry; the contractor, Abdul Kader Bannah; and the architect, Sharjah Architects, established by Adnan Abu Shaar and Ziki Homsi. The document, dated October 10, 1970, is an example of how such contracts were often issued in handwriting and formulated as correspondence. Collection of Abdul Kader bin Mohamed Bannah, courtesy of Humaid Abdul Kader Bannah, Al Naser Engineering & Contracting Co.
03. UAE Minister of Public Works opens a symposium on challenges in the UAE construction sector, 1970s. UN consultant Naman Al Jalili stands left. UAE Ministry of Information, Photography Department. Courtesy of Dr. Naman Al Jalili Archives Collection.
04. In his Sharjah office, Syrian architect Adnan Abu Shaar points to a model of a building on Al Arouba Street, late 1960s. Collection of Mohammed Fawaz Abu Shaar.
05. Adnan Abu Shaar's Al Arouba Street building before extension. Mahmood AlSawan.
06. The same building after completion of two more stories. Mahmood AlSawan.

Commonly referred to as the Grey Building, this mixed-use project was one of Sharjah's first modern buildings, in terms of design and its offering of residences above a commercial ground floor. Commissioned by Sharjah's new petroleum department, the building may have been the launch of Turkish Cypriot architect Mesud Cagdas's prolific career in the future UAE. Its ground floor was leased for a time by Lebanese entrepreneur Merched Baaklini for his contracting company Orient Trading & Contracting Company (OTAC) until it moved to Dubai.

The Grey Building also housed the local offices of design firm Khatib & Alami, according to its later general manager Samir Abdulhadi, before being moved to the BBME Building. In the foreground is Government Square. The building has been demolished. Images: Mahmood AlSawan.

GUARANTEE INSURANCE SERVICES
SHARJAH OPTICALS

Above: For the heart of Al Mareija, one of Sharjah's oldest districts, British engineer Alistair McCowan designed this building with apartments above ground-floor storefronts for local businessman and investor Ali Gargash.

Left: A twelve-story, mixed-use building that led Sharjah's shift to larger and higher buildings, Al Arouba Street, Arab Engineering Bureau, 1977. Images: Prem Ratnam, Hemlyn Photography Studio.

01

Expo Centre Sharjah

In name, Expo Centre Sharjah was a trade fairground. In actuality, it was the most important event on Sharjah's cultural calendar. On various occasions of the year, manufacturers and distributors were invited to sell their wares from its leasable booths. Hosting during the cooler months, the candy-colored tents of Sharjah Expo attracted not only traders and buyers but also families and tourists. Large crowds gathered for musical concerts, 3D movie screenings, fashion shows, and a temporary ice rink. The expo's most memorable act was the Lebanese singer Fayrouz, who attracted more than 5,000 people to the main event tent.

The event's founder and longtime producer, Frederick Pittera, allegedly had his hands in every aspect of Sharjah Expo, from recruiting and marketing to securing the live acts. Described by his colleagues as "the showman," Pittera assembled the team that constructed the first and subsequent premises, including Canada-based Sprung Instant Structures, which provided the iconic striped tents. Though the huge canvas membranes and aluminum parts were manufactured in Calgary, Canada, Sprung Instant Structures insisted that the structures owed "so much in their basic appearance to the nomad culture of the native Bedouin."

During the years of its existence, the expo took place in three different locations, usually relocating to find larger, and more permanent, premises. In 1977, Pittera organized the first trade show on a 200-cabin ship, billed as a floating hotel, or "flotel." At a time when Sharjah's population was estimated at under 100,000, the original sixteen-day event attracted 151,327 visitors. The idea of an annual Sharjah Expo was born from that success. In 2002, the event found a permanent, if less playful, home. Its tents have now been decamped, but Sharjah Expo deserves credit for instigating essential ongoing cultural events in Sharjah, including the Sharjah International Book Fair and the Sharjah Biennial.

Consultants
Sprung Instant Structures

Years of Operation
1977–2001

02

العدد ٩٦٣ — الخميس ٢٩ محرم ١٤٠٢هـ - ٢٦ نوفمبر ١٩٨١م

ملحق اعلاني عن اكسبو الشارقة

صفحة ١٠ — الخليج

اكسبو «٨١» بالصور

لأول مرة في الشرق الأوسط

المعرض السنوي العالمي الخامس

اكسبو ٨١

من ٢٦ نوفمبر إلى ٦ ديسمبر ١٩٨١

يقدم

سينما ١٨٠ درجة

3D

شاشة تحيطك من ثلاث جوانب

وتعطيك صوت من ٦ أقنية

عروض متواصلة من الاثارة والتشويق وانت على مقعدك تشعر وكأنك تقود سيارة سباق في ميدان سباق مونت كارلو بسرعة ١٨٠ ميلا في الساعة أو تتزلج فوق امواج هوآي المشهورة

مركز اكسبو

الشارقة - دولة الامارات العربية المتحدة

03

04

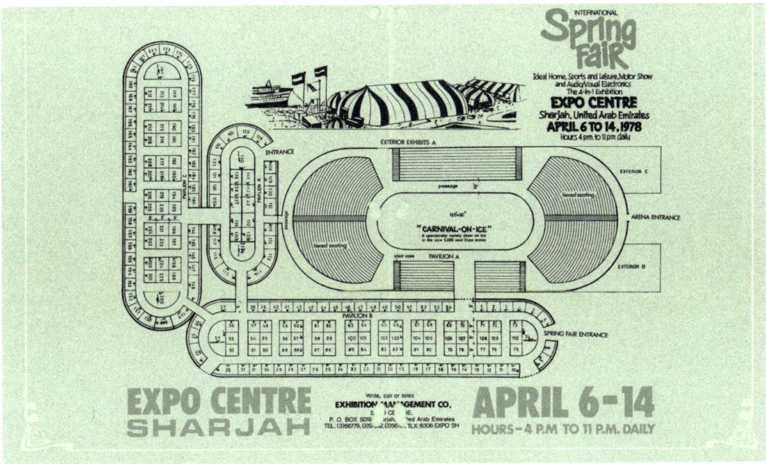
INTERNATIONAL
Spring Fair
Ideal Home, Sports and Leisure, Motor Show and Audio/Visual Electronics
The 4-in-1 Exhibition
EXPO CENTRE
Sharjah, United Arab Emirates
APRIL 6 TO 14, 1978
Hours 4 pm. to 11 pm. daily
EXTERIOR EXHIBITS A
EXTERIOR C
ARENA ENTRANCE
EXTERIOR B
"CARNIVAL-ON-ICE"
PAVILION A
PAVILION B
ENTRANCE
SPRING FAIR ENTRANCE
EXPO CENTRE
SHARJAH
Write, call or telex
APRIL 6-14
HOURS - 4 P.M TO 11 P.M. DAILY

05

06

07

01. Although colonial officers and roving seafarers had for centuries slept on ships anchored off the Gulf's shores, Frederick Pittera claimed Sharjah's first floating hotel in 1976. His company Sharjah Hotel Enterprises Ltd., in which Sharjah's ruler Sheikh Sultan bin Muhammad Al Qasimi held shares, was part of the larger plan of Sharjah Expo. At one time named the *St. Lawrence*, the ship had previously functioned as a cruise ship between Toronto and Montreal before sailing to Copenhagen. Pittera brought the 109-meter ship there and renovated it to meet "luxury hotel standards," including 242 well-appointed cabins, a ballroom, and a restaurant. It was moored off Sharjah's coastline to provide ready-made guest accommodations, until being replaced the following year by the *Grand Floatel*, pictured here during the 1977 Sharjah Expo in Al Khan, behind the vegetable souk. The successor ship provided a 900-square-meter exhibition hall for seminars and conventions in addition to 200 cabins, two restaurants, two cocktail bars, a nightclub, a cinema, and a swimming pool. Formerly known as the *Ile de Beauté*, the ship had hosted the climactic final scenes of the action film *Darker Than Amber*. Barry Cruse, Sprung Instant Structures.

02. Night scene during an expo in the 1980s. Prem Ratnam, Hemlyn Photography Studio.

03. Promotional media coverage of the 1981 Sharjah Expo, in local daily *Al Khaleej*, covered a fashion show and advertised a 180-degree, 3D cinema, allegedly the first in the Middle East. Dar Al Khaleej Printing & Publishing.

04. Scenes from the expo's interior with various product booths on display. Khaled Malik, Sprung Instant Structure's regional manager in the early 1980s, told a local reporter that the structures were not "'tents' in view of their high quality weather proofing, fire resistance, wind and sand loads and aerodynamic design." Prem Ratnam, Hemlyn Photography Studio.

05. Plan, 1978 Sharjah Expo. Barry Cruse, Sprung Instant Structures.

06. The various sizes provided by Spung Instant Structures made multiple kinds of events possible, including a circus show. Barry Cruse, Sprung Instant Structures.

07. The Sharjah International Book Fair, one of Sharjah's largest events today, originated in one of the expo tents. Sharjah Documentation & Archives Authority.

08. Advertisement in Lebanon-based magazine *Achabaka* dated April 9, 1979, announcing singer Fayrouz's upcoming performances at Sharjah Expo: "For the first time in the United Arab Emirates, Fayrouz and the Lebanese Popular Troupe will perform traditional and dance music written and composed by the Rahbani Brothers. Tickets sold at major hotels in the UAE and the Expo Centre." Achabaka, courtesy of Omar Thawabeh.

للمرة الأولى في دولة الإمارات العربية المتحدة
فيروز
والفرقة الشعبية اللبنانية، في تنوعات غنائية راقصة
من تأليف وتلحين الأخوين رحباني
على مسرح مركز اكسبو "القبة الكبرى" - الشارقة
أيام
١٩ - ٢٠ - ٢١ - ٢٢ - ٢٢
ابريل ١٩٧٩
إبتداءً من
الساعة ٩ مساءً
تباع التذاكر في معظم الفنادق الرئيسية في دولة الإمارات العربية المتحدة وفي مركز اكسبو الشارقة
- ٤ -
PUBLICO

SIEMENS
Emirates Neon
AL SHAMS GROCERY
AL JASAR SUPERMARKET
TOPAZ RESTAURANT

01

Al Saud Co. Building

Al Saud Co. Building, also known as Sultan Building, was built on land the owner received upon naming his third son after Sharjah's ruler. Located on Al Arouba Street, which was quickly being filled with Sharjah's largest mixed-use buildings, the site made for a generous gift. A good friend of the new landowner, contractor Ismail Al Zarooni, recommended that British engineer Alistair McCowan, also Al Zarooni's tenant, be commissioned to design the project. The resulting tower housed the head office of Al Saud Co. for 38 years, as well as families and small offices in its six floors of apartments. The ground-floor anchor tenant, Al Jasar Supermarket, was named after the bridge over Al Arouba Street just in front of the building. At least three generations of Arab and Asian families lived in the building before its demolition.

The building's facade featured a series of seven vertical slabs jutting out at angles across the upper six floors. The memorable triangular balconies offered views of Al Ittihad Park and King Faisal Mosque; the apartments in the back looked over Al Jubail Cemetery, the official burial ground of Sharjah's ruling family. A large, red neon Siemens billboard stood on the roof of the building for twenty years, accentuating its prominence in Sharjah's skyline.

Alistair McCowan designed several other residential buildings in Sharjah, including one for the late Dubai businessman Ali Gargash in Sharjah's Al Mareija district. He also designed the Police Training Academy and a mixed-use building on Al Arouba Street for the Al Zayani family from Bahrain.

Architect
Alistair McCowan & Associates

Contractor
Al Zarooni General Contracting Company

Client
Saud bin Khalid Al Qasimi

Completed
1980

Status
Demolished, 2021

01. Al Saud Co. Building from Al Arouba Street overpass. Ismail Al Zarooni.
02. Front elevation, as submitted to Sharjah Municipality by Alistair McCowan & Associates, 1978. Alistair McCowan, courtesy of Sharjah Municipality.

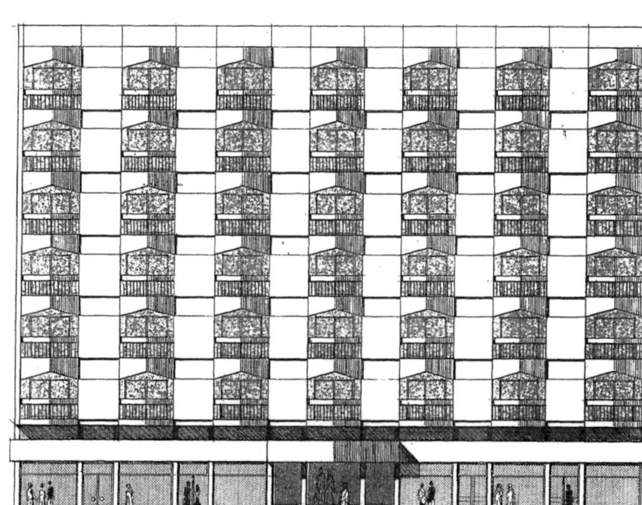

02

The large, oblong roundabout at the junction of Al Meena and Al Arouba Streets once hosted one of Sharjah's most spectacular lighted fountains, but it was not long before it was succeeded by this overpass that extended Al Arouba Street toward Dubai. Early development projects along Al Meena Street (seen under the overpass) soon lost their allure to Al Arouba and Bank Streets. The building with the DNATA storefront was designed by Syrian architect Sulaiman Towfic, 1976. Mahmood AlSawan.

KOHLER

Winston
JVC
NATIONAL TRAVEL & TOURIST AGENCY
DUBAI
SHARJAH
SLOW
DOWN

01

SNTTA Building

A Madrid-based engineering firm with a nondescript name, Tecnica y Proyectos (TYPSA), produced some of Sharjah's most iconic modernist buildings. This eleven-story building's ground floor housed the headquarters of Sharjah National Travel and Tourist Agency, whose acronym provided the building with its commonly used name. Officially, the building was commissioned as Sharjah Tower. The upper apartments had views of Sharjah's growing commercial artery, Al Arouba Street, and the transforming skyline beyond Al Ittihad Park. One of the city's most prominent buildings at the time, the tower announced Sharjah's ambitions to be a center of tourism and travel, offering beach resorts, an international airport, and the promise of authentic Arab culture. The location at the end of Al Meena Street at the corner of Al Arouba Street signaled the city's shift from Sharjah's early modern artery to the large-scale buildings proposed for Al Arouba Street. Though diminishing the building's visual prominence, the eventual overpass on Al Arouba Street brought drivers even closer to the building's upper-story curves and striations.

The building demonstrates an economical use of prefabricated concrete elements assembled to create repeating forms that make its components of living, working, and circulation legible to the viewer.

The project client was Sheikh Abdulaziz Mohamed Al Qassemi, brother of Sharjah's ruler. The tower's design and development phases proceeded in tandem with those of the twenty-four mixed-use buildings, which TYPSA designed along Bank Street.[1]

02

Architect
Jesús Velasco, José Carlos Laredo, Tecnica y Proyectos (TYPSA)

Contractor
Gulf General Projects Company

Client
Sheikh Abdulaziz Mohamed Al Qassemi

Completed
1977

Status
Existing

1. See p. 99.

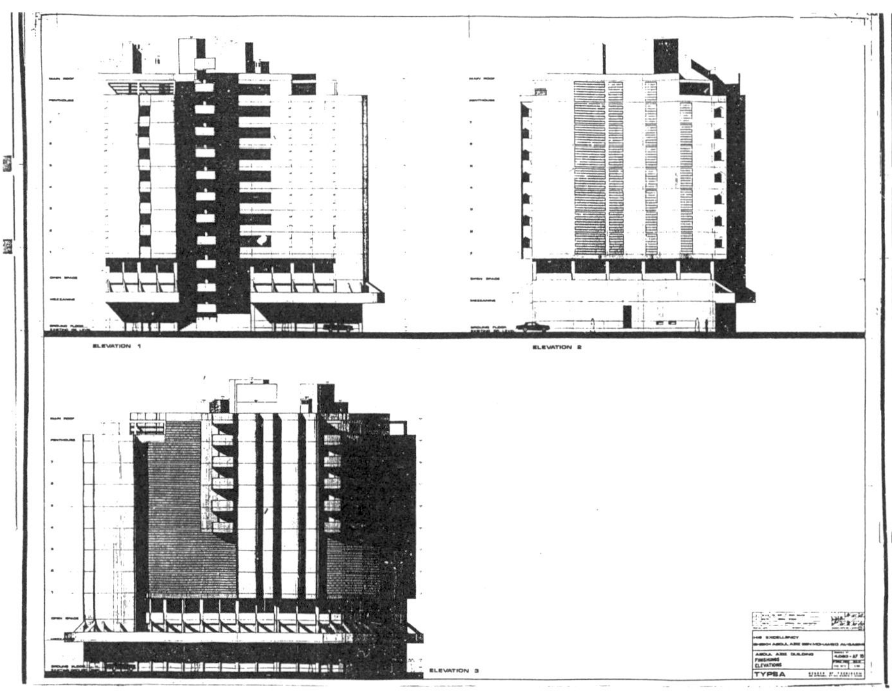
ELEVATION 1
ELEVATION 2
ELEVATION 3
FINISHINGS
ELEVATIONS
TYPSA

03

04

L TRAVEL & TOURIST AGENCY
الشارقة الوطنية للسفريات والسياحة
PIA

05

06

07

01. SNTTA Building seen approaching Sharjah city center from the direction of Dubai. In the years after its completion, the building was painted white. A streetlamp has been removed from this image. United Colour Film, Ajman, courtesy of Abdulla Al Murad.
02. Watercolor rendering includes neighboring Sharjah Cinema (see p. 197) on Al Meena Street. TYPSA.
03. Three elevations show the tower's peculiar siting at an oblique corner, 1974. TYPSA.
04. SNTTA Building during construction, mid-1970s. Far right, a building designed by Khatib & Alami and another residential block, under construction, designed by Professional Group Australia in 1974. TYPSA.
05. SNTTA Building behind Al Khan overpass, mid-1980s. Mahmood AlSawan.
06.–07. SNTTA Building captured in the background of rooftop snapshots by longtime residents of Al Saud Co. Building, 1980s. Prema Babu.

01

02

03

04

Al Seef Palace

Architect and Engineering Consultants
International Consultation Office for Developing & Construction

Contractor
Contractors Group International

Client
Sheikh Sultan bin Muhammad Al Qasimi

Completed
1979

Status
Existing, renovated

The ruler's palace embodies the architectural references that started to define Sharjah's architectural landscape in the late 1970s. While the architectural styles manifested in the palace's facades might seem in agreement with the ongoing adoption of a so-called "Islamic architectural identity" elsewhere in Sharjah, the building departs from other designs that were more often inspired by Islamic Cairo.

As told by the project's contractor, Sharjah's ruler Sheikh Sultan bin Muhammad Al Qasimi, who had studied in Cairo, requested that the palace's design be a modified replica of Al Haramlik Palace inside Alexandria's Al Montaza Palace complex. He had allegedly seen the early twentieth-century residence in the Egyptian film *Al Wessada Al Khaliya* (*The Empty Pillow*). The palace's original design was accordingly prepared by the prominent Egyptian engineer Ibrahim Gaafar, whose Cairo-based Gaafar Engineering Consultants had executed significant infrastructure contracts in Egypt under Nasser's and Sadat's presidencies, as well as in Saudi Arabia. After Gaafar submitted the palace designs, the project underwent several significant modifications in the contractor's hands. The resulting building lacked several of the architectural elements that recalled the Alexandrian palace, including the entrance's spiral stairs and two unmistakable towers. The architect Shafik Nasr designed each elevation of the seaside palace from a catalogue of Islamic-inspired details: pointed arches, arcades, *muqarnas*-inspired cornices, and decorative reliefs.

01. Al Seef Palace under construction, late 1970s. It is considered the first residence that Sheikh Sultan bin Muhammad Al Qasimi commissioned for himself after becoming Sharjah's ruler. Images: Mohammed Abdul Haq Musa, Globe Constructors.
02. During a construction site tour, Dutch architect Reinder de Vries, who helped oversee the project, discusses project progress with Sharjah's ruler Sheikh Sultan bin Muhammad Al Qasimi, May 1977.
03. Sharjah's ruler greeted by the construction team at the construction site of Al Seef Palace, May 1977.
04. Dutch architect Reinder de Vries makes a note on the ruler's car during the tour, Al Seef Palace, May 1977.
05. Construction worker stands on roof arcade during construction, 1977. Kuwait Tower (p. 149) in background.

05

01

Al Qassimi Hospital

The phases of Al Qassimi Hospital's development, including its demolition, reveal Sharjah's constant recalibration of its health care services. By the time work had begun on the hospital, the emirate already counted six operating clinics and four more under construction. Before this, except for clinics and health care facilities for British officers, the closest hospital was Al Maktoum Hospital in Dubai. Since the 1950s, Sharjah's leadership had sought a semblance of modern health care more substantial than the modestly sized clinics. In 1970, when work finally began on such a project, it was announced as "one of the most modern and best equipped medical centres in the Arabian Gulf area." In reality, it was based on an unassuming template commissioned with the expectation of distributing adequate health care throughout the Trucial States.[1] The first phase was intended to accommodate a 206-member staff and advanced amenities provided by the West German company Hospitalia, in general a more ambitious result than the original template intended.

Around 1970, the British partnership Page & Broughton had been commissioned to design a hospital prototype for use throughout the Trucial States. Partner Brian Broughton recalled submitting the final conceptual design to engineers in the Trucial States Development Office but had understood that the design did not advance because of costs. During preparation for this publication, he learned that the hospital in Sharjah had at least implemented his two-story, fan-like proposal, its male and female quarters linked together at a central hub.

Within two years of the hospital's completion, Sheikh Sultan bin Muhammad Al Qasimi appointed the Lebanese office Code International to design a new fully air-conditioned hospital to provide the city's growing population with more advanced care. Even though the original building no longer met current standards and expectations, it was renovated, according to the Lebanese architect, to compensate for the limited funding available for the new wing. Consolidated Construction Company completed the new one-hundred-bed addition while Bin Laden Organization, today known as Saudi Binladin Group, built the staff accommodations in 1974.

The hospital operated through the mid-1980s until the 320-bed Sharjah General Hospital was completed.

1. Jonathan Wallace, ed., *Sharjah 1970* (London: *Middle East Economic Digest*, 1970).

Architect
Page & Broughton

Architect, extension
Code International

Engineering Consultant
Najeeb Maktari

Contractor
Consolidated Contractors Company, Bin Laden Organization

Construction
Nagi Samih Barbir

Client
Government of Sharjah

Completed
1976

Status
Disused, partially demolished

01. Al Qassimi Hospital extension under construction, mid-1970s. Hamid Durani, Honeymoon Studio.
02. Al Qassimi Hospital, designed by Page & Broughton, shown in a model made by Code International. Code International.

02

Holiday Inn Khor Fakkan

Efforts to create a tempting tourist destination were not limited to Sharjah city. They also extended to the eastern exclaves of the emirate, with prized coastlines on the Gulf of Oman. As early as 1976, the road to Khor Fakkan was described as "jammed with holiday campers, picnickers and trailers, all heading for the 'Arabian Riviera.'"[1] In the tourism narrative sold by the government and its collaborators, the city offered the luxuries expected of world-class resorts. Beyond this was the desert of the imagined Arabia, accentuated with dusty souks and palm groves and backdropped by severe-looking mountains. The Holiday Inn promised modern comforts amid the pre-oil "authenticity" of Khor Fakkan. It rose up from a seemingly empty beach, encircled by barren mountains that only heightened the sense of comfort available inside the hotel's 180-room shelter.

1. Kathleen Bishtawi, "Tourist Efforts," *Financial Times*, December 10, 1976.

Architect
Ashok Mody, Architectural Consultants

Contractor
Eastern Contracting Company

Client
Sheikh Sultan bin Muhammad Al Qasimi

Completed
1979

Status
Existing, renovated

Aerial photograph of the $13.2-million hotel under construction with workers' temporary barracks to the right of hotel. Dr. Naman Al Jalili Archives Collection.

Above: Architectural photographer Henk Snoek used several commissioned trips to the Trucial States to document some of Sharjah's ongoing building projects. These two photographs of bank buildings on Al Arouba Street are rare instances of a professional camera specifically focused on Sharjah's architecture. The First National City Bank Building was designed by Consolidated Engineering Company, eventually named Khatib & Alami, as part of the same contract that included their design for the BBME Building (see p. 81), both completed in 1972. Photographed in 1975.

Right: The Grindlays Bank Building, also known as Zamawi Flats after its owner, still stands opposite the BBME Building on Al Arouba Street, Geoffrey Salmon, Speed Associates, 1974. Images: Henk Snoek / RIBA Collections.

GRINDLAYS BANK

SHARJAH CINEMA
PEKING RESTAURANT

Sharjah Cinema

Sharjah Cinema had its roots in Sharjah city's first open-air cinema known as Haroun Cinema. Soon after Ahmed Al Mulla took it over and renamed it Sharjah Cinema, he began plans to build a proper cinema in 1966 on Al Meena Street. The movie theater would reign over the increasingly busy Port Roundabout and its water fountain. At first, the two-story cinema was sited amidst vacant building lots, and moviegoers could easily reach it from all sides. Strings of colorful lights and illuminated signage distinguished the cinema from the scattering of two-story apartment blocks nearby, some of which were designed by British architects Hubbard Ford and Partners.

The cinema is remembered for its landmark forms: the corrugated baby-blue cylinders that encased the spiral stairs and the impressive upper-floor cantilever looming over the main entrance. The marquee spanning the cantilever also announced the 200-seat Peking Restaurant, reached by negotiating the uneven risers of the spiral stairs. Its menu was considered fine dining in Sharjah until it closed in the early 1980s.

Crowds of Arab and South Asian men gathered in the evenings at the cinema's base, some of whom paid to watch movies, mostly Egyptian and Bollywood, while others merely took in the place as a site to behold. Inside, the single theater accommodated up to 1,200 viewers. On August 8, 1972, the cinema opened with the film *Babul Ki Galiyaan*, a 1972 Bollywood film by S. D. Narang. As more cinemas appeared in Sharjah and Dubai, they shared film reels by means of a taxi that shuttled the films from one cinema to the next. Late at night, a ticket stub from the 9:00 p.m. screening was a good thing to have if the police suspected you of loitering.

The cinema was designed by Dutch architect Reinder de Vries, who designed the St. George Hotel and a major office tower on Bani Yas Square in Dubai. He often collaborated with the Glasgow-based firm W. A. Fairhurst and Partners. According to the cinema's owner, De Vries had to convince the head of Sharjah Municipality to approve the twelve-meter cantilever without the addition of structural columns. He allegedly sought certification from the British Council that the building would stand without them. It is not clear, however, how the British Council could have certified structural drawings.

Increasingly dilapidated, the cinema was demolished in 2005 when it could no longer compete with the new cinemas opening in nearby mall complexes.

Architect
Reinder de Vries

Consulting Engineer
W. A. Fairhurst & Partners

Client
Ahmed Al Mulla

Completed
1972

Status
Demolished, 2005

01. Even at its opening in the hot month of August, Sharjah Cinema attracted large crowds below its marquee. Images: AlMulla Family Archive, courtesy of Ahmed Amin Ahmed AlMulla.
02. The cinema's Arabic signage employed a peculiar typeset with isolated letterforms, normally connected to form words.

SHARJAH
PEKING RESTAUR

NEMA

Shell Filling Station

Architect Brian Broughton believes that this Shell filling station in Sharjah was built according to his conceptual design. Broughton and Keith Page, as Page & Broughton, had designed Dubai's airport, a commission they had secured by being quick to make a proposal. Among other projects, the partnership completed a headquarters for Shell in Deira, the design of which was replicated in Bur Dubai. According to Broughton, work with Shell led to commissions for at least two filling station prototypes. While Page procured work and maintained contacts in the Gulf, Broughton produced designs in his UK office. The partnership did not last long. Several projects, for which Broughton produced designs, materialized without his knowledge, including Al Qassimi Hospital and—probably—this filling station.[1]

1. See p. 191.

Client
Royal Dutch Shell

Architect
Page & Broughton

Completed
1970s

A Shell filling station somewhere in Sharjah built per Brian Broughton's prototype design, perhaps near the original airport, 1971. Henk Snoek / RIBA Collections.

Rendering, Khor Fakkan Cinema, 1976. The cinema replaced an earlier open-air theater and operated until 2006, screening Hindi, English, and Arabic movies. The owner, Abdulla Akram, commissioned Karachi-based ASAN Associates for the design. The perspective rendering was created by someone recalled only by his last name, Shahnawaz, who studied architecture in Karachi but never completed his degree. Hassan Abdulla Akram.

BRQ
ASAN ASSOCIATES
ARCHITECTS & ENGINEERS

01

King Faisal Mosque

In 1986, the Dubai-based daily *Gulf News* observed that Sharjah was "fast emerging as a city of mosques." In only two years, the city gained twenty-eight new ones. The most distinguished came to be known as King Faisal Mosque. Named after Saudi Arabia's assassinated ruler, the mosque was built along the road that also bore his name. The design was chosen from an invited competition for a mosque to be partially funded by Saudi Arabia as a gift to Sharjah. Complete responsibility was eventually handed over to Saudi Arabia's finance ministry.

Competition entries included those by Galal Momen and A. Moez & Moh. Hegazy Architects of Egypt and Vedat Dalokay of Turkey, whose design for Islamabad's King Faisal Mosque (1969) is one of the most published modern mosques. Riyadh-based architect Abdulrahman Al Junaidi won the competition. His winning entry, however, has not been located. Al Junaidi was an accomplished architect in Riyadh with several institutional buildings to his name, including the photogenic Ports Authority building.

Sharjah's government originally designated a site for the new mosque immediately adjacent to the recently completed Central Souk. Upon hearing of a planned building nearby that would obstruct views of his design, Al Junaidi claims that he insisted on a more prominent and open location. Today, the mosque stands monumentally at the opposite edge of Al Ittihad Park, visible from countless vantage points in the city. At least three hundred people worked on the site, where construction lasted from August 1982 until December 1984. It took another eighteen months to complete the mosque's finishings. Costs totaled around AED 37 million, about $10 million.

Sharjah's modernist mosque, according to the architect, eschewed ostentatious design, instead keeping worshippers focused on "performing their duties toward God." Still, Japanese mosaic tiles clad the dome's interior, and star-patterned surfaces in Pakistani steel cover the arch openings. The mihrab, the niche in the mosque to indicate the direction of Makkah, is made from elaborate woodwork.

On January 23, 1987, the mosque opened with a 12,000-square-meter prayer hall and two seventy-meter-high minarets. The architect estimated that the mosque could accommodate 16,670 worshippers, more than 5% of Sharjah's population at the time. The mosque's second floor houses Sharjah's Department of Islamic Affairs and Endowments as well as a library.

After Sharjah's residents watched the erection of what seemed to be a monumentally white, concrete mosque, the final stage of construction saw the building recede a bit, behind sand-color tiling.

Architect
The Technical Office for Architectural & Engineering Consultancy

Contractor
Globe Constructors

Client
Government of Sharjah

Completed
1987

Status
Existing

02

03

04

05

06

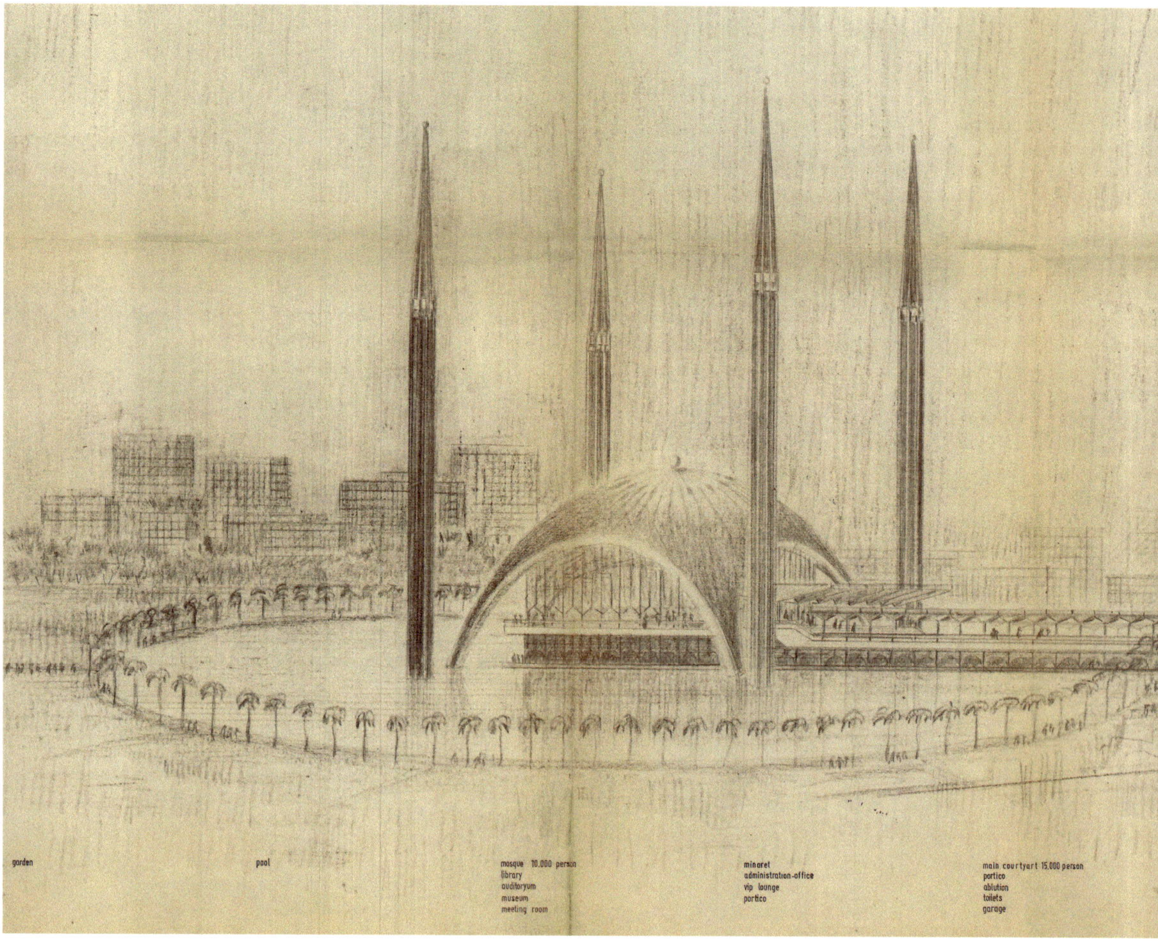

07

01. Mohammed Abdul Haq Musa of Contractors Group International (Globe Constructors) in front of King Faisal Mosque during construction, before the facades were clad in brown tiling, early 1980s. Mohammed Abdul Haq Musa.
02. King Faisal Mosque appears in the background of Al Ittihad Park's berm with the city's slogan "Smile, You Are in Sharjah," circa 1990s. Hamid Durani, Honeymoon Studio.
03. A snapshot captures King Faisal Mosque and its surroundings from Al Saud Co. Building, 1991. On the left is a residential block designed by Nicolas Bou Rjaili, New Form Consultants. Prema Babu.
04. Snapshot of King Faisal Mosque from Al Saud Co. Building with Al Ittihad Park still under construction, 1991. Prema Babu.
05. Jaseera Sayed Abobaker photographed by her father in front of King Faisal Mosque, late 1980s. Collection of Sayed Abobaker Mohammed.
06. Eastern elevation, undated. Hamid Durani, Honeymoon Studio.
07.–08. Turkish architect Vedat Dalokay submitted a design proposal for the Saudi-sponsored mosque in Sharjah, after having won the competition for Islamabad's \$35-million King Faisal Mosque. Islamabad's mosque, still under construction at the time of the Sharjah project, rises from a square plan with a faceted, tent-like roof pinned on four corners with minarets. Dalokay's proposal for Sharjah was more similar to his winning, unbuilt design for the Kocatepe Mosque, which also employed a dome-like roof seemingly held down by its minarets. The tent motif has been described as a nod to Bedouin cultures. (See Kishwar Rizvi, *The Transnational Mosque: Architecture and Historical Memory in the Contemporary Middle East* [Chapel Hill: University of North Carolina Press, 2016].) Dalokay Archive, courtesy Sibel Dalokay Bozer.
09. Detail drawings of the dome from a proposal for King Faisal Mosque, Momen Architects & Consulting Engineers. The proposal was based on an octagonal plan with a detached minaret. Its elevations bear similarities to the firm's design for Cairo's Gamal Abdel Nasser Mosque. Another known proposal was submitted by A. Moez & Moh. Hegazy Architects, which designed Dubai's Jumeirah Mosque. Momen Architects.

den covered crescent
in entrance
ormation
front garden
Sharjah
Sheikh Sultan bin
Muhammad al. Qasimi
mosque

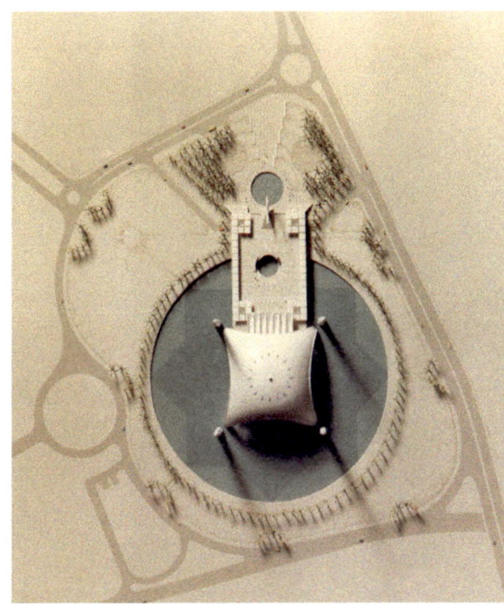

08

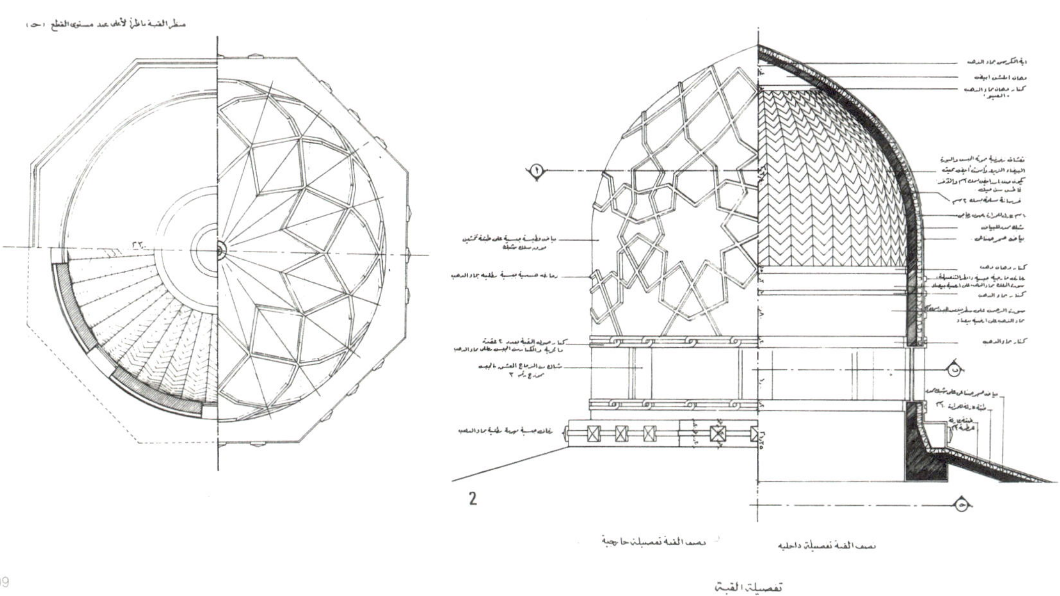
2
نصف القبة تفصيلة خارجية
نصف القبة تفصيلة داخلية
تفصيلة القبة

09

Sheikh Khalid bin Mohammed Al Qasimi commissioned the construction of this perimeter for a *musalla al eid*, an outdoor area for prayers during Eid, late 1960s. It was designed by Syrian architect Mohamed Al Azhari, who designed the Airport Mosque (p. 41) and the police towers (p. 126). The walls and gates were built by DAFCO. It is still in use today. DAFCO.

Children at play in the courtyard of the former Al Qasimiyah School before it moved to Al Manakh district, circa 1980. Archive of Al Qasimiyah Primary School, courtesy of Kambar Mahmood Al Mazem.

01

Talal Al-Rashoud

SCHOOLS FOR THE ARAB HOMELAND: KUWAIT'S EDUCATIONAL MISSION IN SHARJAH

At the dawn of the 1950s, when the Arabian Gulf stood at the precipice of a period of great social, economic, and political upheaval, two small sheikhdoms embarked upon an enterprise that would have a profound impact on the development of the future United Arab Emirates (UAE). Kuwait was larger and wealthier than its southern neighbor Sharjah. Additionally, though both had signed protection treaties with the British, Kuwait enjoyed far greater autonomy, enabling it to attain independence a decade before the other small Gulf monarchies. Crucially, Kuwait also had a head start in the development of modern education. Sharjah, the first among the Trucial States to seek to modernize its schools, thus turned to Kuwait for assistance.

Kuwaiti educational aid began on a small scale, gradually growing until it extended to all but one of the Trucial States and had broadened in scope to include medical and development assistance. This aid was based on a vision of inter-Arab cooperation shared between Kuwaiti authorities and Sharjah's ruler Sheikh Saqr bin Sultan Al Qasimi. Some scholars characterize Kuwait's educational assistance program as subservient to Britain and opposed to the regional policies of Egyptian president Gamal Abdel Nasser. However, an in-depth examination of Kuwait's educational role in Sharjah demonstrates the Pan-Arabist and anti-colonial nature of the program.

Well before Kuwait's educational aid began, Sharjah was an established cultural center of the Trucial States. This had much to do with its success as a pearling and trading port. In the early twentieth century, Sharjah claimed one of the largest pearling fleets in the region and had sizeable communities of Indian and Iranian traders. It benefited greatly from a boom in the global pearl trade during this period, which led to the emergence of an influential merchant class. These merchants maintained close contact with Bombay, the center of the regional pearl trade. They became part of that city's vibrant Arab community, which was in close touch with the modern ideological trends sweeping the Ottoman and Arab worlds. Inspired by these ideas, Sharjah's merchants embarked upon novel charitable and cultural endeavors in their hometown. They founded libraries, cultural clubs, and schools combining traditional religious education with aspects of modern, Western-style pedagogy. The earliest and most significant was the Taymiyah School, founded in the first decade of the twentieth century. In the late 1920s, the collapse of the pearling economy, a result of the Great Depression and the emergence of the cultured pearl, caused these early schools to close.[1]

The development of education in Sharjah remained hindered by financial difficulties until after World War II when the emirate's ruler, Sultan bin Saqr Al Qasimi (who ruled 1924–1951), began supporting education. He reopened a school that had closed in

1. Muhammad Morsy Abdullah, *The United Arab Emirates: A Modern History* (London: Croom Helm, 1978), 103–111; Abdullah Al Tabur, *Rasail al rail al awwal min ruwwad al yaqza fi Al Imarat Al Arabiyya Al Muttahida* (Sharjah: Department of Culture and Information, 1999), 45–49, 78, 107; Sultan bin Muhammad Al Qasimi, *Sirat madina*, vol. 1 (Sharjah: Al Qasimi Publications, 2015), 82; Frauke Heard-Bey, *From Trucial States to United Arab Emirates: A Society in Transition* (London: Longman, 1982), 133, 190–191.
2. Notes on Visit to the Persian Gulf, Keight, 4–9 Feb. 1952, NA, BW 114:11; Sultan bin Muhammad Al Qasimi, *Sard al dhat* (Sharjah: Al Qasimi Publications, 2009), 65–67, 87, 95; Arif Al Shaikh, *Tarikh al talim fi Al Shariqa 1900–1972* (Sharjah: Al Qasimi Publications, 2016), 272–279; Al Tabur, 110–112.
3. Bahrain Intelligence Summary, 16–31 Jan. 1948, BL, IOR L:PS:12:3769B; Bahrain Intelligence Summary, 16–31 Dec. 1947, BL, IOR L:PS:12:3769A; Samih Shabib, *Muhammad Ali Al Tahir: Tajrubatihi al sahafiyya fi Misr*

the 1930s and offered free education to its students. Named Al Qasimiyah, the school went further than its predecessors in incorporating modern methods of teaching and organization, introducing new subjects such as English and civic education, and importing textbooks from various Arab states. In the late 1940s, it opened a class for girls, apparently the first of its kind in the Trucial States.[2]

A poet of classical Arabic verse, Sheikh Sultan also established two private libraries, hosted a literary salon, and corresponded with men of letters abroad. His son and heir Sheikh Saqr bin Sultan (who ruled 1951–1965) inherited his literary inclination and cultural reach. Influenced by events in Palestine and the increased British interference in the Trucial States, both sheikhs espoused anti-colonial ideas. Sharjah's British-run airfield also kept its rulers in contact with the outside world. In the 1950s, Sheikh Saqr made use of it to travel extensively in the Arab world, further exposing him to Pan-Arabist ideology.[3]

This intellectual background is vital to understanding Sheikh Saqr's drive to develop Sharjah through assistance from Kuwait and other Arab states. A 1957 British document describes him as "modern in his outlook" and as the only Trucial States ruler "who has any real interest in, or knowledge of, the affairs of the Western world." It adds: "He is the foremost among the Trucial Rulers in having constructive ideas for the improvement and development of his Shaikhdom." Education was high on his agenda. The British political resident reported that the first thing the new ruler raised with him following his recognition ceremony in May 1951 was the construction of a proper building for Al Qasimiyah School, which operated out of a traditional house.[4]

PHASE I: KUWAITI EDUCATIONAL ASSISTANCE 1952–1961

Around the same time that Sheikh Saqr acceded to power, the Kuwaiti government was preparing to launch an educational assistance program for less fortunate Arab states. Several factors enabled Kuwait to embark upon this program. To begin with, the export of oil starting in 1946 and the renegotiation of its oil concession agreement in 1951 made Kuwait one of the wealthiest states in the region. A second factor was the relative development of Kuwait's public educational system, founded in 1936 and significantly expanded in the 1940s with help from the Egyptian government. In the early 1950s, Kuwait became one of the few states in the Arabian Peninsula to offer secondary school certification, making it a desirable destination for students from the region wishing to complete their studies.

02

Finally, although Kuwait would remain under British protection until 1961, it had much greater freedom than other Gulf states in managing its internal affairs and conducting relations with other Arab governments. This increased interaction with the Arab world led high-ranking bureaucrats and even certain ruling family members to espouse Pan-Arabist views. Such an ideological orientation was particularly evident in Kuwait's educational department, which was administered by Kuwaiti intelligentsia, Palestinian expatriates, and educators seconded by the Egyptian government. The department's director, Abdulaziz Husain, was an Egyptian-educated Kuwaiti and an ardent Nasserist who played a central role in Kuwait's educational assistance program. While the department was not a tool in the hands of Cairo, as some British officials believed, it did maintain close ties with the Egyptian government.[5]

min khilal suhufihi Al Shura, Al Shabab, Al Alam 1924–1939 (Nicosia: Al ittihad al am li al kuttab wa al sahafiyyin al filistiniyyin, 1990), 278–279; Sultan bin Muhammad Al Qasimi, *Sirat madina*, vol. 2 (Sharjah: Al Qasimi Publications, 2017), 41, 130–157; Saqr bin Sultan Al Qasimi, "Liqa ma Al Sheikh Saqr bin Sultan Al Qasimi Hakim Al Shariqa al sabiq," http://youtu.be/KKwf42sKb9c; Sultan bin Muhammad Al Qasimi, *Nashij al wada* (Sharjah: Al Qasimi Publications, 2011), 8.

4. Leading Personalities of the Persian Gulf, 1957, NA, FO 371:126870; Robert L. Jarman, ed., *Political Diaries of the Persian Gulf*, vol. 19, 1951–1954 (Cambridge: Archive Editions, 1990), 65; Al Qasimi, *Sard al dhat*, 95.
5. Talal Al-Rashoud, "From Muscat to the Maghreb: Pan-Arab Networks, Anti-colonial Groups, and Kuwait's Arab Scholarships (1953–1961)," *Arabian Humanities*, no. 12 (2019): 2–6; Talal Al-Rashoud, "Modern Education and Arab Nationalism in Kuwait, 1911–1961" (PhD diss., School of Oriental and African Studies, 2016), 256–262, 301–304.

Kuwait's educational department framed its assistance to the Trucial States in terms of Arab nationalism and Gulf unity. Its annual reports speak of Kuwait's "great responsibility toward the Arabian Gulf" and of "this beloved segment of the Arab homeland." Another report emphasizes that this assistance is "motivated by the call of [common] blood, origins, and creed."[6] Muhammad Diyab Al Musa, a Palestinian teacher seconded by Kuwait to Sharjah, considers this discourse to reflect the actual motivations behind Kuwaiti aid. In his memoirs, he recalls that the prevalence of modern political ideas and movements in Kuwait produced "a very good nationalist sentiment toward the poor emirates of the Gulf."[7]

As the first emirate to request educational assistance from Kuwait, it was Sharjah that prompted the Kuwaitis to begin helping the Trucial States. In late 1951, Kuwait's ruler, Abdullah Al Salim Al Sabah, visited the emirate. At a palace reception, an Al Qasimiyah School student delivered a speech that appealed for Kuwait's help in obtaining teachers and books. Moved by the student, the ruler promised that his educational authorities would study the matter. In January 1952, a group of Al Qasimiyah students followed up with a written request for funding to establish a literary club. They received 6,000 rupees—Kuwait's first contribution to education in Sharjah. More substantial support soon followed. After sending delegations to Sharjah in March 1952 and March 1953, the Kuwaiti educational department agreed to host students from the emirate in Kuwait and to provide Al Qasimiyah School with a grant for renovations, textbooks, and educational materials as well as two teachers and their salaries.[8]

The two teachers, Palestinians Mustafa Taha and Ahmad Al Burini, arrived in Sharjah in late 1953. The former became headmaster of Al Qasimiyah School, overseeing the implementation of the Kuwaiti curriculum, which was adopted by all Trucial States except Abu Dhabi. In 1954, Kuwait sent two more Palestinian teachers to Sharjah: Muhammad Diyab Al Musa and a woman, Sharifa Al Ba'ba', who oversaw girls' education.[9] The number of teachers seconded by Kuwait subsequently fluctuated, reaching ten by the early 1960s.[10]

Sheikh Saqr energetically sought educational aid from other Arab countries in addition to Kuwait. The British, who were wary of his regional ties, spoke pejoratively of this behavior.[11] Sharjah's meager resources and the inadequacy of British assistance, however, left few avenues for the ruler to develop his emirate's educational system. In 1955, he visited Egypt and convinced its government to second two teachers. Around the time of the 1956 Suez Crisis, Britain temporarily banned further Egyptian teachers from entering Sharjah despite Sheikh Saqr's protests.[12] Nevertheless, their numbers increased steadily thereafter, reaching twenty-four in 1961.[13] In 1958, Qatar also began sending teachers to Sharjah, followed by Bahrain in 1961.[14]

As a result of this Arab assistance, by 1960 Sharjah hosted "nearly half the expatriate teachers in the Trucial States and more than half the United Arab Republic teachers."[15] This led a British official to remark: "Sharjah has more education for less cost than any of its neighbors." Despite having one of the Trucial States' most advanced educational systems, in 1960 the British estimated that Sharjah paid only £1,800 annually toward education compared to £15,000 in Dubai and £4,500 in Ras Al Khaimah.[16]

6. *Al taqrir al sanawi li al am al dirasi 1961–1962* (Kuwait: Ministry of Education), 160; *Al taqrir al sanawi li al am al dirasi 1960–1961* (Kuwait: Educational Department), 160; *Al taqrir al sanawi li al am al dirasi 1958–1959* (Kuwait: Educational Department), 190.
7. Muhammad Diyab Al Musa, *Sira ala darb al masira* (Sharjah: Department of Culture and Information, 2008), 42; Muhammad Diyab Al Musa, in discussion with the author, Sharjah, 11 Apr. 2013.
8. The equivalent of about $80. Minutes of the Educational Council, Kuwait (MEC), 21 Jan. 1952, Session (S):13; 16 Apr. 1953, S:62; Jarman, 19:278–279, 436; Al Qasimi, *Sard al dhat*, 91. For more on the scholarships in Kuwait, see Al-Rashoud, "From Muscat to the Maghreb."
9. Yaaqub Al Ghunaim, *Ahmad Al Bishr Al Rumi: Qiraa fi awraqihi al khasa* (Kuwait: Center for Research and Studies on Kuwait, 1997), 228–240; Al Musa, 43, 59; Al Shaikh, 381–385; *Al taqrir al sanawi 1961–1962*, 161; MEC, 16 Apr. 1953, S:62.
10. Annual reports by the Educational Department/ Ministry of

03

Although by the early 1960s most of Sharjah's teachers came from other Arab states, Kuwait continued to administer the emirate's educational system, also providing all educational materials, stationery, furnishings, and even school uniforms. Its teachers also offered adult literacy classes. Education in Sharjah developed rapidly under Kuwaiti direction, with the number of students soaring from 251 in 1955 to 1,377 in 1961. Sharjah became the first emirate to complete the intermediate level for boys in the academic year 1957–58 and to introduce secondary classes the following year. From 1961, students completing the second year of secondary school could continue their studies in Kuwait. Girls' education did not lag far behind: the first female students completed the intermediate level and started secondary school in 1960. Elsewhere in the Trucial States at that time, no other class of girls had yet to complete the primary level.[17]

Kuwaiti educational assistance to Sharjah eventually extended to the building of schools, a field that Britain initially regarded as its domain. Several months after Kuwait promised to provide teachers to Sharjah, the British announced that they would construct a purpose-built structure for Al Qasimiyah School. Completed in mid-1954, it was the first such building in the Trucial States.[18] In 1955, the British adopted a Trucial States development program that included a plan for Britain to build schools and for Kuwait to staff them. However, it is unclear what commitments the Kuwaiti authorities actually made in this regard.[19]

The British were thus disappointed when Kuwait's educational department began building its own schools in the Trucial States without coordinating with them. In 1956 and 1958, the department agreed to expand existing schools in Sharjah.[20] Over the next several years, it built new schools in the emirate, starting with Fatima Al Zahra School for girls, which had hitherto occupied "a crumbling old house." In the eastern town of Kalba, the department constructed a single building to house two schools: Saif Al Yarubi for boys and Djamila Bouhired for girls.[21] Both were named after anti-colonial figures: the former an Omani ruler who resisted the Portuguese and the latter a contemporary Algerian female freedom fighter.

ARAB NATIONALISM AND KUWAITI-SPONSORED EDUCATION

Kuwait's school building program was part of a broader pattern of non-cooperation with Britain over education in the Trucial States. This attitude had its roots in the 1940s, when the Kuwaiti educational department resisted British attempts at controlling the educational system in Kuwait. The department adopted a more radical Nasserist line following the 1956 Suez Crisis, hardening its anti-British position.[22] It was also at this time that Britain sought to assert greater control over education in the Trucial States to counter the political influence of Arab expatriate teachers.

In 1957, Britain established an education committee under the Trucial States Council, a British-led coordinating body including all seven emirates, with the goal of centralizing educational administration. This scheme failed, however, due to the Kuwaiti authorities' refusal to deal with the committee coupled with Sheikh Saqr's "lack of enthusiasm."[23] A similar scenario occurred between 1960 and 1961 when Kuwaiti opposition played a key role in foiling a British attempt at imposing a Sudanese director of education on Dubai. British officials had hoped that the director's authority would eventually extend to Sharjah.[24] Kuwait's educational staff also

04

Education, Kuwait: *1961–1962*, 170; *1960–1961*, 166; *1959–1960*, 313; *1958–1959*, 191; *1957–1958*, 149; *1956–1957*, 126.

11. Annual Report, 1959–1960, NA, BW 114:6; Jarman, 19:324.
12. Tripp to Gault, 29 Jun. 1958, NA, FO 371:132884; Jarman, 20:58, 66, 75, 183, 197, 212, 220.
13. See footnote 10.
14. *Al taqrir al sanawi 1961–1962*, 162; *Al taqrir al sanawi 1958–1959*, 191.
15. Hawley to Middleton, 11 Sep. 1960, NA, FO 371:149143. The United Arab Republic (UAR) was formed following the unification of Egypt and Syria in 1958. Although Syria seceded from the union in 1961, Egypt continued to be officially known as the UAR until 1971.
16. Annual Report, 1959–1960, NA, BW 114:6; Man to Earl of Home, 7 Nov. 1960, NA, FO 371:149144.
17. *Al Kuwait wa nahdatuha al talimiyya: Sanat 1955–1956* (Kuwait: Educational Department, 1956), chart 10; Annual reports of the Educational Department/ Ministry of Education, Kuwait: *1961–1962, 160–161*, 164; *1960–1961*, 162; *1959–1960*, 75, 316; *1958–1959*, 191; *1955–1957*, 147.

05

refused to cooperate with various British educational projects in the late 1950s and early 1960s. These included the British-run Sharjah Trade School, a plan to train local teachers in Bahrain (where British influence over education was stronger), and the appointment of an English language teacher to Sharjah and Dubai.[25]

The Arab nationalist environment in Sharjah's Kuwaiti-run schools remained a key point of tension between the Kuwaitis and the British. The British could not close these schools because they did not want to appear to be depriving the Trucial States of education. Moreover, they were unable to provide alternative teachers themselves. They therefore monitored the teachers seconded by Kuwait and expelled those they regarded as troublemakers.[26] A notable example of the latter was the aforementioned Muhammad Diyab Al Musa. Prior to arriving in Sharjah in 1954, the young teacher had engaged in political activism in Palestine and Kuwait and was involved with both the Arab nationalist Baath and the Islamist Tahrir Parties. In his memoirs, Al Musa recalls that his "ideological makeup" inspired him to transfer to the emirate where he thought he could better aid his fellow Arabs.[27]

Al Musa, who became Al Qasimiyah School's headmaster in 1955, emphasizes that he and his fellow teachers believed they had a mission "to connect students ... with the affairs of their Arab nation." He elaborates: "The school fortified [the students'] awareness of the Arab homeland ... and spoke to them about their Arabism, Islam, ancient Arab glories, and their situation today, and the students were greatly affected." Al Musa inculcated these ideas through both classroom instruction and extracurricular activities. He put on one of Sharjah's first student plays, introduced an annual sports day, encouraged students to write a wall magazine during the Suez Crisis, and established the Trucial States' first Boy Scouts troop.[28] The British blamed the latter activity for producing "militarism" among schoolboys.[29]

The Suez Crisis ignited a wave of anti-British activity among Sharjah students, which Al Musa describes as spontaneous and fueled by what the boys heard on the radio. Though he did not engage in direct agitation, it is clear that his teaching at least partly paved the way for this groundswell. Pupils pelted British military forces with stones and shouted hostile slogans. Moreover, Sharjah's current ruler Sheikh Sultan bin Muhammad Al Qasimi, then an Al Qasimiyah student, recalls leading classmates in sabotage operations on British political and military facilities.[30] British officials blamed Al Musa and his colleagues for these incidents, threatening them with expulsion if they did not subdue their students. Although Al Musa subsequently persuaded the schoolboys to stop their activities, the British nevertheless prohibited him and another Palestinian teacher, Fayiz Abu Al Naaj, from returning to Sharjah from Kuwait in the fall of 1957. Al Musa believes that the last straw was his refusal to show a British propaganda film on the Suez Crisis in his school.[31]

The conduct of Al Musa and his colleagues not only reflected their individual political proclivities but was also very much in line with the Pan-Arabist policies of the Kuwaiti Educational Department. Kuwait's 1956 national curriculum made the fostering of Arab national awareness a primary goal of education, and Arab nationalist rhetoric pervaded classroom instruction, extracurricular activities, and the department's public celebrations and sports days. Indeed, Al Musa recalls that the director of education Abdulaziz Husain commended him for refusing to screen the

18. Burrows to FO, 26 Mar. 1954, NA, FO 371:109859; Jarman, 19:463.
19. Tripp to Gault, 29 Jun. 1958; Tripp to FO, 23 Jun. 1958, NA, FO 371:132884; Annual Report, 1958–1959; Annual Report, 1956–1957, NA, BW 114:6; FO Minute, Denson, 20 Dec. 1955; Trucial States Development Programme, Appendix D, n.d., NA, FO 371:114656.
20. Tripp to Gault, 29 Jun. 1958; Tripp to FO, 23 Jun. 1958; MEC, 5 Sep. 1956, S:37; 30 Oct. 1954, S:5; Jarman, 20:194.
21. Craig to Tripp, 4 Feb. 1962, NA, FO 371:163035; Tripp to Gault, 24 Jun. 1958, NA, FO 371:132884.
22. Al-Rashoud, "Modern Education," 169–174, 291–325.
23. Tripp to Gault, 29 Jun. 1958.
24. Tripp to Walmsley, 4 Sep. 1961; Hawley to Luce, 29 Jun. 1961, NA, FO 371:157066; Hawley to Luce, 14 Jun. 1961, NA, FO 371:157065; Winchester to Ford, 9 Nov. 1960, NA, FO 371:149144; Hawley to Middleton, 11 Sep. 1960.
25. Explanatory Notes, Taylor, 27 Apr. 1964, NA, FO 371:174512; Craig to Lamb, 13 Sep. 1962, NA, FO 371:163070; Winchester to Tripp, 7 Sep. 1961, NA, FO 371:157066; Hawley to Walmsley, 14 Jul. 1960, NA, FO 371:149142; Hawley to Luce, 14 Jun. 1961.

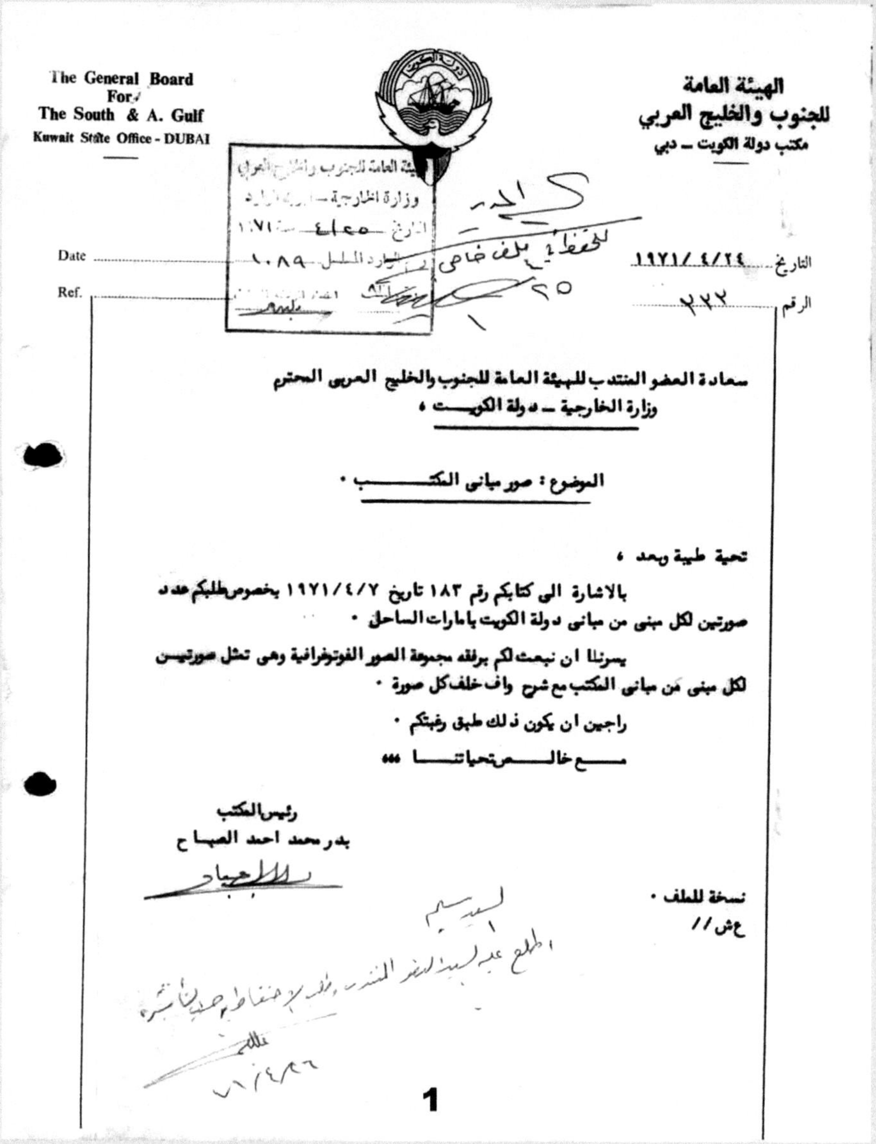

The General Board For The South & A. Gulf
Kuwait State Office - DUBAI

الهيئة العامة للجنوب والخليج العربي
مكتب دولة الكويت ــ دبي

Date — التاريخ ١٩٧١/٤/٢٤
Ref. — الرقم

سعادة العضو المنتدب للهيئة العامة للجنوب والخليج العربي المحترم
وزارة الخارجية ــ دولة الكويت ،

الموضوع : صور مباني المكتب .

تحية طيبة وبعد ،

بالاشارة الى كتابكم رقم ١٨٣ تاريخ ١٩٧١/٤/٧ بخصوص طلبكم عدد صورتين لكل مبنى من مباني دولة الكويت بامارات الساحل .

يسرنا ان نبعث لكم برفقه مجموعة الصور الفوتوغرافية وهى تمثل صورتين لكل مبنى من مباني المكتب مع شرح واف خلف كل صورة .

راجين ان يكون ذلك طبق رغبتكم .

مع خالص تحياتنا ...

رئيس المكتب
بدر محمد احمد الصباح

نسخة للملف .
ع ش //

1

06

26. Gault to Walmsley, 3 Jul. 1958; Tripp to Gault, 29 Jun. 1958, NA, FO 371:132884.
27. Al Musa, 33, 38, 45.
28. Al Musa, 63–65, 70–71; Al Shaikh, 385; Al Qasimi, *Sard al dhat*, 100–102, 156.
29. FO Minute, M.H.N., 9 Apr. 1957, NA, FO 371:126998.
30. Al Qasimi, *Sard al dhat*, 135–150.
31. Ibid., 145–146, 156; Jarman, 20:273, 276–277; Al Musa, 68–74.
32. Al Musa, 73; Al-Rashoud, "Modern Education," 299–325.
33. Hawley to Middleton, 11 Sep. 1960.
34. Jarman, 20:276–277, 378.
35. Al Qasimi, *Sard al dhat*, 156.
36. FO Minute, Black, 26 Jan. 1962, NA, FO 371:163034; Annual Review 1961, NA, FO 371:162879.
37. Abdulaziz Husain, "Taqrir an al talim fi Sahil Uman," 25 May 1960, in *Wathaiq madaris Al Khalij*, a bound collection of documents held by the Center for Gulf and Arabian Peninsula Studies (CGAPS), Kuwait University; Political Agent Kuwait to Political Resident, 2 Jun. 1960, NA, FO 371:149140.
38. Cranston to Craig, 31 Oct. 1962, NA, FO 371:163037; Cranston to Lamb, 24 Jun. 1962; Tripp to Craig, 26 May 1962; Cranston to Tripp, 18 Apr. 1962, NA, FO 371:163036; Craig to Tripp, 4 Feb. 1962, NA, FO 371:163035; Richmond to FO, 25 Jan. 1962; Craig to Lamb, 30 Jan. 1962; Lamb to Craig, 18 Jan. 1962, NA, FO 371:163034; *Al kitab al sanawi* (Kuwait: Ministry of Guidance and Information, 1967), 170; *Al Kuwait al yawm* (Official Newspaper, Ministry of Guidance and Information, Kuwait), 7 Jul. 1966.
39. Craig to Cranston, 7 Jan. 1963, NA, FO 371:168925; Cranston to Craig, 15

aforementioned British propaganda film, stating: “You did the right thing. Protect the school and its students and do not compromise on your Arabism.”[32]

These Pan-Arabist policies found an advocate in Sheikh Saqr. British officials noted his tolerance of teachers’ political activities, which they attributed to his being “to some extent hypnotised by the United Arab Republic.”[33] In 1956, the British complained that the ruler “failed to stop the schoolboys in Sharjah from shouting anti-British slogans.” At that year’s sports day, the flags of the Arab League, Egypt, and other Arab states were raised. The following year, the British pressured Sheikh Saqr to “fly only the Kuwaiti and Sharjah flags.” Although he yielded on this point, he “declared himself unable to fly the Union Jack.”[34] In 1957, the ruler also tried to prevent the British from deporting the Palestinian teacher Abu Al Naaj.[35] Sheikh Saqr’s tensions with the British would come to a head in the subsequent decade.

PHASE II: THE EXPANSION OF KUWAITI ASSISTANCE 1962–1972

After independence in June 1961, Kuwait significantly increased its aid to the Trucial States and broadened its scope to include medical and development assistance. This policy was in line with the state’s campaign to win regional support against the Iraqi claim on its territory through aid distribution.[36] However, it should be noted that the provision of medical assistance to the Trucial States had already been proposed as early as May 1960.[37]

The expansion of Kuwaiti assistance to the Trucial States necessitated new institutional arrangements. In the spring of 1962, the assistance program, no longer administered by the educational department, came under an interministerial committee headed by the finance minister Jabir Al Ahmad Al Sabah. This followed the visit of a Kuwaiti mission in February to survey development needs. In October 1962, the information minister Sabah Al Ahmad Al Sabah assumed control over the committee, which acquired an independent budget and became known as the Permanent Committee for Gulf Assistance (PCGA). In 1966, the PCGA became the General Authority for the Arabian South and Gulf (GAASG), a semi-independent body under the Ministry of Foreign Affairs.[38]

In January 1963, the Kuwait State Office opened in Dubai to administer the country’s projects in the Trucial States. These projects, which the Kuwaitis insisted on administering independently of the British, targeted four key sectors: education, public health, social and religious services, and natural resource development.[39] A GAASG report from the late 1960s lists the following facilities that the Kuwaitis built, equipped, and—in large measure—staffed in Sharjah: seven schools, two hospitals, one clinic, and two mosques.[40] The GAASG’s last major project in Sharjah was a new secondary school, work upon which began in 1971. The Kuwaiti authorities continued to fund and administer these facilities until September 1972, when they were handed over to the recently formed UAE government.[41]

Two additional forms of Kuwaiti educational assistance from this period deserve mention for their social impact. The first was the provision of university scholarships to Trucial States pupils. From as early as 1961, Kuwait’s educational department allocated exchange scholarships provided by other countries such as Iraq to graduates from the area. In 1963, the department began sponsoring these graduates to study in Egypt. Kuwait University also provided scholarships after opening in 1966. In the academic year 1968–69, the university counted nineteen students from Sharjah, the second largest contingent of scholarship holders.[42] A second policy introduced during this period was the training of local teachers. From 1963, graduates from the Trucial States received scholarships to attend Kuwait’s teacher training academy. In 1966, Kuwaiti authorities established teacher-training classes for men in Dubai and for women in Sharjah. Two years later,

Aug. 1962; Cranston to Lamb, 24 Jun. 1962; Al Mutairi to Economic Counsellor, British Embassy Kuwait, 2 Jun. 1962, NA, FO 371:163036.

40. “Al mashari allati qamat al haya al amma bi inshaiha fi Imarat Al Sahil,” n.d., GAASG Archive, Center for Research and Studies on Kuwait. British correspondence from 1964 also mentions an ongoing project to pipe water to coastal towns including Hamriyah in Sharjah. Information could not be found on the project’s outcome. See Craig to Crawford, 26 Jan. 1964, NA, FO 371:174712.
41. “Al haya al amma li Al Janub wa Al Khalij Al Arabi,” April 1976, Ministry of Foreign Affairs, Kuwait, CGAPS archive, Kuwait University, 5:A:800; Bahbahani to Al Saqqaf, 22 Mar. 1971, GAASG Archive; Abdullah, 147.
42. *Al taqrir al sanawi li al am al dirasi 1968–1969* (Kuwait: Ministry of Education), 127; *Al taqrir al sanawi li al am al dirasi 1963–1964* (Kuwait: Ministry of Education), 173; “Al ihtimam bi tatawwur al talim fi Al Khalij wa Al Janub Al Arabi wa ma qamat bihi dawlat Al Kuwait fi hadha al shan,” n.d., *Wathaiq madaris Al Khalij*; *Al Kuwait al yawm*, 18 Jun. 1961, 19.
43. “Adwa ala sayr al talim wa mashakilihi fi Imarat Al Shariqa,” Al mutamar al thalith li Wizara Al Tarbiyya wa Al Talim Al Arab, Al Kuwait, 17–22 Feb. 1968, *Wathaiq madaris Al Khalij*; *Al kitab al sanawi*, 171; *Al taqrir al sanawi 1963–1964*, 112; Cranston to Craig, 6 Apr. 1963, NA, FO 371:168926.
44. The head of Kuwait’s PCGA participated in or oversaw many of these developments, documenting them in

07

the first cohort of trained local teachers, both men and women, began teaching in Sharjah's schools.[43]

During this period, Kuwait was drawn into a struggle over the future development of the Trucial States that ultimately contributed to the downfall of its primary partner in the area: Sheikh Saqr bin Sultan. In 1964, the Arab League advanced a scheme to provide development aid to the Trucial States in areas including infrastructure, agriculture, and public health. Kuwait played a central role in inspiring and supporting this scheme. It joined the Arab League's Gulf Committee, which was created to oversee the aid, and was the only state to actually transfer money to its fund. Moreover, Kuwaiti personnel facilitated and participated in all Arab League diplomatic and technical missions to the Trucial States between 1964 and 1965. The Arab League planned to operate from Kuwait's Dubai office until it could establish its own headquarters.[44]

Among the Trucial States rulers, Sheikh Saqr of Sharjah was the primary advocate for Arab League aid. According to the PCGA head Badr Khalid Al Badr, the ruler saw in the scheme "the embodiment of his patriotic and nationalist aspirations." Sheikh Saqr organized a warm welcome for the Arab League delegation that visited Sharjah in October 1964. The town was festooned with banners bearing "patriotic and nationalist slogans" while folk bands performed and crowds thronged the streets. Sheikh Saqr even erected a small guesthouse for the visitors that he named after the Arab League.[45]

The Arab League's aid scheme was a step too far for British officials concerned about an even stronger Pan-Arab presence in the Trucial States. They did everything in their power to oppose it, demanding that all external aid to the Trucial States be channeled through a British-controlled fund. The Kuwaiti authorities repeatedly refused to contribute to this fund and asserted their commitment to the Arab League scheme. They also attempted to mediate between Britain and the Arab League, but to no avail.[46]

Meanwhile, Sheikh Saqr remained steadfastly committed to accepting Arab League aid and convinced other rulers to do

detail in his memoirs: Badr Khalid Al Badr, *Rihla ma qafilat al hayat, al juzan al thani wa al thalith* (Kuwait, 2004), 274–300, 309, 312–317, 324–325. See also the account of the Assistant Secretary General of the Arab League: Sayyid Nawfal, *Al awda al siyasiyya li Imarat Al Khalij Al Arabi wa Janub Al Jazira: Al kitab al thani, Imarat Sahil Uman* (Cairo: The Arab Educational, Cultural and Scientific Organization, 1972), 13, 38, 41, 137, 141–143, 207, 230.

45. Al Badr, 299–300.
46. Matthew MacLean, "Spatial Transformations and the Emergence of the 'National': Infrastructures and the Formation of the United Arab Emirates, 1950–1980" (PhD diss., New York University, 2017), 178–182, 187, 190–196; Al Badr, 320, 322, 326; Nawfal, 230.

so as well. When the British denied visas to Arab League officials and closed airports in the area, Saqr responded by offering them Sharjah passports and chartering a private flight for them.[47] These efforts failed, however, and Arab League personnel were barred from entering the Trucial States to commence their aid program. In June 1965, the British overthrew and banished Sheikh Saqr for daring to defy them, installing the more amenable Sheikh Khalid bin Mohammed Al Qasimi as his successor.[48] The Kuwaiti authorities responded by reaffirming their refusal to cooperate with the British development program, threatening to close their Dubai office if forced to do so.[49] With the Arab League threat eliminated, however, Britain no longer pressed Kuwait on this point.

Kuwait continued to administer its aid as it had previously. In 1967, the British political agent complained that the Kuwait State Office "is under instructions from the Kuwait Government not to co-operate with the Trucial States Council in education and health matters." He added that the teachers seconded by Kuwait "are inclined to use education as a vehicle for putting over Nasirist propaganda." The same year, the political resident went so far as to describe Kuwaiti assistance as "an instrument for bringing revolutionary influences into the area" and even suspected the Kuwait State Office of instigating violent protests in Dubai against the Arab-Israeli War.[50]

CONCLUSION

Sheikh Saqr's overthrow ended a formative chapter in Sharjah's modern history. By no means a passive recipient of Kuwaiti assistance, the ruler was an active partner in constructing an educational system that was, for a time, the most advanced in the Trucial States. This partnership rested on a shared vision of development through inter-Arab cooperation, irrespective of British colonial authority. Ultimately, however, Britain proved unable to tolerate the expansion of this project beyond the educational field. Kuwait's assistance program nevertheless persisted, retaining its Pan-Arabist and anti-colonial character, and the facilities it created went on to form a substantial part of the independent UAE's welfare state.

47. MacLean, 198.
48. For more details on the coup, see ibid., 181–199; Abdel Razzaq Takriti, "Colonial Coups and the War on Popular Sovereignty," *American Historical Review*, 124, no. 3 (June 2019). Sheikh Sultan bin Muhammad addresses the British role in the coup in his book, *Sard al dhat*, 251–252.
49. Al Badr, 329–330.
50. Roberts to Melhuish, 8 Nov. 1967, NA, FCO 8:617; Crawford to Brown, 29 Jul. 1967, NA, BW 114:9. Rosemarie Said Zahlan, *Palestine and the Gulf States: The Presence at the Table* (New York: Routledge, 2009), 45.

08

09

Images:

01. Students demonstrate in Sharjah around the time of the Suez Crisis, 1956. Hatem Mohammad Al Mosa.
02. During a visit aboard British naval ship *Newcastle* in the 1950s, Muhammad Diyab Al Musa, headmaster at Al Qasimiyah School, poses with some of his students in scout uniforms. Students from left to right: Sultan bin Muhammad Al Qasimi, Abdallah Omran Taryam, Taryam Omran Taryam, Mahmoud Khairallah Al Hajji, Saeed Obaid Al Shaer, Humaid Obaid Humaid, M. D. Al Musa, Sultan bin Sagr bin Sultan Al Qasimi, Mohammed Hamad Al Shamsi, Sultan Mohammed Al Mazrou, Mohammed Sultan Abdallah, Ali Abdallah Al Noman, Jassim Saif Al Midfa. Taryam Omran Taryam is the student who appealed to the Kuwaiti emir for educational funding. Courtesy of Hatem Mohammad Al Mosa.
03. The Kuwait-funded Sharjah School for Girls was constructed between 1968 and 1969. As of April 1971, it counted 594 students, 25 teachers, and 11 classrooms. Center for Research and Studies on Kuwait.
04. A motorcade conveys Kuwait's leader through a crowd of onlookers in Sharjah, May 1966. People wave flags of both Sharjah and Kuwait. Hassan Al Khayal.
05. Sharjah native Saud bin Khalid Al Qasimi served as the first treasury secretary at the Kuwait Office in Dubai. He applied for the job while working in Kuwait. Photograph taken mid-1960s. Shaikha Nama bint Majid bin Saqr Al Qasimi.
06. Letter from Badr Muhammad Ahmad Al Sabah, head of the Kuwait Office in Dubai, responds to a request from Kuwaiti foreign affairs ministry for two photographs of each project funded by Kuwait in the coastal emirates, April 24, 1971. Center for Research and Studies on Kuwait.
07. Kuwait-funded Al Arouba Secondary School for Boys, a second campus with the same name, separate from the original, constructed near the ruler's palace. Center for Research and Studies on Kuwait.
08. In addition to schools, the Kuwait Office in the Trucial States also funded this maternity hospital and outpatient clinic in Sharjah. Center for Research and Studies on Kuwait.
09. Khalid bin Mohammed Al Qasimi, ruler of Sharjah, left, and Sabah Al Salim Al Sabah, emir of Kuwait, during a ceremony near what later became Rolla Square. In the background is Al Hisn, or Ruler's Palace, 1967. Estate of David Neild, courtesy of Medina Publishing Ltd.
10. Crowd stands under a banner designed by Sharjah natives Ibrahim Yousef Al Qaseer and Yaacoub Yousef Al Qaseer that reads "Al-Shaab Club Welcomes His Highness the Emir of Kuwait." Kuwait's leader visited Sharjah and the rest of the Trucial States in May 1966. Hassan Al Khayal.

10

Children celebrating Eid and enjoying rides in front of Al Rolla Tree and Abdullah Al Salim School (renamed Al Arouba School), 1968. The location is now Rolla Square. Mahmood AlSawan.

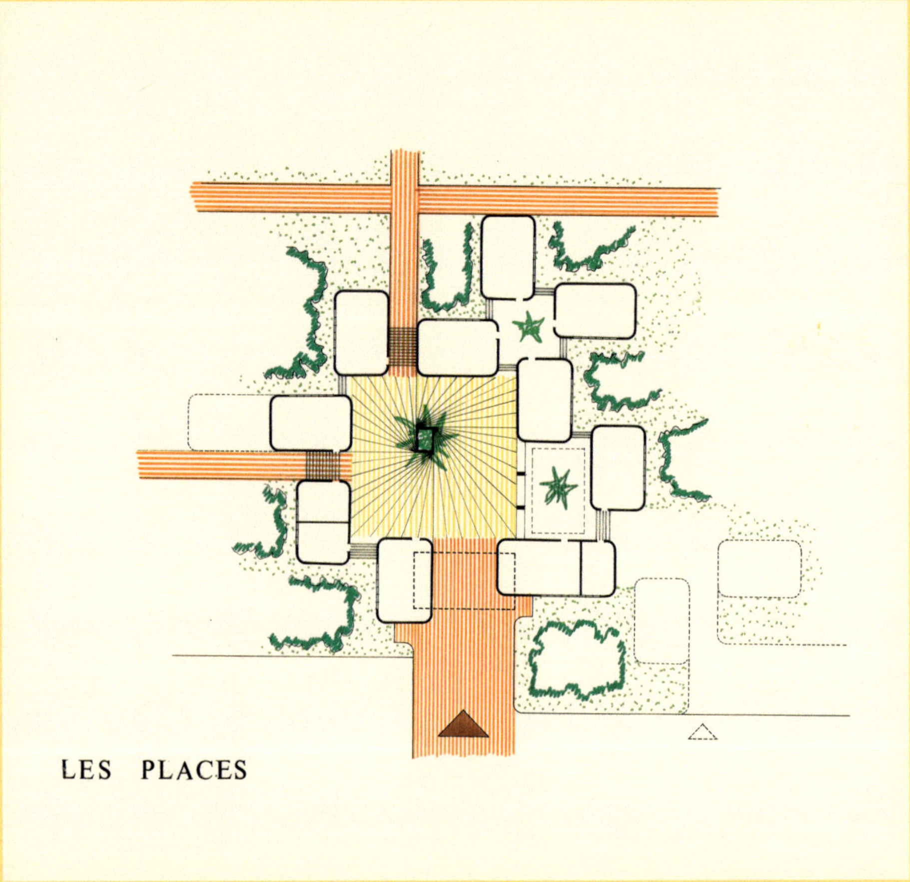

01

École Française de Sharjah

Architect
Regnault & Partners

Engineering Consultant
Six Construct

Construction
Société Entrepose G.T.M. pour les Travaux Petroliers Maritimes (ETPM)

Client
ETPM

Completed
1977

Status
Existing, expanded

While the UAE's oil industry attracted expatriates from around the world, Sharjah allegedly received the greatest number of French families in the 1970s. The French oil-industry contractor, ETPM, arrived in Sharjah in 1975 and soon counted three hundred employees, many with families. The company first built its offices and installed the necessary industrial equipment. It then started the École Française de Sharjah as a primary school located in a small villa on Kuwait Road, managed by ETPM's local director and only accepting children of the company's staff. In 1977, it built a school not only for employee families but also others, including Sharjah's Belgian community.

French architect Jean-Michel Regnault established his architectural office in Sharjah in 1976. Soon thereafter, he introduced the idea of a French school to the brother of Sharjah's ruler, Sheikh Sager bin Mohamed Al Qassemi, who approved it. The ruler subsequently gifted land for the school and—according to the architect—AED 400,000, or about $100,000, in funding. The Belgian engineering consultants Six Construct also provided services with the expectation that the school would accommodate its Sharjah-based families.

Regnault designed the 3,900-square-meter compound in relation to the existing trees and established water wells surrounding it. At the time that the French school was being designed and built, the surrounding landscape had not yet been transformed into the suburb of Halwan. Adjacent to the site was the existing German School designed by Rudi Eller. The site of the French school itself had been previously used for farming. The developers' preferred schedule was in fact delayed by the final vegetable harvest, with construction eventually starting in April 1977. The school was completed a few months later and opened for its first students in October 1977.

Inspired by the interrelation seen in traditional homes, Regnault formulated the school as a complex of intimate, pod-like buildings, including eight for classrooms, a director's office block, and another for restroom facilities. The pods were organized in clusters to create shared outdoor spaces for school activities, with a large central courtyard used for school gatherings and theater performances. The compound also provided three villas for staff. The clustering organization created shaded alleys between the buildings, some covered with wooden lattice. Regnault made subtle references to regional architectural details with archways that linked some of the blocks and rooftop casings that mimicked *barajeel*, or wind towers, to cover air-conditioning units.

The layout followed an axis with the flexibility to accommodate future extension plans. In 1984, an expansion provided a gymnasium hall. A secondary education program was added to the school in 1990 when the school's name was changed to Lycée Français International Georges Pompidou.

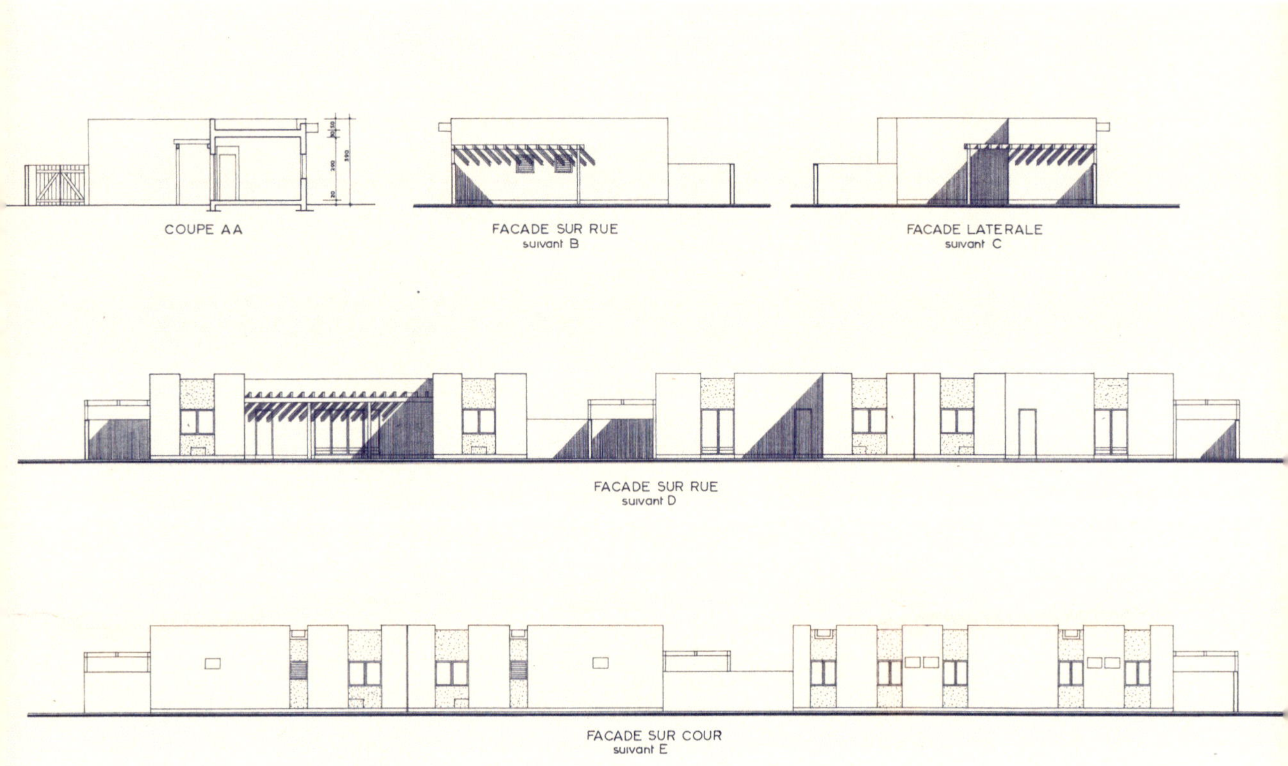
COUPE AA
FACADE SUR RUE
suivant B
FACADE LATERALE
suivant C
FACADE SUR RUE
suivant D
FACADE SUR COUR
suivant E

02

03

04

01. Site plan submitted in 1976 as part of a preliminary proposal. Images: Regnault & Partners.
02. Elevation and section drawings of faculty accommodations, dated March 20, 1977.
03. Students and teacher in school's main yard, late 1970s.
04. Aerial view of classrooms, late 1970s.

01

02

03

National College of Choueifat

After civil war broke out in Lebanon in 1975, the Lebanese National College of Choueifat struggled to keep its doors open for students. When enrollment dropped from 2,000 to a few hundred students, the school administration started looking for another location beyond Lebanon to keep the institution going.

With a history reaching back to 1886 and currently hosting more than 30 branches in 20 countries, Choueifat's campus in Sharjah was its first outside Lebanon. The new campus also functioned as the school's temporary headquarters. Some might have considered Sharjah as an unexpected choice for the elite private school, but by gaining the school's presence, the government of Sharjah also aimed to strengthen its reputation in education and international allure.

In 1976, in the midst of the Lebanese Civil War, fifty of the school's teachers found refuge in Sharjah, launching the new branch on part of the evacuated British Royal Air Force camp.[1] Military barracks were converted into classrooms while new facilities were being built.

Sharjah's ruler Sheikh Sultan bin Muhammad Al Qasimi not only offered a spacious site near other schools in the emirate but also provided financial aid to build premises for 600 boarding students and 1,800 day students. With funding and a site secured, Choueifat's in-house architect, Emile Khoury, was able to begin work on the new facilities.

The new school's program included accommodations for the faculty, a classroom building, a gymnasium, and outdoor sports facilities. According to the architect, everything was laid out on an orderly grid with the expectation that additional facilities for a growing student body would one day be attached. The school built piecemeal additions before a major expansion was designed in 2009 by the firm ATI Consultants.

After the war, the main school branch moved back to Beirut while the Sharjah branch continued serving local and expatriate residents, thereby continuing a scholastic relationship between Sharjah and Lebanon. Today, the school is known as the International School of Choueifat.

1. See p. 45.

04

Architect
Emile Khoury

Contractors
MOBIC

Client
National College of Choueifat

Completed
1979

Status
Existing, expanded

01. Outdoor sports areas at the school's purpose-built facilities. Jamal Hazbun, courtesy of the International School of Choueifat–Sharjah.
02. Suleiman Mansour, Ralph Bistany, co-founder of the school, and director Dorothy Miles, during a site visit. The school's faculty was involved in the transfer and in the eventual design of purpose-built facilities and classrooms. Emile Khoury.
03. Entrances to two rows of utilitarian classrooms. Students of thirty-five nationalities attended the Lebanese school after its headquarters was moved from Beirut to Sharjah in 1976. Jamal Hazbun, courtesy of the International School of Choueifat–Sharjah.
04. Some of Choueifat's earliest students in Sharjah, 1976–77. In the background, one of the British military barracks repurposed for Choueifat before completion of new facilities. Back row, left to right: Bariya Ataya, Daliah Khoury, Marwan Al Saleh. Front row: Houry Abrahamian, Raed Al Saleh, Nizar Adasani. Courtesy of Bariya Ataya.

CHEVROLET

01

Elementary and Intermediate School Prototype / Al Qasimiyah Primary School for Boys

Text by
Mona El Mousfy

Architect
Nabil Kanafani, Consolidated Engineering Company (Khatib & Alami)

Client
Ministry of Public Works

Proposed
1976

Completed
1981

Status
Existing

Al Qasimiyah Primary School for Boys was established during a period of significant national investment in education and civic projects across the UAE. In the 1970s, the Ministry of Education commissioned Khatib & Alami to design a primary school typology. Accordingly, the Ministry of Public Works built numerous, nearly identical schools throughout the country, with more than twenty versions in Sharjah alone, including Al Qasimiyah School located in Sharjah's Al Manakh district, built in 1981. The ubiquitous typology became synonymous with modern educational facilities.

The school is a two-story building that groups twenty-four classrooms, twelve on each floor, as well as five labs, a large library, and a double-height theater. Accessible via covered walkways, educational spaces are organized around a series of visually interrelated courtyards of different sizes: a large covered central courtyard, an adjacent long and narrow courtyard, and four smaller courtyards flanking them. The weaving of indoor classrooms, outdoor areas, and covered spaces endows the building's spatial organization with permeability. Perforated screens, bookending covered hallways, and delineating small courtyards add to the building's porous quality. Each classroom is defined by a trio of flat, vaulted bays, a relatively closed facade lining the walkway, and a glazed facade that opens directly to an adjacent courtyard. A trademark palette of soft earthy tones enlivens the concrete surfaces and the school's iconic water tower. Through its spatial strategies and architectural elements, the architecture demonstrates a sensitivity to both the climate of the UAE and the well-being of students and teachers.

In an effort to preserve the modern architectural heritage of Sharjah and to demonstrate an example of the adaptive reuse of an existing building, the Sharjah Architecture Triennial took on the challenge of renovating the abandoned Al Qasimiyah Primary School to serve as its headquarters and main venue. The Triennial was keen to occupy this particular building not only because of its diverse spatial possibilities but also because it bears witness to a time of great investment in the UAE's civic and educational spaces.

01. Entrance reveals various kinds of indoor and outdoor spaces created by the prototype design. Archive of Al Qasimiyah Primary School, courtesy of Kambar Mahmood Al Mazem.
02. The prototype water tower quickly became a recognizable and replicated landmark on the UAE landscape. Dr. Naman Al Jalili Archives Collection.
03. Elevation and section drawings of the twenty-four-classroom prototype, April 1976. Khatib & Alami, courtesy of DAFCO, Basil M. Al Farhan.

02

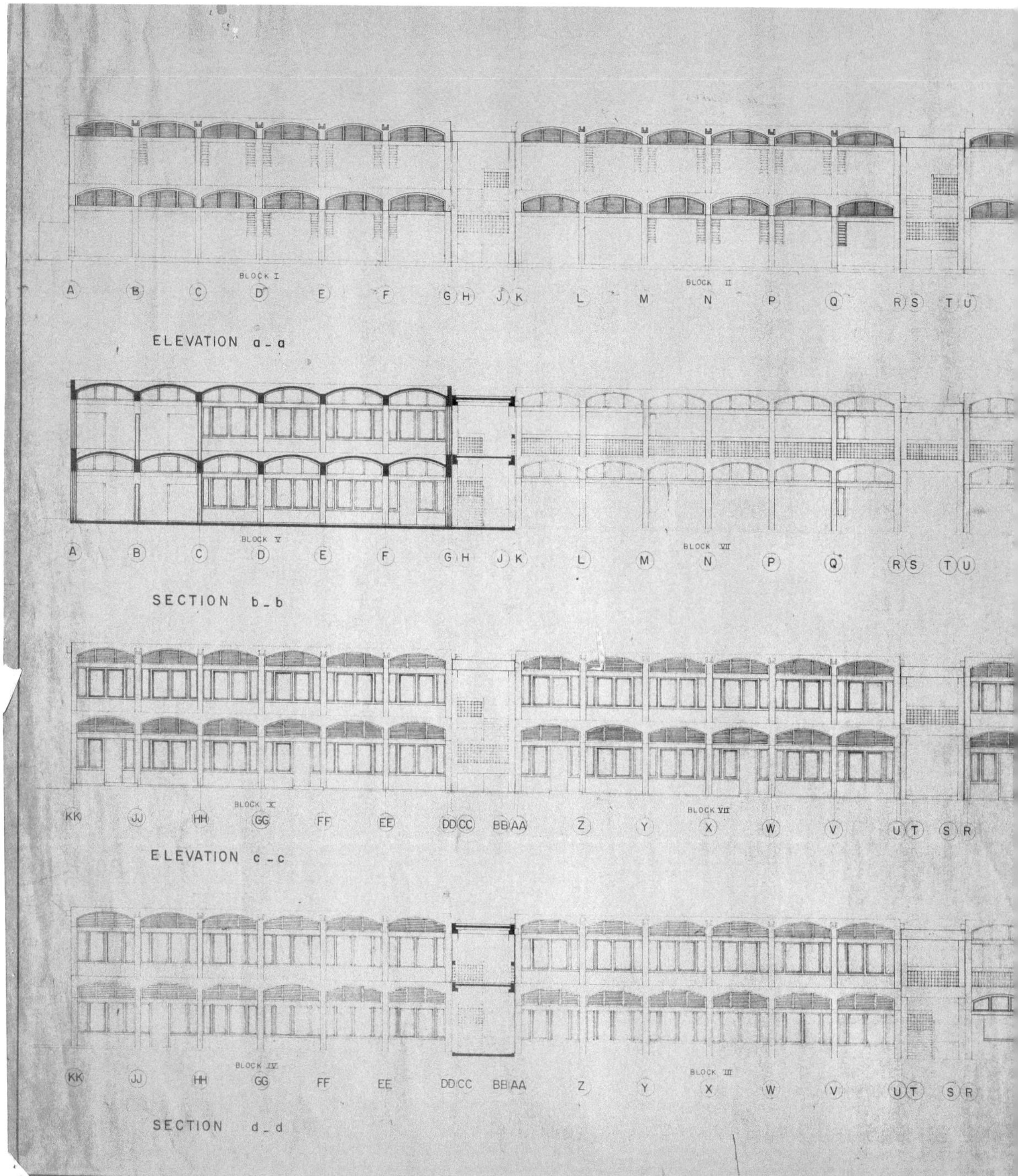
BLOCK I
BLOCK II
A B C D E F G H J K L M N P Q R S T U
ELEVATION a_a
BLOCK V
BLOCK VII
A B C D E F G H J K L M N P Q R S T U
SECTION b_b
BLOCK X
BLOCK VIII
KK JJ HH GG FF EE DD CC BB AA Z Y X W V U T S R
ELEVATION c_c
BLOCK IV
BLOCK III
KK JJ HH GG FF EE DD CC BB AA Z Y X W V U T S R
SECTION d_d

03

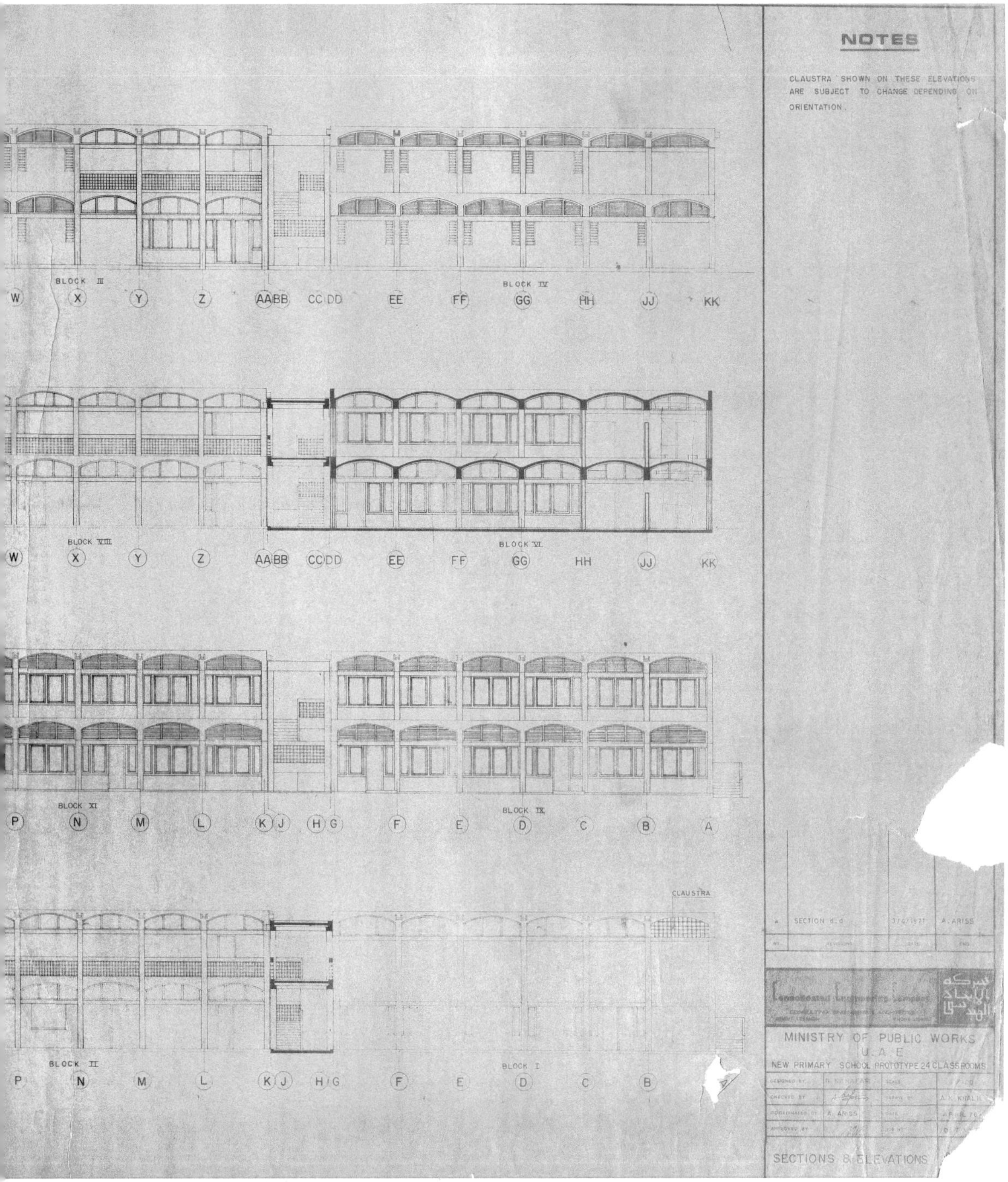
NOTES
CLAUSTRA SHOWN ON THESE ELEVATIONS ARE SUBJECT TO CHANGE DEPENDING ON ORIENTATION.
BLOCK III
BLOCK IV
BLOCK VIII
BLOCK VI
BLOCK XI
BLOCK IX
BLOCK II
BLOCK I
CLAUSTRA
SECTION
A. ARISS
MINISTRY OF PUBLIC WORKS
U.A.E
NEW PRIMARY SCHOOL PROTOTYPE 24 CLASSROOMS
SECTIONS & ELEVATIONS

Kindergarten Prototype

After Rais and Tukan Architects secured the contract to design a kindergarten prototype for the UAE Ministry of Public Works, Jafar Tukan traveled to study various precedents in France and the Levant. To develop the concept, the architect told ministry officials that he had imagined himself as a child walking around the school, which helped him build a narrative around the arrangement of clusters that a child would comprehend. The prototype provided another kind of narrative as well, one about the visible distribution of a government service. Its architectural strategy coincided with other projects to reform and coordinate the UAE's public education system. With Rais and Tukan's prototype in hand, the federal government could pursue the quick and equitable establishment of an educational system throughout the new nation's seven emirates.

Rais and Tukan Architects, a partnership formed in 1973 between Lebanese architect George Rais and Palestinian-Jordanian architect Jafar Tukan, submitted their design in 1974. The practice, hardly a year old, was introduced to the ministry by Sultan bin Khalifa Al Habtoor, who worked at the ministry from 1972 to 1974 and later commissioned the office to design his mixed-use tower in Sharjah's Al Majaz district.[1]

The kindergarten prototype prescribes a perforated, concrete-block wall to enclose a campus of about 300 square meters. Inside is a building composition reminiscent of Dutch structuralism, not unlike Herman Hertzberger's Amsterdam orphanage. The prototype called for twelve classrooms, two multi-purpose rooms, administration offices, open galleries, patios, and service amenities. The single-story network of articulated blocks maintains an intimate scale with four discernible zones, each made up of three classrooms arranged around a multi-purpose courtyard. The four zones are oriented around a larger central courtyard, which functions as an open-air playground and circulation space.

The design's recognizable, pyramid-like roof pieces were cast in concrete on site and rest atop a system of exposed concrete columns and tie beams. Smaller pyramids sheltered classrooms while larger ones roofed the multi-purpose spaces. Each pyramid is topped with a contemporary, and functional, wind tower slotted with concrete louvers, thus integrating the modern architecture vocabulary with elements of vernacular architecture.

Although replaced later by another—much larger—kindergarten prototype, several instances of Rais and Tukan's design still stand, albeit often abandoned and in bad shape. A version of the prototype in Sharjah's Al Manakh district has been converted into an education center. Another in the town of Kalba has been acquired by Sharjah Art Foundation and is used for Sharjah Biennial events.

Now standing modestly, if not abandoned, in urban locations throughout the UAE, the schools' prismatic water towers are often seen looming in the distance, weary witnesses of their rapidly changing surroundings.

1. See p. 159.

02

Architect
Rais & Tukan Architects

Client
Ministry of Public Works

Proposed
1974

Status
Existing, renovated, and demolished

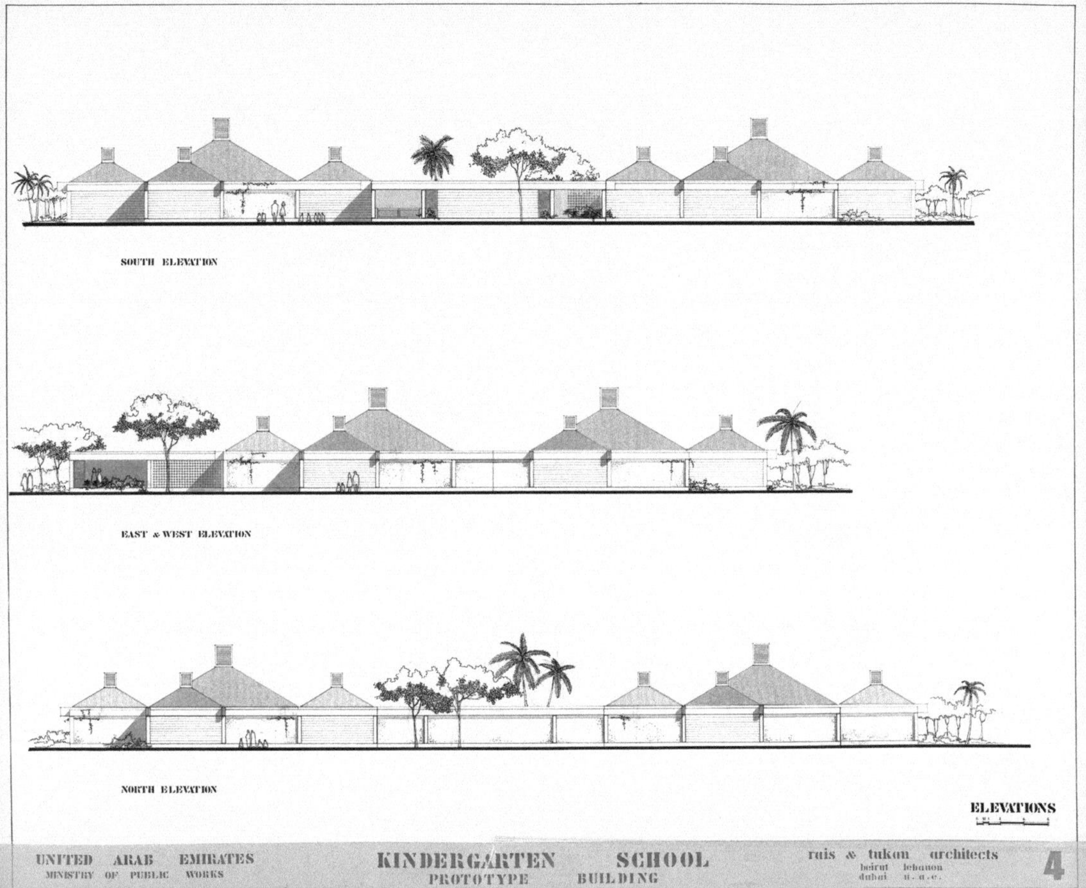

03

01. Execution of Rais & Tukan prototype, Al Khan district, photographed 1977. John R. Harris Library, courtesy of Mark Harris.
02. Construction worker dampens cast-concrete roof during construction, Al Khan, undated. Osama Hassanein.
03. Elevations of the prototype reveal the hierarchy of zones as represented by the sizes of pyramidal roofs. Rais & Tukan Archives, courtesy of the Arab Centre for Architecture.
04. The floor plan displays similarities to Dutch structuralist design and Alison and Peter Smithson's mat-building concept. Rais & Tukan Archives, courtesy of the Arab Centre for Architecture.
05. Perspective section drawing of a multi-purpose space and its transition to classroom spaces. Drawing includes demonstration of a wind tower. Its title has been adjusted for the layout. Rais & Tukan Archives, courtesy of the Arab Centre for Architecture.

04

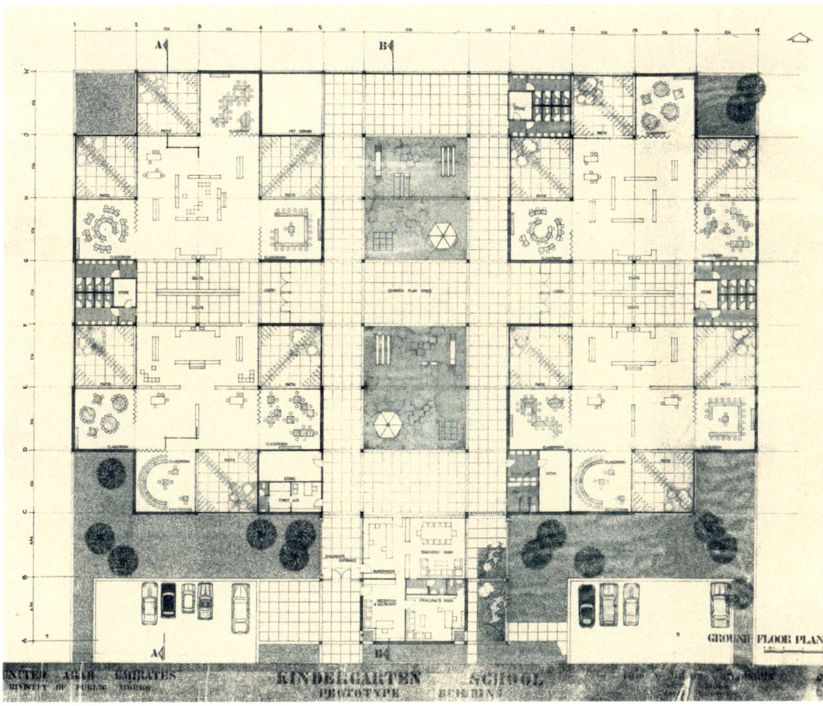
GROUND FLOOR PLAN
KINDERGARTEN SCHOOL

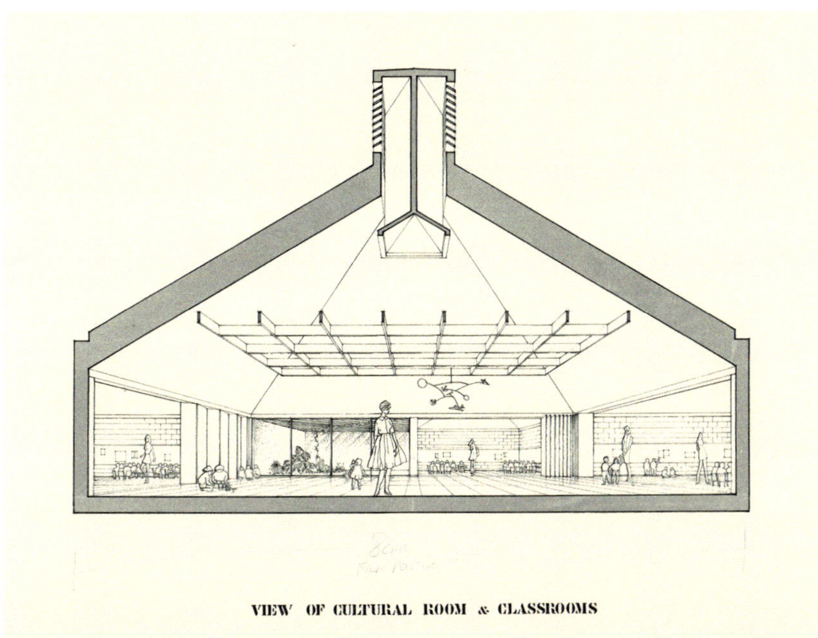
VIEW OF CULTURAL ROOM & CLASSROOMS

05

Modern Miniatures, Sharjah National Park

On the most inland edge of Sharjah International Airport is a linear park, 1.5 kilometers in length. At its center is an interrupted project to celebrate Sharjah's architectural achievements, in miniature form. All of the completed components of the project represent architectural and infrastructural projects from the late 1970s and 1980s.

Naim Khan, a Pakistani official in Sharjah Municipality's sewage division, organized the project after his British director, Trevor Starkey, received instructions from Sharjah's ruler to rebuild "all of Sharjah in small scale." Khan and other municipal workers finished six scaled-down replicas, including: a row of the Córdoba Buildings on Bank Street, Sharjah Post Office, the vegetable souk, the fish market, King Faisal Mosque, and the reclamation projects by Halcrow connecting Sharjah Creek to Lake Khalid. For a short time, water even flowed through a miniature channel. Sometime in the early 1990s, work on the mini-city stopped while plans were underway to add the Central Souk to the landscape, apparently due to limited funding and lack of workforce capacity.

With the largest reaching four meters high, the miniature structures have partially accessible ground-floor spaces, and some pose a challenge to children scaling the edifices to reach the roofs. King Faisal Mosque, outfitted with a full-scale air-conditioning unit, also functions as a women's mosque.

Sharjah's infrastructural landscape resulted from engaging a global economy of consultants; its miniature version was designed and delivered by the in-house officials of Sharjah Municipality.

Design and Oversight
Sewage Treatment Works, Sharjah Municipality

Client
Sharjah Municipality

Opened
Early 1990s

Status
Existing

Miniatures of the central post office, vegetable souk, and Córdoba Buildings. Early paving may have been an interpretation of the Sharjah roadways. Sharjah Municipality, courtesy of the Maraya Art Centre.

01

02

Abdulla Saad Moaswes

LAND, HOUSES, AND HOMES: A PALESTINIAN HISTORY OF AL FAYHA

In early 1971, Ali Moaswes and his family settled into a purpose-built house in Sharjah's Al Fayha district. Several months prior, Ali and his family had arrived in what would soon become the United Arab Emirates, initially renting a house in a new compound owned by the Al-Owais family in Port Saeed, Dubai. Ali's wife, Hiyam, was immensely proud of her role in designing the layout of the Dubai house, intended to be a replica of the family's previous home in Kuwait. Despite this immense pride and attachment, however, renting a house was not the same as owning a home, and it was with this in mind that the Moaswes family moved to Sharjah.

Like many Palestinians, Ali struggled to find a place to settle his family after the Nakba of 1948, when Israel expelled hundreds of thousands of Palestinians from their homes. The need for stability and dignified domicile became an existential pursuit, all the while keeping alive the memory of—and the hope of a return to—a peaceful Palestine. To the Moaswes family, the promise of land ownership in Sharjah represented the most ideal form of stability upon which they could rebuild their lives: it offered them both a home of their own and a higher quality of life for the family. In exchange, the Moaswes family and other Palestinians worked hard to contribute to the rapid growth and development of the emirate.

THE ARRIVAL

During the family's brief time in Dubai, fate reconnected Ali with Haseeb Rasoul from Nazareth. Ali knew Haseeb from his days working at Aramco in Dhahran, Saudi Arabia before he moved to Kuwait. To this day, Ali fondly considers Haseeb one of his closest friends and confidants, speaking highly of him in a manner only reserved for a select few of the many people he has met during his long life. Haseeb, a wealthy man, resided in Sharjah where he owned a furniture factory in addition to several properties close to the Clock Tower Roundabout. He introduced Ali to Sheikh Khalid bin Mohammed al Qasimi, then the ruler of Sharjah. Sheikh Khalid, known to be a principled and generous man, persuaded Ali to move with his family to Sharjah by offering a plot of land, seventy-five feet by seventy-five feet, in the Fayha district. In order to keep the title to the property, Ali was required to build a house. Al Fayha was not far from Palestine Street and the Palestine Roundabout, both landmarks before Palestinians came to the area and early evidence of Sheikh Khalid's support for the Palestinian cause.

The offer represented an ideal opportunity for Ali, who had for years lamented the inability of Palestinians to own land in the countries to which they fled. His son Saad recalls how his father often stated, half-jokingly, that he would be happy to own even a "grain of sand" so long as it was undeniably his. Owning a plot of land with a house he built instilled in Ali a sense of gratitude that formed the foundation for his continued commitment to residing in and serving the Emirate of Sharjah for the following half century. Contrary to the norm in neighboring countries, where non-citizens were excluded from land ownership, Palestinians were encouraged and trusted in Sharjah. They were in critical need of stability to secure dignified futures for themselves and their families on land they owned, and the local community welcomed them not just as brisk builders of the community but also as teachers, doctors, business owners, and skilled professionals.

THE MOASWES FAMILY HOME

To build his house, Ali hired Odeh Al Banna's Union Contractors. Both Odeh, from Gaza, and the project architect Fathi Wafa, from Yafa, were already prominent members of Sharjah's growing Palestinian community. Ali chose Union Contractors on the recommendation of Haseeb Rasoul, and because they were widely considered to be the best local contractors of the nascent Palestinian community. The house represented one of Ali's most crucial ambitions, and therefore hiring the best in the business was a logical choice. Haseeb's recommendation only strengthened his conviction in doing so.

Selecting Union Contractors worked out well for the Moaswes family, and the house was completed within a few short months. Ali's son Saad recalls how Haseeb's brother-in-law, Abdullah Taha, employed by Sharjah's armed forces at the time, would say that construction was accelerated by the fact that, rather than paying installments upon completion of milestones as per the norm, Ali paid installments in advance. There also seemed to be a tacit agreement between client, contractor, and consultant that constructing homes was key to building a stable, semi-permanent homeland where Palestinians could live and attempt to heal from the collective trauma of losing their ancestral homeland, and construction should thus be swift.

Upon completion, Ali's one-story house included three spacious bedrooms and one bathroom on 2,055 square feet. Ali's children, Sami and Saad, shared the bedroom adjoining that of their parents while the third bedroom was used as a study. The room contained, in addition to a desk and chair, a large filing cabinet and a broad window overlooking the street; the neighborhood girls came to jokingly refer to it as *burj al moraqabah* (the watchtower). When

03

Sami left home to attend university in Iraq, he left his place in the second bedroom next to Saad to his younger brother Khalid, born in 1972 and named after Sheikh Khalid.

When the Moaswes family moved into the Fayha house, where they were to live for almost four decades, they had very few neighbors. The nearest building of note was the Ruler's Court, roughly 400 meters away. The house was so remote at the time that it was inaccessible by car until Sharjah Municipality installed an improvised road leading to it, made from *sabkha*.[1] Browsing through photos of Al Fayha from the time, it is difficult to believe that what is such a densely settled area today, with narrow roads and countless houses, was once little more than a sandy expanse populated by a small handful of families.

Ali's house was also among the first houses in Sharjah to have a telephone line. It was installed a few days after Hiyam mentioned applying for one to Sheikh Khalid's wife, Sheikha Noura, one afternoon while delivering her a pot of *waraq enab* (stuffed vine leaves). Given the scarcity of home telephones at the time, this privilege was another indication of

the stability and belonging that the Moaswes family were to enjoy in Sharjah. The Moaswes' sons still remember their first four-digit phone number: 8636.

Over the coming years, many families from Palestine and other parts of the Arab world built homes on similar plots within the neighborhood. The Moaswes family's closest neighbors were the Dajani family from Yafa. Mamdouh Al Dajani, who had built houses in Al Fayha for himself as well as for his nephews, was a particularly close friend. He owned a terrazzo tile factory in partnership with Sheikh Khalid, and his floor tiles adorned parts of Ali and Hiyam's house. Other notable early neighbors included Dr. Ramadan Shubair and his family from Gaza and the Dagher family from Lebanon. Dr. Shubair was notable for being the first physician in Ras Al Khaimah as well as for establishing the first blood bank in the UAE. His wife, Najah, was also well known as an Arabic teacher at several UAE schools.

THE ARAB WORLD IN MICROCOSM

As the 1970s progressed, Al Fayha grew into one of Sharjah's most important Arab neighborhoods. A large number of Gazan families arrived in Al Fayha, thanks to Odeh al Banna. Many of them immigrated directly from Gaza, fleeing the brutal Israeli expansion into the territory in the summer of 1967. Among them were the Bayidh, Aidi, Enany, Ghalayini, and Banna families. As they arrived, Palestinian families from other parts of the country also joined: the Abu Quba family from Yafa, Tahboub from Al Khalil (Hebron), and families from other parts of the Arab world such as Egypt and Lebanon.

Each was offered a plot of land, similar to the Moaswes family, in Al Fayha on the same condition that they build a house on it. Diverse Arab families formed a tightly knit community, a microcosm of an idealized Arab world. Just as how the Palestinian cause had become the central rallying point for Arab unity and the lifeblood of dreams of a virtuous Arab future, new arrivals found an existing social bedrock of Palestinian families and businesses in Al Fayha. Following the typical procedures of acquiring a plot of land and building a house on it, they became acquainted with and befriended community figures, many of whom worked in construction and related industries. In this sense, not only did land ownership manifest ideas of stability, domicile, and belonging, but it also held a practical, utilitarian value: through building private homes, families built a new public.

Although Al Fayha was largely settled by Palestinians, in the 1970s it was also home to some notable Emirati families. Saad, Ali's middle son, recalls living in proximity to members of the Al Qasimi and Al Noman families. Ali Al Noman was then director of what later became the Sharjah Electricity and Water Authority. Another well-known resident of Al Fayha in the 1970s was the UAE Minister of Education at the time, Dr. Abdullah Omran Taryam, who regularly visited Ali's house in order to use his telephone.

EVERYDAY LIFE IN 1970S AL FAYHA

Life in Al Fayha suited the Moaswes family. They were one of only a few migrant families to own more than one car. Ali had brought with him from Kuwait an air-conditioned, fully automatic, white Dodge Monaco with red leather seats that was one of the fanciest cars around; and Hiyam, with her more modest Morris, was the only female motorist in the neighborhood. She was also among the first women in Sharjah to obtain a driver's license. Given that Ali still worked in Dubai and that both of his older sons went to school there, having two cars was hugely convenient.

As its population grew, Al Fayha became a site of strong friendship and camaraderie. The neighborhood boys used to gather frequently to discuss important matters of the day while taking long walks through the area's gridlocked streets. On Thursday afternoons, a few of them, including Ali's son Saad, Sadiq Al Muzaini and Amin Ataya from Gaza, and Amjad Dweik from Al Khalil, would borrow a car and drive to the popular hangouts, Wimpy Burger in Deira or Bake-O-Mat on Al Arouba Street. Like Saad, Sadiq's family also moved to the UAE from Kuwait, where his father had been a district attorney, initially renting a house in Al Fayha before building his family's own home a few years later. Amjad was the son of Judge Yusri Dweik, well known for his role in advising Sheikh Khalid during the 1960s and for representing the emirate during legal negotiations leading to UAE federation.

Like the neighborhood boys, the adults also benefitted from the burgeoning sense of camaraderie. The everyday practice of sharing important household resources such as telephones, cooking ingredients, and other essentials became the foundation for decades and generations of friendship. By way of entertainment, weekends became synonymous with small gatherings at neighbors' houses. The Moaswes house was a common site of such gatherings, with many of Ali and Hiyam's friends, such as the Dajanis and the Daghers, joining them in games of *tarneeb*, a card game popular among Levantine Arabs.

A HOME TO MULTIPLE GENERATIONS

The late 1970s and early 1980s witnessed several changes in the daily life of the Moaswes family. In 1978, Ali added a second floor to his house. With both Saad and Sami studying abroad, he moved into the smaller upper level with Hiyam and Khalid, their youngest son, and rented the ground level out to the Sarhans, another Palestinian family whose father worked in insurance.

A few years later, in 1981, Ali left the Kuwait Insurance Company and moved to Sharjah Insurance. As part of his new job, he set up the company's Dubai branch and became its first branch manager. That same year, Saad completed his master's degree at the University of Southern California, returning to Al Fayha to begin a career as a civil engineer. In 1986, after a brief sojourn working in Oman, he set up Abdullah Al Sheikh General Maintenance and Decoration Contracting (ASGM) in partnership with Ghassan Somah from Syria and Joseph Assi from Lebanon. By this point, Ali had been promoted to general manager at Sharjah Insurance, working at their head office on Al Burj Street, also known as Bank Street.

With Saad now an established interior contractor, the Moaswes family house underwent renovation in late 1988. The sea salt and sand-based concrete, used in building many houses at the time of construction, had created structural problems that required urgent attention. With Saad looking to expand his business into working with special epoxies, then a new building technology in the UAE, the house represented an ideal terrain for experimentation.

During the renovation period, which lasted about a year, Saad got engaged and married Houda Eldah. Rather conveniently, the timing of Saad's marriage coincided with the completion of the house's renovation. This meant that the same house in which Saad began his life in Sharjah became the place where he and Houda started their family. Along with their two children, they continued to live in Al Fayha until 2007 when they moved to a larger house in another part of Sharjah. By this point, Saad had become the managing director of Bond Interiors, a company headquartered in the Sharjah Industrial Area owned and run by the Moaswes family.

Many refugees and other migrants put down roots in Al Fayha in the 1960s and early 1970s, and they only grew deeper over the following decades as new generations were born and raised in the area. The younger generations had, and continue to have, little to no memory of any other home, even in the most romantic sense of the word. The Moaswes family memory of Sharjah goes back three generations,

1. *Sabkha* is a clay-like concoction of saline minerals found naturally in the region's landscape hard enough (when not wet) to sustain automobile traffic.

04

and many other families of old Palestinian arrivals are now entering their fourth generation. Although many family residences have since moved away from Al Fayha, they are still bound to the area by the land ownership that they have refused to relinquish.

REFUGE AND DIGNITY

Al Fayha, currently one of Sharjah's oldest and most storied areas, remains one of the few places in the UAE where much of the land is still owned by foreign nationals. It also remains a place of refuge for those fleeing war and other tragedies. At least three generations have watched Al Fayha grow from a quiet area to one of Sharjah's most central and vibrant neighborhoods as newcomers built houses representing powerful hopes of a bright future. Although many of the families that originally built and lived in Al Fayha's homes have since moved to other parts of Sharjah and the UAE, the spirit of community birthed within its narrow streets has persisted in the legacy of the district as a place affording refugees due dignity. While many who gathered to play tarneeb in the early 1970s have passed, their children and grandchildren still gather to indulge in comparable, albeit trendier, pastimes.

The hope of an eventual return to Palestine complicates the question of permanence for many Palestinian refugees and their descendants. It is nearly impossible to dislodge a person's love for home, especially when that home is all of a sudden snatched away in an act of a violence that renders the displaced life instantaneously unrecognizable from the known past. To reinstate feelings of belonging, appreciation, and stability can restore a sense of dignity despite the agony of life in exile. By providing a cohesive space for Palestinians and other Arabs to once again realize feelings of ownership, responsibility, and the hope of investing in a bright future, Al Fayha made many feel for a long time like active citizens rather than transient refugees trapped in a state of passive waiting for a return to the hills, plains, rivers, and coastlines of Palestine.

05

01. Saad Moaswes takes a self-portrait before a mirror beside the main foyer of the house, circa 1971. Images: Private collection, Moaswes Family.
02. The Moaswes family home in Al Fayha upon completion in early 1971. Architect: Fathi Wafa. Contractor: Union Contractors.
03. Ali Moaswes (center, in glasses) and his wife Hiyam host friends from the Abdulwahab family at the Moaswes family home in Al Fayha.
04. Ali Moaswes parks his wife's Morris in the driveway of their home as son Sami stands alongside.
05. Hiyam and Sami Moaswes in the study, known in the neighborhood as *burj al moraqabah*, or the lookout tower.

Adnan Saffarini in Sharjah

Once its commercial quantities of oil were announced in 1966, Dubai became even more attractive to regional Arab professionals. This new pool of white-collar labor would serve Sharjah well, too. One of the arriving experts was the Cairo University–trained Palestinian Adnan Saffarini. Although he was an engineer, Saffarini practiced like an architect. While most buildings were going up as quickly as possible to take advantage of capricious rent prices, Saffarini took time for the artistic hand- rendering of what his buildings would look like once the surrounding city was completed. His street views often included the latest car models, mature trees, and people, even children with balloons. According to his descendants, Saffarini worked on hundreds of buildings in Sharjah, where he opened an office in 1968 or 1969. The staggering number of commissions also meant that he worked on a diverse range of projects, including social housing, palaces, a dog pound, luxury hotels, factories, hospitals, mosques, and schools. This 1974 drawing was for a mixed-used building for Dubai businessman Rashid Ahmad Lootah. It was to be situated on Al Zahra'a Square, also known as Clock Tower Roundabout, which the 1969 master plan had envisioned as becoming the city's main urban square. The building is currently slated for demolition.

Perspective rendering of a mixed-use building at Clock Tower Roundabout, 1974. Courtesy of Sharjah Municipality.

Al Meena Street Housing

In the years prior to Sharjah's boom, Al Meena Street was one of two paved roads branching out from the roundabout welcoming traffic from Dubai. Its destination was of significance at the time: BP's compounds.[1] By 1968, some of the city's first streetlamps lined the road, which eventually veered from the compounds to connect a row of new banks and offices to the new jetty extending out over the Gulf waters. The name Al Meena Street, or Port Road, signaled its sustained prominence. By the 1970s, ongoing road construction in Sharjah's existing city required the rehousing of Sharjah residents in large numbers. New buildings erected on Al Meena Street were intended to be allocated as "compensation buildings," given to landowners who lost property as a result of major redevelopment efforts. In exchange for vacating, they were given apartments in the rows of repetitive, three-story, mixed-use buildings to lease to expatriates, who sought proximity to Sharjah's business center. The British firm Hubbard Ford and Partners delivered three corresponding prototypes for this swift trade-off, each with its own "pseudo-Arab" elevation featuring rounded vault forms and different styles of arches.

The buildings' restrained scale was dwarfed by the larger buildings that eventually rose across the street and at the road's terminus with Al Arouba Street. Left behind as new development began to accumulate along Al Arouba Street, the distinct row of buildings proved an inefficient response to Sharjah's housing shortage and an inadequate draw for arriving businesses and banks. With the completion of the Bank Street buildings in 1979, Sharjah's business district sealed its departure from Al Meena Street.[2]

1. See p. 43.
2. See p. 99.

Architect
Hubbard Ford & Partners

Client
Government of Sharjah

Completed
1976

Status
Partially demolished

Al Meena Street buildings, 1977. Some of the roof arches were later removed to accommodate mechanical systems and water tanks. Henk Snoek / RIBA Collections.

01

02

Al Majarrah Buildings

As Sharjah's oldest districts faced a real estate boom, neighborhoods and old houses were reconfigured or eradicated. New housing projects with ground-floor shops were commissioned to accommodate local families displaced by redevelopment. The shops and flats of these new blocks were originally designed for locals but are now rented by foreign residents.

The four mixed-use blocks, originally built with corniche views, have receded behind the gold-domed Sharjah Museum of Islamic Civilization, previously Al Majarrah Souk.

The Majarrah Buildings' facades adopted the prevailing architectural language of 1970s Sharjah—including pointed and semi-circular arches that crest the ground-floor arcade of shops and other subtle references to Islamic architecture. Screens with decorative geometric patterns cover some of the building's openings, allowing natural light and air into circulation spaces. The building's orientation seems intended to maintain visual privacy for residents and to provide communal spaces between buildings.

Architect
Regnault & Partners

Contractors
Energyco

Client
Sheikh Sultan bin Muhammad Al Qasimi

Design
1976

Status
Existing

03

04

05

06

07

01. Al Majarrah Buildings employed two facade designs, featuring pointed and rounded arches. Images: Regnault & Partners.
02. View of planned road between the mixed-use blocks, along the arcades, during construction.
03. Early clay study model.
04. Detail, facade screen used for shading and privacy.
05. Construction crew on site, late 1970s.
06. Elevation drawing, mid-1970s.
07. Project announcement board punctured by a bullet and vandalized with text "Freedom comes from the barrel of a gun."

01

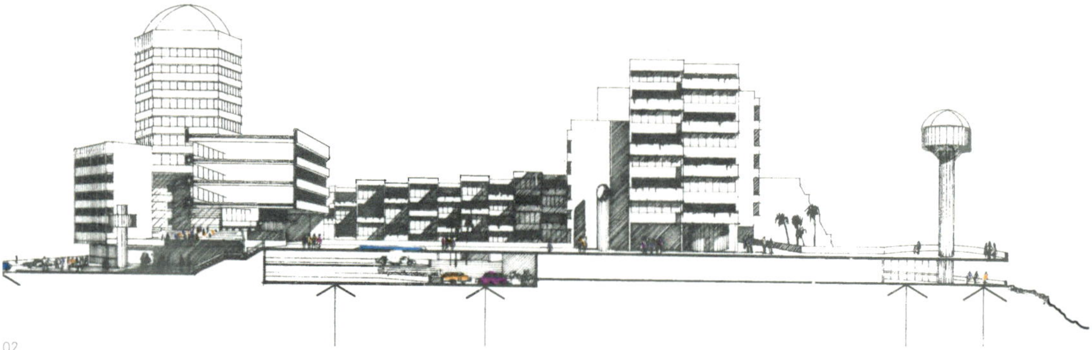

02

Golden Gate Project

In 1974, the Australian consortium PGA secured the contract for the master plan of Golden Gate as part of a constellation of mostly unbuilt seaside schemes for Sharjah.[1] This component, as described in Sharjah's 1969 master plan, was to form part of Sharjah's planned harbor development, filling Al Layah's promontory with a sprawling mid-rise district of high-end housing, retail, and underground parking. Located on reclaimed land across the recently dredged Sharjah Creek from the existing corniche, the new district promised the existing city an array of recreational and leisure facilities—all raised a meter higher than the area's high-water level.

The plan's land-use proposal prioritized privacy, pedestrian circulation, and access to services. Elevated walkways and pleasantly landscaped promenades provided residents access to the project's two beaches and the waterfront commercial district—mirroring the city's original corniche on the other side of the creek. Residential units were oriented toward the Gulf, taking advantage of northern frontages as PGA's other projects did. The project's northern corniche, with views over the horizon, adopted a more intimate scale for the residential area.

Even though the scheme was never realized—the new Port Khalid ended up needing all of the land—the investigation reports, proposed sketches, and artists' impressions reveal the ethos and ambitions of development in Sharjah at that time. No master-planned, mixed-use project of this size was ever completed in Sharjah's city center.

Architect
Professional Group Australia (PGA)

Client
Sheikh Sultan bin Muhammad Al Qasimi

Status
Unbuilt

1. See p. 149.

03

01. Aerial perspective, mid-1970s. Images: Professional Group Australia.
02. Sectional perspective reveals proposed underground parking and road system, undated.
03. Sectional perspectives, undated. The project included interlocking public and private spaces at various levels.

01

02

Sharjah Carlton Hotel

Architect
Sabah Abi Hanna & Associates

Contractor
Consolidated Contractors Company (CCC)

Client
Mubarak Abdul Aziz Al-Hassawi

Completed
1973

Status
Existing, renovated

After designing Kuwait's hexagon-themed Al Messilah Beach Hotel, Lebanese architect Sabah Abi Hanna was commissioned by the hotel's Kuwaiti developer, Mubarak Al-Hassawi, to design his new venture in Sharjah. It was not Abi Hanna's first commission in the UAE; before that, he had designed two unrealized projects, one each in Abu Dhabi and Dubai. For those projects, he opened a Dubai office in 1970.

Opening in February 1974, the 170-room Sharjah Carlton Hotel was more than just one of Sharjah's earliest modern hotels. Its air-conditioned and upholstered lobbies functioned as welcoming halls to Sharjah's visiting dignitaries, including those attending the 1976 African-Arab Symposium as well as UAE president and ruler of Abu Dhabi, Sheikh Zayed bin Sultan Al Nahyan, and UAE prime minister and ruler of Dubai, Sheikh Rashid bin Saeed Al Maktoum. Located on Al Khan's shoreline, next to the eventual Hotel Meridien Sharjah, the Carlton gave the emirate's visitors "an alternative to the Sheba," offering more guest services, entertainment facilities, and a beachfront.[1] The Inter-Continental Group was approached to operate the hotel but turned the offer down.

The architect claims to have originally proposed a larger hotel, but the client requested a more modest scale that could be expanded later. The final design comprised a seven-story main hotel along with a collection of one- and two-story chalets. The design program also included gardens and ample parking for hotel visitors and evening guests of the hotel's nightclub.

The hotel has largely maintained its original form from the early 1970s, including the facade's precast perforated panels that provide shading and privacy to the rooms.

Following the Carlton's success, Sabah Abi Hanna was commissioned to design another, lesser-known building in Sharjah—a housing and commercial complex on Al Arouba Street.

1. See p. 93.

01. Seaside elevation, 1970s. Bernard Gérard, Éditions Delroisse.
02. Photographs of event held at the Carlton, perhaps connected to Sharjah's African-Arab Symposium, December 1976. Sharjah Carlton.
03. Front entrance along Al Khan's beach strip, undated. Mahmood AlSawan.

03

Marbella Club of Sharjah

Architectural Consultant
Peter Hudson & Partners

Concept Designer
Prince Alfonso zu Hohenlohe-Langenburg

Landscape
Blakedown Gulf

Consulting Engineers
Ian Banham & Associates

Quantity Surveyors
D. G. Jones, McCoach & Partners

Contractors
Conforce Gulf

Completed
1978

Status
Existing

Although 1975 was a peak year for Sharjah investment pitches, European "playboy" Prince Alfonso zu Hohenlohe-Langenburg claimed he was merely visiting Sharjah when the idea of launching a version of his Spanish resort concept came to him. Three years later, in April 1978, the Marbella Club of Sharjah opened on the edges of Khalid Lagoon, then under transformation. It was described as a village-like compound of luxury, "a garden landscape on barren desert." Really, it was reconstituted land sealed off from the lagoon, according to Halcrow's 1969 plan. The architectural consultant was British engineer Peter Hudson, a recurring name in Sharjah's development, but news reports claimed the resort was "designed by Prince Alphonso himself ... in the exact style of his successful clubs in Spain, right down to the pigeon tower." One report counted 7,000 imported plants and trees, and another 28,000 "carefully chosen by Blakedown Landscapes of Kidderminster." An estimated 80,000 gallons of water per day, supplied by a sewage treatment plan, were required to keep them alive.

Today, the Marbella is bounded by one of Sharjah's busiest roads and jumbled skyline of tower blocks; back then, it was "'a lush jungle' in a hostile desert," tethered only to the adjacent Holiday Inn tower. Its access to the shore is now cut off by a cloaked fence, but the complex was purported to have once included a marina "full of power boats." The grounds lay in ideal proximity to most of Sharjah's notable sites including the Central Souk, Sharjah Expo, and the Bank Street offices.

Inside its walls, the Marbella offered an earthy kind of modernity, stuccoed and tiled in Spanish colonial. Each of the fifty cottages, according to the *Financial Times*, was painted "to echo the tone of the plants and flowers which border it." The design's flexibility allowed the 130-square-meter units to be rented with or without kitchens and living rooms. The central club building and tennis courts were connected to the rental units by meandering concrete paths, preferably navigated by golf cart. Marbella's promoters said there were too many people interested in making the cottages permanent residences. They remained committed, they said, to keeping some available for "visiting businessmen."

The cottages' domed tops were merely ornamental, made of a concoction of concrete, wood, and glass-reinforced plastic and seen only in photographs or from the Holiday Inn's upper floors. The 1,860-square-meter central club building is topped by a 15-meter-wide roof made of glass-reinforced plastic and shaped to conjure up a Bedouin tent.

The itinerant Spanish prince, carrying a Liechtenstein passport, was supposed to attract glamor. Rumors abounded about all the celebrities who would stay at the club. The only one noted in the local press was Scottish actor Sean Connery, who attended the first-anniversary bash. Billed the "the lushest spot in the entire Gulf," the Marbella survived its first year at 20% occupancy and quickly began offering "cut-rate weekend prices." In 2019, the resort started a major renovation.

02

01. Aerial view from neighboring Holiday Inn, with Central Souk and Sharjah Expo site in background, late 1970s. Terry Kirk, courtesy of Camera Press Ltd.
02. Visitor at the Marbella Club stands atop one of the domed chalets. In background, the Holiday Inn (Architects: David Firmin & Partners, Consulting Engineers: Brown, Corzier & Wyatt, 1977). Collection of Mohammed Shamis Al Mazemi, courtesy of Ahmed Al Mazemi.

01

Seashore Development Proposal, Khor Fakkan

Text by Łukasz Stanek

Architect
Józef Zbigniew Polak

Client
Sheikh Sultan bin Muhammad Al Qasimi

Completed
1977

Status
Unbuilt

Polish architect Józef Zbigniew Polak's career took him across four continents. Long before he produced a design proposal for a seashore development in Sharjah's eastern exclave of Khor Fakkan, he had started out with blueprints for post-war Poland, where he designed several cultural centers. By the late 1950s, he embarked on a peripatetic career, garnering awards for his architectural and urban planning competition designs throughout Central Asia, the Middle East, and Africa. While his work in Afghanistan (1967–70) reflected the goals of socialist technical assistance to developing countries in the midst of Cold War rivalry, by the time he arrived in the UAE in 1977, authorities in socialist Poland were focused on the profit potential of architectural export. Across these changing geopolitical contexts and along with some time spent in the United States, Polak developed a vision of urbanism defined by curvilinear layouts that negotiated topography, historical landmarks, and vernacular urban fabric.

The Khor Fakkan project, delivered by Polak's Dubai-based team, was interpreted along these lines. Polak used a found postcard showing a dramatic view of the shoreline landscape to convey his development concept. He delineated the proposed buildings, roads, and decks by etching white lines into the postcard, retouching it with a black pen. Roads on the mainland follow terrain contours and provide access to a mosque at the top of the hill and to clusters of villas that cascade toward the sea. Via a new bridge, the project then extends into the Gulf of Oman to the rocky Shark Island, where a hotel, exhibition center, and marina were planned. The island's buildings vary between spheres set against the sky and decks stretched between the cliffs. Concave forms cling to the rocks, and convex forms float in the sea.

This project remains unrealized. The adjacent shoreline was transformed into a deepwater port that opened in 1979.

02

03

04

01. The architect sketched his proposal onto an aerial-view postcard. Most of the mainland coast was eventually developed into Khor Fakkan Port.
02. Polak and team consider a site model, perhaps in the UAE office, 1977.
03. Sketch of proposed development along coastal road, 1977.
04. Elevation of Shark Island and proposed bridge, 1977. Images: J. Z. Polak.

GOOD VIBRATIONS
When Special evenings require that Special Touch, think of
THE fantasy SUPPER NIGHT CLUB
Romanticii
The elegant night club with the finest nouvelle cuisine, international show **Good Vibrations,** Resident band **Romanticii** and our Arabic Belly Dancer.
The Fantasy Supper Night Club for those memorable moments ...
PALMOTEL
SHARJAH
Al Wihda Street, Sharjah – Tel : 352249/355020

01

Hind Mezaina

GOOD VIBRATIONS: LIVING IT UP IN SHARJAH'S HOTELS

Not so long ago, Sharjah was the UAE's premier party town. Over the years, I've heard many family friends and friends of friends reminisce about the good old days in Sharjah and read many posts on social media about them.

"We Sharjah folks rarely ventured across no man's land, there were more pubs and discos in Sharjah than all the other six emirates put together!"
A.W., Dubai — "The Good Old Days" Facebook group (April 22, 2019)

I have come across recollections like this time and again in print media, too, in back issues of *What's On*, for example. The monthly publication, said to be the first English-language magazine in the Gulf, was established in Dubai in 1979 and found its niche as the entertainment guide for Dubai and Sharjah. By 1981, it also covered Abu Dhabi and, soon after, the rest of the United Arab Emirates and Oman. As it turns out, this entertainment magazine may be one of the definitive historical archives on Sharjah of the late twentieth century.

In the 1980s, *What's On* targeted English-language readers who could no longer be reached simply by word of mouth. Ian Fairservice, the founding editor of *What's On* and also the managing partner and group editor of the magazine's parent company Motivate Media Group, explained his initial business idea in an article in *The National* (June 17, 2009):

"If I wanted to advertise my hotel, I'd have to make 5,000 copies of my own leaflet, drive to Sharjah, which was a long way on not very well made-up roads, and then I'd have to pay money for them to staple the leaflets into the day-old news. And that was the only print advertising that existed in 1978."

By aggregating all those leaflets into a single magazine, Fairservice helped promote Sharjah's party-town status. There was a plethora of Sharjah nightclubs, all located in hotels, including:

. Club 58 and Al Khama Room at the Beach Hotel
. Coral Bar Disco La Belle Epoque at Hotel Meridien
. Coins Disco at the Palmotel
. Disco 21 and Queen's Night Club at the Palace Hotel
. Peaches at the Marbella Club
. Juliana's at the Holiday Inn
. Al Matador at Al Andalus Hotel.

The oil boom in Sharjah began in the mid-1970s, several years later than in Abu Dhabi and Dubai. The oil reserves enabled Sharjah's government to create infrastructure serving newly monied locals seeking to establish businesses and international brands aiming to set up shop with local sponsors.

"Sharjah at the time (mid-1970s) was about to boom, with large numbers of people with high disposable incomes, rushing to take up residence."
Mike Hennessy, *What's On* (July 1984)

The boom funneled an influx of expatriates from across the world into newly constructed residential apartments and villas. The building of hotels and entertainment venues soon followed: they accommodated international business travelers and tourists, in search of contracts and sunshine, who enjoyed the thrill of visiting a destination that was new, affordable, and off the beaten track. By luring tourists with sun, sand, and the exotic flare of "Arabia," Sharjah's tourism efforts aimed to boost the economy. One of the earliest advertisements for the Sharjah Tourist Centre promoted themed nights like Dishdash and Caftans, Day in the Dunes, and Desert Disco. Even Sharjah's oldest hospital, Al Qassimi, hosted at least one night of revelry: the Razzle Dazzle party.

Hotels in Sharjah and across the Gulf became social centers, for local residents and expats in addition to travelers, who mingled in the array of restaurants, cabarets, discotheques, and concert venues—places to experience the music played back home, the drinks familiar from back home, the food eaten back home. Expats paid to access the memories, and locals paid to experience novelty: the pub lunch, discos playing "the latest sounds—direct from the UK," restaurants serving European and Asian cuisine, oriental nights, a German *Bierkeller*, an Italian pizzeria, and all the cultural festivals, from Indonesian to Lebanese and South African.

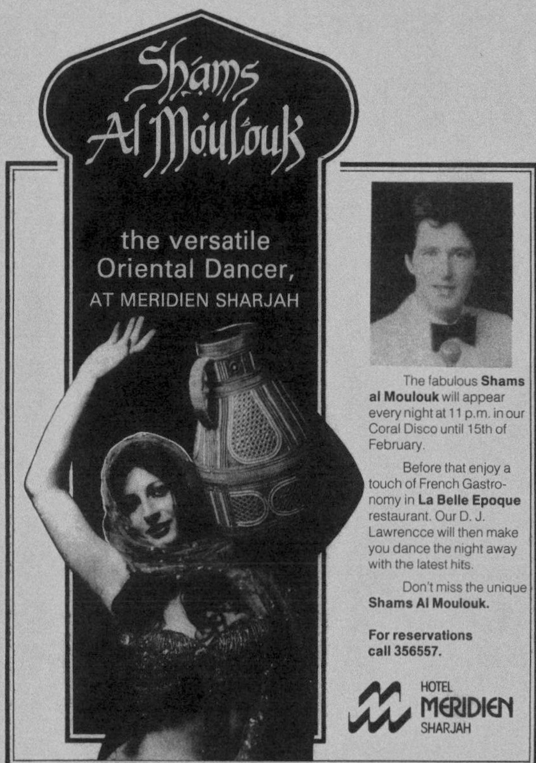

02

03

Many today consider malls in Gulf countries to be public spaces, and hotels have also served a similar function for expats and locals, predominately men, over the years. Although the venues were limited in number, they offered environments where Sharjah residents could enjoy a cup of coffee or tea in the hotel lobby; order a meal and drink in a restaurant; use hotel facilities that might include a gym, swimming pool, or beach; and then boogie down at night in one of the entertainment venues—if they could afford it, of course. To build a clientele of more than tourists, these hotels also attracted the local community with membership offerings. Before the word "staycation" was a thing, hotel ads promoted weekend package deals and family weekend getaways to the *What's On* readers. Sharjah's hotels fueled a joint campaign for the city to become "the ultimate in business and leisure," a superlative once claimed by Hotel Meridien Sharjah.

Before the idea of dine-in cinema as we know it today existed, Hotel Meridien was screening films with dinners every Sunday. Although the films themselves were never listed in the monthly *What's On* ads (which makes me wonder whether the screenings were licensed), there was one advertisement for a special screening of *Trishul* on February 6, 1980. The 1978 Bollywood film, directed by Yash Chopra, starred Amitabh Bachchan, Sanjeev Kumar, Shashi Kapoor, and Hema Malini. Malini was booked as the evening's host.

It's important to note there were cinemas in Sharjah at the time, including Sharjah Cinema and Rivoli Cinema, that screened films in Arabic, Hindi, Malayalam, and English. They offered popcorn but, unlike the hotels, couldn't serve cold beer from the tap. Venues like the Sharjah Wanderers Sports Club also had weekly film nights.

When disco was dying, or really was already dead, in the late 1970s, it found a lifeline on Sharjah's dance floors. The Dune Beat Disco, a mobile disco started by *What's On*, kept it flowing at events and parties with hits by Gloria Gaynor, the Bee Gees, Boney M., and the Village People. The DJs also played the punk-rock numbers dominating the UK charts at the time; but, according to *What's On* (June 1979), "Everyone stops dancing as soon as they come on ... so we don't even carry them with us anymore."

I get the impression that other discos in the city also kept a similarly dated repertoire. They satisfied a crowd holding on to the music of its dance-hall days back home. Don't we all jump to our feet when we hear a song we once loved dancing to? I also imagine the dusty hits were a way to find common ground, to share memories of pop culture with new friends, and to create new memories in spaces of familiarity and comfort. Nevertheless, people eventually wanted new ways to party. This probably explains the emergence of RamRock. In June 1982, Palmotel organized a "Woodstock-style music festival" featuring local bands and musicians. RamRock, because it took place during Ramadan, was an offer for the non-fasting crowd to party during that month, something I am certain would not pass today.

The parties were not limited to just hotels. Sharjah had its share of desert disco as well:

"The idea is to avoid hotels and to choose venues, clubhouses, or open areas to 'boldly go where no roadshow has gone before.'"
What's On (December 1981)

We must also remember that it wasn't just Western customers dancing to Western music in these hotels. One hotel would host a club with a live Filipino band and another with an Egyptian belly dancer or disco music. The adverts of the time convey a wide range of music and entertainment cultures, reflecting the multinationalism of these venues' patrons. Local, Arabic-language newspapers also promoted discos, cabarets, and live acts which makes me think: the population may have been less fragmented compared to today.

In 1984, Sharjah's hotels faced a changing market, and even *What's On* reported on the economic downturn in the September issue of that year:

"Where once the area was flooded with businessmen and entrepreneurs, and later, European package-holiday makers, the world recession has affected Sharjah the same as it has everywhere else. The result is a diminishing market."
What's On, September 1984

By October 1985, the government of Sharjah banned the sale of alcohol and introduced restricted regulations for live acts, greatly impacting nightlife in Sharjah. In the *What's On* directory, the list of clubs in Sharjah became shorter and shorter, until there were hardly any at all. Sharjah's alcohol ban remains in effect today, but there are several dedicated music venues, museums, and art spaces, all playing a role in gathering local communities for a shared experience and playing live music on many occasions. Who knows, maybe the clubs will soon follow, and we can once again dance to "Be My Lover" by La Bouche, just a few years too late.

04

05

06

Images:

01. The Fantasy Supper Night Club, Palmotel, advertisement, December 1982. Images: Motivate Media Group.
02. Shams Al Moulouk, Hotel Meridien Sharjah, advertisement, February 1981.
03. Al Matador, Andalus Hotel, advertisement, November 1981.
04. The Cottage, Novotel, advertisement, March 1981.
05. Coins Disco, Palmotel, advertisement, December 1979.
06. Hotel Nova, advertisement, November 1984.

مسموح...وممنوع

● هذه صورة من اعلان بالحجم الكبير نشر بجريدة الفجر يوم الخميس ١٤/٦/١٩٧٩م العدد ٤٧٥ وهذا الاعلان كما جاء فيه فعلا « الجديد الفريد من نوعه في الامارات » فهو يدعو افراد هذا المجتمع المسلم بكل جرأة وبهذا الشكل السافر إلى قضاء ليلة من ليالي الجمعة في سهرة حتى الصباح مع كأس الانتاج بالمجان بشرط اصطحاب النساء !

وكان الاعلان حريصا على اظهار اللباس الوطني في المرقص والبار بقصد جذب الشباب للفساد .. وفي الوقت الذي تمنع احدى الامارات الخمور يعلن عن دعوة مفتوحة لشربها في امارة أخرى وبالمجان . فيا له من تناقض .

عبد الله احمد
الشارقة

07

07.

Translation
Above: Palace Hotel welcomes you to the opening of Disco 21, a new, one-of-a-kind venue in the UAE. Thursday, June 14, 1979, 9:00 p.m.–3:00 a.m. Open invitation, free drink included (only couples allowed).

Below: Allowed and Forbidden
This is an image of a large advertisement published in *Al Fajr* newspaper, Issue 475, on Friday, June 14, 1979. As advertised, the "new, one-of-a-kind venue in the UAE" is brazenly and openly inviting members of this Muslim community to spend the night before Friday at an all-night party by offering a free drink, provided they are accompanied by women!

The advertisement intentionally showed revelers in traditional Emirati attire at the disco and bar with the aim of attracting youth to sin; and while one of the emirates bans alcohol, it advertises an open invitation to drink free alcohol in another emirate. Oh, the contradictions!
—Abdullah Ahmad, Sharjah
(*Al Azmenah Al Arabiya*, Issue No. 18, July 4–10, 1979)

Long before newspapers were refereeing online comments and social media tags, there was the old-fashioned letter to the editor. A reader of Sharjah-based magazine *Al Azmenah*, Abdullah Ahmad, wrote the above letter about an advertisement he encountered in Abu Dhabi–based *Al Fajr* newspaper, expressing the disgruntlement shared at the time by other religiously and culturally conservative readers. What made this ad all the more offensive to Ahmad was that a man photographed on the dance floor was wearing a *kandoora*, traditional Emirati attire for men and also a signifier of an Arab Muslim. Beyond the single photo, the reader points out the contradictory nature of alcohol's easy availability in one emirate versus another. Ease of access tempted "the youth to sin." The angry letter reveals sentiments of the everyday man or woman in UAE society and evinces a freedom of expression, articulated in print in the local papers, that we no longer see today. Letters like this one likely helped bring about stricter rules for advertising alcohol in UAE media and the occasional "No National Dress" sign seen outside bars and nightclubs.

Current UAE advertising media regulation prohibits the promotion of "alcoholic beverages, narcotic substances, tobacco, smoking, or any related goods and services." Today, Arabic-language press stays clear of the topic altogether. English-language outlets imply alcohol with words like *house beverages*, *grapes*, and *bubbles*. Doublespeak. —H. M. Image: Al Azmenah Al Arabiya.

01

Hotel Meridien Sharjah

Architect
Henri Colboc & Partners

Contractors
Al Masaood Engineering & Contracting Co. (METCO)

Client
Mohammad bin Masaood & Sons

Completed
1978

Status
Existing

Along with a large French expatriate community, the 1970s brought a significant number of French development proposals to Sharjah, including the Hotel Meridien Sharjah, a tourism development project associated with the Air France/ Le Méridien chain of hotels. The 200-room hotel opened on May 24, 1978, one of the early marquee international hotels intended to promote the city as a tourism capital. The hotel's ideal patrons were businessmen in search of seaside luxury without luxury prices. The $10-million hotel was built in Sharjah's Al Khan district, a village assimilated into Sharjah and, with a string of hotels before the Meridien, set to become Sharjah's attempt at a beachfront tourism district.

Unfortunately, the opening coincided with "a slackening of world demand for oil" and therefore also a decline in the global travels of mid-market businessmen. In its first couple of months, the hotel suffered through a phase of 25% occupancy, causing management to cut about two hundred staff positions. "There are too many hotels," the hotel's French manager complained to the *Financial Times*.

The Abu Dhabi–based client commissioned Henri Colboc to design the hotel after his firm had completed Abu Dhabi's iconic Zayed Sports City Stadium in 1975. The French architect created a playful curved floor plan for the hotel in Sharjah. The guest rooms' fenestration was recessed behind balconies—a design decision, according to the architect, meant to achieve two goals: privacy and shading for the interiors. Inside, venues adopted distinctive themes to attract clientele, like the plush red decor of the restaurant La Belle Epoque, which was outfitted with Parisian street lighting to suggest a "French way of life." Other dining rooms and lounges, like Al Khaimah and L'Aquarium, presented staged versions of Arabian and aquatic life, not only for the sparse tourists but also for residents of Abu Dhabi and Dubai lured to spend weekends in Sharjah's comfort.

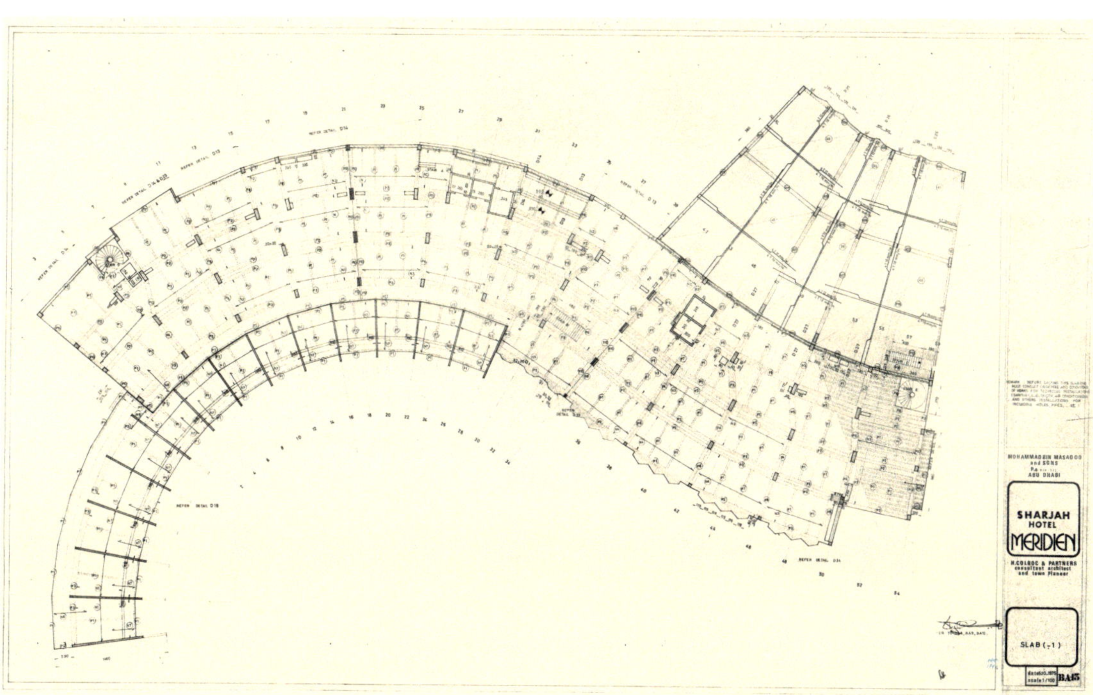

02

03

01. Aerial photograph of beachside frontage, late 1970s. H. Brey, Peichär.
02. Lower-level plan for casting floor slabs, H. Colboc & Partners, October 5, 1975. Henri Colboc & Partners, courtesy of the Grand Hotel.
03. "Façade Coté Mer," H. Colboc & Partners, July 1975. Henri Colboc & Partners, courtesy of the Grand Hotel.

MOHAMMAD BIN MASAOOD
and SONS
PO Box 322
ABU DHABI
SHARJAH
HOTEL
MERIDIEN
H. COLBOC & PARTNERS
CONSULTANT ARCHITECT
AND TOWN PLANNER
FAÇADE
COTÉ MER
AD
5009
DATE JUILLET 75
SCALE 1/400
B
402

Sharjah's hotel service workers participate in a waiters' race, balancing water bottles and glasses on Beck's service trays on their way to the finish line. Hotel clubs, cocktail bars, and restaurants offered a pastiche of international themes, but the servers were predominantly South Asian. By the early 1980s, Al Khan's beachside road was the UAE's definitive beach strip. On the right, Beach Hotel, Hotel Meridien, and Carlton Hotel. On the left, Summer Land Motel, designed by Lebanese engineer Gabriel Matta, early 1970s. Photograph, early 1980s. Khaleej Times Archives.

Crush
BECK'S BIER

01

Alia Al Sabi

AN UNRELENTING LENS: SOCIAL ENGAGEMENT AS JOURNALISM IN *AL AZMENAH AL ARABIYA*

The year is 1979, eight years after Sharjah's incorporation into the United Arab Emirates. The newly formed country is undergoing expansive efforts to unify the seven emirates under a single federal government. A small independent magazine out of Sharjah runs an in-depth report about Sharjah Radio and the consequences of its merger, one year prior, with its Abu Dhabi counterpart. The article begins with a quick summary of the station's state of affairs: Sharjah Radio officially opened in October 1972 and grew to employ a team of 62 people, including 26 Emiratis. By 1981, just two years after the merger, there were only 27 employees with little to do beyond witnessing the station's pre-merger progress quickly dissipate, its momentum—of training local talent, broadcasting to wide networks across the globe, and building a content library of 30,000 tapes—lost. Along with deteriorating, abandoned equipment and unequal distribution of funding, the grievances are real. The tensions are evident; the voices recorded.[1]

The reporting unearths deep frustrations with the transformations taking place at the station. The merger entailed a complete transfer of human resources and technology from the Sharjah station to Abu Dhabi, with Sharjah Radio acting as a support base dedicated to amplifying the broadcasting and production facilities of the capital station. The report's tone is inquisitive, curious; the content reveals the veritable birthing pains of a union and the resulting effects on an institution intended to serve its people. One passage is particularly striking: "The last work of local drama presented on Sharjah Radio was *Candle on the Way*....The station's production facility was then converted into a church by order of Sheikh Sultan Al Qasimi. The merger took place on January 4, 1978, at 5:40 p.m., the last presenter on shift was Ahmad Abd El Razzaq, and the last technician in the technical department was Muhammad Mathkour. The station concluded its programming with the voice of presenter Abdel Wahhab Qataya, of the successful literary program *Souk Okaz*, which he now presents on Abu Dhabi Radio." And just like that, it was the end of an era.

A thoroughly investigative lens that serves to trace the outlines of change forming in the sand, *Al Azmenah Al Arabiya* (Arab Times) took on the role of the active observer, concerned about the affairs of the society in which it was created. In 1979, *Al Azmenah*'s Emirati founders Abdullah Ali Al Sharhan and brothers Muhammad and Ghanem Ghubash mobilized writers, thinkers, artists, poets, and local residents to participate in reflecting on and engaging with the epic transformations defining their lives.[2] Asking questions that needed to be asked, pursuing answers to local issues looming without any resolution on the horizon, bearing witness to marginalized communities in the northern emirates who felt left behind by the oil boom, *Al Azmenah* can be read today as a historical document that holds within its pages many issues still existing in the Emirati landscape today. These include citizenship, foreign labor, identity and values, development and preservation of tradition, the social ideals at stake, the massive disparity in the ratio of citizens to expats in the population, and what this means for the local minority population.

Today, those with an interest in understanding the evolution of the region's cities and societies, searching beyond officially sanctioned sources, can gain significant insight from *Al Azmenah*'s groundbreaking coverage. *Al Azmenah*'s lens captured the landscape's diversity: from interviews with tailors and barbers to political analysis of imperialist forces at play in the region, to an array of cultural criticism seeking to implore local artists and theater actors to dig deeper. The voices in the magazine are wide and varied: there are thinkers assessing the state of intellectual life in the UAE and the ramifications of oil discoveries; there are laborers attesting to the hardships of life and the difficulty of keeping up with the increasing expenses that accompany efforts to modernize; there is talk of unions and protests, with responses from the leadership; and there is a direct and visible line of inquiry that demands answers from silent or apathetic officials.

As a historical document, *Al Azmenah* is a blueprint for the state of things today—how was space transformed and used? How did people inhabit cities and villages as active agents and subjects of transformation? What remains of the old ways, and how might they shed light on things today? Countless references to various sites in Sharjah and other cities, and their outskirts, give us an idea of just how much has changed over the past thirty or forty years, not only in terms of physical change and urban development, but also in terms of the discourse around this change and how people inhabited it.

Reading old issues of *Al Azmenah* is fascinating, not because the reporting is unusual but because it is matter-of-fact. Take, for example, an article published in the December 5, 1979, issue, which documents a local debate on the evolution of traditional coffeehouses. Titled "The 'Gahwa' Enlivens Culture and Gathers Writers and Poets ... If Not for Wasted Time," the piece begins with an overview of Sharjah's erstwhile traditional coffeehouses:

> Traditional coffeehouses were meeting points for community leaders and fishermen—places where conversations took place, local issues were raised, and scores were settled between dhow captains and sailors.

The article then presents more contemporary local coffeehouses, in particular the popular *gahwa shaabiya* (a local coffeeshop) on Sharjah's Khalid Lagoon. A handful of frequent patrons provide us with a glimpse of how this social space has evolved from "a small storefront made of mud (with four big chairs, two *gadu*, a large teapot, and a container for washing the tea glasses)" into a bigger coffeehouse in a more central, touristy part of town, though still made of palm fronds.[3] The expansion of the centrally located coffeehouse, the provision of additional seating and other amenities, and the expanded food and drink menu attracted a broader range of patrons, with various and sundry ways of using the coffeehouse as a social space. To some, it was a community meeting

02

point; to others, perhaps the younger generation, simply a place to pass time.

What's really striking about this article are the photographs accompanying the piece. They give a glimpse of a world now almost entirely replaced by modern state building projects. This magazine feature on the evolution of traditional cafes, published four decades ago, evokes dormant memories of place. Looking at the black-and-white photographs from 1979, we see scenes from a local gahwa depicting everyday life: serving food, drink, and gadu; young men playing dominoes; an old record player setting the mood. The images show the modest aesthetics of the place and a slice of its all-male demographic—little boys, young men from different ethnic backgrounds (including a coffee server of African descent), and the older coffeeshop owner, who also doubles as the accountant.

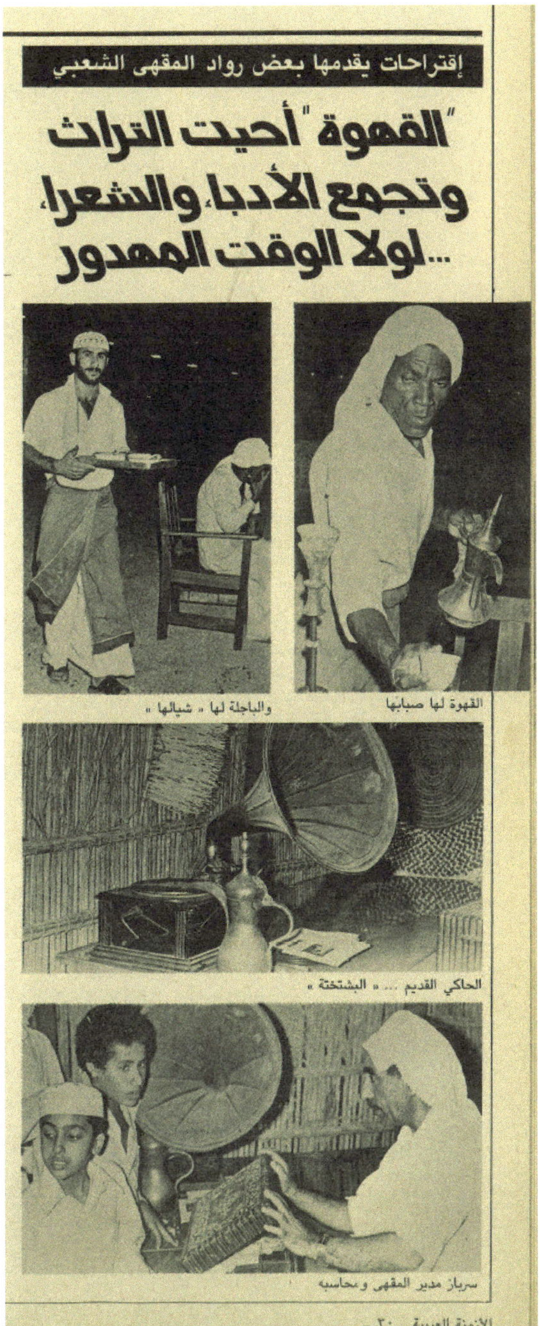

إقتراحات يقدمها بعض رواد المقهى الشعبي

"القهوة" أحيت التراث وتجمع الأدباء والشعراء لولا الوقت المهدور...

القهوة لها صبابها

والباجلة لها « شيالها »

الحاكي القديم ... « البشتختة »

سرباز مدير المقهى ومحاسبه

الأزمنة العربية – ٣٠ –

03

The various observations throughout the report capture how coffeehouses were being reshaped more as places of leisure than as sites of civic community gatherings, with the coffeeshop in the profile showcased as an example of modernization firmly rooted in culture and tradition. It is easy, however, to sense the undertones of lament about the larger societal changes resulting from the expanding world of the city in the nation: "This place is a rebuttal to the cultural encroachment of Western lifestyles such as nightclubs and the like." The article continues, "The gahwa used to be a meeting point for conversation and debate, but now it is a place for passing time and showing off cars," and—portending future political discussions—"there should be a prayer area, a women's section, and a kabab joint in the coffeeshop." The coffeeshop is also a destination for writers and artists, some of whom suggested installing a bulletin board in the gahwa to announce upcoming lectures and plays for those interested in theater and literature.

As the title indicates, the author suggests that "wasted time" is a direct consequence of the gahwa's changing role in the city. The gahwa owner provides several statistics, including how many patrons frequent the coffeeshop daily and the average number of hours they spend there. His calculations demonstrate the author's point: "300–350 a day, and up to 500 on Fridays and holidays ... spending from 15 minutes to 6 hours sometimes." These numbers show that the gahwa was increasingly a space where people could be idle, where time could slow down as the pace of the city was picking up. Some patrons wished for the coffeehouse to be an ideal communal space, "a place where issues and problems can be discussed, and eventually

الأزمنة العربية
AL-AZMENA AL-ARABIA SOCIAL AND POLITICAL WEEKLY ISSUE No.64-28/5-3/6-1980
اسبوعية ـ سياسية ـ إجتماعية ـ العدد الرابع والستون ـ الاربعاء ٥/٢٨ ـ الثلاثاء ٦/٣ ـ ١٩٨٠
المثقفون ...
إضاءات لواقع الوطن

04

موضوع الغلاف

وفي أم القيوين بقي وحيداً

الجدران عالية والجنود مسلحون

ولكن مدن الأشباح لا توجد سوى في كتب الأطفال

بقلم : غانم عبيد غباش

05

resolved," according to one patron, Sheikh Muhammad Al Qassimi. This desire for a public sphere and citizen engagement, notions often underscored by the magazine's editorial line, clashed with the indolence that threatened Sharjah's intellectual and cultural life as development and so-called "progress" materialized in the increasingly wealthy nation.

"But Ghost Cities Only Exist in Children's Books" is the riveting title of another critical exposé, this one about the unraveling of Umm Al Quwain. Up to 200 families were uprooted as a result of tensions with the emirate's ruling family, details of which remain unexplored in the article. Written by one of *Al Azmenah*'s founding journalists, Ghanem Ghubash, the article chronicles the deteriorating living conditions suffered by these families who sought help and guidance from their community leaders and those of the other emirates. They eventually found refuge in neighboring Sharjah. Later in the article, Ghubash touches upon an issue that soon became central to many future initiatives and conversations within Emirati society, namely modernization's impact on an Emirati population increasingly in the minority. At the time of this article's publication in 1981, Emiratis constituted 25% of the total national population. Using a simple calculation, Ghubash predicted that by 1985 Emiratis would constitute 18% of the population, with a mere 3% annual increase through births compared to a 12% annual increase in the expatriate population. Ghubash raises this issue as a way to address the imminent repercussions of urban displacement. "Ghost cities" refers to what could happen if Umm Al Quwain residents continue to migrate to Sharjah and the UAE's other commercial centers, leaving behind an urban void gradually filled with an influx of expats. Ghubash concludes the article with a question:

> What kind of relationship will form between [Umm Al Quwain] and the federation, and between Emirati society and this "alternative society"? These are serious questions ... and while we wait for a response, it would be good to remember the lands of the Apache, Cheyenne, and Iroquois. These are some of the Native American tribes that only 200 years ago formed nations that inhabited the North American continent ... and they have become extinct, with tribal leaders and figures existing only in some history books and Westerns.

Today, Emiratis make up less than 12% of the total UAE population; and less than a decade after the union, this was already a pressing concern.

... تركوها وراءهم والمرارة بعض الزاد

وليست وحدة ، وطالما أن لكل امارة حكومتها المحلية وحدودها الاقليمية وبما أن ما جرى في الآونة الأخيرة وصلت به الأمور حتى الى حد تقليص هذه العلاقة الاتحادية ، مما جعل مظلة الاتحاد تنكمش لتتحول بدورها إلى الامارة الثامنة التي يقتصر الاعتراف بحدودها على سجلات هيئة الأمم المتحدة والجامعة العربية لذلك لابد من قطع حديث الانسان وحوار الذكريات لنطرح القضية على صعيد قد يكون أقل دفئا ولكنه يجسد الواقع كما تريده القيادة السياسية .

نستنتج من أكثر من احصاء حول نسبة المواطنين في دولة الامارات ككل ، ان هذه النسبة كانت تصل حتى وقت قريب الى حوالي ٢٥ بالمئة من المجموع الكلي للسكان ، وهذه النسبة هي أقل بمرات مما كانت عليه قبل سنوات ، وسوف تكون أقل بمرات ايضا مما ستكون عليه بعد سنوات ، وحتى لا نضيع في متاهات الأرقام نأخذ بأبسط أنواع المنطق ، وهذا النوع البسيط يقول أن النسبة الطبيعية لتزايد المواطنين سنويا هي في حدود ٣ بالمئة بينما يتزايد عدد السكان الآخرين حوالي ١٢ بالمئة ، وهذا يعني أننا لن نصل العام ١٩٨٥ إلا وتبلغ نسبة المواطنين الى باقي السكان حوالي ١٨ بالمئة فقط ، وهذه النسبة هي مشكلة بحد ذاتها ، وربما كان باستطاعة المواطن أن يتفاءل بطرح الحلول لها ، إلا أن هذه الحلول ترتبط بقرارات سياسية تنبثق عن دراسة علمية واعية ، للوضع الاقتصادي والاجتماعي في الدولة الواحدة ، وهذه القرارات لابد أن تصدر عن قيادة سياسية واحدة ، تملك شرعية الحسم في تنفيذ ما يصدر عنها من قرارات في جميع انحاء الدولة .

ولكن لأن واقعنا الحالي يختلف عن مفهوم الدولة الموحدة ، وبالتالي فان تلك الحلول العلمية الشاملة لا تنسجم مع واقع التجزئة ، فلا بد إذن ، في هذه الحال ، من وضع تلك الحلول ، ولو مؤقتا ، على الرف ، لنناقش الأمور على طبيعتها ، فوق أرض الواقع الراهن .

مدن الأشباح اسطورة

ومن هنا نحاول أن نناقش ما جرى في أم القيوين مؤخرا على ضوء هجرة بعض المواطنين مع عائلاتهم منها .

إن جميع الأرقام والنسب الواردة سابقا ، تصبح منذ النظرة الأولى لاغية ، فهذه النسب والأرقام تتعامل مع أوضاع محسوبة رغم انها غير طبيعية ، وتبنى عليها النتائج العلمية ، ولكن ما جرى في أم القيوين يمثل استثناء حتى لتلك الأوضاع غير الطبيعية ، فهجرة عدد من المواطنين ، تمثل من ناحية ، سابقة ، مرشحة إذا لم تبتر اسبابها للاستمرار ، وهي من ناحية ثانية تمثل دعوة سافرة لمزيد من الوافدين .

بكلمات أخرى ، ان هجرة أولئك الأهالي من بلدهم بدأت بعشرة أفراد ، ولكنها في خلال ٣ أسابيع فقط ارتفعت لتصل الى ٢٠٠ عائلة ، وهذه العائلات ، كحل مؤقت استقرت في الشارقة . ان عدم تقديم حل جذري لمشكلة هذه العائلات المهاجرة أدى الى تزايد عددها وترك الباب مفتوحا أمام من تبقى كي يحمل أسرته وأمتعته ويرحل ... مما يعني ان يوما قد يأتي تتحول معه أم القيوين الى مدينة مهجورة تسكنها الأشباح .

ولكن مدن الأشباح أسطورة لم تعد موجودة سوى في كتب الأطفال ، لأن قوانين الواقع تقول أنه حتى في المدن التي يضربها الوباء ويعصف بكل ما فيها من أحياء ، تعود الحياة لتنبض فيها من جديد ، حيث يتوافد اليها قادمون جدد ، يبدأون فيها حياتهم .

وهؤلاء القادمون سيحلوا مكان المواطنين في أم القيوين ، ولن يكونوا في حال من الأحوال ، من أبناء الامارات ، بل من الآسيويين الوافدين وأمامنا اكثر من نموذج صارخ ، فمنطقة مصفح في أبوظبي ، ومنطقة الكرتون في دبي ، لم يكن فيهما الى سنوات خلت أي بناء ، كانت منطقة مصفح خالية ، ومثلها منطقة الكرتون ، ولكن الأبنية قامت ، وبدأت مجتمعات صغيرة تتشكل وهي اذا استمرت على هذه الوتيرة من النمو ، فقد تتحول قريبا الى مدن كاملة .

... هذا في المناطق الخالية ، فكيف يكون الحال في مدينة قائمه ولكنها خالية من السكان ؟

الجواب مخيف ، فالمجتمع البديل الذي سيأخذ مكان المجتمع الأصيل سيتكلم لغة تختلف عن اللغة التي يتكلمها سكان باقي الامارات ولعل بعضهم يجد في هذا الاختلاف الحل المنشود ، بعد أن عجزت اللغة الواحدة عن الحيلولة دون افتراق العشيرة عن شيخها ، وهذا المجتمع البديل لأنه غريب وطارىء ، ولم تأكل الصخور والأصداف من لحمه الحي ، فانه على المدى القريب ، لن يشعر بحقه في جني ثمار لم يزرعها .

وأمام هذه الصورة لابد أن نتساءل : أي نوع من العلاقة سيقوم بين هذه الامارة ودولة الاتحاد وبين مجتمع الامارات وهذا « المجتمع البديل » ؟

وهي أسئلة جادة ، برغم انها تكاد تبلغ حد السخرية السوداء ... وبانتظار أن تجد أجوبتها لا بأس من التذكير بأن أرض الأباش وأرض الشايين وأرض الأوواكوا : أسماء لشعوب من الهنود الحمر كانوا قبل ٢٠٠ عام يشكلون دولا تغطي القارة الأميركية الشمالية ... وقد انقرضوا ، ولم يبق منهم شيخ ولا عشيري .. إلا في بعض كتب التاريخ .. وأفلام رعاة البقر ●

من الدستور

مادة (٦) : شعب الاتحاد شعب واحد ، وهو جزء من الأمة العربية .

مادة (١٠) : أهداف الاتحاد ... وحماية حقوق وحريات شعب الاتحاد وتحقيق التعاون الوثيق فيما بين إماراته لصالحها المشترك من أجل هذه الأغراض . ومن أجل ازدهارها وتقدمها في كافة المجالات وتوفير الحياة الأفضل لجميع المواطنين .

مادة (١٤) : المساواة ، والعدالة الاجتماعية ، وتوفير الأمن والطمأنينة ، وتكافؤ الفرص لجميع المواطنين من دعامات المجتمع ، والتعاضد والتراحم صلة وثقى بينهم .

مادة (٢٥) جميع الأفراد لدى القانون سواء ، ولا تمييز بين مواطني الاتحاد بسبب الأصل أو الموطن أو العقيدة الدينية أو المركز الاجتماعي .

This article debunks the popular notion that the demographic explosion in the UAE only began in the mid-2000s, when the population doubled in size from 4.1 million in 2005 to 8.3 million in 2010, with less than one million Emiratis in the populace.

What is compelling about Ghubash's concluding statement is the comparison he draws between post-union Emiratis and the indigenous communities of North America, who, although clearly not eradicated to the degree implied, indeed underwent genocidal ethnic cleansing at the hands of European settlers and were chosen to illustrate a cautionary tale in light of the influx of foreigners to the UAE and the subsequent erasure of local identity and culture resulting from this demographic imbalance. In drawing this drastic comparison, the Sharjah magazine offers insight into the intellectual discourse of the late seventies, revealing a sense of nativism heightened by dramatic demographic changes. The early questions about the fate of local residents amid a booming expatriate population are laced with notions of indigeneity and authenticity.

There are other instances in the magazine where local issues are presented in the context of global struggles. An investigative report titled "No... to the Dishdasha, No... to Arabs" documents the case of a private club along Dubai's Jumeirah Beach that was established in 1970.[4] The report opens with a description of scenes at the club's entrance, manned by an Indian employee. The article recounts how Arabs and Emirati nationals were barred from entering the facility on the grounds that the club is for members only and that government mandate prohibited the entry of nationals into such clubs.

The report's investigative methodology is significant in that it relies on witness reports that test the exclusionary practices firsthand. The journalists Kawthar Muqabel and Abdul Hamid Ahmad accompanied a British woman, an Arab woman, and an Emirati man to four different clubs in Sharjah and Dubai to witness how each person was received at each venue.[5] The results were consistent across the board: the British woman was welcomed with few questions asked, the Arab woman was informed that she needed to apply for membership and wait for approval, and the Emirati was denied any option to facilitate his entry. *Al Azmenah* concludes the report with a question to both Sharjah's and Dubai's municipalities: were these clubs licensed to impose discriminatory policies? The answer they received was one of unanimous denial, that no such laws would allow this.

07

The report's tone is critical of the perceived "white man's privilege"—typified by exclusive access to entertainment facilities—and by extension of the Western imperialism ravaging the Arab world on the macro scale. The following excerpt in the report deserves pause:

> UAE locals are the negroes of the American South, barred entry to the white man's country club, their children undeserving of its special film programs, and their eyes unable to even glimpse its swings and slides. The sound of their local laughter might spoil the purity of this European atmosphere.

Tying the segregation implemented in local spaces in the UAE with American discrimination against the black populace in the US is a powerful example of the magazine's literary and journalistic efforts. The writer positions the subject matter within geographies and populations that exist on the periphery of contemporary global capitalism and simultaneously as part of the wider anti-imperial movements sprouting throughout the region. This comparison also sheds light on how Emiratis may have perceived themselves as being, not unlike Native Americans, in a sea of foreigners, with the particular experience of exclusion from European establishments, undergoing a local racial discrimination reflective of colonial history.

In a 2005 interview with the Dubai-based daily newspaper *Al Bayan*, Muhammad Ghubash discusses the intellectual currents defining the era in which *Al Azmenah* emerged: Baathism, Nasserism, Sayyid Qutb's brand of Islamism of the 1960s, and other nationalist projects; along with Marxist thought as adopted by movements in the Global South in the 1970s.[6] The magazine's founders identified with those social movements from within a region plagued by poverty and corruption. The political disposition of the magazine was squarely anti-colonial and leftist in tone and substance, echoing the Arab world's zeitgeist at the time and the anti-imperialist waves sweeping through the region.

Despite *Al Azmenah*'s ideological bend, the magazine's greatest contribution arguably lies in its role as a critical mirror reflecting the seismic shifts of nation formation and how these changes were impacting those on the margins, whose social and economic status left them unprepared for the deep transformations around them. Through its hard-hitting reporting on these cracks in a newly formed reality, *Al Azmenah* urged people to ask more critical questions and to take stock of how their lives were being affected and transformed, almost overnight. In its ethos, the magazine encouraged active participation in nation building, promoting ideas of accountability, duty, the fulfillment of promises, and an inclusive society that bears witness to the experiences of those on the fringes.

The stories of the early union days are rich and complicated. Marked with sacrifice, they are not without their tales of woe. The gradual evacuation of Sharjah Radio being one such tale of the price that unity demands, its fate ringing premonition bells of what was yet to come. *Al Azmenah*'s sharp, analytical tone and its examination of the federal experience eventually brought on its demise, with orders from the UAE Ministry of Information closing it down.[7] Despite numerous efforts to continue publishing from outside the UAE, the magazine eventually faded, ending with it an important chapter in the UAE and for Sharjah's intellectual and political circles. *Al Azmenah Al Arabiya* was published weekly in Sharjah between March 1979 and October 1981. Some 140 issues are kept today at the National Archives in Abu Dhabi, a testament to their role in local history and a ready reservoir for the curious.

Notes:

1. All translations from the Arabic are provided by the author.
2. Muhammad Obaid Ghubash (b. 1952, Dubai) earned a PhD in philosophy of political science from University of Wales, UK, and was assistant professor of political science at UAE University from 1994 until 2004. Ghanem Ghubash (1946–89, Dubai) returned to Dubai just prior to federation after travels in India. He was deputy director of Dubai's labor department and was later appointed associate director of labor affairs at the UAE Ministry of Labor. His column in *Al Azmenah Al Arabiya*, under the pen name Ballouty," offered satirical accounts about local issues written in colloquial Arabic. Abdullah Ali Al Sharhan (b 1940, Ras Al Khaimah) was a member of the Federal National Council and the licensing founder of the magazine. His fierce pen found resonance among local readership.
3. *Gadu* is an Emirati term for shisha or hookah.
4. The dishdasha is a white robe traditionally worn by men in the Gulf.
5. Abdel Hamid Ahmad is currently editor in chief at the Dubai-based daily *Gulf News*.
6. Muhammad Ghubash, interviewed by Muhammad Al Ansari, *Al Bayan*, October 7, 2005, https://www.albayan.ae/sports/2005-10-07-1.983564.
7. In 1983, the magazine was briefly published in London, Cyprus, and finally Beirut until 1996.

الأزمنة العربية

أسبوعية ـ سياسية ـ إجتماعية ـ العدد الواحد والثمانون ـ الأربعاء ٩/٢٤ ـ الثلاثاء ٩/٣٠ ـ ١٩٨٠

AL-AZMENA AL-ARABIA SOCIAL AND POLITICAL WEEKLY ISSUE No. 81-24/9-30/9-1980

ممنوع من التداول
مع تحيات إدارة الرقابة

08

Images:

01. "No to Arabs," Issue 13, May 30–June 5, 1979. The issue features an article on discriminating practices at private beach clubs in the UAE. Permission to reprint pages from various issues provided by Mohammed Obaid Ghubash.
02. "Sharjah Radio and the Consequences of Its Merger with the Capital Station," Issue 37, November 21–27, 1979.
03. "The *Gahwa* Revives Heritage and Gathers Writers and Poets…If Not for Wasted Time," Issue 39, December 5–11, 1979.
04. "Intellectuals: Luminaries of a Nation," Issue 64, May 28–June 3, 1980.
05. "But Ghost Cities Only Exist in Children's Books," Issue 17, June 27–July 3, 1979.
06. "But Ghost Cities Only Exist in Children's Books," Issue 17, June 27–July 3, 1979 (continued).
07. Shades of discrimination in UAE private clubs, "No … to the Dishdasha, No … to Arabs," Issue 13, May 30–June 5, 1979.
08. A mostly vacant cover with text, "Banned from circulation. With regards from the censorship administration," Issue 81, September 24–30, 1980. The weekly *Al Azmenah Al Arabiya*'s critical tone and sharp examination of the federal experience eventually brought about its demise.

مؤسسة الإمارات للاتصالات
EMIRTEL
مؤسسة الامارات للاتصالات ترحب بحضرة صاحب السمو حاكم البلاد المفدى ومعالي وزير المواصلات والضيوف الكرام

Sharjah State Telecommunications Building

According to Cable & Wireless's *Zodiac Magazine*, what follows an oil boom is a "telephone boom."[1] And indeed, the discovery of oil brought a spiked demand for telephone lines to Sharjah.

The British company Cable & Wireless (C&W) secured the contract to oversee the laying of lines in Sharjah and the outer regions of Dhaid and Khor Fakkan. Given a location in the district of Al Qassimiyah, C&W commissioned its own Architectural Services Group to design the new headquarters. As demand continued to increase through the late 1970s, the company needed to construct another office nearby.

While C&W facilities around the world were known for their functional efficiency, officials in Sharjah expected more sophistication and attention to aesthetics. According to Fred Hammond, C&W's chief architect at the time of the initial conceptual design, "Gulf rulers expect you to come up with an artistic design. If they like it, you build it." Sharjah's ruler, Sheikh Sultan bin Muhammad Al Qasimi, did indeed demand revisions after noting some unseemly drain pipes on the front facade. Upon their removal from the drawings, Hammond recalled, the ruler found the design to be "beautiful."

1. *Zodiac Magazine*, Summer 1978.

Architect
Fred W. Hammond, Cable & Wireless

Client
Government of Sharjah

Completed
1974

Status
Existing

Front view of early-phase building during a welcoming ceremony at Sharjah's telecom agency, which eventually became part of the Emirates Telecommunications Corporation, or Emirtel. At the time, the agency employed a logo featuring the dial of a rotary telephone. Sharjah Documentation & Archives Authority.

01

ETPM Building

Design
Fadi Chammas

Consultant
Hussain Mohamed Saleh, Al Arooba Establishment for Design & Supervision

Contractor
Al Nahda Contracting & Trading Company (ALCO)

Proposed
1975

Status
Existing

Having first rented space in the BBME Building on Rolla Square, Société Entrepose G.T.M. pour les Travaux Petroliers Maritimes, or ETPM, opened its prominent offices in Sharjah's Al Layah district in 1976, just as the emirate was becoming home to the UAE's largest French community. The company had begun to build and manage its own facilities and services, including a school and housing for employee families.[1]

In a scenario not uncommon in Sharjah at the time, ETPM's eventual two-story office building resulted from at least two hand-offs in the design process. ETPM's Lebanese business partner and civil engineer Fadi Chammas had originally submitted conceptual drawings to the Iraqi architect Hussain Mohamed Saleh for him to develop into construction drawings. In the end, the Sharjah-based contractor ALCO completed the design work and oversaw the building's construction.

The client had initially requested a smaller, single-story office building before approaching ALCO for a two-story office building with central air conditioning. The final T-shaped floor plan offers straightforward, functional circulation among offices, meeting rooms, and services. The unpretentious exterior design is dominated by repeating full-floor, vertical fins that shade receded windows. The central air conditioning's distribution system required loftier floor heights, making the building more prominent than most two-story buildings at the time.

The building is currently the headquarters for the Sharjah Museums Authority.

1. See p. 231.

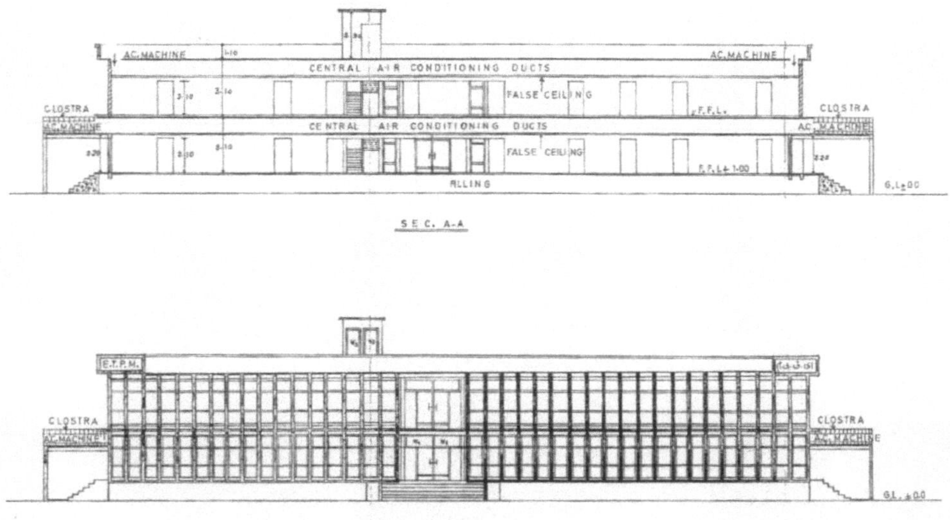

02

01. Ruler of Sharjah Sheikh Sultan bin Muhammad Al Qasimi, Sharjah dignitaries, and ETPM officials attend the building's inauguration, 1976. © Ramesh Shukla, Four Seasons Ramesh Gallery.
02. Section and elevation drawings, as submitted by architect of record Hussain Mohamed Saleh to Sharjah Municipality, July 30, 1974. Hussain Mohamed Saleh, courtesy of Sharjah Municipality.

Elevated Water Tanks

Built at a cost of AED 10 million, or $2.7 million, each, Sharjah's once-famed water towers loomed over residential neighborhoods for three decades. Centered on roundabouts at major road intersections of the Halcrow plan, they were landmarks and guideposts for an expanding city. Employees of the Sharjah Electricity and Water Department referred to the tanks as tulips, with "petals" painted yellow and white. The shape reminded many of similar water towers in Kuwait and of the submergible tanks made for Dubai's oil storage.

In fact, the same company, Chicago Bridge & Iron Company, that supplied Dubai's oil storage tanks also provided this method of storing Sharjah's water, referred to in Arabic as a *khazzan*. The design for the water towers was ultimately realized in Sharjah between 1982 and 1985 in the districts of Ezra, Rifa'a, and Qadisiya. One would replace a more rudimentary storage tank in Al Layah. Reaching between 40 and 50 meters high, the tanks stored two million liters of water for daily use in the surrounding districts. In 2012, the final water tower was taken down in Al Rifa'a, much to the chagrin of residents. Two years later, a twelve-minute film, *Hidden Songs from the Past*, chronicled the dismantling and residents'reactions. It debuted at the Abu Dhabi Film Festival.

Engineering Consultant
Halcrow International Partnership

Contractor
Chicago Bridge & Iron Company

Client
Sharjah Electricity & Water Department

Completed
1982–1985

Status
Dismantled, 2012

01. Construction of one of four water towers, Al Layah district. Dar Al Khaleej Printing & Publishing.
02. Sectional elevations and plans for an "elevated water tank," Halcrow International Partnership, May 1984. SEWA.

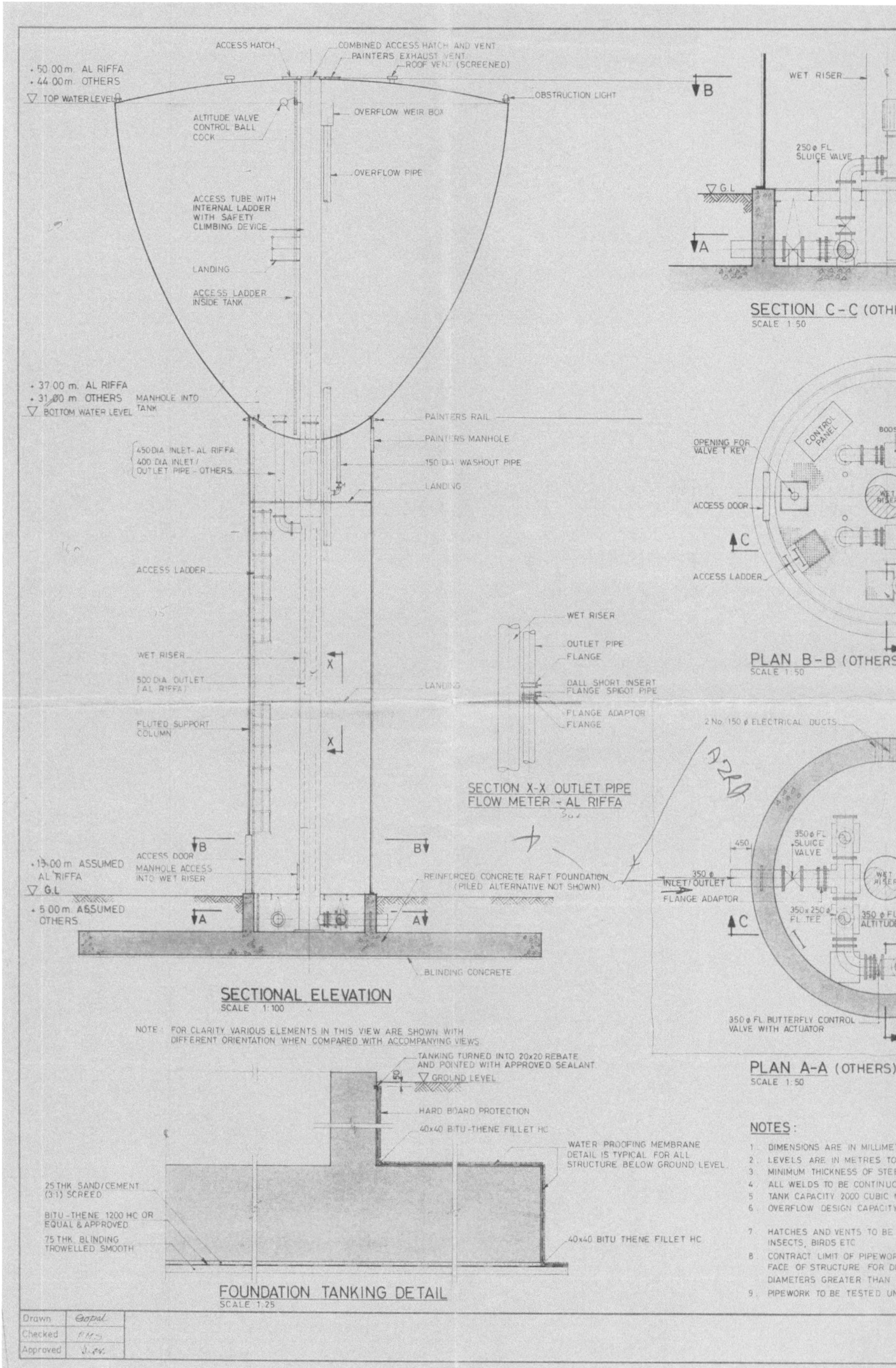
ACCESS HATCH
COMBINED ACCESS HATCH AND VENT
PAINTERS EXHAUST VENT
ROOF VENT (SCREENED)
+ 50.00 m. AL RIFFA
+ 44.00 m. OTHERS
TOP WATER LEVEL
OBSTRUCTION LIGHT
ALTITUDE VALVE CONTROL BALL COCK
OVERFLOW WEIR BOX
OVERFLOW PIPE
ACCESS TUBE WITH INTERNAL LADDER WITH SAFETY CLIMBING DEVICE
LANDING
ACCESS LADDER INSIDE TANK
+ 37.00 m. AL RIFFA
+ 31.00 m. OTHERS
BOTTOM WATER LEVEL
MANHOLE INTO TANK
PAINTERS RAIL
PAINTERS MANHOLE
450 DIA INLET - AL RIFFA
400 DIA INLET / OUTLET PIPE - OTHERS
150 DIA WASHOUT PIPE
LANDING
ACCESS LADDER
WET RISER
500 DIA OUTLET (AL RIFFA)
LANDING
FLUTED SUPPORT COLUMN
+ 13.00 m. ASSUMED AL RIFFA
G.L
+ 5.00 m. ASSUMED OTHERS
ACCESS DOOR
MANHOLE ACCESS INTO WET RISER
REINFORCED CONCRETE RAFT FOUNDATION (PILED ALTERNATIVE NOT SHOWN)
BLINDING CONCRETE
SECTIONAL ELEVATION
SCALE 1:100
NOTE: FOR CLARITY VARIOUS ELEMENTS IN THIS VIEW ARE SHOWN WITH DIFFERENT ORIENTATION WHEN COMPARED WITH ACCOMPANYING VIEWS
WET RISER
OUTLET PIPE
FLANGE
DALL SHORT INSERT
FLANGE SPIGOT PIPE
FLANGE ADAPTOR
FLANGE
SECTION X-X OUTLET PIPE FLOW METER - AL RIFFA
WET RISER
250 ø FL. SLUICE VALVE
G.L
SECTION C-C (OTHE
SCALE 1:50
CONTROL PANEL
OPENING FOR VALVE T KEY
ACCESS DOOR
ACCESS LADDER
PLAN B-B (OTHERS)
SCALE 1:50
2 No. 150 ø ELECTRICAL DUCTS
350 ø FL SLUICE VALVE
450
350 ø INLET / OUTLET
FLANGE ADAPTOR
WET RISER
350 x 250 ø FL TEE
350 ø FL. ALTITUDE
350 ø FL BUTTERFLY CONTROL VALVE WITH ACTUATOR
PLAN A-A (OTHERS)
SCALE 1:50
TANKING TURNED INTO 20x20 REBATE AND POINTED WITH APPROVED SEALANT
GROUND LEVEL
HARD BOARD PROTECTION
40x40 BITU-THENE FILLET HC
WATER PROOFING MEMBRANE DETAIL IS TYPICAL FOR ALL STRUCTURE BELOW GROUND LEVEL
25 THK. SAND/CEMENT (3:1) SCREED
BITU-THENE 1200 HC OR EQUAL & APPROVED
75 THK. BLINDING TROWELLED SMOOTH
40x40 BITU THENE FILLET HC
FOUNDATION TANKING DETAIL
SCALE 1:25
NOTES:
1. DIMENSIONS ARE IN MILLIMETR
2. LEVELS ARE IN METRES TO
3. MINIMUM THICKNESS OF STEEL
4. ALL WELDS TO BE CONTINUOU
5. TANK CAPACITY 2000 CUBIC ME
6. OVERFLOW DESIGN CAPACITY
7. HATCHES AND VENTS TO BE D INSECTS, BIRDS ETC
8. CONTRACT LIMIT OF PIPEWORK FACE OF STRUCTURE FOR DIA DIAMETERS GREATER THAN 3
9. PIPEWORK TO BE TESTED UND
Drawn Gopal
Checked
Approved

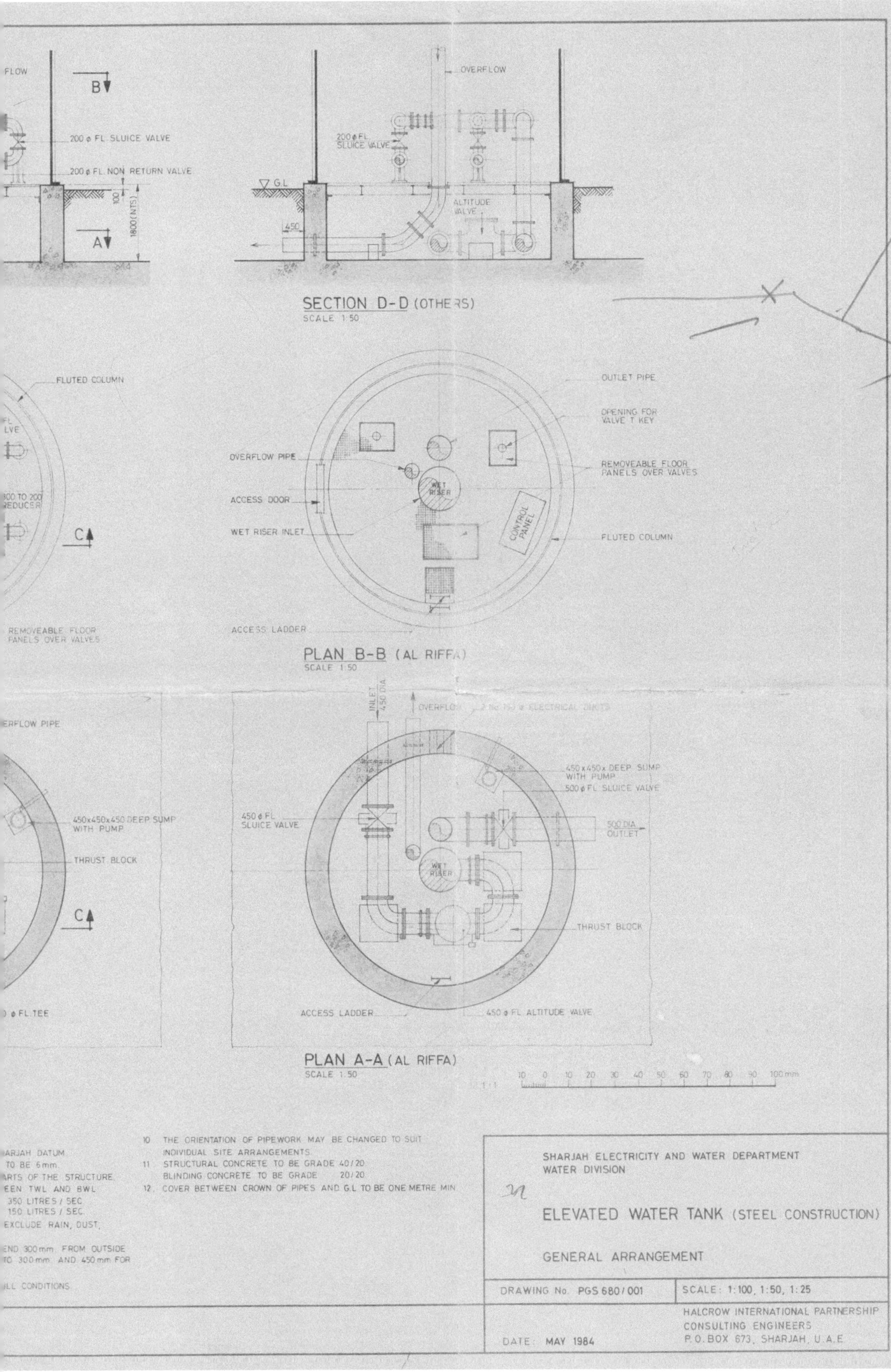
FLOW
B
200 ø FL SLUICE VALVE
200 ø FL NON RETURN VALVE
100
1800 (NTS)
A
OVERFLOW
200 ø FL
SLUICE VALVE
G.L
ALTITUDE
VALVE
450
SECTION D-D (OTHERS)
SCALE 1:50
FLUTED COLUMN
300 TO 200
REDUCER
C
REMOVEABLE FLOOR
PANELS OVER VALVES
OUTLET PIPE
OPENING FOR
VALVE T KEY
OVERFLOW PIPE
ACCESS DOOR
WET RISER INLET
WET
RISER
REMOVEABLE FLOOR
PANELS OVER VALVES
CONTROL
PANEL
FLUTED COLUMN
ACCESS LADDER
PLAN B-B (AL RIFFA)
SCALE 1:50
INLET
450 DIA
OVERFLOW
ERFLOW PIPE
450x450x450 DEEP SUMP
WITH PUMP
THRUST BLOCK
450 ø FL
SLUICE VALVE
450 x 450 x DEEP SUMP
WITH PUMP
500 ø FL SLUICE VALVE
500 DIA
OUTLET
WET
RISER
THRUST BLOCK
ø FL TEE
ACCESS LADDER
450 ø FL ALTITUDE VALVE
PLAN A-A (AL RIFFA)
SCALE 1:50
10 0 10 20 30 40 50 60 70 80 90 100 mm
ARJAH DATUM
TO BE 6mm
ARTS OF THE STRUCTURE
EEN TWL AND BWL
350 LITRES / SEC
150 LITRES / SEC
EXCLUDE RAIN, DUST,
END 300mm FROM OUTSIDE
TO 300mm AND 450mm FOR
ULL CONDITIONS
10 THE ORIENTATION OF PIPEWORK MAY BE CHANGED TO SUIT
INDIVIDUAL SITE ARRANGEMENTS
11 STRUCTURAL CONCRETE TO BE GRADE 40/20
BLINDING CONCRETE TO BE GRADE 20/20
12 COVER BETWEEN CROWN OF PIPES AND G.L TO BE ONE METRE MIN
SHARJAH ELECTRICITY AND WATER DEPARTMENT
WATER DIVISION
ELEVATED WATER TANK (STEEL CONSTRUCTION)
GENERAL ARRANGEMENT
DRAWING No. PGS 680/001
SCALE: 1:100, 1:50, 1:25
DATE: MAY 1984
HALCROW INTERNATIONAL PARTNERSHIP
CONSULTING ENGINEERS
P.O. BOX 673, SHARJAH, U.A.E.

Above: Flyover on Al Wahda Street, as prescribed by a 1969 master plan to supersede the busy roundabout. Al Wahda Street was built as an extension of the Sharjah–Dubai road to deflect traffic from Sharjah's older and denser districts. The precast infrastructure for early flyovers was purchased from Japan. Their construction was contracted to the Japan-based Pacific Consultants Company, which also worked on Al Khan Bridge and the cement factory. Khaleej Times Archives.

Left: Sharjah coastline is transformed into the expectations of a regional corniche, replete with streetlights, landscaping, and walkways. Keeping the wooden ships, or dhows, moored at the water's edge was already considered an act of historical preservation, late 1970s. Background left: Inter-Continental Hotel (p. 313) and Hotel Aladin (p. 407). Khaleej Times Archives.

01

Sharjah Cricket Association Stadium

Text by
Hammad Nasar

For a certain generation of cricket fans from India and Pakistan, the Sharjah Cricket Association Stadium (SCAS) still resounds with the reverberations of *that* six hit more than three decades ago: the Austral-Asia Cup Final, India versus Pakistan, 1986. Chetan Sharma to Javed Miandad. Four runs needed from the last ball. Sharma's attempted yorker is hoisted for six—the perfect climax to a match that cemented Sharjah's entry into world cricket. Part of that perfection was the stadium itself. With a seating capacity of more than 15,000 and an imported turf wicket, SCAS quickly moved beyond its "rolled sand" beginnings and came to hold its own as a ground of international stature.

Its distinctiveness was not conventional. It offered neither a starchitect-designed, dazzling media center nor the standard, telegenic vistas on par with those of St. Lucia, Galle, or Cape Town. What made SCAS singular was that teams from both India and Pakistan—nations often literally and metaphorically at war—felt as if they were playing in front of a home crowd, drawn from the millions of South Asian migrant laborers, themselves feeling their way toward being at home in the UAE. SCAS has since served as a home ground for national cricket teams not only from the UAE but also from Afghanistan and Pakistan, countries where the security situation has required them to play home games abroad. SCAS has thus become a site of belonging, enacted through cricket, for the teams as much as for the audience.

So how does one design a home ground for cricketers without a home?

Money helps—it provides facilities and attracts players. So does geographic proximity to the cricket-mad populations of the South Asian subcontinent. But the magic ingredient is neither a matter of the stadium's construction nor its location. Abdulrahman Bukhatir, the Emirati businessman who was smitten by cricket as a student in Pakistan, anchored Sharjah's cricket field in the love of the game, building it for cricketers rather than for its commercial potential. He inaugurated the stadium in 1981 with exhibition games for the financial benefit of retired cricketers from India and Pakistan.

From these modest beginnings, Sharjah became a fixture in global cricket, and SCAS still holds the world record for the most one-day international games staged. Greater financial incentives and grander stadiums are available elsewhere—in Abu Dhabi since 2004 and in Dubai since 2009. These may have shifted Sharjah's status within the UAE's contemporary cricket infrastructure, but the game's foundations in the UAE were first laid at SCAS.

Architect
Peter Hudson Buckle & Partners

Contractor
Eastern LLC

Client
Abdulrahman Bukhatir

Completed
1981

Status
Existing

03

01. Aerial view along Second Industrial Street, February 1984. © Gulf News, Dubai.
02. Outside public stands, undated. Khalaf Bukhatir.
03. Emirati businessman Abdulrahman Bukhatir on the pitch, undated. Khalaf Bukhatir.
04. Some stadium seating was shaded and cooled by perforated walls and concrete-shell vaults. Khalaf Bukhatir.

Sharjah Sports Club

After completing work on upgrading the Dubai International Airport runways, British firm RMJM, popularly referred to as "Rumjum," opened a Sharjah office under senior engineer Peter Hudson's management. The firm was commissioned to design Sharjah's first sports complex on a large plot of land not too far from the Sharjah Cricket Association Stadium. The $7.4-million complex comprises a football stadium encircled by a 400-meter running track, a sports hall, a 50-meter swimming pool, and a social center. Its standardized components were the project's most important elements: only the stadium, with its concrete "umbrella" roof and precast pattern screens, was given any extra attention in terms of architectural expression. Designed for the local football club and for paying neighborhood residents, the complex stood as a testament to Sharjah's commitment both to entertainment and to rising standards of public health and hygiene.

Fifteen minutes away from RMJM's stadium, another British firm, Brewerton, Guyan & Howland, was commissioned to design a complex for the rival Shaab Club in Sharjah's Al Hazannah neighborhood.

Architect
William Smith, Robert Matthew, Johnson-Marshall & Partners (RMJM)

Contractor
Mothercat LTD

Client
Government of Sharjah

Completed
1977

Status
Existing

Sharjah Sports Club, late 1970s. Henk Snoek / RIBA Collections.

Above: Celebrations, perhaps for a wedding, and traditional *razfa* dance outside Government Square, Sharjah, late 1960s. Images: Mahmood AlSawan.

Left: Funeral parade along Al Arouba Street in honor of deceased Egyptian President Gamal Abdel Nasser, September 1970. Background right: the Arab Bank under construction, in front of the British Bank of the Middle East (see p. 81). Images: Mahmood AlSawan.

01

Inter-Continental Hotel, Sharjah

Even before its Dubai location was completed, Inter-Continental Hotels signed on to build another one twenty kilometers away in Sharjah. With an initial price estimate of AED 50 million, or more than $13.5 million, the Inter-Continental provided Sharjah with what was becoming a staple signifier of technological opulence in the region: a self-contained, air-conditioned environment centered around a lofty indoor atrium. And as with most of the regional atria, this one reenacted a tropical oasis, protected from Sharjah's high temperatures by glass, steel, and thousands of tons of concrete. Inside, water trickled along creeks into ponds, and tropical vegetation blossomed.

US-based The Architects Collaborative (TAC), a firm co-founded by the famous modernist architect Walter Gropius, began work on the resort-style hotel in 1976. Whereas Dubai's Inter-Continental "dazzled" with a sunken lounge and indoor garden, Sharjah's version reached upward and outward, aiming for a biosphere. The final design included a twelve-story, pyramid-shaped atrium defined by two sloping concrete wings of rooms and a cascading glass wall. The building's complex shape necessitated computer calculations to ensure structural stability and maintain the atrium's freedom from columns and bracing. The design team also claimed to have modeled the atrium's thermal movement and ventilation systems to ensure enough daylight for the atrium's tropical plants while keeping the temperature comfortable for guests among fountains and pools.

Rising on two sides of the atrium are twelve floors of 380 guest rooms along single-loaded corridors overlooking the atrium—an architectural feature credited to the American architect John Portman. The hotel's lobby and ground floor housed everything else enticing guests not to leave the property: guest services and administrative offices, restaurants, cafes, shops, bowling alleys, squash courts, and a barber shop. The Inter-Continental was also a popular hangout in the 1980s, drawing patrons beyond just visiting guests to its bowling alleys in particular, which at one point were licensed to serve alcohol. The hotel's banquet halls were the city's most coveted venues for wedding celebrations.

One of Sharjah's most vast and decadent spaces was initially not a success. Even before it opened, Sharjah was suffering from a glut of luxury hotels and the serious debts from having built them. In 1977, just as oil prices led high-end hotel companies to start pulling out of deals in the region, there were nearly thirty hotels with a total of 4,500 guest rooms in Sharjah. It is no surprise, then, that the Inter-Continental's first two years reportedly achieved an occupancy rate of less than 15%. In 1982, in a resuscitative effort, the Kuwaiti investor Mubarak Abdul Aziz Al-Hassawi purchased the hotel, the most prestigious of his investments in Sharjah's hotels, housing, and cinemas.

Architect
Alexander Cvijanovic, Michael Prodanou, The Architects Collaborative

Construction Manager
Bechtel International Corporation

Construction
Conforce Gulf

Client
Mubarak Abdul Aziz Al-Hassawi

Completed
1980

Status
Existing

02

03

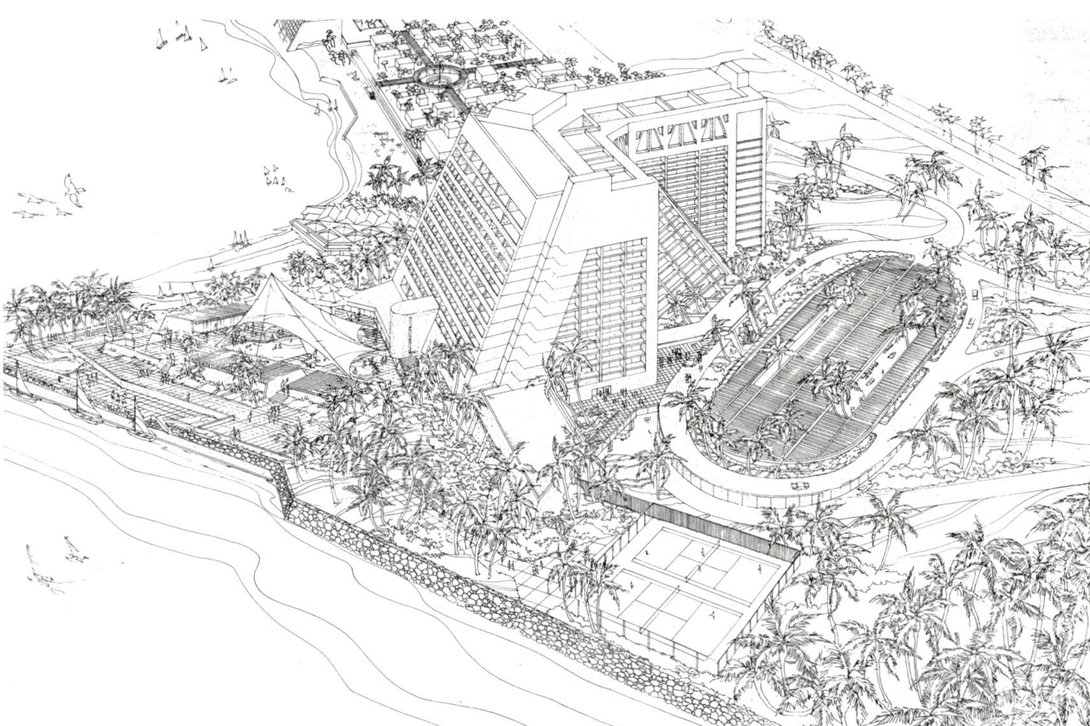

04

05

Inter-Continentalism: The Architects Collaborative in Sharjah

Text by Michael Kubo

The construction of the Inter-Continental Hotel in Sharjah marked the expanding footprint of two US entities that had a heavy hand in the urbanization of Gulf cities after the 1960s: the Inter-Continental Hotel Corporation (IHC), one of the hospitality chains that spearheaded the proliferation of hotels designed by US architects as instruments of US foreign policy during the Cold War; and The Architects Collaborative (TAC), founded in 1945 by eight partners including Walter Gropius and the designers of major cultural and commercial commissions throughout the Gulf by the 1970s.

The Inter-Continental Hotels Corporation (IHC) was established in 1946 as a fully-owned subsidiary of Pan American World Airways. Its growing roster of international hotels charted the expanding map of the airline's travel routes in the decades that followed. Business began in South America, where US President Franklin D. Roosevelt lobbied Pan Am's founder Juan Trippe, the head of the largest air carrier on the continent, to build hotels to boost US-related commerce under the Good Neighbor Policy. By the 1970s, IHC had extended its reach to Asia, Africa, and the Middle East, specializing in building in locations where a luxury hotel in itself would create a commercial and tourist market.

Unlike its main competitors in this era of expansion, the Hilton and Sheraton Hotels, who preferred a leasing business model, IHC typically held an ownership stake in each property it operated abroad. The company often financed projects by securing loans from governmental entities like the Export-Import Bank of the United States (EXIM) and the U.S. Agency for International Development (USAID) alongside lenders with interests in regional development, including the Aga Khan. Following the opening of Hilton hotels in Istanbul (1955) and Cairo (1959), IHC first arrived in the MENA region with the construction of the Phoenicia Inter-Continental in Beirut, designed by Edward Durell Stone and completed in 1961. By 1976, IHC's eleven projects in the Middle East included hotels in Dubai, Abu Dhabi, Al Ain, and Jeddah.

The Architects Collaborative (TAC) was the largest dedicated architecture firm in the US by the time work on the Sharjah hotel began in 1974, a position directly linked to the firm's successes in the Arab Gulf. In 1968, TAC began working in Kuwait, where the firm collaborated with Pan-Arab Consulting Engineers (PACE) as local consultants for as many as thirty projects by TAC in the 1980s. PACE's first two projects in Kuwait, a pair of housing blocks designed by Rifat Chadirji/Iraq Consult, were built for a single client: Kuwaiti developer Mubarak Abdul Aziz Al-Hassawi, who later came to own the Inter-Continental in Sharjah. One of PACE's founding partners, Sabah Al-Rayes, claimed that his firm later designed another project in Sharjah for Al-Hassawi as well.

TAC's design for the Sharjah project ran in parallel to the firm's work on the Abu Dhabi National Library and Cultural Centre (1974–81), its other major building in the Emirates. Alex Cvijanovic, partner in charge of the hotel project, and Michael Prodanou, the job captain, worked on related coastal hotels in Piran, Yugoslavia, such as the Hotel Bernardin (1971–76), and in Sithonia, Greece, including the Porto Carras Resort (1975–79), that also featured long, sloping concrete slabs of guest rooms facing the water.

Construction of the Inter-Continental Hotel, Sharjah, was contracted to Bechtel, the US engineering conglomerate responsible for building the Tapline and other major oil infrastructures across the Middle East (a list that soon included the oil port town of Jubail in Saudi Arabia, master planned by TAC after 1977). According to consulting engineer Wayman C. Wing, at least eight structural schemes in concrete were studied prior to the final design, in part due to the difficulties of accommodating the thermal movement caused by Sharjah's extreme temperature swings between day and night. As realized, the building features two wings of guest rooms oriented perpendicular to each other in plan, each sloping at a structurally optimum sixty-eight degrees in section. Vertical glass curtain walls face toward Sharjah, encasing the hotel's soaring interior atrium, one that amply satisfied the desire for a self-contained, environmentally controlled oasis that would announce Sharjah's presence on an intercontinental stage.

06

07

08

01. Aerial view of Inter-Continental Hotel, Sharjah, 1980s. Kuwait Tower in background, left, see p. 145. Background right: Sultan Bin Ali Al Owais's building, designed by A. Moez & Moh. Hegazy Architects, 1978. Prem Ratnam, Hemlyn Photography Studio.
02. The hotel's banquet hall was a prized venue for weddings in the 1980s and 1990s, 1987. Prem Ratnam, Hemlyn Photography Studio.
03. Documentation of construction progress, late 1970s. Radisson Blu–Sharjah.
04. Aerial perspective, TAC, April 23, 1976. Courtesy of MIT Museum.
05. Concrete work at staging area, late 1970s. Radisson Blu–Sharjah.
06. Inter-Continental Hotel's atrium lobby during installation of palms and succulents to create the interior's oasis theme, circa 1980. Radisson Blu–Sharjah.
07. Construction of the stepped garden and pond terraces on lower level of the atrium lobby, circa 1980. Radisson Blu–Sharjah.
08. Inter-Continental Hotel, under construction, late 1970s. Radisson Blu–Sharjah.
09. Documentation of construction progress, late 1970s. Radisson Blu–Sharjah.

09

A traffic jam along Sharjah's coastal road. Looming in background center is the large, monumental *barjeel*, or wind tower, located in Al Majarrah district before it was demolished. Halcrow's master plans in 1963 and 1969 strove to move traffic and people away from Sharjah's old center, toward ring roads further inland and purpose-built markets with abundant parking. See, for example, the vegetable souk (p. 143). Jim Thomas, courtesy of Nicholas Cornhill.

masafi
مسافي
SHAKER HAMOUD TRADING EST.

Rendering for a hotel and cinema at Al Zahra'a Square, or Clock Tower Roundabout, mid-1970s. In the early 1970s, Sharjah Real Estate commissioned Bombay-based Architectural Consultants to design a hotel for the site. The 1969 master plan had proposed a hotel for the opposite end, a fitting location at what was designated as Sharjah's new center. Drawings for a 132-room hotel were prepared in Bombay, and construction began in 1975. Halfway through construction, architects added the 1,500-seat Concorde Cinema upon request. Near the point of completion in the late 1970s, the client sensed that Sharjah needed not a new hotel but another hospital. While Architectural Consultants were not involved in the conversion, their original structure, layout, and service areas were maintained. Hotel rooms were converted to serve new functions, including patient rooms. On November 15, 1981, the AED 60-million hospital opened with 100 beds, 11 suites, and two operating rooms.

As reported in *Al Azmenah Al Arabiya*, October 20, 1981, about the future Al Zahra Hospital: "Although the location is unsuitable for a hospital, the municipality did not reject the request [to convert the hotel into a hospital]. It met all requirements, though ignoring internationally recognized regulations about constructing hospitals in locations away from noise and activity." Images: Architectural Consultants, Ashok Mody.

01

Momen Architects in Sharjah

Text by
Mohamed Elshahed

One of Nasserist Cairo's most prominent landmarks is the mammoth Radio and Television Administration, designed by architect Galal Momen and opened in 1960. The building, sometimes referred to as the Maspero television building, consists of a square tower rising from a semi-circular base facing the Nile. In the previous decade, Mostafa Momen, Galal's brother, had a hand in the massive nearby Mogamma government building on Tahrir Square. Both buildings typify how state commissions of the 1950s needed at once to house large numbers of employees and to create architectural symbols of state power. Both Mostafa and Galal Momen pursued their professional training in Cairo and belonged to a generation of architects and engineers who participated in large state projects that interlinked modern architecture with power structures after World War II and the 1952 military coup.

Another state commission in Cairo won by Galal Momen was the Gamal Abdel Nasser Mosque, a state-funded project completed in 1966 and the eventual burial site of Nasser. That building, smaller in scale and characterized by simplified motifs borrowed from or sometimes inspired by the city's Islamic architecture, is a formal precursor to Galal Momen's buildings in Sharjah, distinguished by their town-hall scale, simple forms, and low-profile appearances.

With increased contact between Egypt and members of the ruling elite of the Trucial States in the 1960s, Momen Architects expanded their practice to open offices in Sharjah and Abu Dhabi in 1972 which continue to operate today. In Sharjah, the office completed several modernist government commissions including Sharjah Municipality and Africa Hall, the police headquarters, and the fire department. Momen Architects designed these buildings in response to the vision of Sharjah's ruler, Sheikh Sultan bin Muhammad Al Qasimi, that the new government buildings share a unified identity.

After a 1971 law tasked the Sharjah municipality with urban affairs and management, the expanded municipal bureaucracy required a new building to house it. Momen Architects was commissioned to design the municipality building and oversaw its completion in 1976. The 12,000-square-meter building contained two distinct programmatic elements: the new municipality's offices and an auditorium named Africa Hall after the inaugural event that took place in the building, the African-Arab Symposium. The police headquarters and the fire department were both completed in 1975, each conceptualized as a long rectilinear block with a modular structural and facade design. Other projects in Sharjah by Momen Architects include apartment blocks commissioned by the Sharjah Department of Islamic Affairs, as well as an unbuilt proposal for the King Faisal Mosque.[1]

1. See p. 207.

Architect
Momen Architects

Consulting Engineers
Galal Momen and Mostafa Momen

Contractors:
Municipality and Africa Hall: DAFCO

Fire Department: DAFCO

Traffic Department: DAFCO

Police Headquarters: Bin Laden Contracting

02

01. Africa Hall, adjacent to the Sharjah Municipality. In December 1976, over forty politicians, scholars, and experts from African and Arab countries assembled in Sharjah to attend the African-Arab Symposium. When the conference was announced, only the hall's foundations had been completed. DAFCO, the contractor, had forty-five days to complete the hall. It was demolished in 2015 and replaced with new premises. DAFCO.

02. Originally based in the old fort, Sharjah's police force moved to its new headquarters in 1975, the same year the architects finished the new fire department (see p. 20). Nitin Tavkar.

03. Sharjah Department of Traffic, under construction, mid- to late-1970s. DAFCO.

04. Contractor DAFCO provided a logo design for the traffic department as part of its building design submission, 1975. The hands represented the "stop" and "go" gestures of a traffic guard. DAFCO.

03

04

بلدية الشارقة
ادارة التخطيط والمساحة
قسم التخطيط

العمارة الإسلامية المحلية

الجزء الثاني

01

A Mandate for Local Islamic Architecture

By the mid-1980s, government authorities were consciously shaping Sharjah's identity to express what they described as Arab and Islamic ideals. Stricter regulations were put in place throughout Sharjah, including restrictions on certain forms of public assembly and the ban on alcohol in hotels in 1985. In the years after, further regulations would follow, including the ban on mixing unwed males and females, the institution of a more conservative dress code, and the prohibition of mannequins with facial features in shop windows.

The city's urban landscape also came to reflect these restrictions. At the 1981 meeting of the Arab Towns Organization, British engineering firm Halcrow's design for Sharjah International Airport "won much admiration" for its adherence to Islamic design.[1] At the organization's March 1986 meeting in Riyadh, Sharjah "came up for special praise." The Sharjah delegation presented a "comprehensive report" on how public buildings were "in line with the Islamic architectural heritage." They also assured conference attendees that new, and presumably private market, buildings "will follow this basic pattern." Around that time, Sharjah Municipality had issued its first guidelines for how new developments should reflect an Arabic-Islamic heritage.

In February 1988, the Dubai-based *Gulf News* reported that Sharjah Municipality was about to release guidelines for this new "basic pattern" that would "make Islamic designs compulsory for buildings." Planning officials claimed to be searching for "the best formulae" that would "link modern buildings to Islamic designs." Mandated to ensure that private development shared the concerns expressed in recent public buildings, municipal officials met with locally active design offices to review the new rules. They insisted on meeting the consultants, not owners or developers, to safeguard the unmitigated execution of an architectural sensibility now set on paper.

On May 9, 1988, Sharjah's Planning and Survey Department informed officials in other municipal departments that "the actual implementation of Local Islamic Architecture ... has started." There were three sets of guidelines produced around this time: the first before the implementation notice, the second around the time of its delivery, and a third in the early 1990s. The latter also reported on the success of the program, noting that 83.4% of new buildings had conformed to the guidelines. The last batch of guidelines, furthermore, underscored that the domes of buildings and the coverings for ever-present water tanks would guarantee Sharjah an appropriately authentic skyline. Several public buildings were highlighted for their exemplary design: the Emiri Diwan, Sharjah Municipality, and the headquarters for the police and traffic departments as well as the civil courthouse, the vegetable souk, Central Souk, and the main post office.[2]

Accompanying images are taken from the second set of guidelines. The pages of instructional drawings advise architects and other building-industry professionals on how to detail the exteriors of residential, commercial, and governmental buildings. References include details derived from regional forts and *barajeel*, or wind towers. They also include columns, arches, and domes representing the emergence of a "Neo-Islamic architecture" inspired by Fatimid, Umayyad, and Ottoman motifs. With this document in hand, municipal planners and architects easily rejected building designs that employed features they considered overtly Western—like red-clay roofing tiles (even though these might have been a half-hearted reference to Andalusia).

1. See p. 387.
2. See pp. 331, 415, 324, 325, 333, 139, 127, 87.

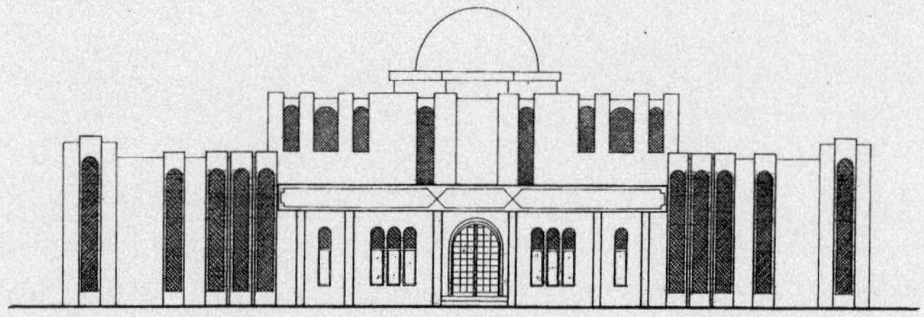

مبنى حكومي (عام)

02

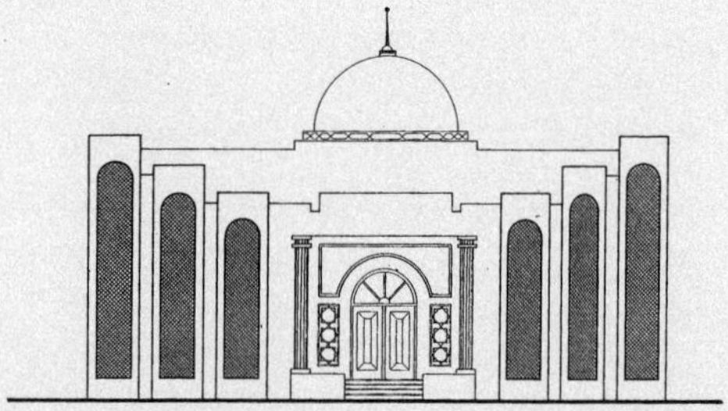

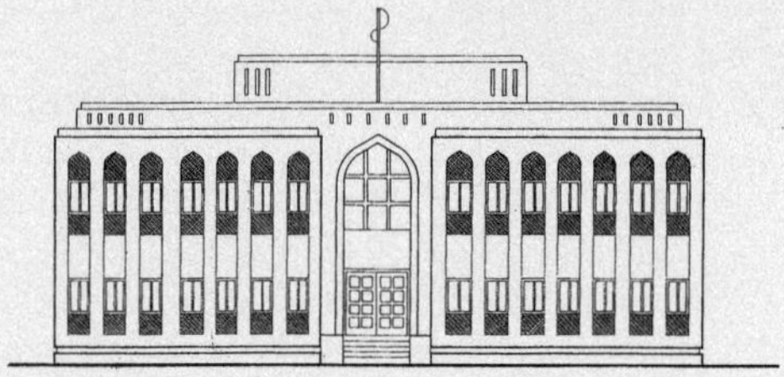

مباني حكومية (عامة)

03

04

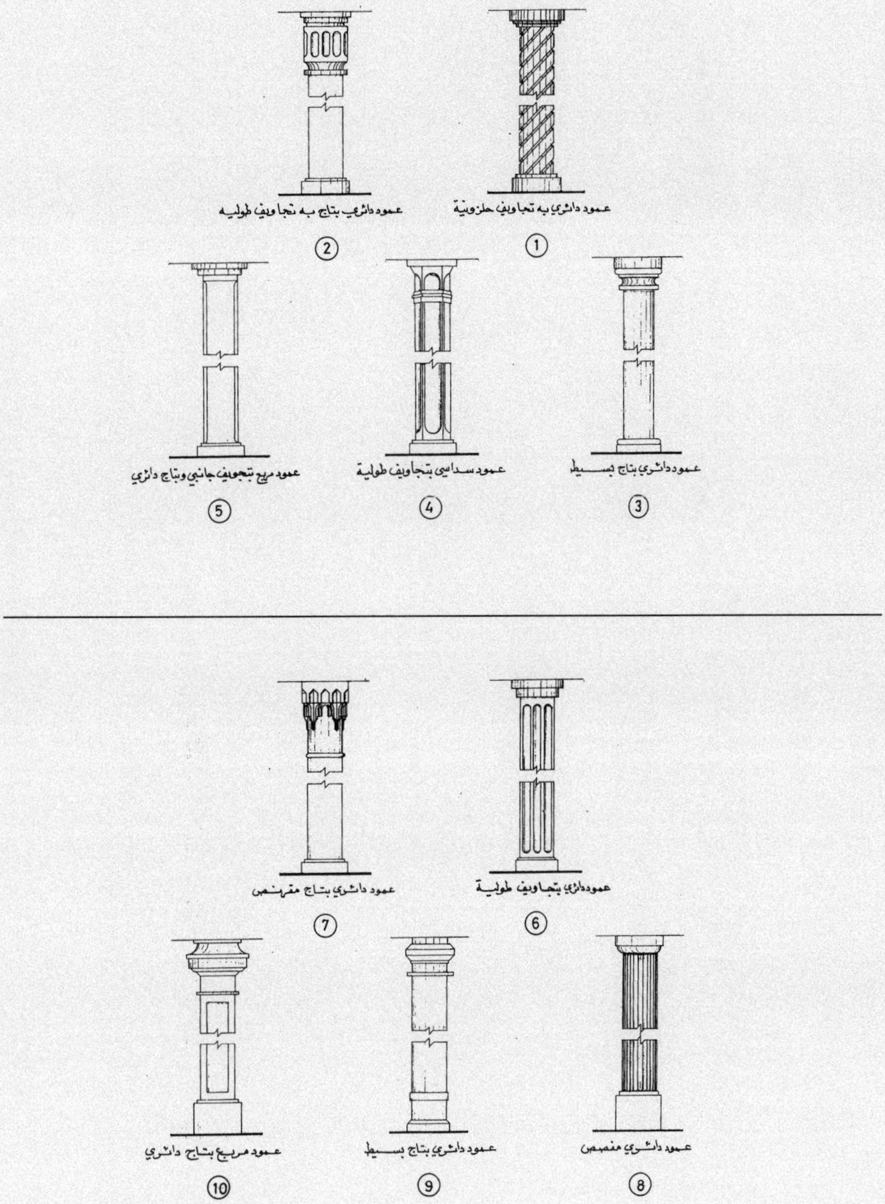

05

01. "Local Islamic Architecture," cover page, no date. Images: Sharjah Municipality, courtesy of Jafar Tukan Library.
02.–03. Government buildings (public).
04. Window designed with adjacent hollow squares; window designed with unchained circles; window designed with chained circles.

05. 1. Circular column decorated with spiral-shaped carvings; 2. Circular column topped with crown decorated with vertical carvings; 3. Circular column topped with a simple crown; 4. Hexagonal column decorated with vertical carvings; 5. Square column topped with a circular crown and decorated with side carvings; 6. Circular column decorated with vertical carvings; 7. Circular column topped with a leveled, decorated crown; 8. Circular column decorated with vertical fluting; 9. Circular column topped with a simple crown; 10. Square column topped with a circular crown.

01

02

03

04

Emiri Diwan

The Emiri Diwan, or Government House, was one of the earliest commissions by Sharjah's ruler Sheikh Sultan bin Muhammad Al Qasimi, who assumed power in 1972 after the assassination of his brother. The new ruler sought a clean slate of premises to house his majlis and the offices of his closest advisors. He hired Egyptian architect Mohamed Essam Eldin Fahmy, founder of Arab Engineering Bureau, or AEB, which had opened an office in Sharjah in 1975.

The project benefited greatly from the first of Sharjah's oil exports in 1974, which bankrolled significant investments in more imposing government buildings. One British travel writer described the result as a "vast white-domed edifice resembling the sort of railway station the British might have built in India."[1] Its design was a bellwether of future designs of government buildings that claimed more traditional, Islam-inspired architecture.

The diwan gave Government House Square its name. Its arriving neighbors—Sharjah Municipality, Africa Hall, and the central post office—however, did not as explicitly correspond in form to the Emiri Diwan.[2] It seems that the diwan building may have prefigured the design guidelines eventually set by the municipality.[3]

In 1994, the facade was overhauled by Emirates Stone, a Sharjah-based precast concrete manufacturing company, resulting in an exterior that foretold the elaborately decorated facades of today's Cultural Palace and other Sharjah government buildings. The post office, through a dramatic renovation, and Africa Hall, demolished and replaced, were both brought more in line with the city's architectural guidelines while the municipal building was demolished.

In 2002, Sheikh Sultan awarded Mohamed Essam Eldin Fahmy the golden key to the City of Sharjah.

Architect
Arab Engineering Bureau

Contractor
Contractors Group International

Client
Sheikh Sultan bin Muhammad Al Qasimi

Completed
1978

Status
Renovated, 1994

Notes:

1. Christine Osborne, *The Gulf States and Oman*, (London: Routledge, 2016), 111.
2. See pp. 415, 322, 87.
3. See p. 327.

Images:

01.–04. Photographs taken during Sheikh Sultan bin Muhammad Al Qasimi's construction site visit. Globe Constructors.
05. Workers operating a concrete mixer for subsurface works along Government House Square, with Emiri Diwan under construction in background. DAFCO.

05

Sharjah Civil Court

The Sharjah Civil Court is an example of Cairo-inspired architecture in Sharjah delivered by an Egyptian architecture firm. The commission was one of Arab Engineering Bureau's earliest for the city before it designed several government offices that even more emphatically mimicked Old Cairo.

Before its demolition in 2007, the court building stood on the Clock Tower Roundabout opposite Al Zahra Hospital.[1] Commissioned five years after the establishment of the emirate's first court of law in 1967, the building was designed with an attention to detail that required the skilled craftsmanship arriving in Sharjah for the construction boom. The project's design complexity resides not only in its ornamental elements but also in the vast array of materials, including marble, granite, and mosaic tiles used to clad the exterior.

Uncommon for most Sharjah projects, detailed ink drawings were produced to illustrate the proposed embellishments: the claustra-patterned screens, the floral patterns on the entrance columns' shafts and capitals, and even the proposed light fixtures. The building program arranged offices around an open-air courtyard adjoined to the central courtroom. Four Corinthian columns were installed at the main entrance, presumably to express the court's grandeur.

1. See p. 321.

Architect
Arab Engineering Bureau

Contractor
Bin Laden Contracting

Client
Ministry of Justice

Completed
1975

Status
Demolished, 2007

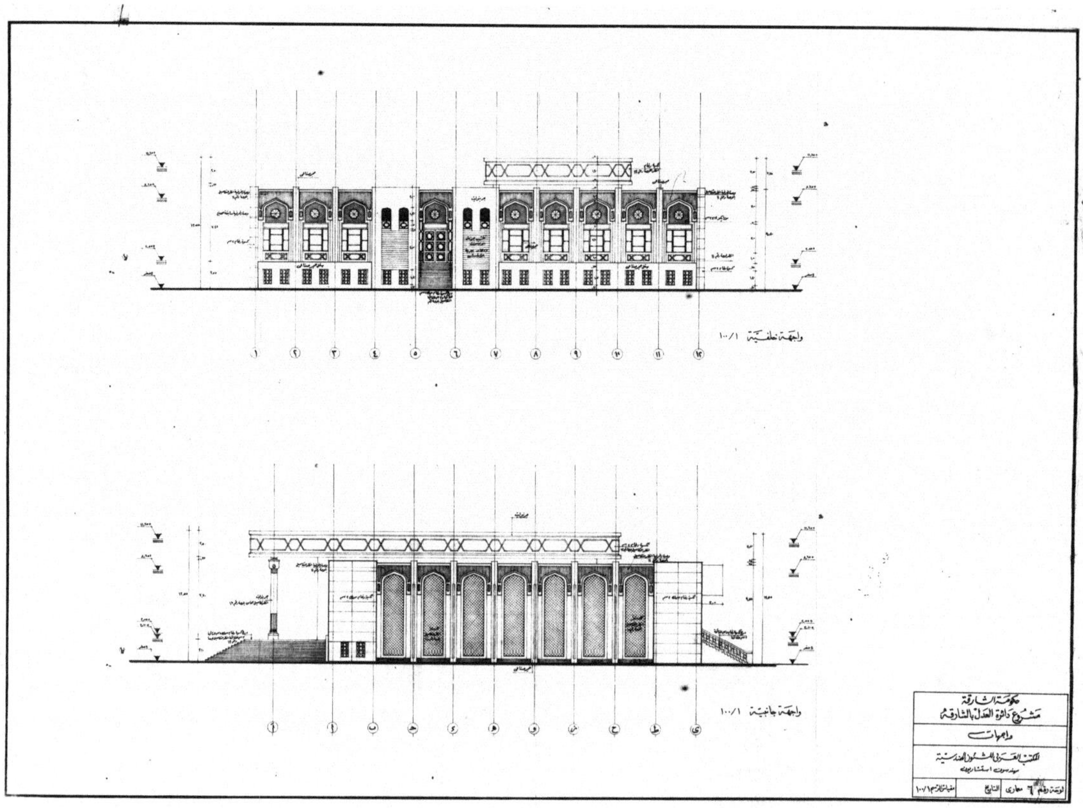

واجهة خلفية ١/١٠٠
واجهة جانبية ١/١٠٠
حكومة الشارقة
مشروع دائرة العدل بالشارقة
واجهات
المكتب الفني للشؤون الهندسية

02

03

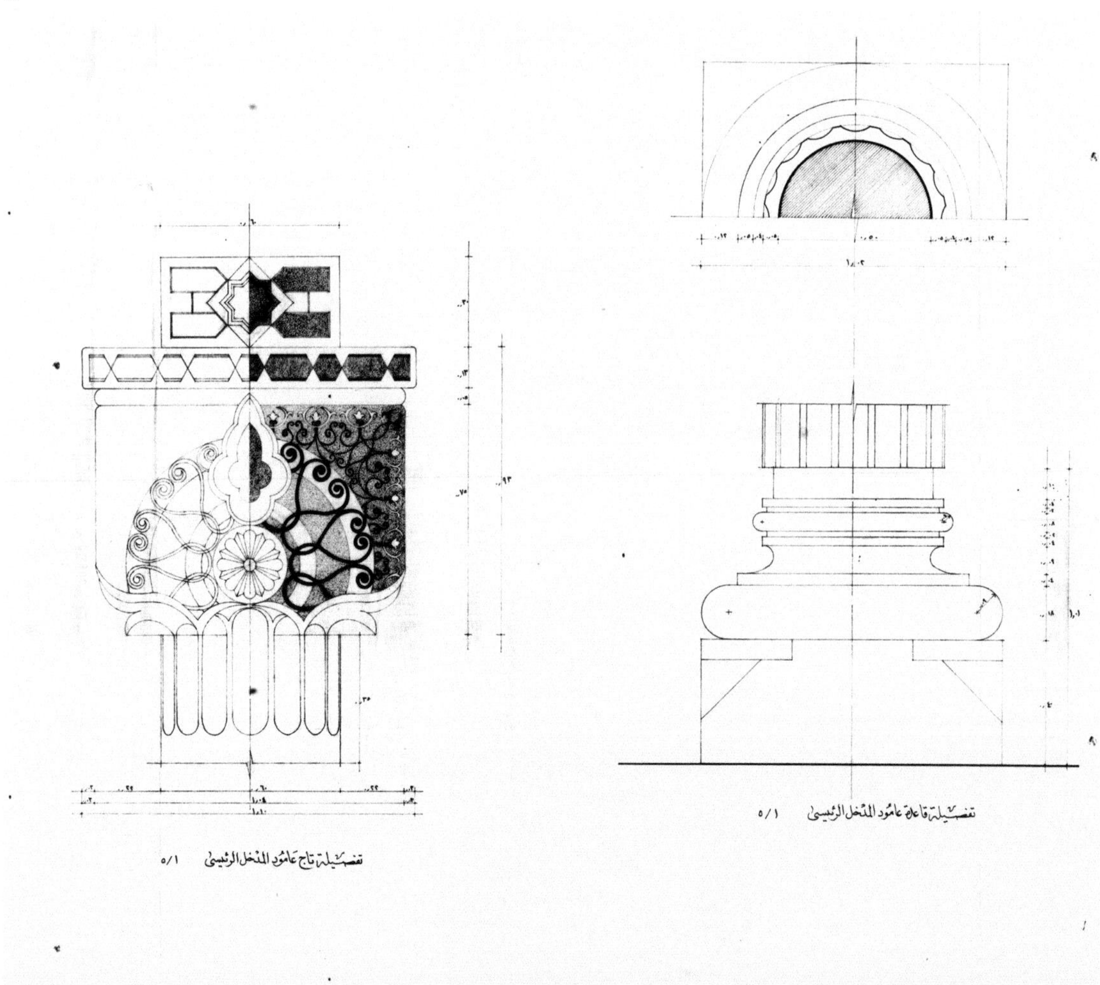

تفصيلة قاعدة عامود المدخل الرئيسي ١/٥
تفصيلة تاج عامود المدخل الرئيسي ١/٥

04

01. Main entrance off Al Zahra'a Square, late 1970s. Dr. Naman Al Jalili Archives Collection.
02. Rear and side elevations, undated. AEB, courtesy of DAFCO.
03. Ink and graphite detail drawings for main entrance, Arab Engineering Bureau, undated. AEB, courtesy of DAFCO.
04. Main entrance portico with four Corinthian columns, late 1970s. Dr. Naman Al Jalili Archives Collection.

A construction crew and supervisors, unknown location in Sharjah, 1970s. DAFCO.

Volvo / Caterpillar Buildings

Text by Roberto Fabbri

Designed in 1976, the office buildings and adjunct warehouses for Volvo Trucks and Caterpillar (CAT) are representative of an epoch of local business expansion within the Gulf. The Mohamed Abdulrahman Al-Bahar LLC was founded in Kuwait as a trading company in 1937 and later specialized in selling heavy equipment for earth-moving, infrastructure, and building construction. The enterprise successfully tied its name to international brands such as CAT construction machinery, Koehring Cranes, and Volvo Trucks. Kuwait was among the first countries in the Gulf to experience rapid urban development, and Kuwaiti companies found lucrative opportunities in other states' later post-oil development, including Bahrain, Qatar, Iran, Oman, and the UAE. In order to head off CAT's direct supply, Al-Bahar opened a purpose-built Volvo/CAT facility in Sharjah, likely taking advantage of local incentives to run light industries on the outskirts of town.

Al-Bahar's vast Sharjah complex was in the city's designated Industrial Area, well served by a major artery connecting Sharjah and Dubai. The nine-hectare site was split in two by a central access road, with two buildings on either side. As Al-Bahar's largest facility in the Gulf, the project was pragmatic and efficient, implementing a prefabricated modular construction system. A porch-like element was situated slightly preceding the main facades, with the intention to mitigate sunlight entering the office interiors and break the monotony of the facade's composition. The precast vertical components were painted so that they stood out in contrast to the rest of the building.

Architect
Milan Kovac
Arkitektkontor

Client
Mohamed Abdulrahman
Al-Bahar LLC

Completed
1978

Status
In use

Exterior view, undated.
Henk Snoek / RIBA
Collections.

01

Choithrams Building

Architect
Gulf Design Group

Contractor
Architectural Construction Team

Client
Gulf Design Group

Completed
1978

Status
Existing

Popularly referred to today by the supermarket chain that occupies the ground-floor showroom, the iconic King Faisal Street structure was designed as an office building. The building was commissioned, designed, and built by a single party, unusual for Sharjah. Three architects, formerly architecture-school classmates in Delhi, founded a design firm, Gulf Design Group, and a contracting company, Architectural Construction Team, in 1975—a move that likely explains how Sharjah got one of its most unusual buildings. Not only did they create the project, they also owned it.

The Sharjah-based Gulf Design Group produced a peculiar design whose shapes are reminiscent of work by Charles Correa and Le Corbusier.

In place of repetitive floor plans stacked up on a square plot, the architects produced an erratic arrangement of volumes that at least seem to consider shading as a design generator. Clad in aluminum and concrete panels, the five-story building's dynamic composition was achieved with precast elements mirrored across the elevations. Its structural system adopts a visibly layered approach, which its waffle-slab elements also reinforce. The ambiguous, even if symmetrical, composition offers a playful set of forms that alternate between negative spaces and protruding vaulted masses, suggesting a more playful interior than what is actually offered.

01. Building from King Faisal Street, 1980s. Images: Dr. Naman Al Jalili Archives Collection.
02. Before the supermarket chain Choithrams occupied it, the ground floor was a furniture store showroom.

02

Above: A residential block owned by Hamad Hilal Thabit Al Kuwaiti, Al Qassimiyah District, Helal & Partners, 1982.

Right: Mixed-use building, Al Wahda Street, Helal & Partners. The design called for a ten-story mixed-use block. Because of financing problems, construction was halted at six stories. Images: Nicolas Bou Rjaili.

Al Shamsi Housing

The Aga Khan Documentation Center at MIT holds preliminary drawings credited to Rifat Chadirji for a project in Sharjah with the name "M. Shams Housing Project." M. Shams is an incorrect reference to Mohammed Al Shamsi, who commissioned the drawings from Chadirji's firm Iraq Consult. The drawings are stamped with "IQC," the initials used for Chadirji's firm Iraq Consult. Sami Alwash, an Iraqi architect who ran Iraq Consult's office in Bahrain, recalls discussions about the project in 1974 and maintains that Chadirji himself was not involved in creating the drawings. Al Shamsi commissioned the work, perhaps with his fellow board member at the Bank of Sharjah, Abdulrahman Bukhatir, for a private development on property the former owned along Sharjah's coastline near the Ajman border. Alwash recalls that the perspective drawings, not based on any detailed plans or sections, were a quick production in order to help raise the necessary funding for an actual project. Al Shamsi failed to secure the funding.

Available drawings reveal a twenty-six-unit housing compound, organized around its own supermarket and afforded direct access to Sharjah's beachfront. The two- and three-bedroom houses with spacious garages were proposed with cast-concrete shapes one might recognize from Chadirji's built work. Interior walls were extended to the exterior, with deep eaves to shade the living spaces' expansive glazing. Evidently designed for high-income residents, the houses nevertheless lack the overly scaled security walls already expected of such projects in the 1980s, with gardens remaining visually available to the neighborhood. Iraq Consult also submitted design proposals to the UAE Ministries of Education and Public Works for gymnasiums and stadiums, none of which was executed.

Architect
Rifat Chadirji, Iraq Consult

Client
Mohammed Al Shamsi

Proposed
1974

Status
Unbuilt

Perspective street view, Iraq Consult, undated. Kamil and Rifat Chadirji Photographic Archive, courtesy of Aga Khan Documentation Center, MIT Libraries (AKDC@MIT).

01

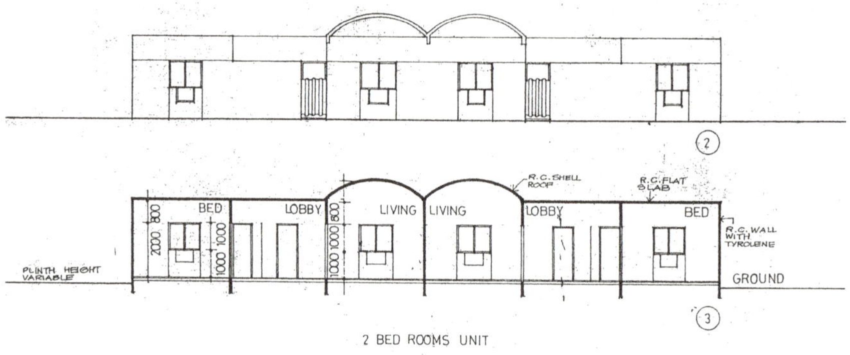

2 BED ROOMS UNIT

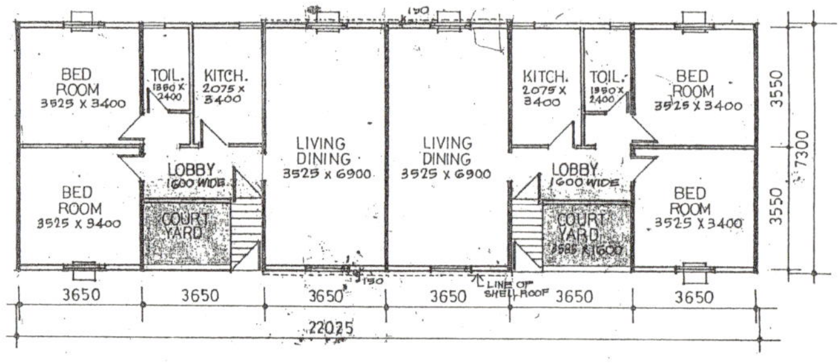

2 BED ROOMS UNIT

02

1000 Villas

Text by K. V. Shamsudheen

I cannot forget the youthful years we spent in 1000 Villas.

Starting in 1970, my bachelor friends and I lived in a two-story building on Al Arouba Street. We had no air conditioning because there was no steady supply of electricity. By 1974, we had electricity and had set our eyes on the 1000 Villas project being built in Al Gubeiba under the orders of Sheikh Sultan bin Muhammad Al Qasimi.

Things kept getting better, and in 1976, we bachelors moved to 1000 Villas, each in his own villa but very close to the others. Two of our older friends, Appu Kuttan and Narayana Swami, got married before we did and rented houses adjacent to ours. Then Cheeran Varkey got married. So did P. C. Simon and myself. I moved into Villa No. D-21 with my wife and my one-year-old son Sameesh Shamsudheen in 1978. My second son was born while we were living in 1000 Villas.

The houses, we were told, were Sharjah's first precast concrete structures. The living and dining areas were laid out under vaulted ceilings as were the bedrooms. In between them were the bathroom and the kitchen. Perfect for a small family. The living room's arched roof was impressive and long, but not even a two-ton air conditioner could keep it cool. Some families had to install a drop ceiling to keep temperatures down.

1000 Villas was home to a community of Indians from Kerala, Tamil Nadu, and Gujarath and to Pakistanis, Sri Lankans, Egyptians, Jordanians, Syrians, and Sudanese. Most of the Asian men worked for private companies and the UAE Defense Force. The Arab expatriates were teachers and government workers and also worked in defense. It seemed everyone got along. We had only one grocery store in the complex. It meant that we all had a chance to say hello to all nationalities.

We celebrated Eid, Christmas, New Year's Eve, Onam, and Vishu together. Our children played together, studied together, and lived together. Our wives are still close friends.

Most of the houses were gifted to nationals by Sharjah's ruler. My landlord was more than ninety years old, a widow named Mariyam Mohammed. She used to come to our home to collect the rent every three months (AED 2,000, or $500). We offered to bring the rent to her home, but she always wanted to visit my family. She was like our grandma, telling us to look after the house as if it were our own. She enjoyed seeing our garden.

Everyone kept a garden. I planted a coconut plant and a drumstick (Moringa) plant in our villa's courtyard on the day we moved in. By the time we left 1000 Villas, the coconut tree had started bearing coconuts, and drumsticks were available every day. We also planted beans, okra, tapioca, and more in our courtyards.

There were no asphalt roads inside the 1000 Villas complex in those days. Cars were regularly stuck in the sand, so residents had to help each other out.

Architect
Fowler Hanley Inc., Architectural Consultants

Urban Designer
Hosni Iskandar

Contractor
Bucomac

Client
Sheikh Sultan bin Muhammad Al Qasimi

Completed
1977

Status
Existing

03

1000 VILLAS FOR
H.H. SHEIKH SULTAN BIN MOHAMMED AL-QUASIMI
THE RULER OF SHARJA AND ITS DEPENDENCIES
CONTRACTORS
oucomac
CONSULTANTS
FOWLER HANLEY INC.
ENGINEERS - ARCHITECTS - PLANNERS
P.O BOX 88 TEL 24591 SHARJAH TELEX 8033 BK
ARCHITECTURAL CONSULTANTS
TEL:24145 P.O.BOX 1850 SHARJAH U.A.E.

04

05

01. Residential units during construction, 1970s. Architectural Consultants, Ashok Mody.
02. Elevation, section, and plan for two-bedroom unit, as submitted to Sharjah Municipality. Drawing by architect Kiran Jathal, August 1976. Sharjah Municipality.
03. Author's sons, Sameesh and Shamil, and wife Samiyya, seen through window, in driveway of No. D-21, Al Gubeiba, early 1980s. K.V. Shamsudheen.
04. Construction announcement, late 1970s. Michael Fowler, Fowler Hanley Inc.
05. Haidar Abdulrahman Ali poses on a motorbike in front of his family's two-bedroom house, 1979. His sister Asma recalls, "I have very fond memories of 1000 Villas. It was such an amazing, tight community. To this day, my parents call their circle of friends, 'Watu wa Ghubaiba,' the people of Gubeiba." Asma Ali.

Al Ramla Houses

The ruler's brother Sheikh Sager bin Mohamed Al Qassemi allegedly asked French architect Jean-Michel Regnault to propose a modest three-bedroom house as a home for his gardener. Regnault's design, priced at around AED 70,000, about $18,000, pleased the client enough that soon a billboard announced "32 Villas" in Sharjah's Al Ramla district. The design, by then a template, was used to create housing for local families.

Lined up on a single lot and attached by party walls, each house was afforded a small front porch or a garden and featured an open roof terrace, enclosed by most inhabitants to increase indoor space. Regnault's design embellished the simple concrete-brick construction with delicate details in wood, an indulgent import at the time and features not likely to last long in Sharjah's climate. The houses, reminiscent of homes of the 1950s, are a fraction of the size allotted to locals today.

Architect
Regnault & Partners

Contractor
Energyco

Client
Sheikh Sager bin
Mohamed Al Qassemi

Completed
1978

Status
Existing, modified

02

01. Two residents outside Al Ramla Houses, late 1970s. Images: Regnault & Partners.
02. Each L-shaped house had a roof terrace accessed by wooden stairs, late 1970s.
03. While some residents kept the wooden doors, others installed larger metal gates decorated with colorful symbols, including the UAE flag.

03

SPINNEY'S

Spinney's Supermarket and Office Block

Starting in the 1960s, Spinney's Supermarket occupied a small shop on Sharjah's Al Arouba Street. The city's growing population was good reason to relocate to a larger location on King Faisal Street, Sharjah's thoroughfare of rapid development that housed the latest newcomers. For the British architecture firm, the project was one of their early designs overseas. It consisted of two adjoining volumes. The first was a five-story office block lifted on pilotis that created a shaded entry and parking. The precast concrete facades of the northern and southern elevations formed a grid of vertical louvers that shaded recessed windows. In addition to the prominent precast scuppers, concrete awnings over small windows contributed to the building's simple geometries that played easily with shadow. The second volume, a box retail space, accommodated an expanded and further accessorized Spinney's. The supermarket chain started as a purveyor of British goods in British Mandatory Palestine before opening a branch in Dubai in 1959. Through the mid-1990s, the Sharjah branch was one of the city's top alcohol retailers for license-holding customers. While the supermarket still serves Sharjah residents, the site of the office block remains vacant.

02

01. Exterior view, King Faisal Street, 1977. Images: Henk Snoek / RIBA Collections.
02. Interior, Spinney's supermarket, 1977.
03. Office building's brise soleil and scuppers, 1977.

Architect
George Trew Dunn
Beckles Willson Bowes

Engineering Consultant
White Young & Partners

Contractor
Conforce Gulf

Client
Spinney's Limited

Completed
1977

Status
Demolished, renovated

Above: Night scene at unidentified fountain, Sharjah, 1970s. The lights for several fountains throughout Sharjah were provided by Dutch electronics company Philips. The fountains were built by Consolidated Contractors Company for a beautification project led by Sharjah's ruler Sheikh Khalid bin Mohammed Al Qasimi.

Left: Fishing on the paved edge of Lake Khalid. Landscaping details take shape—waterside parking, lampposts, and paving stones (though no railings yet)—projecting a sense of recreation and leisure, 1980s. The *Financial Times* described the selected streetlight model as a "fake gas lamp." Images: Mahmood Alʿawan.

01

Deepak
Unnikrishnan

WHEN MEN GLOW IN SHARJAH

In my sophomore year at Sharjah College, billed at the time as the American University of Asia, I had my first bout of insomnia. There was no history of the illness in the family. At first, I blamed it on my classes.

Sharjah College was a practical space, with manageable tuition, American-like education, and a high acceptance rate, why my brown parents were sold on the idea. Importantly, the college had an arrangement with University of Houston–Clear Lake, where our credits got recognized, if any of us hoped to transfer to the States. Later, I heard that the arrangement with Clear Lake had fallen through. As Troy University was touted as a potential substitute partner, the American University of Asia billing got replaced with the motto of "Technology Today for Tomorrow." I suppose we didn't know any better. I suppose we all got hustled. I suppose we should've run when we discovered there was not a single American on staff at the American University of Asia.

The American system wasn't easy. I came from an Indian high school by Muroor Road in Abu Dhabi, where the school continues to be housed, where teachers suggested, then demanded, that we acquiesce. Bereft of options, Fuck sure, we said. So when I wrote about daffodils and Wordsworth, I wrote what was expected of me, that Wordsworth found worth in flowers I'd never seen in person. In an American school (possibly), teachers may have been open to the suggestion that the daffodil, like Wordsworth, was an overrated flora, but such rebellious thinking wasn't afforded to the likes of me, or my peers.

Flora aside, American freedom(s) had nothing to do with my lack of sleep. It would be fair to say my first semester at university in Sharjah was bland, almost anti-climactic. I wasn't wowed or cowed. Just bored.

Then, because it was convenient, I assumed I couldn't sleep because I was reluctant to dream, because dreams were oracles. If all else fails, as they say, blame a parent. Or genes.

My gran suffered from migraines, code in my family for depression. My mother had migraines, too, code for periods and depression. Both had trouble sleeping. Gran, I remember, when our family visited the homeland, would go to her room and lock the door. Mum popped Panadol. Neither liked doctors because physicians, whether male or female, asked intimate questions, about bowels and breath, and smelled like disinfectant.

02

01. Next to the title is the logo of erstwhile Sharjah College. Opposite page: the Flying Saucer at dusk, circa 1977. Haro Levonian.
02.–03. Along Sharjah Creek's corniche, circa 1977. Sue Simpson.
04. Streetlights at night along Al Arouba Street, possibly Al Khan Bridge, 1980s. United Colour Film, Ajman, courtesy of Abdulla Al Murad.
05. View of Port Khalid over Sharjah Creek, 1980s. United Colour Film, Ajman, courtesy of Abdulla Al Murad.

I refused to see a doctor because I wasn't going to take anything based on five-minute doctor-patient banter. And I couldn't ring my parents because they would've panicked. Besides, meds weren't cheap, and there was no money at home. The only solution would've been to take the semester off, wait out the problem. Basically, do nothing or drop out. I didn't want either. To cope, I walked.

I walked after dinner, past Baluchi taxi wallahs who honked even after I said no. It's hot, they'd say. It's fine, I'd say.

I walked after chats with friends in the dorms, sipping Sun Top through a straw, munching Pofaki cheese curls.

I walked after phone calls with a girl on a borrowed mobile, until the wee hours of the morning, in time to see delivery vans drop one-dirham cheese croissants, chicken mayonnaise sandwiches, and sausage rolls into the arms of grocery store uncles, cheap protein to sate hundreds of hungry tummies.

*

In the beginning, before the campus—once pinned to the heart of the city—got moved to the Industrial Area, I walked around campus grounds, past the asphalt football pitch, the girls' dorms, where the boys smoked, and the patch of green where couples necked and felt each other up in the open. I walked around in circles, to a point where security frisked me (quickly) for booze and dope.

They asked if I was high. No, I said. I wasn't believed. I could be a mule, I was told in the little Tamil I understood. Find something, I said in English, then we talk. We will, they said, then we reach understanding. Whatever, I said. Otherwise, they laughed, you big trouble. One time they urged me over: Come, we tell something. Okay fine, I said. Yesterday, they said, we caught hiding boy under bed in girl room. Hiding boy screwed up, I said. No, they chuckled, hiding boy fucked up. What we learned from this was that if you must hiding boy in girl room, put hiding boy's clothes back on.

One night, fed up of security watching me, stopping me, I chose to slip out into the street, breaking curfew (the main gate got locked after 11:00 p.m.). It became habit until I graduated.

The college, which doesn't exist anymore (rumor goes some smart schmuck from administration embezzled a shitload of cash), was twenty minutes from Rolla Square on foot. As you stepped off university grounds (a few trees, some benches, a couple buildings here and there, a makeshift cafeteria), you made a left, walking away from Dubai, turning your back to Dubai completely, passing a straight road stripped of beauty, turning into a tunnel some distance away, making your way towards markets and restaurants, getting sand in your sneakers from taking shortcuts, following the lights, flanked by the smells of smoke, food, trash, life––towards the water by the corniche, where I sat for hours, slammed by breeze, salt, humidity.

I often brought cookies on such trips, red packets of Hit, licking the chocolate cream first and only then biting the biscuit. And as I ate, I thought about my place in the world, my laziness and burgeoning emptiness, because Sharjah wasn't taking me anywhere.

I also wondered about my lack of sleep, sex, and the girl I was falling in love with. I wanted to live with this person, raise her kids.

03

I also wanted shorter hair, to be cool, slick, and lanky, a combination of Dean and Hepburn (Audrey), to be admired and envied for my body, but I also wanted Katherine's (Hepburn) voice, her bite, as well as Hasselhoff's jacket from *Knight Rider*. Throw in the Pontiac Firebird, which I'd ride to school with the top down, pretty gal in the front, Lighthouse Family on the stereo, and just like that life would be all set. I wasn't white, yet I thought I could be. Back then, no brown role models, no desire (yet) for women who looked like Smita (Patil) on VHS, even though I looked like a boy who could play Smita on film.

No understanding of textiles either, of why clothes could be comfort, or how color and drape (and shape, dumbass) offered visibility and invisibility at the same time, based on when the man or woman or child looked at you, or where. Or what they thought, or the questions that hit them as soon as they saw your face. Hello, who is your mother? What is your name? Country? Faith? What do you look like in the shower, as you sleep, if you kiss? Or because of my brown frame, my gait, my life, the time––what are you? All these thoughts about the self, and I was barely eighteen.

I watched the sea like others before me, pretending I knew what it must've felt like to wonder whether a family member (or lover or friend) had lived, survived, or perished at the mercy of waves, fire, war, and/or pirates. Sometimes I just watched the water, and the spirits of the deep returned the gaze and, like others before them, they wondered what I was, whether I had been ostracized by my tribe, whether my mother was related to any of their mothers, or whether I, the Mallu, spoke Khaleeji in pidgin. And as they quarreled, I saw an old man asleep on a bench, an empty ice cream cup by his side.

By the seventh week, little had changed. I couldn't sleep for long periods and found myself at the corniche again, desperate to rest, tired. When I spotted the seven men, brown, mustachioed, in baggy track pants, dusty chappals, walking at a clip, fifteen minutes must have passed. Two of them held cricket bats. Another taped a ball with yellow insulation tape, swearing/laughing vociferously (the lot of them) in Urdu/Dari/Punjabi. I followed them. For the most part, they paid me no mind, although they turned around a few times. They carried on walking.

I tried to guess where they were going, which patch of asphalt, sand, or grass appealed to them, whether they lived near the Industrial Area, whether their games were legal, who they pretended to be––Akram, Miandad, Gavaskar, Imran, Kapil, Tendulkar? Importantly, I wanted to see how they were going to keep it down.

I checked my watch: past one in the morning. Where *could* they go? Mentally, I compiled a list of spaces available to them and couldn't think of any nearby, but Sharjah wasn't my city.

The men led me to a circular structure, building-like yet oddly dressed in glass and concrete, a thing with sharp edges, something that seemed to have been thought up at a party by a hatmaker. Years into the future, I would lunch with an architect who knew the building, a man who wore red shoes and a watch with a white dial and a red strap, someone who smiled right. "When I once knocked on the glass door," he shared, "there was a feeling of instability, as if all the glass trembled." I asked him for the name of the architect. "A mystery," he said.

I assumed the men would situate themselves close by, near the parking lot lined by sleeping cars with lukewarm engines, the base of street lamps morphed into wickets. Instead, their captain rapped his knuckles on the glass door and let himself in. His friends/teammates followed.

I hesitated. I didn't know these men. I'd assumed I'd pass time watching them cuss, run, bat, bowl. This felt different. I was about to turn homebound when the lights switched on.

Through the glass, caked with weeks' worth of grime, I watched the men don their gear: kneepads, helmets.

I spotted a woman (dark as burnt wood, like my father) in a nurse's uniform handing them things.

The space, flanked by glass, was empty. There was no furniture, pictures, or signs, only ample room to run, and white tiles. The men, with the nurse's help, rolled out the pitch, a rubber mat, bright enough to add color, short enough to feel right and not dominate the space. Trashcans got placed on either side. And as the wicketkeeper stretched his hamstrings, fielders sauntered to their positions, while the batsmen took guard, as the umpire found his hat, a white sports cap.

As I waited for the opening bowler to steam in from the bowler's end, the man skipped once, twice, then bowled underarm. As the ball got thrown back to the bowler, I noticed the nurse exit the building and walk towards me, finding a spot not far from where I sat, and taking color pencils and a sketchbook from a plastic bag.

I was sneaking glances at her—she looked like my favorite aunt Beena—when the streetlights went out. Within seconds, I realized I was sitting in a city pocket emptied of light. All around the building's perimeter, as well as two hundred meters across, little was clear, except the beams of the occasional passing car. Yet as I squinted in the direction of the players, I found parts of them bathed in light, like fish in the deep. The batsmen's helmets glowed green, as did their gloves, chappals, and bats. The ball, hurled underarm with speed towards wickets colored like autumn, looked like a burning fruit, while the bowler's fingertips glowed blue, as did his shoes, knees, and elbows. And as it dawned on me that the bowling team was blue, and those batting green, the nurse lit a kerosene lamp and sketched the men as they huffed, ran, dove.

It was the first and only time I'd watched cricket without the noise or the interference of English commentary, adverts, or jingoism. This wasn't the usual Indo-Pak shit the radio, then Star TV, loved to hawk. This was sport as practice, where little mattered except the game. It was the only time in my life I can recall cricket feeling beautiful/dangerous/vulnerable, sport that mimicked dance/life. And through the rules of the game, doctored to respect the space, as the batsmen ran, as wickets tumbled, as catches were caught or spilled, cricket became movement, rhythm and beat, and game became drug, pure and uncut, even unreal. As though the game had been played at the bottom of the seabed, cheered on in silence by the spirits of those who knew the land before petrol fired up the Khaleej and by those who swam towards Khaleeji shores following the scent of oil.

It was also one of the few occasions my nose paid attention to the smell of the sleeping sea, as I sat on land burning, stockpiling and selling crude, as a man in a green helmet, who looked like one of the servers at the Kashmiri Restaurant I frequented, hopped down the pitch to whack a ball. But then, as bat met ball, it got hit with care, not ferocity, because the rules of the game they played were different, softer.

I'd played their version of cricket, one-bounce cricket, with the boys of my high school, Indian School lads, in a little room at the India Social Center by Mina Road in Abu Dhabi, where my father drank Chivas on ice with other Mallu men. In one-bounce cricket, the body had to dive—to catch the ball before the second bounce—onto tile, wood, rock, wherever the game got played. One-bounce wasn't tempestuous like gully cricket or obsessed with codes and rituals among those who continued to believe in the lie that cricket, invented by Empire, was a gentleman's game. One-bounce was a game

05

birthed by need, requiring players who weren't afraid to play with soft hands. One-bounce needed craft, guile, and imagination. One-bounce was invented, I suppose, to kill time, like x-n-zero or rock-paper-scissors. But one-bounce was also about men, brown men remembering their childhood/ homes through sport. And cricket, then and now, was a place for men. With its expensive gear (bats, cork balls, pads, guards) and push for real estate—concrete pitches and thousands of yards of grass—the game didn't have a place indoors; one-bounce did. One-bounce felt like hip-hop, raised out of need.

In the morning, as light returned, as the game ended, and the woman and the men disappeared, I returned to the college grounds, greeted by the familiar. I skipped classes, slept six hours straight, then went to lunch at the Yemeni place (which would also close years later) a block down, where I ordered my usual, while the owner, tiny, skinny, shortsighted, and mustachioed, greeted me in sunglasses and day-old stubble. In my college days in Sharjah, only two things mattered when I lunched at the Yemeni joint: the peppered lamb soup, served with a slice of lemon, spiced right to wake my brain; and the scrambled eggs with tomato and chili, served with warm bread that flaked and warmed and coated your fingers with charred sesame seeds.

I must've told myself I needed to go back, to observe the games (and the men), to see how spaces could be appropriated with stealth, then put back together as it were, as well as to watch and feel the joy and euphoria of sport in the presence of strangers. It was as though the building in question, erected to be something specific (or significant), had been treated (by those who were into sport) as an excuse to become something else, like the makeshift badminton set-up—lines of chalk on the stone floor, net hung across poles—inside the abandoned warehouse on campus grounds. Yet the cricket I'd witnessed, the game the nurse documented in her sketchings, meant something more to me, as though I had also participated, as a rule/law breaker, part of a secret I was delighted to keep.

I returned to the spot many times over, hoping to catch more games or introduce myself to the nurse, to check if she *was* Mallu. She must've been, but I didn't run into them again. And yet over the years, as I've caught gully cricket in alleyways and sandlots, talked Ambrose and Thompson with aficionados & cheats, as T20 went mainstream, arguably prostituting the game's soul, I've thought about that night. And I've often wondered whether I was allowed to remain because of what I was supposed (or assumed) to be, a young man with cropped hair, or what I was, a young lady who resembled a boy, dressed in a baggy tee, pants, and sneakers.

*

In my classroom, fifteen years later, in the role of teacher, I once told this tale to my students. A young lady put her hand up. Professor, she said, you need to see *There Was Nothing—Kuch Bhi Naheen Tha!*

Made by artist Yaminay Chaudhri, shot at Seaview, a public beachfront in Karachi, *TWN—KBNT!* is a short film about beachgoers, property barons, vendors, light, and darkness. It is also a film about the work of men who rely on the sand and the sea, stealth, the commodification of fun, and, as I said before, darkness.

When I played the film at home, I didn't know any of these things. My students felt the less I knew, the better. And as my eyes adjusted to the night shot(s) on screen, I made out a buggy fitted with LED lights, only parts of its silhouette visible to the eye. Then I saw/heard another motorized vehicle, strips of light, bursts of color. Memories—smells and sound—came back, and I smiled and wondered whether any of the players I'd seen all those years ago boasted Karachi roots. Or how they came about their arrangement with the woman who drew them, whether she had drawn their blood at the clinic she worked for, whether they lunched/flirted in the open, in multiple languages, whether their bodies hung on a frame in someone's drawing room, bars of light etched onto paper, evidence of a game once played with the kind of honesty I've yearned for and missed and craved in my life but have yet to find, the only night in my life where I nursed my vulnerable heart and body in front of strangers.

Shortly after the Flying Saucer's completion, the Lebanese company Misal Gulf was contracted to renovate the interior and add exterior cold storage, December 1978. Haro Levonian.

The Flying Saucer

Text by
Mona El Mousfy

The Flying Saucer lies at the meeting point of multiple residential areas, namely Dasman, Gubeiba, Yarmouk, and Ramla, and overlooks what was previously known as "The Flying Saucer Roundabout." This iconic building from the 1970s has a unique and relatively simple silhouette defined by a circular footprint and a central dome. V-shaped, angled pillars foreground the triangular glazing that rounds the building, and a star-shaped canopy projects further beyond the facade, giving it that flying saucer quality. It was likely built between 1974 and 1976 (evidenced in aerial archives), facing the entrance of a former British camp. It remained isolated on the roundabout for a long time. During its construction, the government was relocating families from older coastal neighborhoods to the newly developed Dasman and other surrounding neighborhoods.

In stark contrast to its surroundings, the building references Western space-age pop culture of the 1960s and 1970s and Brutalist architecture of the same period. Over the years, the site has undergone substantial urban transformation. The building is currently positioned on the corner of Sheikh Zayed Street and Al Wahda Street, both busy multi-lane thoroughfares. Al Wahda bridge, having replaced the historical roundabout, now overlooks the building.

After its initial short-lived occupation by a French-inspired patisserie, the Flying Saucer underwent a number of programmatic changes.[1] This led to a series of architectural and interior transformations by various tenants, altering the building's character and the quality of its interior space. In 2015, the building's exterior cladding was stripped, and interior elements, including the ceiling and partitions (added in 2008), were taken down to reveal its 7.3-meter-high dome, an impressive structure. Eight columns support the dome, and sixteen peripheral spaces fan around the central space. Tapered and tilted, the V-shaped pillars create a complex three-dimensional, structural diagrid, their arrangement in a circle allowing for a fully glazed facade. The result is a 360-degree view of the surroundings. Beyond the facade extends a sixteen-point, cantilevered canopy that partially merges into the annex structure.

The Flying Saucer's unique character allowed it to adapt to various occupants without losing its identity and formal features. Its history speaks of the adaptability and resilience of an iconic building that has undergone decades of change and transformation. This resilience has enriched its history, in turn inscribing it in the collective cultural memory and place identity of Sharjans.

Client
Sheikh Sultan bin Muhammad Al Qasimi

Completed
Mid-1970s

Status
Renovated

1. An advertisement in Dubai-based *Khaleej Times* promised "space age shopping" at the Flying Saucer (December 18, 1978).

FRONT ELEVATION
SCALE(1/50)

SIDE ELEVATION
(SCALE.1/50)

01

Arab Academy for Science, Technology & Maritime Transport

Architect
William Brown, Charter Oil Company, and Tunisia & United Arab Emirates Engineering Company

Contractor
Al Nahda Contracting & Trading Company (ALCO)

Client
Government of Sharjah, Arab Academy for Science, Technology & Maritime Transport

Completed
1979, 1981

Status
Demolished, 2005. Planetarium, disused

In the late 1970s, the Sharjah government commissioned US-based Charter Oil Company to design and deliver seven precast buildings, their intended end use never clear. Charter's in-house engineer and architect, William Brown, completed the drawings. Upon the project's completion, the buildings remained vacant.

The 1979 Camp David Accords presented the complex with a purpose. Since 1972, the Arab Academy for Science, Technology & Maritime Transport had been based in Egypt, a founding member of the Arab League. When Egypt signed a peace treaty with Israel, the Arab League voted to expel Egypt from its organization. Subsequently, the academy was moved from Alexandria to Sharjah and took refuge in the seven buildings.

The academy operated in Sharjah throughout the 1980s. A small but iconic planetarium was added to the site for astronomy instruction, with the Tunisia & United Arab Emirates Engineering Company established specifically to build the structure. It was completed in 1981.

Before the end of the Gulf War in 1991, Egypt rejoined the Arab League, and Cairo once again became the organization's headquarters. The academy returned to Alexandria.

The facilities served Sharjah College for some time until 2005 when they were demolished. The planetarium's demolition, to make way for a widened Al Arouba Street, was halted after it had already begun. Its future is undetermined.

01. Elevations of the planetarium, as submitted to Sharjah Municipality, 1981. Tunisia & United Arab Emirates Engineering Co., courtesy of Sharjah Municipality.
02. Arab League ministers of transportation and communications inspect facilities during ministerial meeting, March 1986. Arab Maritime Transport Academy Magazine, courtesy of Juma Al Majid Center for Culture and Heritage.
03. Students learning to use nautical sextants, 1989. Arab Maritime Transport Academy Magazine, courtesy of Juma Al Majid Center for Culture and Heritage.

View from upper floor of the Holiday Inn, over its empty fountain, designed by the hotel's architect David Firmin & Partners, to the Buhaira Corniche road. Across the road are mid-rise residential buildings, constructed in the 1980s to house Sharjah's arriving populations. The rightmost building on the road was designed for then Minister of Education Saeed Abdullah Salman by Egyptian architect Fayek Howeedy. Further back to the right is the Rostamani Building on King Faisal Street, Khatib & Alami, 1977. The green and white building on the left was designed by Arab Engineering Bureau, 1975. Alexander Gnezdilov.

Some Sharjah sites caught on film: Buhaira Corniche, Al Khan Bridge, Al Khan Overpass, Al Wahda Street, Hotel Aladin, Arab Maritime Academy, Sharjah police headquarters, Bank Street, Central Souk, Flying Saucer, Holiday Inn, Inter-Continental Hotel, King Faisal Mosque, Marbella Club, interior of a cinema, Novotel, Rolla Square, Sharjah International Airport, Allied Building (The Deal Building), Lake Khalid. Mariam Kamal. Courtesy of South and Southeast Asian Video Archive, University of Wisconsin–Madison, Boston College Libraries

Vilkkanundu Swapnangal | 1980, India (Malayali), Azad, Director

Some Sharjah sites caught on film: Airport Mosque, Al Khan Bridge, Lake Khalid, Bank Street, Carlton Hotel, Central Souk, Emiri Diwan, Sharjah Corniche, Inter-Continental Hotel, Sharjah Cinema, Sharjah Central Post Office, Al Qassimi Hospital, Sharjah International Airport. B. K. Menon, Marunadan Movies.

There almost seemed to be a film genre, sourced from Pakistan, India, Egypt, and other places from where people came to the Gulf, in search of moving up a notch in the hierarchy of life. There were at least two films intended to be shot in Dubai, neither of which was granted the necessary approvals from the city. Except for some furtive, roadside filming at Dubai Creek, both films instead secured permission to shoot in Sharjah. Sharjah starred as Dubai.

By then, *Dubai* was anyway a stand-in term for any place where, with a little luck, you could make a fast buck on the slippery terms of petroleum trade. In 1980, the Malayali film *Vilkkanundu Swapnangal*, or Dreams for Sale, was released, with the celebrity actor Mammootty in his first credited role. In 1984, the Punjabi film *Jat Kamala Gaya Dubai*, or Jat Kamala Goes to Dubai, was released. Each film opens in a rural village where the male protagonist faces countless frustrations, for one of them even death threats. A new start in Dubai, that is Sharjah, seems to be each character's only option. The first survives a wretched journey at sea, carrying his dead companion to shore and walking over desert mountains to arrive at the Airport Mosque in Sharjah.[1] The second uses wily means to raise the cash to buy a work opportunity that turns out to be a swindle; he departs from his sweetheart by horse-drawn cart. We see him next at Sharjah International Airport, trying to go up the down escalator.[2] Once in the city, both heroes try the litany of usual jobs available to an undocumented migrant: construction worker, lunchroom waiter, hotel bellhop, car washer, and even human mannequin. One gets a break to become a nightclub crooner; the other arrives at the brink of losing an executive job in real estate development. No gain is permanent. In the end, one hero returns victorious, shaded by his resort beach hat, atop a newly purchased tractor—his beloved again by his side, his position in the village recast; the other returns home to settle a score—for love, for honor—his destiny not fulfilled but certainly shaped by his days in Sharjah.

1. See p. 37.
2. See p. 387.

01

Ammar Al Attar in Conversation with Prem Ratnam

SHARJAH IN A PHOTOGRAPHY STUDIO

In the late 1960s, when the territory now named the United Arab Emirates (UAE) was still known as the Trucial States, there was a wave of migration, mainly men from India and Pakistan, to this land of nascent opportunity. Some set up businesses, including photography studios that came to document both the transient and the more settled population.

In 2013, following my passion for archival photography, I visited the oldest studios in Deira, Dubai, and was inspired to start Reverse Moments, a research project focused on visual archives of the UAE's social history. My initial goal was to outline the origins of photography in the UAE, but Reverse Moments grew into much more than that. I found not only portraits on slides and negatives but also images of life in the UAE's cities that had been featured in regional publications, all of which I hope to compile and make accessible in a public archive in the future.

To date, photographer Prem Ratnam has been my most important collaborator. I met him in 2014 when I visited his studio, located next to where Sharjah Cinema once stood. We began rummaging through drawers and boxes of old slides, many of which Prem had lost track of through the years. So many archives had accumulated that he added a floor between his ground and mezzanine floors to store it all. Since that day, our weekly meetings have become crucial to the development of the Reverse Moments archive as well as to the formation of this book.

Ammar: Can you tell me your personal story with photography?
Prem: It was my father who got me interested in photography. He was a mechanical engineer, but he began learning photography at school. He had a very old camera that he allowed me to use. I remember one day, when I was about eight years old, he took me to the beach, and I took a picture of the sunset with a boat on the horizon. That was my very first picture.

Did that lead you to study photography?
No. I graduated in physics from college in India, and I also studied chemistry and mathematics. But I always loved photography. During my college days, I used to take a small pocket camera with me everywhere. Every morning, I would load a roll and go to college, which was on top of a hill. At the end of each day, I would take the roll for processing and get another one. I finished college in 1967 and started looking for a job. I applied to a local film institute, but didn't get in. My cousin had a photography studio in Abu Dhabi, so he sent me a visitor's visa and asked me to come. I had to go to the British Embassy in Madras to get the visa, and then from there I traveled to Bombay and took a ship to Port Rashid in Dubai. I landed on June 5, 1971, and my cousin took me by car to Abu Dhabi. His studio was in an old building by the post office.

What were your main duties in the studio?
I worked there from 1971 to 1974, and used to take portraits in the studio, but a lot of my work was in outdoor commissions as well. Large oil companies such as Crescent Petroleum and Dana Gas would hire me to take aerial shots from helicopters, and there was also a hotel called The Baalbeck. I covered their parties and functions. I was always very busy especially during National Day celebrations. I have, however, lost many of my photographs from this period.

How did you end up moving to Ajman?
In 1974, I went back to India, to Kerala, for vacation, and when I came back, I saw an advert in the newspaper for a job with United Colour Film (UCF)

in Ajman. I applied, and got a job working with Mr. Abdullah Al Murad. At the time, the office was situated opposite the Ruler's Palace, and I took a great many images for royal functions and at the sheikh's palace. I also worked a lot with the Trans-Arabian Pipeline Company, taking images of pipelines in the desert.

Why did you decide to leave UCF and open your own studio?
At the time, I was single and a bachelor. I sent some money home to my mother, but everything else I earned I would spend on books and equipment. In 1982, there was an issue with salary increases, so I decided to set up my own business. I knew a lot of people by then, and whenever they needed me, I would get a call.

Why did you move to Sharjah?
While I was working at UCF, I became familiar with Sharjah. I spent my leisure time there with my friends, either watching movies or going to the Sharjah Book Centre, which is where I bought a lot of my photography books. At the time, the Sharjah Expo Centre was also there, and I had a lot of work from their events and functions. I also did a lot of weddings, and I was one of the first photographers to collate images into albums for my clients. Thanks to this and to my reputation, I was really busy.

Can you describe your studio as it was in 1982?
When I started, the studio was bigger than most. I had an entire hall with enough space to photograph large groups and to provide a small dressing room. Downstairs, there was a small dark room; back then I was only shooting in black and white. By that time, my younger brother had joined me, and he was working at UCF. Together we also worked with photo enlargement, which was a large part of our business.

Have your images ever been published?
Yes, plenty of times. My images have appeared in numerous newspapers over the years. Also, in 1992, one of my friends was commissioned to make a book about Dubai. I took a lot of pictures for him. The book was called *Images of Dubai*. It was commissioned by Dubai Municipality and published in two editions. When I was working at UCF, I was also commissioned by Emirates Post to take landmark images of all the emirates, which were later used for postage stamps.

I think you were also creative and innovative—perhaps that helped you to develop your practice?
I used to read, read, and read some more so that I was familiar with all the theory before putting it into practice. In the 1980s, I covered the expansion of Khor Fakkan Port, which was a difficult job, and I also had to think on my feet at the many functions and weddings that I attended. Once, I was commissioned by Al Huzaifa Furniture to do a product shoot in their show room. I decided to take the furniture to the park to get more interesting shots. This was considered quite experimental at the time.

Why do you have so many images of architecture?
In Sharjah, I covered a lot of events and took many portraits, but in my free time I was interested in the architecture of the city. Buildings were my passion, and I always had my camera with me. I liked getting as high up as possible. I went up in helicopters and took great shots. Even when I wasn't working, I climbed to the top of the highest buildings. These were the images that I loved to take and also the ones that I kept.

Why didn't you keep all your images?
I used to keep all my pictures, but later had to throw some away due to space. It became a matter of keeping the ones I was interested in, especially those of friends and family and also of architecture. Luckily, I met you, and all of these are now being shared. Otherwise they probably would have remained in storage and eventually lost.

When did you switch to digital?
Honestly, I don't remember the exact year, but it was as soon as it came out. We always had to stay up-to-date by getting the newest models and brands whenever they were released. If we didn't stay ahead, we would lose business.

Did your children follow in your footsteps?
I got married in 1983, and my wife is a mathematics teacher in Sharjah. We have two daughters. One is a chemical engineer, and the other is a graphic designer. It is a nice balance between art and science.

Thank you very much for sharing your story.
Thank you. It is really my pleasure.

02

03

01. Photographer Prem Ratnam at work at the United Colour Films studio, Ajman. Images: Prem Ratnam, Hemlyn Photography Studio.
02. Hemlyn Photography Studio operated out of a storefront in a mixed-use block on Al Arouba Street, early 1980s. The building was designed by Arab Engineering Bureau, 1977.
03. Interior of Hemlyn Photography Studio, early 1980s.
04. Prashanth Mukundan, assistant to Prem Ratnam at Hemlyn Photography Studio, early 1980s.
05. Prem Ratnam and his brother Deva walk the flooded streets of Sharjah. On March 3, 1988, Dubai-based daily *Gulf News* reported on severe flooding and the resulting "atrocious living conditions" in Sharjah, especially for South Asian expatriates. Deva Ratnam rests above the flood level on a raised building dais along King Faisal Street, designed by Dutch architect Reinder de Vries. The fact that the building is raised is evidence that such floods might have been expected. The building's facade was significantly renovated in 2018.
06. Deva Ratnam at a recently installed railing along the reclaimed land of Lake Khalid. Holiday Inn, background right, late 1980s.
07. Deva Ratnam on King Faisal Street, late 1980s. On the right is a residential building designed by Adnan Saffarini. The same design was implemented for a building on Al Wahda Street.
08. The Ratnams' tour of Sharjah ended on drier ground in front of the Central Souk. In the background, between the souk and King Faisal Mosque is the Union Monument, 1984, commemorating the establishment of the UAE. The surrounding Al Ittihad Park was designed by Arab Engineering Bureau and Carlos Marinas Rubio, late 1980s.

c needs like Nikon.
Nikon
cameras Kodak film Kodak pape
melt your icy heart.

insist on
Kodacolor VR
Film and see the difference
Kodak film Kodak paper
Kodak
FILM
منتجات
كوداك
Kodak
FILM
Kodak
FILM
film

05

06

07

08

Sharjah International Airport

Architect
Edward Mansfield, Sir William Halcrow & Partners

Sub-Consultant
Alan F. Meldrum, Halcrow International Partnership

Structural Engineers and Consultants
Nathan Croft & Leggatt, Project Engineers Partnership

Contractor
Khansaheb Gammon Ltd., Khansaheb Civil Engineering

Construction
Halcrow International Partnership

Steelwork Consultant
A.E. Watson Ltd.

Facade Consultants
Anmac Ltd.

Quantity Surveyors
Widnell & Trollope

Client
Government of Sharjah

Completed
1977

Status
Renovated

In 1975, Sharjah's ruler Sheikh Sultan bin Muhammad Al Qasimi reportedly asked Sir William Halcrow and Partners to pick out a site for Sharjah's new airport. The firm, with more than twenty years of experience in Sharjah, had been pushing for such a contract since as early as 1963. Its engineers chose a location fifteen kilometers east of Sharjah's built-up city, far enough away from the city's urban fabric to support a tale about a "rise out of the desert."[1]

Sharjah's new terminal had to take into consideration environmental factors, including noise pollution, and the more dominant Dubai International Airport just a little more than twenty kilometers away. In addition to accommodating the prescribed 3,670-meter runway, proximity to road networks and state boundaries also influenced the site selection process. The airport was also only six kilometers away from the neighboring emirate of Ajman.

Halcrow's multi-faceted engineering and planning office was able to secure significant aspects of the eventual $108-million (AED 430 million) project, including its architectural design. In December 1979, Sharjah International Airport opened with an unforgettable 35-meter, minaret-inspired control tower and three massive domes that were, according to Halcrow, "designed to reflect traditional Islamic geometrical patterns."[2] Sharjah's airport was reportedly "controlling the air minaret style."[3] According to Halcrow, the airport's design, interior and exterior, reflected an Arab or Islamic identity, as instructed by Sharjah's ruler, whose hand-drawn sketches for the project illustrated his investment in the design. The three-domed terminal building signaled the airport's various uses, with the largest dome covering the airport's main concourse with its 48-meter diameter span. Each of the other two smaller 30-meter domes capped the arrival and departure halls. In each of these, an upper mezzanine with waiting areas and cafes brought travelers closer to a richly decorated ceiling. Pedestrian arcades and bridges connect the main hall with the arrival and departure areas.

A fourth and smaller dome near the control tower houses VIP areas, which the ruler allegedly also sketched, including its ceremonial stairs.

Each double-layered dome, in consideration of "cost, ease and speed," was created with a steel frame clad with glass-reinforced plastic on the exterior and textured Pyrok on the interior. The total weight of the three domes is 203 tons, with some of the weight transferred to the concrete frame below and the rest to "rocker assemblies."[4]

While the reinforced-concrete structure of the control tower mimics a minaret, additional minaret-themed lighting units were used in the main terminal's parking lot to incorporate more Islamic-inspired design. The interiors of the airport were also carried out with elaborate attention to detail. Walls are adorned with Islamic arches clad in patterned, ceramic window screens. "Sumptuously furnished and bedizened," Sharjah airport opened with the reputation of being "the most beautiful airport in the world," replete with an illuminated water fountain reaching toward the apex of the main concourse's dome, though there were at first only three flights a day.[5]

Notes:

1. "Sharjah's Man Made Oasis Set for Take Off," *New Civil Engineer*, April 19, 1979.
2. Ibid.
3. Edward Mansfield, "Controlling the Air Minaret Style," *Chartered Quantity Surveyor*, January 1980.
4. G.M. Pinfold, "The Dome Roofs at Sharjah International Airport," *Building with Steel*, May 1980.
5. Alex Hamilton, "Dhows, Deserts and Dirhams," *Guardian*, November 21, 1981.

02

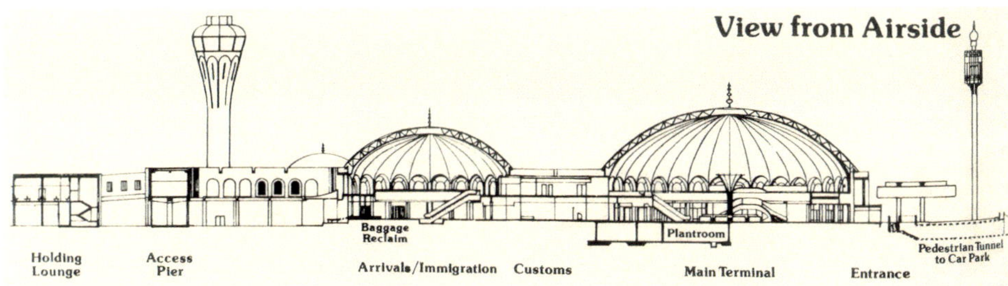
View from Airside
Baggage Reclaim
Plantroom
Pedestrian Tunnel to Car Park
Holding Lounge
Access Pier
Arrivals/Immigration
Customs
Main Terminal
Entrance

03

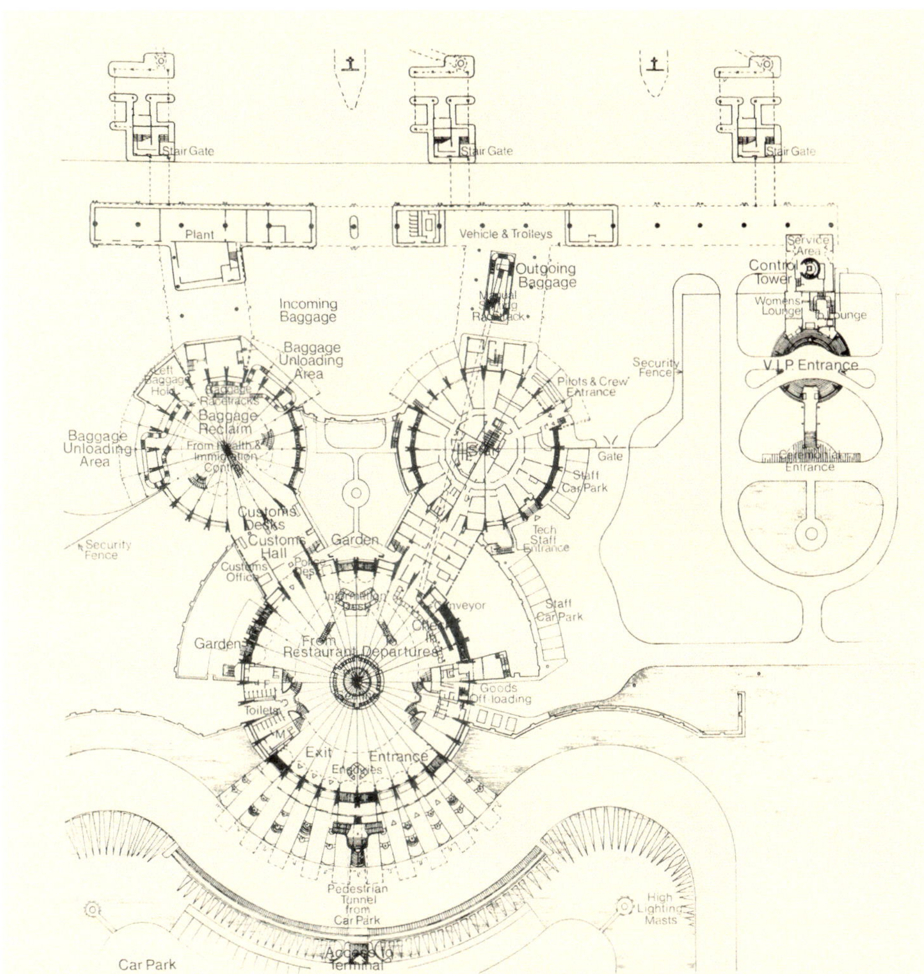
Stair Gate
Stair Gate
Stair Gate
Plant
Vehicle & Trolleys
Service Area
Control Tower
Outgoing Baggage
Incoming Baggage
Womens Lounge
Lounge
Baggage Unloading Area
Security Fence
V.I.P Entrance
Pilots & Crew Entrance
Baggage Reclaim
Baggage Unloading Area
Gate
Entrance
Staff Car Park
Security Fence
Customs Desks
Customs Hall
Garden
Tech Staff Entrance
Customs Office
Conveyor
Staff Car Park
Garden
Restaurant
Departures
Goods Off-loading
Toilets
Exit
Entrance
Pedestrian Tunnel from Car Park
High Lighting Masts
Car Park
Access to Terminal

04

05

06

07

08

Images:

01. Hamid Durani, of Honeymoon Studio, traveled to Sharjah International Airport to say goodbye to his friend Gulam Alim (right) an employee at Sharjah's post office, late 1970s. Prem Ratnam, Hemlyn Photography Studio.
02. According to Halcrow, a preliminary sketch by Sharjah's ruler Sheikh Sultan bin Muhammad Al Qasimi, undated. Courtesy of Halcrow/Jacobs.
03. Schematic section, Halcrow, undated. Airport Forum, courtesy of Halcrow/Jacobs.
04. "Islamic architecture," according to Dubai-based *Khaleej Times*, "gives a touch of class at Sharjah," (October 16, 1981). Site plan, Halcrow, undated. Airport Forum, courtesy of Halcrow/Jacobs.
05. Hamid Durani (second from right) and other friends have a final cup of tea with Gulam Ali (third from right) under one of the airport's dome, late 1970s. Hamid Durani, Honeymoon Studio.
06. The airport's escalators were an exhibition of technology, late 1970s. Hamid Durani, Honeymoon Studio.
07. Hamid Durani's brother poses in front of the reservation desks before departing to the UK, late 1970s.
08. Forty-eight meters in diameter, the main dome is carried on a reinforced-concrete, load-bearing base and has a double-layer frame of steel lattice. Photograph, 1980. Tata Steel, courtesy of RIBA Collections.
09. An aerial view of Sharjah International Airport reveals an air monitor designed to recall a minaret. The high-mast lighting, capped with their own domes, were intended to heighten the "Islamic effect" by lighting the airport's domes at night. Cars approached the primary dome via a tunnel under the drop-off overpass. "On entering the dome-shaped main terminal building they will find a modern system geared to speed and comfort." H. Brey, Peichär, Sharjah Airport Authority.

Water boosters for packaged hotel

Expertise in modular construction enabled a Scottish firm, Anchor Construction Co Ltd, of Edinburgh, to design, supply and complete a 40-room motel in Sharjah in just five months. This performance led to a second order from the client, Sheikh Faisal, calling for a fully modular package comprising the 102-bedroom Anchor Motor Inn, complete with lounges, restaurants, etc, for erection at the new international airport in Sharjah.

This considerably larger complex, demanding an abundance of cold water for drinking, etc, and hot water for baths and kitchens, called for careful specification of pressure boosting equipment for the water services. An answer was found in Megator booster sets which, in addition to facilitating the supply of all cold water services in the hotel, also supplies a calorifier to provide hot water.

The continuously running packaged pressure set incorporates three vertical multi-stage pumps, each with a capacity of 24 litres/min, a hydraulic accummulator, control equipment and all wiring and pipework. The duty pump runs continuously, and the support pump comes into operation when demand rises beyond the capacity of the duty set. The third pump is a standby. The support and standby pumps are started and stopped automatically by pressure switches and the duties of all the pumps can be interchanged periodically to ensure uniform use.

The booster sets were supplied by Megator Pumps and Compressors Ltd, of London.

☐ 326

Top: Anchor Motor Inn under construction in Sharjah. Above left: model of the completed hotel. Above right: modules for the project were factory made. Water services are pressurised by a Megator booster set.

01

02

Anchor Motor Inn

Engineering Consultant
Anderson Associates

Contractor
Anchor Construction Company Limited

Client
Sheikh Faisal bin Khalid bin Mohamed Al Qasimi

Completed
1979

Status
Existing

Their speediness made Scotland-based Anchor Construction Company popular in Sharjah, and they were particularly adept at handling modular prefabricated construction. After completing a forty-three-room guesthouse, known as Marhaba Hotel, for the French concern ETPM in only five months in 1978, the company was commissioned by the same client to design, supply, and assemble a "packaged hotel," located within a five-minute-walk from Sharjah's recently completed international airport.

The company chartered a ship from Edinburgh's Leith port to deliver the new hotel's six-by-four-meter prefabricated units. Each unit was a complete bedroom and sanitary cell. The dimensions and spatial organization of the hotel's rooms were designed exactly like a Holiday Inn in London, as requested by the client Sheikh Faisal bin Khalid bin Mohamed Al Qasimi.

The $3.3-million hotel, also known as the Airport Hotel, offered 102 bedrooms, several spacious lounges, a tennis court, swimming pool, nightclub, bars, and restaurants. Financing for the project came from both the Bank of Scotland and the Bank of America, with guarantees from the British Export Credits Guarantee Department, suggesting that British commerce authorities considered the prefabricated systems to have a lucrative future as an export to the Gulf region.

The fully modularized project was the first of its scale in the UAE; although two pre-fab housing factories already operated out of Sharjah with an output of four houses per day. With the Anchor Motor Inn, an imagined prefabricated world crept closer to reality.

01. British press covering the achievements in modular construction that brought about Sharjah's Anchor Motor Inn, 1979.
02. Exterior view, 1980s. International General Stores/Farook Stationery.

A flyover added to alleviate roundabout traffic on Arabian Gulf Street, 1980s. Top left: Municipality Souk (demolished), designed by Pakistani architects Sagheer Ahmed Khan and Kamal Khorsheed of Sharjah Municipality. Tanweer Ahmad Zaidi, the municipality's chief engineer, 1970–87, designed the souk's steel structure built by local contractor Bin Hadda, 1974. Courtesy of Ahmed Rukni Al Awadhi.

Mini-city project

The Charles de Gaulle centre in Sharjah is one of the most exciting projects in the Gulf region. In its final form the centre will be a mini-city where 15,000 people will live and work as a self-contained community with all its needs catered for in the complex. It will have five high-rise blocks varying in height from nine to 40 storeys, linked by a ground floor and mezzanine complex of air conditioned walk-throughs with banks, boutiques and foodshops. "It will be the Bullring of the Gulf" say the developers.

The first stage of construction will comprise two of the lower blocks in the foreground of the photograph below, one nine storeys high with 8,000 sq. m. for shops and 4,000 sq. m. for offices, and second, on the right, 15 to 18 storeys high with 15,000 sq. m. of space. Estimated cost is Dh.30m. No exact figure for the whole centre can be given as yet, but based on present building costs, the five block centre is expected to cost in the region of Dh.300m. at least. The decision to continue construction on the other three main blocks is to be taken at a later stage when the economic needs of the Emirate can be more accurately assessed.

The whole project is being developed by ADRECO (Arabian Development Real Estate Company) which comprises the Renault Development Overseas Corporation, and a number of Kuwaiti and Lebanese interests including the Beirut-based Investment and Financing Bank SAL, and local merchants of Sharjah. The Sharjah Government itself has taken 20 per cent. The centre is being designed by a prize-winning French architect, Jean Dubuisson.

Perhaps the most exciting prospect in the centre is that foreign companies may be able to buy space in the blocks. The developers have not yet decided whether to sell or rent the office accommodation, but under a new law which should come out shortly in Sharjah foreigners would be able to buy office space.

At the moment, though, the whole project has been held up by the Dubai/Sharjah border dispute, for Dubai has been claiming the land it is built on. Until the dispute is finally settled by the Supreme Council, piling work on the first blocks has been halted. In the meantime the company estimates that building costs are going up at the rate of 2 per cent. a month, and that already they have lost Dh.6m. in delayed returns. The developers are now seeking compensation.

K.B.

Source: Kathleen Bishtawi, *Financial Times*, December 10, 1976, "Mini-city Project."

Charles de Gaulle Center

It is difficult to determine just how far this project came before it evaporated. There is little evidence of it outside of some promotional reporting in a Sharjah-focused supplement for the *Financial Times* on December 10, 1976. The short piece describes a new "mini-city" made up of five abstract slab buildings, reaching as high as forty stories and promising high-end apartments, resort-style hotel rooms, business suites, and commercial opportunities. There were to be 15,000 residents—equal to about a third of Sharjah city's population at the time.[1]

Much of the project's equity and its designer were French. The French carmaker Renault was allegedly involved through a short-lived, ancillary, overseas development corporation. It was also a shareholder in another short-lived entity called the Arabian Development Real Estate Company, which pooled further commitments from Kuwaiti, Lebanese, and Sharjah investors, including a 20% stake from the Sharjah government.

The project's size was incongruous with the rest of Sharjah, but it was a direct response to Dubai's recent announcements: There was the World Trade Centre, made public in 1974, with renderings circulating of the region's future tallest building, not to mention a high-end hotel, exhibition halls, and the potential to include a vast shopping mall. Also in 1974, Dubai Municipality received designs for a vast new city designed by Doxiadis Associates International for a massive development abutting the no-build zone still under contention with Sharjah. It was proposed as a "unifying element" for the two rivalrous cities, with the profits flowing to Dubai. By 1976, the project was shelved and replaced by an $85-million proposal for Dubai's "biggest private enterprise building complex"—smooth, abstract high-rise towers, like those proposed for Sharjah, replete with hotel rooms and luxury apartments.

By 1976, new projects were being announced in Sharjah with abandon. The *Financial Times* reported that its ruler had a "flair for design." The year he took out a $20-million loan largely to fund the Central Souk, the government was expected to earn only about $12.6 million from petroleum sales.[2] While Sharjah's debts were to multiply over the next decade, optimism seemed undeterred, though this project signaled the limits to that ambition.

French architect Jean Dubuisson was a late-modernist architect, a contributor to France's post–World War II reconstruction through the deployment of huge and dense projects, most notably at Maine-Montparnasse in Paris. In Sharjah, he applied his overwrought tendencies, this time to accommodate not a shelter-seeking population but real estate bravado.

The project's demise likely had much to do with its ambitions: to overtake Dubai as the developer of spectacular development. Its first phase was only meant to materialize two mid-rise buildings; but, according to the *Financial Times* coverage, a federal court halted construction, based on the Dubai government's claim that the site was inside the no-build zone between the two cities still disputing their shared border. The foundations of the two buildings were reportedly completed before their abandonment. The site was allegedly anchored at the Al Khan roundabout along Al Wahda Street, near but well within today's acknowledged border.

Architect
Jean Dubuisson

Contractor
Setec

Client
Arabian Development Real Estate Company

Status
Terminated

1. The project was also covered in "New Office Centre for Sharjah," *Middle East Construction*, August–September 1976.
2. See p. 127. Kathleen Bishtawi, "The Economy," *Financial Times*, December 10, 1976.

Rendering, Jean Dubuisson, no date. © Dubuisson Fund. SIAF / City of Architecture and Heritage / Archives of 20th century architecture.

PUB RENAULT
INFI
BANK

HOTEL ALADIN
Restaurant

Hotel Aladin

Architects
Ramzi Shaker
Regnault & Partners (conversion to hotel)

Contractor
Contracting Marine Engineering

Clients
Jassim Saif Mohamed Al Midfa, Fikry El Gawly

Completed
1976, converted to hotel in 1978

Status
Demolished, 1995

The brief life of Hotel Aladin, its rise and fall, reflects a chapter of Sharjah's history, particularly the period when the city was marketed to the world. The project began as a twelve-story residential building, filled with three-bedroom apartments atop a ground floor of shops. Designed and built in 1976, the building's owners were Sharjah businessman Jassim Saif Mohamed Al Midfa and Fikry El Gawly, an Egyptian engineer who owned Contracting Marine Engineering. The two owners hired Egyptian architect Ramzi Shaker to design the building.

Less than a year after the building's completion, the two partners sensed Sharjah's more profitable economic sector shifting, from housing Sharjah's well-off expatriates to entertaining them. In 1977, they submitted an application to convert upper floors into hotel rooms and the top floor into restaurants. Not unlike a scene out of a Fellini movie, in 1978 a helicopter hovered over Sharjah with a giant genie lamp tethered to it. It delivered its cargo, made by Greek craftsmen, to the tower's roof, where the lamp was mounted to signal that the building had become a hotel. Hotel Aladin was one of Sharjah's most legendary meeting places. With no adjacent high buildings, the hotel's height bestowed unmatched views of the water, the corniche, and Sharjah's ongoing modern transformation. During his official visit of the premises, Sharjah's ruler was given a commemorative one-kilogram golden lamp, a replica of the one that crowned the building, and shown how restaurant guests had views over the high walls of his recently completed Seef Palace.

The top floor offered one of Sharjah's most fashionable leisure venues with views framed by pointed arches, by then considered a common, restrained gesture of Islamic architecture. The management promoted the hotel's "novelties, artistic structures, aquaria and the mosaic tile works providing an atmosphere entirely different not only in the Gulf but in hotels in the entire Arab world." The hotel's management targeted German tourists especially, perhaps in tune with the Sharjah government's collaboration with the German airline Lufthansa.

Hotel Aladin became a social landmark during Sharjah's boom years. Its French restaurant and cafe hosted numerous musical events, and its bars, especially the Falken-Keller, or the falcon cellar, were favored watering holes in Sharjah. That was at least until October 9, 1985, when the government of Sharjah banned alcohol sales. In "a complete surprise" to the city's nine hotels, according to local reporting, police officers arrived that evening with the fresh decree in hand and ordered all bars and liquor storerooms "completely sealed." The decree also limited the kinds of dance performances and stage shows that could be presented at the city's hotels. Eventually, the government directed wholesalers to accept returns of the hotels' unused inventory, but the hotels suffered a much more devastating financial blow from the dramatic drops in customer patronage. Many say that, when the emirate had financial troubles in the 1980s, the tourism industry could not provide the needed economic relief due, in major part, to the alcohol ban.

The hotel persevered for a full decade after the alcohol ban ... until it could no longer. On February 17, 1995, the tower was imploded. No helicopter rescued the genie lamp before the demolition. It is said, however, that the lamp survived the collapse and has found sanctuary in a warehouse in Sharjah's industrial district.

02

03

04

05

06

07

08

01. View from the corniche road toward Ajman. Alexander Gnezdilov.
02. The Panorama Restaurant on the tenth floor offered a view of Gulf waters and, directly below, Al Seef Palace. Courtesy of Regnault & Partners.
03. According to Hotel Aladin's marketing brochure, the Falken-Keller, its bar, was the only place in the Gulf to serve "live" beer from Germany. Courtesy of Regnault & Partners.
04. Taken from Hotel Aladin's roof, the photograph captures the arrival of the hotel's crowning sculpture, Aladin's lamp, 1978. In the background, a residential tower designed by A. Moez & Moh. Hegazy Architects for Sultan Bin Ali Al Owais, 1975. Attributed to Klaus Gruschwitz, courtesy of Ann and Kenneth Sadolin Pedersen.
05.–08. A photographer for Dubai-based daily *Gulf News* captured the demolition of Hotel Aladin, February 17, 1995. © Gulf News, Dubai.

In the early 1960s, when Al Arouba Street connected Sharjah to Dubai, an unassuming sign—“Smile, You Are in Sharjah”—was staked along the final stretch leading into the city. Various iterations of the sign were created as the

Appendices

Sharjah, 1700–1995

1700–1755
The mercantile dynasty Al Qawasim builds up a commercial base through control of the ports at Sharjah, Khor Fakkan, Dibba, Rams, Ajman, Fujairah, and Umm Al Quwain, a coastal territory that makes up a significant portion of what will become the United Arab Emirates shoreline. The dynasty also controls parts of present-day Iran, including Qeshm and Lingah.

1800
The Qawasim fleet that dominates the Gulf waters includes more than 500 ships. Among other regional powers, it competes for influence with the British, who aspire to control regional access to trade with India.

1819
A third attack by British forces on the Qawisim fleet and its landside strongholds brings forth an era of British control over the region that will last until 1971.

1820
Regional leaders, including Sharjah's ruler, sign the first of several treaties with the British government. A subsequent treaty will name their collective dominions the Trucial States.

1823
The British government selects Sharjah as its regional base on the peninsula, with an Arab resident agent eventually reporting to British officers in Bushehr, Iran. From 1934, he reports to the British political residency in Bahrain.

1866
By the end of Sheikh Sultan bin Saqr Al Qasimi I's rule, Sharjah's inland reaches have increased significantly, allowing a diversification of the emirate's economy to include sea trade, agriculture, and mining.

Circa 1903
The Taymiyah School is established in Sharjah, financed by a pearl trader. The school soon counts 320 students, 120 of whom are boarding students.

1908
The town of Sharjah's estimated population: 15,000. The population of the larger territory of Sharjah: 45,000.

1924
Sheikh Sultan bin Saqr Al Qasimi II assumes power in Sharjah and is "subsequently recognized by the [colonial] Government of India as the new Sheikh."

1927
The municipality is established in Sharjah, although 1961 is also mentioned as a founding date.

1928
The British residency agent, Isa bin Abdullatif Al Serkal, imports the Trucial States' first car (two years before any arrive at Dubai).

1932
In March, Sheikh Sultan bin Saqr Al Qasimi agrees to provide a land lease for British airport facilities. On July 22, he signs an agreement with the British government, which includes payments to him to hire local men as security guards for airport facilities. By October, the "air route" is in operation.

1935
The ruler of Sharjah reports to the British agency that "about 500 people" have left Sharjah in protest of the 1932 airport agreement. At the same time, the ruler's message is that establishment of a British-sponsored post office must be hurried along.

1939
In October, a white British political officer is posted in Sharjah during the year's cooler seasons. Sharjah's estimated population: 5,000.

1948
An estimated population count, likely just for Sharjah town and registering a decline resulting from emigration: 4,000.

1950
For years, the British government has not paid rent for the airport and Royal Air Force camp, citing the hardship of World War II as the reason. Acting ruler of Sharjah requests back pay of rent since the "termination of hostilities with Japan" on May 15, 1945 onward. He is partially motivated by the mounting costs of health care in Bombay for his brother the ruler. He agrees to Great Britain's suggested increased rate of 500 riyals, or about one hundred dollars, per month.

1951
In March, Sheikh Sultan bin Saqr Al Qasimi dies after seeking medical treatment in Bombay and London. His brother and regent during his absence, Mohamed bin Saqr, rules for less than two months. The deceased ruler's son Saqr bin Sultan becomes ruler on May 21. The British-led land force Trucial Oman Levies is founded in Sharjah.

1952
American doctor Sarah Hosman opens a missionary medical clinic in Sharjah and offers free consultations, but patients must leave with a complimentary copy of the Bible. In March, British aid to Sharjah is considered at the first meeting of the Trucial Council, an advisory body of local leaders convened by the British Political Agency.

1953
Kuwait's government, still overseen as a British protectorate, provides teachers for a new school in Sharjah—Al Qasimiyah School, considered the first modern school for boys in the Trucial States.

1954
In the same year the British government moves from Sharjah to a new compound constructed in Dubai, it also commissions British engineering company Sir William Halcrow & Partners to complete studies of both Dubai and Sharjah's harbors. Their analysis, published in early 1955, will endorse the development of Dubai's at the expense of Sharjah's. The British Political Agency moves from Sharjah to Dubai. Fatima Al Zahra School for girls opens in Sharjah.

1956
Non-British employees at the RAF camp strike against working conditions for five days. Sharjah's ruler collaborates with the British Political Agency to negotiate resolution. Two months later, in August, Sharjah shopkeepers threaten to close shops in alliance with Egyptian president Gamal Abdel Nasser's call for regional strikes. Traveling abroad at the time, Sheikh Saqr persuades them to stay open. Students of the new Qasimiyah School nevertheless demonstrate in support of the nationalization of the Suez Canal. In November, British records chronicle persistent public demonstrations in response to aggressions against Egypt. "There is no doubt," according to a British government account, "that some of the schoolmasters have vented their anti-British feelings and were able to instigate their boys in shouting abuse at the British Officers." On November 26, an unknown man attempts to burn a British officer's car. Sharjah's ruler employs a "well-known tracker" to find culprits. By December, "the situation has become progressively quieter. Shaikh Saqr holds another meeting with Arab and Persian merchants and closes a coffee-shop belonging to a certain Harith for three days, allowing it to re-open on the understanding that the owners will not allow his customers—mainly young men—to discuss politics there." Early in the year amidst the unrest, Sheikh Saqr visits Kuwait, where he is "entertained by most of the senior Shaikhs," spends a day in the new town of Ahmadi, and meets the director of education.

1957
A job posting for British headmaster of the new vocational school describes Sharjah as "a picturesque town of some 8,000 inhabitants stretched along a shallow tidal creek. ... It consists mainly of mud and palm-frond houses, and has a market where all the necessary and basic tinned food and supplies can be obtained." Although tension between residents and the British government is still palpable, the air station's four weekly flights are one reason to keep relations intact. In January, Sheikh Saqr announces he will "restrain his Egyptian and Jordanian schoolmasters" in response to continuing protests regarding the Suez Crisis. A few days after his announcement, British-led Trucial Oman Scouts (formerly the Levies) hold a formal parade in Sharjah and bestow medals for exceptional service. Perhaps as a meager sign of appeasement, the British government pays local contractor Khansaheb Hussain bin Hassan to complete repairs to a school's roof.

1958
Sheikh Saqr bin Sultan visits Cairo and meets Gamal Abdel Nasser, the same year he demands British funding to build a hospital and other forms of assistance. The British-sponsored trade school opens.

1961
Hunting Aerosurveys completes an aerial photographic survey of Sharjah based on photographs taken in 1960. Sharjah's ruler establishes Sharjah Municipality and Land Department. Early students of the trade school help build a second trade school in Dubai.

1963
Sharjah town's estimated population: 20,000. In an ongoing boundary disagreement, the ruler of Dubai orders the removal of oil drums that had marked the border with Sharjah since 1957. Sheikh Saqr receives his commissioned study from British consulting engineers Sir William Halcrow & Partners, effectively approving Sharjah's first town plan. A post office department is established.

1964
An Arab League delegation visits Sharjah and the Trucial States. Sheikh Saqr commits to building the organization an office in Sharjah.

1965
It is said that the Arab League office opens and the British government thwarts the arrival of staff members at the airport. The British government appoints a British official to run a development office for the Trucial States, the timing of which makes it seem a response to Arab League interests. Against British plans, Sheikh Saqr supports ongoing urban development of the city and pays for the start of constructing a new jetty according to proposals by Halcrow. Without seeing the jetty completed, Sheikh Saqr is deposed and replaced by his cousin Sheikh Khalid bin Mohammed Al Qasimi. The exact role of the British government in this coup remains uncertain since relevant documents remain classified today, but it is clear that British officials are concerned about Saqr's ties to Pan-Arabists.

1966
Sharjah now has a total of fourteen schools, including two high schools, thanks largely to the former ruler's collaboration with the Kuwaiti government and other Arab countries. On June 24, Egyptian president Gamal Abdel Nasser celebrates Sharjah Day in Cairo, still recognizing Sheikh Saqr as the emirate's rightful ruler. Following plans prepared by Halcrow, local contractor Khansaheb Civil Engineering paves the Dubai–Sharjah road. The project is completed in November, linking the two cities more smoothly, but the border dispute remains unresolved.

1967
Sharjah's police force is established and led by a British police officer. Sheikh Khalid founds a finance department and a lands and survey department. The Arab League's attempts at extending development aid continue to be frustrated, with British officials insisting it must be channeled through their government's development aid program. They do, however, allow Saudi Arabia to fund the extension of the Dubai–Sharjah road to Ras Al Khaimah, contracted to the forerunner of today's Saudi Binladin Group. The British departure from the Yemeni port city Aden makes the British land base in Sharjah even more significant.

1968
On January 16, British Prime Minister Harold Wilson announces that Britain will withdraw its forces from the Gulf by the end of 1971. On February 25, the rulers of seven Trucial States plus Bahrain and Qatar begin negotiations to create a federation. British officials sign Sharjah's first traffic regulations into law, and the first streetlights are turned on in Sharjah, likely along today's Al Arouba Street. The first census in the Trucial States, carried out by Bahraini officials, counts 31,668 residents in the Sharjah emirate, including all towns and settlements.

1969
Sharjah has a total of fifty beds in two British-government hospitals. German contractor Beton- und Monierbau completes the deepwater jetty. The project dramatically increases Sharjah's import capacity. The first road in Sharjah is paved. Halcrow's updated master plan estimates the city's population at 30,000, even though the company claims in a report that "it is not possible to determine the rate of growth of the population of Sharjah as there are no available statistics." Sheba Hotel, perhaps Sharjah's first "modern" hotel, opens.

1970
Sharjah is home to an estimated 55,000 residents and 12 fountains, which have been wired with multicolor lights installed by Dutch electronics company Philips. *Middle East Economic Digest* publishes a report extolling Sharjah as an "outstanding example of a developing country effecting the maximum utilisation of limited resources." The issue is supported by Sharjah-based advertising. Sheikh Khalid is reportedly optimistic about finding alternative revenue sources in light of pending British withdrawal, including a fishing scheme. US-based First National City Bank opens a branch in Sharjah.

1971
British officials continue pressuring local rulers to found a new national federation by end of year. Bank Melli Iran opens a branch in Sharjah. British-based Cable & Wireless secures a seventeen-year contract to re-equip and administer Sharjah's telecommunications system, currently served by only 350 lines. British forces clear out the leased airbase and RAF camp by selling surplus. The rushed sales cause a regional drop in market prices for trucks. Some of Sharjah's first churches and schools will occupy the vacated buildings. A "green belt" of trees and parkland is planned to buffer the city from its environs. In November, Halcrow completes first-phase dredging work at Sharjah Creek. One week after the creation of the United Arab Emirates, with Sharjah as one of the six initial emirates, on December 9, the new nation is recognized by the United Nations.

1972
In late January, mere weeks after federation, a "leftist coup" attempt is made by former ruler Sheikh Saqr. The predicament is an early test of the new nation's stability and its national defense force. It ends in the death of Sheikh Khalid. On January 25, Sheikh Sultan bin Muhammad Al Qasimi succeeds his assassinated brother as ruler. He ascends at a time when his state is said to be nearing a petroleum windfall estimated at around $54 million, possibly as soon as the following year. Based upon this prediction, Sheikh Sultan maintains the development fervor of his predecessor. The UAE dirham is introduced as the national currency.

1973
Sharjah's estimated population: 38,000, plus another 32,000 living in the emirate's other towns and settlements. British-based engineering firm Halcrow prepares studies for an international tender on plans to expand Sharjah's port, soon known as Port Khalid. Sheikh Sultan visits the US, attended by oil company representatives. The ruler, who has a degree in agriculture, takes interest in learning more about hydroponic agriculture advancements. As part of Sharjah's preparations for becoming an oil producer, the Bank of Sharjah is founded, the first bank to be headquartered in Sharjah. Operations begin in May the following year. Its capital is raised through investors that include the Government of Sharjah, the investment arm of Kuwait-based Mubarak Abdul Aziz Al-Hassawi, and Dutch-French Banque Paribas.

1974
Sharjah city's estimated population: 55,000. In April, Belgium-based Six Construct and Greek–West German partnership Archirodon-Hochtief are awarded $40 million in contracts for constructing what will become known as Port Khalid. The opening of Sharjah's beachside Carlton Hotel adds to the city's luster, offering travelers comfort and air conditioning. In May, the emirate secures a $50 million, multi-lender loan to accelerate development, the same month in which Sharjah's government signs contracts for a cement plant (the UAE's fourth in one year).

In July, oil production begins, but wealth predictions are reduced: Sharjah will have to share proceeds with Iran and another UAE emirate, Umm Al Quwain. Production estimates are reduced by a third. A list of infrastructural projects funded by the new wealth is already well-known: a new port, new airport, new power station, dredging work, a hotel, a drainage system, a bridge over the lagoon, and a slaughterhouse. Having advocated for a new, larger airport outside the city, British engineering company Halcrow is hired to scout out its location and will later secure contracts for its construction.

1975
The new airport officially opens, at first without the new buildings for which Halcrow has secured contracts. The UAE's first national census counts Sharjah city's population at 58,053, with a predominantly male population. The British embassy deems the number "enhanced." The Investment Bank for Trade and Finance (today Investment Bank) is founded largely with reserves from locally based Sharjah merchants and the ruling family and as a public shareholding company. Sharjah shops for a loan of about $25 million on the European financial markets, according to reports from London.

1976
Sharjah's oil production dips below the previous year's numbers. In January, Sharjah's government says it will cut spending after experiencing "cash-flow problems," resulting in delays and confusion for ongoing development projects. The following month, it tenders for the proposed Central Souk, estimated at the time to cost $20 million. Eventual cost is several times more. The 1976 census estimates Sharjah's population at 88,188, including the exclaves. The British embassy again questions the count's accuracy. The *Financial Times* estimates that about half of the population lives in Sharjah city. UK-based Jouzy & Partners secures a consulting contract for a $16.6 million, 46-kilometer road network in Sharjah. A 33-kilometer extension to the sewer network and new water supply system are also announced. Seatrain Lines Inc. secures a four-year management contract for Port Khalid, raising the stakes in port facility provisions in the UAE. In May, Sheikh Sultan visits the governor's mansion of the US State of Tennessee and the ongoing infrastructure projects by the Tennessee Valley Authority.

In October, the Dubai–Sharjah border dispute appears close to settlement, possibly with the agreement on a no-build zone but, in the end, a resolution remains elusive. The souk, recent hotels, and the airport under construction are part of Sharjah's announced plans to develop facilities for a tourism sector. The first phase receives funding of AED 1.5 million ($380,000), for various projects including construction of "forty tourist cabins" on what is called Liberty Beach. The London-based *Guardian* describes Sharjah's ongoing construction boom as "reminiscent of Abu Dhabi's six years ago. Whole streets and quarters are going up at once, and returns on property development are soaring; buildings built earlier this year are now worth almost three times their original cost of construction." Africa Hall opens with the hosting of the African-Arab Symposium.

1977
A new well at Sharjah's offshore Mubarak oil field is activated, renewing optimism in Sharjah's oil production, but profits are still below those of previous years. Despite the disappointment, new projects are completed: Al Qassimi Hospital opens with 100 beds; initial temporary passenger facilities open at the new Sharjah International Airport; a Novotel and Holiday Inn are completed; Sharjah's cement plant opens. And more projects are started: Sharjah's government secures a $20-million loan, "with little difficulty," to finance the new Central Souk and construction begins on the beachfront Inter-Continental Hotel. The National Bank of Sharjah is founded with $3.8 million in capital.

The first Sharjah Expo is organized under the theme "Exposition of Progress." It takes place on a ship outfitted as a floating hotel and managed by Holiday Inn. During its sixteen-day run starting on November 17, organizers count 151,327 visitors, more than Sharjah's entire population.

In the face of a national housing glut most evident in Sharjah, the local government institutes the country's first rent control laws, effectively freezing prices indefinitely. Favorable prices compared to those in Dubai are a strategic advantage to be maintained. It is reported that for the first time, developers have to advertise new rental units. The *Financial Times* estimates that Sharjah is the emirate hit hardest by the ongoing recession.

1978
Sharjah's government announces a new $512 million portfolio of development projects, including the expensive Central Souk project. In February, it secures a $200-million loan from a consortium of banks, its financing terms made manageable by guarantees signed by the ruler of Abu Dhabi. No local banks participate. The loan's amount is six times Sharjah's income from petroleum the previous year. In May, plans for three new hotels are shelved, the economic slowdown cited as the reason. Hotel Meridien Sharjah opens, suffering through a 25% occupancy rate during its first couple of months. With the floating hotel transformed into a ferry for cars between Jeddah and Suez, the second Sharjah Expo moves to tensile structures erected on the airport's former site.

In the midst of a regional recession caused by sinking oil prices, the *Financial Times* reports that Sharjah is home to "an almost embarrassing number of empty buildings," causing "the air of a ghost town." This is a "near-catastrophe," "not because it is the place in the Gulf hardest hit by the recession (which it is) but because its planners have created a state infrastructure and are now searching for an economy to drop into place." There are reports of "regular power cuts, leaving homes without air conditioning for up to 8 miserable sweaty hours a day."

1979
In January, Sharjah's oil production is reported to have dropped to "barely commercial" levels. A container terminal opens in Khor Fakkan, Sharjah's exclave on the Gulf of Oman. The port is part of the strategy to make Sharjah into a transshipment hub connecting the new port with the one in Sharjah city and the Sharjah International Airport—all projects overseen by Halcrow.

Sharjah International Airport's partially completed passenger terminal opens. City hotels experience a boost as a result of uncertainty about a potential alcohol ban in Dubai's hotels. "At night Sharjah blossoms through numerous cabarets, discos and supper clubs as the hotels attempt to make [up] for empty bedrooms through lucrative food and drink sales." Port Khalid welcomes its first tourist ship, MS *Europa*.

The Indian Association of Sharjah opens the city's first Indian school. Three hundred students and fourteen teachers occupy the former premises of the English School, still roofed with corrugated sheet metal.

1980
Sharjah city's estimated population: 125,149, 66% male. The government's outstanding debt is estimated at $1 billion, largely defined by development projects, including the increasing costs at the Central Souk and new airport. Developers report unpaid bills for finished and ongoing projects. The new airport averages twelve flights per day.

New oil deposits confirmed at the Sajaa oil fields offer an optimistic counterpoint to Sharjah's mounting debts "during a 1970 economic boom that went wrong." Within a week after the announcement, land transactions top AED 1 billion ($250 million). Investors from neighboring Arab countries also join in Sharjah's renewed real estate market, "making sure they are not left out." Rents in Sharjah soar.

By end of year, the number of houses has doubled since 1975; the number of businesses operating out of Sharjah has increased five-fold since 1972, to 3,907; and Sharjah Municipality counts 730 commercial buildings in the city, up from 12 in 1975. The oil announcement helps stimulate growth, as does the "relative cheapness of land and rents." The most prevalent type of business: auto repair shops. Four pedestrian subways open in response to wider and busier thoroughfares. The relatively new Sharjah Tourist Centre finalizes executive services and a tourism program intended to attract businessmen to the emirate.

1981
Emboldened by new petroleum discoveries, the Sharjah government, according to Dubai-based *Gulf News*, "is moving ahead with plans to step up the industrialisation of the area in a big way." Sharjah's exports through Port Khalid have more than tripled since 1977. Sharjah's ruler founds the emirate's economic department by decree. Municipal planners estimate that oil revenues will reach $1 billion by 1986, an approximation noticeably equivalent to the emirate's estimated debt.

Escalators are installed in the Central Souk to attract more shoppers. Sharjah claims 25 hotels with 3,000 guest rooms, a ten-fold increase in rooms since 1977. In March, despite the previous year's new water reserves, a months-long water shortage begins, blamed partially on rising population. By May, the situation worsens when rainstorms damage up to two-thirds of Sharjah's water infrastructure. Recently opened hotels scramble to find additional water sources outside Sharjah as guests are limited to a few hours of running water per day. It is reported that residents of Al Wahda Street, one of the city's main residential and commercial corridors, go ten days without running water. In July, a desalination plant in Al Layah opens, estimated to provide about five million gallons daily, enough water to meet needs until 1983.

Water shortages are succeeded by electricity shortages. During Ramadan that summer, Sharjah experiences three hours of daily "load shedding," when the energy supply is "shut off for periods during the day and night in all localities by rotation." Local magazine *Al Azmenah* reports that "the looks of horror on the faces of people trapped in elevators due to sudden outages says it all." In October, Sharjah Expo opens in the "largest air-conditioned purpose-built exhibition facility in the Middle East with over 40,000 square meters of exhibition space." Work begins on construction of four new mosques to accommodate an additional 4,000–8,000 worshippers at a time.

1982
A local newspaper declares "the bad days for landlords are over" in Sharjah, as housing rents continue to rise. Air conditioning and escalators have revived business at the Central Souk.
French companies lead as fastest growing exporters to Sharjah, in a year when Sharjah port suffers a modest reduction in overall traffic and a 17% decrease in imports after significant growth in previous years. Additionally, the number of banks with offices in the city falls from 55 in 1980 to 50. Hotels average a 35% occupancy rate during the peak months between January and March. After recording 12% occupancy rates "during most of its existence," the Inter-Continental Hotel is bought by Kuwaiti investor Mubarak Al-Hassawi.

Global oil prices continue to fall. Citing new earnings from the Sajaa oil fields and new online production of condensate and gas, Sharjah still projects annual earnings of $250 million.

1983
The border dispute between Dubai and Sharjah is reignited over oil exploration rights. Dubai police arrest Sharjah-contracted prospectors at sea for trespassing.

A year after the passenger terminal opens for full operation, Sharjah reveals expansion plans for Sharjah International Airport in February. Sharjah is home to 10,100 villas; 5,783 traditional Arab houses; 800 residential-cum-commercial buildings up to 15 stories high; 2,500 industrial establishments; 70 mosques; 13 markets; 8 police stations; 12 hospitals; 40 schools; 4 post offices; and 1 community center.

Having seen gradual increases in tourism over the last two years, Sharjah counts 8,349 tourists during its 1982–83 season, all but 441 of whom come from West Germany, Switzerland, and Austria—at least partially a result of a collaboration with Lufthansa. The population of Sharjah increases by more than 30% between 1980 and 1982. Government of Sharjah's hired planning and engineering company Halcrow estimates that the end-of-century population will reach between 280,000 and 350,000.

1984
A Dubai-based newspaper reports that half of Sharjah's petroleum revenues goes to paying off debts. Sheikh Sultan announces plans for building new dry docks at Port Khalid while those at Dubai's nearby Port Rashid suffer from disuse. Sharjah's largest employment sectors: 21,897 jobs in building and contracting, 3,482 in the food industries, 5,667 in petroleum services, 1,974 in hotels, and 1,314 in finance. There is no indication of how many workers are immigrants.

A year after a maritime border scuffle, Sharjah and Dubai governments agree to an AED 11.8 million ($3 million) road-widening project to ease traffic between the two cities.

1985
Despite ramped up tourism marketing, Government of Sharjah counts only 2,500 tourists during 1984–85, down a third since the previous year. The strong US dollar (to which the UAE dirham is linked) and limited flights are blamed for the drop. The number of recorded employees in hotels drops by a third in one year. Sharjah's daily petroleum production increases to 60,000 barrels, which helps close the emirate's thirteen-bank, $155-million loan deal. The loan, the *Financial Times* reported, "is an indication of the banking world's confidence that Sharjah ... is moving into the black after several years of financial shortfall." Resolution of the Dubai–Sharjah maritime border dispute includes an agreement that Dubai will buy gas from Sharjah's new inland oil fields. This agreement also helps ease Sharjah's debts, which "continue to be a major drain on revenues." A Dubai newspaper estimates the city's population to be 160,000.

In February, Sharjah Municipality begins a "massive landscaping and beautification project covering all parts of the city." The landmark "Smile, You Are in Sharjah" hillocks—one in Arabic, one in English—are completed. The world's third largest fountain begins operating in Khalid Lagoon. The first phase of the Green Belt Park, billed to become the region's "largest afforestation project," is completed.

On October 9, without prior notice, Sharjah police enter hotels to shut down alcohol sales. The next morning, hotel managers are summoned to police headquarters, and newspapers announce the Sharjah government's ban of alcohol sales in public, which effectively erases a major income source for the city's hotels. The decree builds upon initial restrictions announced in 1983. The hotel ban goes into effect one day before a senior member of the Saudi ruling family arrives in Sharjah for the official opening of King Faisal Mosque, financed by the Saudi government. Alcohol continues to be made available for sale, with a license, in some stores.

1986
Economic diversification programs continue as 80% of Sharjah's annual revenue is from petroleum sales. Global petroleum prices drop yet again. As a result, "Sharjah's dreams of industrialization have evaporated." Shelved projects include industrial plants, a $20-million zoo, road schemes, and a new palace for the ruler. The Union Monument is completed—an upright column bedecked with seven curlicued flutes (representing the UAE's seven emirates) and stylized references to pearls, all inside a fountain and topped with a gold-plated sphere, fifteen meters in diameter.

Sharjah's population is again estimated at 160,000. The Sharjah Municipality director, Obaid Isa Ahmed, describes Sharjah's future growth as horizontal, with a number of model houses planned throughout the emirate: "The general planning of the city, based on the lines of modern international cities, drew its inspiration, in design and structure, from the 'heritage of Islamic architecture.'" More of the Green Belt Project is completed. The 5.5-kilometer-long Green Belt Project is expected to "surround the whole city" and "protect the city from dust storms during the summer."

1987
Passenger and cargo traffic at Sharjah International Airport improves: 659,000 passengers (17.9% increase); 13,000 tons of cargo (33.6% increase); and 23,000 flights (22.3% increase). While Sharjah's ruler is abroad, his brother attempts a coup by having a local radio station report a peaceful transfer of power. The statement claims, "Mistakes were made in planning our financial policy. ... Accordingly damage has developed and debts accumulated in our budget." The *Financial Times* estimates that Sharjah's public debt remains at $1 billion. Major roads and buildings are blocked by military-issue sandbags. Within three days, the UAE Supreme Council negotiates a resolution, and Sheikh Sultan returns to power. Within ten days of the ruler's reinstatement, repayment of outstanding loans is rescheduled. About seventeen creditors agree to reschedule final payments by 1993. The sovereign debt, the highest in the world after Mexico, is said to have accrued as the result of a decrease in offshore production. Repayment negotiations started a year prior, but the coup attempt, according to one banker, "concentrated the mind wonderfully." Sharjah's hotels are reportedly operating at 3% occupancy.

1988
A feasibility study is reportedly completed for a $100-million new town somewhere between the Dubai–Sharjah road and the road leading to Sharjah International Airport. The proposal is said to be a private-sector proposal. In March, "atrocious living conditions" are reported by the Dubai-based *Gulf News* as a result of severe flooding conditions in low-lying districts, inhabited mostly by South Asian expatriates. Sharjah's debt is estimated at $1.3 billion. About a year after issuing its first set of guidelines, Sharjah's planning department sends notices to all departments pertaining to Arab-Islamic guidelines for future private development projects.

1989
Sharjah city's estimated population: 268,700. A Dubai-based daily calls Sharjah "the cultural capital of the UAE." The government counts 157,000 tourists. Local reporting asserts that Sharjah was able to endure the recent recession due to its self-sustaining agricultural and industrial development. Tax holidays and concessions to investors, as overseen by the recently founded Sharjah Chamber of Commerce, have provided a "desired shot-in-the-arm." The Green Belt project appears to be on hold; the city counts fifteen parks. Hopes of Sharjah International Airport becoming a transshipment hub remain buoyed; the airport finds a modest market niche as a stopover for transcontinental charter flights.

1990–1995
In 1990, the government tallies a 500-person increase in tourist visits. A Sharjah official declares the end of electricity and water shortages. In 1992, France-based construction company SOGEA and British engineering firm Halcrow secure contracts for tourism development projects around Lake Khalid, formerly Khalid Lagoon, its shores girded by railings and pedestrian pathways. In 1993, it is announced that Al Saf City, a new town with a man-made lake, will be developed inland from the exclave of Kalba. On February 17, 1995, Hotel Aladin is demolished.

Other Projects in Sharjah

01

02

03

04

05

06

07

08

09

10

11

12

13

14

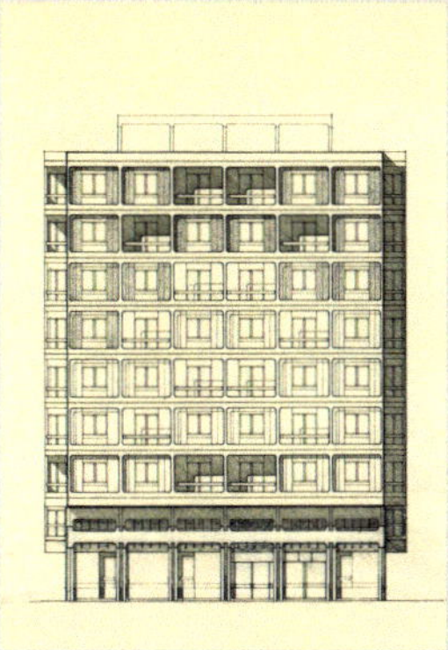

15

16

17

18

19

20

21

22

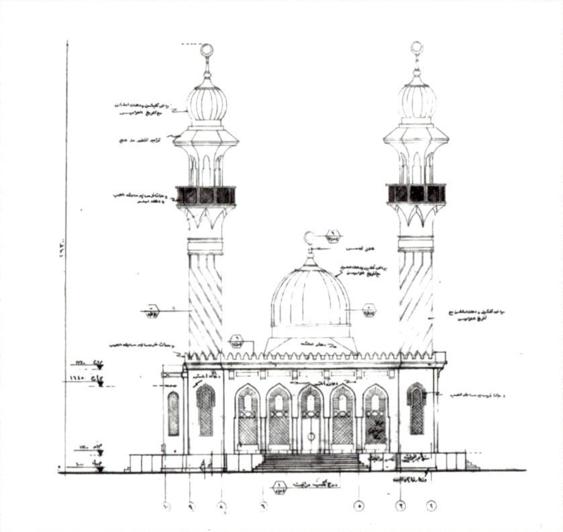

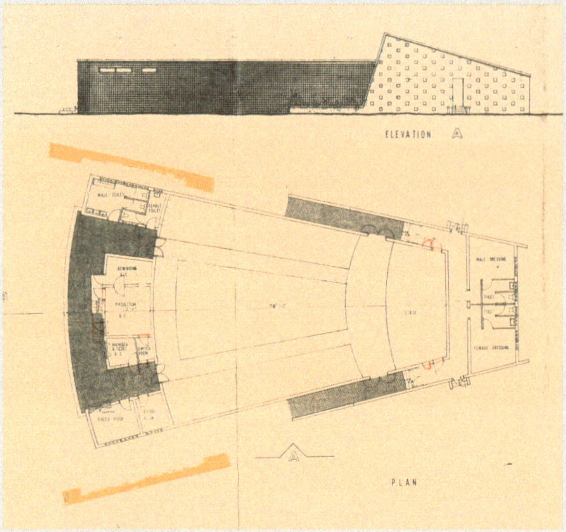

23

24

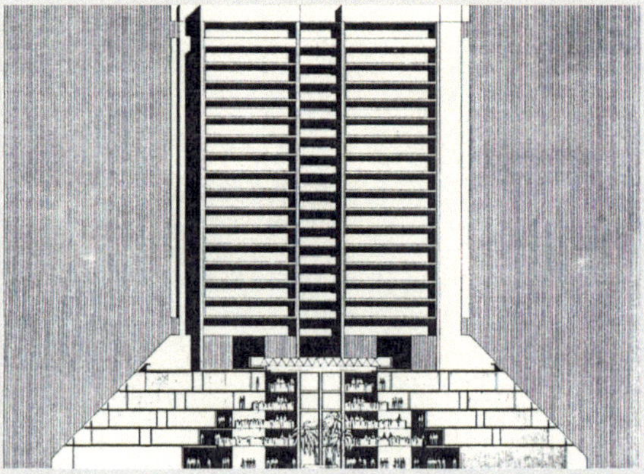

25

26

27

28

29

30

31

32

33

34

35

36

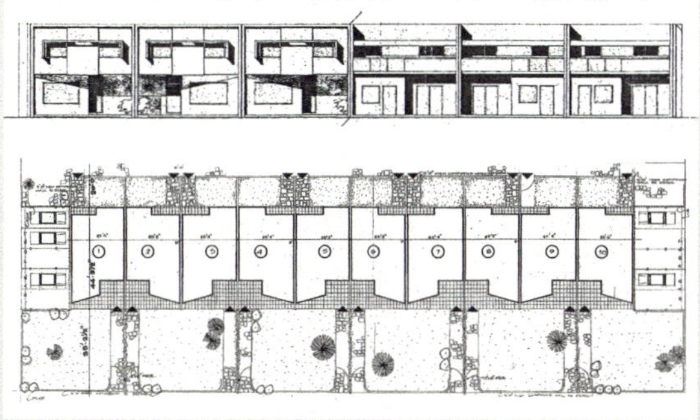

37

38

Other Projects in Sharjah

01. **Novotel Sharjah**, Fowler Hanley Inc., 1976. Existing. Image: Henk Snoek/ RIBA Collections.
02. **Hassan Hussain El Fardan Building**, Arab Engineering Bureau, 1974. Existing. **Butti Bin Bishir Building**, Khatib & Alami, 1975. Existing. **Building for Sheikha Sheikha Sultan Bin Saqr Al Qasimi & Mariam Abdulrahman Saif**, Gulf Consulting Office, 1977. Existing. Image: Sharjah Municipality, courtesy of Juma Al Majid Center for Culture and Heritage.
03. **Corniche Plaza**, Al Salaam Consultants, 1986. Existing. Image: the architect.
04. **Holiday Inn**, David Firmin & Partners, 1978. Existing. Image: the architect, courtesy of Sharjah National Hotels Group.
05. **Verger et Delporte Complex**, Regnault & Partners, 1977. Existing. Image: the architect.
06. **Federal Hotel**, Gabriel Matta, 1979. Demolished. Image: Myrna Ayad.
07. **Rashid Al Makhawi Building**, Singh & Associates, 1980s. Status unknown. Image: Ramesh Singh.
08. **Cultural Palace**, Arab Engineering Bureau, 1980. Significantly renovated. **Flame Monument (Cultural Square Roundabout)**, Arab Engineering Bureau, 1982. Demolished. Image: Hamid Durani, Honeymoon Studio.
09. **Fatima Al Zahra School**, A. Moez & Moh. Hegazy Architects, 1982. Demolished. Image: the architect.
10. **Palace Hotel**, Mohamed Abd El Aziz Al Sulayeman, 1975. Demolished. Image: Khaleej Times Archives.
11. **Rashid Bin Hadda Building**, Singh & Associates, 1983. Disused. Image: Ramesh Singh.
12. **Garden City Villas**, Professional Group Australia, 1974. Existing. Image: the architect.
13. **Sheikh Abdul Aziz bin Rashed Al Nuaimi Building**, Momen Architects (Galal Momen), 1975. Existing. Image: Ramesh Singh.
14. **Hussein Abdul Rahman Khansaheb Building**, Interplan 4 SA, 1979. Existing. Image: Mark Furrer, Interplan Projekt GmbH.
15. **Chartered Bank Building**, Consulting Architecture & Civil Engineering Bureau, 1976. Existing. Image: the architect.
16. **Sheikh Abdulla Al Qassemi Building**, International Company for Construction & Trade, Ali Nassar, 1976. Demolished. Image: Prema Babu.
17. **Orient Travel Building**, Consolidated Engineering Company (Khatib & Alami), 1974. Existing. Image: Hamid Durani, Honeymoon Studio.
18. **Low-cost housing**, International Consultation Office for Developing & Construction, c. 1978. Demolished. Image: the architect.

19. **Sharjah Municipality**, Momen Architects (Galal Momen, Mostafa Momen), 1976. Demolished, 2015. Image: DAFCO.
20. **Sultan bin Srour Building**, Lucien and Bernard Cassia & Associates. Existing. Image: Dr. Naman Al Jalili Archives Collection.
21. **Sheikh Hassan Mohamed Al Khazraji Building**, Adnan Saffarini Office, 1985. Existing. Image: Ismail Al Zarooni.
22. **DAFCO Tower**, Seymour Harris & Partners, 1979. Existing. Image: DAFCO, courtesy of Sharjah Chamber of Commerce & Industry.
23. **Dasman Mosque**, Engineering Consultants Group, 1978. Renovated. Image: ECG.
24. **Cinema**, Royal Air Force Camp, Tripe & Wakeham, 1962. Unbuilt or demolished. Image: Crown Copyright, by kind permission of the Trustees of the Royal Air Force Museum.
25. **Syed Ahmed Building**, Architectural Consultants (Ashok Mody), 1975. Existing. Image: the architect.
26. **Immeuble Albadi** (later **Prime Hotel**), Helal & Partners, 1982. Renovated. Image: Dr. Naman Al Jalili Archives Collection.
27. **Sharjah Business Centre**, Fowler Hanley Inc., late 1970s. Unbuilt. Image: the architect.
28. **Cement Factory**, Pacific Consultants Company, 1977. Existing. Image: Architectural Press Archive/RIBA Collections.
29. **Abdulrahman Al Zayani & Sons Building**, Alistair McCowan & Associates, 1974. Demolished. Image: Cagdas Frank Shaw & Partners, courtesy of Esra Par.
30. **Khansaheb House**, Mohammad Ben Habib, 1935. Demolished. Image: Amer Khansaheb.
31. **Crescent Petroleum Headquarters**, Design Construction Group, 1974. Demolished, 1996. Image: Crescent Petroleum.
32. **Rashid Lootah Building**, Adnan Saffarini Office, 1988. Existing. Image: Ismail Al Zarooni.
33. **Hassawi Complex**, Khatib & Alami, 1985. Existing. Image: Khaleej Times Archives.
34. **Allied Building (The Deal Building)**, Architectural Consultants (Ashok Mody), 1977. Existing. Image: Ramesh Singh.
35. **Coral Beach Hotel**, Helal & Partners, 1982. Existing. Image: Helal & Partners, courtesy of Nicolas Bou Rjaili.
36. **Sharjah Tower**, Halcrow Group Architectural Practice, 1986. Renovated. Image: Randa Kamal.
37. **Heera Beach Houses**, De Vries, Fairhurst & Partners, 1974. Existing. Image: the architect, courtesy of Sharjah Municipality.
38. **Gulf Star Hotel**, Tecnica y Proyectos, 1976. Unbuilt. Image: TYPSA.

Aden Engineering & Contracting Company was founded by Mohammed Saeed Al Husseiny in Yemen in the 1960s. The company worked on the construction of Sharjah's Sheba Hotel, a commission from the firm's founder.

Mohamed Shawki Afifi (1933–1996, Cairo) trained under Ramses Wissa Wassef and Hassan Fathy and graduated with a bachelor's degree in architecture from the Faculty of Fine Arts, Helwan University. He completed his studies in Paris, where he earned his PhD from the École des beaux-arts, before founding his own practice and teaching architecture in Cairo. In 1971, he established the Architectural Bureau for Tropical Zones with offices in Dubai, Sharjah, and Ras Al Khaimah. In addition to his own office, Shawki Afifi also worked for the UAE Ministry of Public Works & Housing on several housing projects in Sharjah, Dubai, and Abu Dhabi.

Mohamed Bahaei Aliyan (1938–2004, Aswan) studied architecture at Cairo University's Faculty of Engineering, graduating in 1963. After several years working in Cairo, he moved to Abu Dhabi to work as an engineer for the education department in 1968. In 1975, he co-founded Consulting Architecture & Civil Engineering Bureau (CAB) in Sharjah with Fayek Howeedy. He left CAB in 1992 and resumed working as an architect in Cairo in 1993.

Abdulrahman Al Junaidi (b. 1938, Makkah) earned a scholarship that allowed him to study at American University of Beirut in 1956. The American invasion of Lebanon in 1958 forced him to relocate to Syria, where he completed his architectural engineering degree at Aleppo College of Engineering. Besides Sharjah's King Faisal Mosque, Al Junaidi designed many projects for the Saudi government, including Dallah Hospital and the Riyadh headquarters of Saudi Ports Authority and the Ministry of Finance.

Arab Consultants was established by Abdul Razzak Al-Nassar in Kuwait in 1969. The company designed projects in Kuwait and the UAE, where it completed facilities for the Ministry of Foreign Affairs in Abu Dhabi and a Kuwaiti-owned residential tower.

Arab Engineering Bureau (AEB) was founded in 1966 by Egyptian architects Gamal Abdul Haleem and Mohamed Essam Eldin Fahmy in Qatar. In the early 1970s, Fahmy established a second office in Sharjah with Egyptian architect Mahmoud Ali Khalifa. In 1975, the partnership ended, and the two regional offices operated independently until the Qatar branch was sold in 1990 to Ibrahim Mohamed Jaidah. Both the Sharjah and Doha offices are still in operation.

Arabian Contracting Company was founded in Beirut in 1968. It later established branches in the UAE, Qatar, Saudi Arabia, and France. With offices in Sharjah, Abu Dhabi, and Al Ain, the company completed various projects for private developers, such as the GIBCA Building in Sharjah in 1977, and for the government, such as the Emiri Diwan's administrative offices in Abu Dhabi in 1981.

The Architects Collaborative (TAC) was founded in 1945 by Walter Gropius, Norman C. Fletcher, Jean B. Fletcher, John C. Harkness, Sarah P. Harkness, Robert S. McMillan, Louis A. McMillan, and Benjamin C. Thompson. After smaller commissions in the US into the early 1950s, the company began pursuing larger commissions abroad starting in the late 1950s. One of its most significant commissions was the campus design for Baghdad University in 1958. The firm established an office in Rome to oversee foreign projects, including those in the Middle East. In the Gulf, TAC started work in Kuwait in 1968 and in the United Arab Emirates and Saudi Arabia in the 1970s. The firm closed in April 1995.

Architectural Construction Team. See Gulf Design Group.

Architectural Consultants was established in Sharjah in 1975 by Indian architect Ashok Mody and local developer Abdulrahman Bukhatir with an office on Al Arouba Street. The firm operated for five years in Sharjah, during which it designed the hotel that became Al Zahra Hospital, Holiday Inn Khor Fakkan, and housing projects in Dibba and Sharjah.

Mohamed Al Azhari (b. 1937, Latakia, Syria) studied architecture at Technical University Berlin. Upon graduation in 1965, he worked in Berlin for two years and then moved to Sharjah where he established his own office. His mosque prototypes were realized throughout the country.

Ian Banham & Associates was founded in Abu Dhabi in 1976. It oversaw projects throughout the UAE, including the Marbella Club of Sharjah in 1978. The firm, now headquartered in Dubai, has expanded its operations to Qatar, Bahrain, Iraq, and Saudi Arabia.

Nagi Samih Barbir (b. 1940, Lebanon) started his studies in France before completing his bachelor's and master's degrees in civil engineering at American University of Beirut. In 1963, he established a structural engineering practice in the UK. In 1965, he completed advanced studies in prestressed concrete in France. He joined the Conseil exécutif des grands projets de la ville de Beyrouth in 1964. In 1971, he became partner at the firm Code International.

Bechtel completed railway, roadway, and bridge projects before winning the bid to construct the Hoover Dam (Nevada, US) in 1931. In 1947, US government contacts helped the company secure construction contracts for the Trans-Arabian Pipeline, from Eastern Province, Saudi Arabia, through Jordan and Syria to the Lebanese port city Sidon. The company continued work in Saudi Arabia, building airports and Jubail Industrial City. In addition to other buildings in the UAE, the firm also completed Sharjah's Inter-Continental Hotel in 1980.

Beton- und Monierbau was a West German construction company founded in 1895 as G. A. Wayss & Co. The company oversaw contracts in both Europe and the Middle East throughout the 1950s, including the Blombachtal Bridge in Wuppertal and several road and bridge contracts in Iraq. The firm also completed several buildings in Algeria, Nigeria, and Saudi Arabia in the 1960s and 1970s. The company won the contract for Sharjah's Port Khalid in 1963.

Bin Hadda was a contracting firm founded by Saeed Sultan Ali Bin Hadda al-Suwaidi in Sharjah in the early 1960s. It oversaw construction of several buildings for Sharjah including the Municipality Souk and various mosques and housing projects. The firm also completed residential buildings for private clients.

Brian Broughton (b. 1934, UK) completed his architecture studies at the Canterbury School of Architecture. He worked for the design practice Covell & Matthews before joining UK contracting company Richard Costain as chief architect for its Kuwait-based subsidiary. He worked with Kuwaiti architect Ghazi Sultan during the time he set up the architecture arm of Kuwait Engineering Office. In Kuwait in the early 1960s, he founded a design partnership with Keith Page. In a moment of good timing, Page & Broughton pitched a design for Dubai's first full-fledged airport and secured the job. The project led to more projects in the Trucial States, including for Shell Markets M.E. Broughton designed projects in the UK, before opening his studio in Cyprus, while Page managed client relations in the Gulf.

Bucomac was founded in Sharjah in 1976 by Abdulrahman Bukhatir. The firm specialized in manufacturing bricks and concrete blocks for construction. In addition to materials, it also provided contracting services for projects in Sharjah, including 1000 Villas.

Abdulrahman Bukhatir (b. 1940, Sharjah) completed secondary studies in Karachi at BVS Parsi High School, where he learned Urdu and English. In 1958, he relocated to Kuwait to work at Gulf Bank before returning to Sharjah in 1961 to work at Eastern Bank. In 1971, Bukhatir started a concrete-mixing firm and began trading in timber, cement, and steel. He subsequently founded several construction-related firms in Sharjah. In the early 1980s, he lobbied the International Cricket Council as well as the national boards of India and Pakistan to endorse the Sharjah Cricket Association Stadium, which he opened in 1981.

Mesud Cagdas (1929–2012, Northern Cyprus) earned an architecture degree from Brighton's College of Art. He established Cagdas Associates in 1970 in Dubai with branches in Sharjah, Muscat, Abu Dhabi, and London. In April 1982, the firm merged with Frank Shaw & Partners and moved to London soon after.

Bernard Cassia (b. 1936, Turkey) earned his degree in architecture and interior design from the Accademia di Belle Arti in Rome in 1960. He taught at the Lebanese Academy of Fine Arts (ALBA) from 1964 to 1970. In 1958, he co-founded Lucien and Bernard Cassia & Associates with his brother in Beirut and directed the firm's interior design projects until retirement in 2010.

Lucien Cassia (1935–2016, Turkey) attended the Lebanese Academy of Fine Arts (ALBA) in Beirut from 1955 to 1958. He then pursued postgraduate studies at the École des beaux-arts, Institut d'urbanisme in Paris in 1960. He co-founded Lucien and Bernard Cassia & Associates with his brother in Beirut in 1958 and served as a founding principal and managing director until 2012.

Lucien and Bernard Cassia & Associates was founded by brothers Lucien Cassia and Bernard Cassia in 1958 with an office in Beirut. The architecture firm oversaw many projects across the Middle East including in Syria, Saudi Arabia, and the UAE, where an office was established in Abu Dhabi in the early 1970s.

Rifat Chadirji (1926–2020, Iraq) earned his architecture degree at the Hammersmith School of Arts and Crafts (London) in 1952 before returning to Iraq and co-founding Iraq Consult in Baghdad. With his practice, Chadirji designed several prominent buildings in Iraq, including Baghdad Central Post Office. He also designed projects in the Gulf: in Kuwait, he designed the Hamad Residence (1967) and housing blocks; in Abu Dhabi, he completed the National Theatre. In 1983, Chadirji left Iraq for the United States where he taught at Harvard through the 1980s.

Fadi Chammas (b. 1946, Amioun, Lebanon) earned his civil engineering degree at American University of Beirut. After graduating in 1971, he moved to Doha and worked for Orient-Zakhem Construction on Doha's airport project. He later moved to the UAE where he co-founded Al Nahda Contracting & Trading in 1972.

Peter Champion (b. 1942, Australia) earned architectural degrees from the Royal Institute of Technology (Melbourne) and Hobart Technical College (Tasmania) in 1969. He joined Alexander & Lloyd in Sydney in 1970, becoming director in 1980. He was involved in overseas projects including multiple housing projects and laboratories in the UAE.

Chicago Bridge & Iron Company was founded in 1889 as a construction company. It later concentrated on bulk liquid-storage projects as it pursued work in oil exploration outside the US. Its first projects in the Gulf were for Aramco in Saudi Arabia in 1960. In 1965, it built Royal Dutch Shell's petroleum production complex in Qatar. In the UAE, the company supplied

Dubai with underwater oil-storage tanks before building aboveground water-storage tanks for Sharjah. In 2018, the company was acquired by McDermott International, which filed for bankruptcy in 2020.

Code International was an architectural and engineering firm established in 1964 by civil engineer Nagi Barbir, architect Kamal Philippe Mujaes, and accountant Nabil Barbir. From its head office in Beirut, the firm expanded to Sharjah after securing a contract for Al Qassimi Hospital in 1972. Offices were later established in Abu Dhabi and Muscat.

Henri Colboc (1917–1983, Le Havre) graduated from l'atelier Tournon de l'ENSBA in 1942. He earned a degree from the Paris Institute of Urban Planning in 1943. In 1947, he co-founded an architectural practice with Georges Philippe in Paris, a partnership that lasted until 1977. After the partnership ended, Colboc established his own practice Henri Colboc & Partners, through which he designed Abu Dhabi's Zayed Stadium.

Henri Colboc & Partners. See Henri Colboc and Georges Philippe.

Conforce Gulf was established in the early 1970s in Sharjah by Abdulrahman Bukhatir. The contracting firm specialized in construction of hotels, including the Marbella Club and the Inter-Continental Hotel, both in Sharjah.

Consolidated Contractors Company (CCC) was founded in 1952 by three American University of Beirut graduates—Palestinians Kamel Abdul-Rahman, Hasib Sabbagh, and Said Khoury. Based in Homs, Syria, and later Beirut, CCC won contracts to build pipelines in Iraq and a refinery and workers' camp in Aden, Yemen. In 1953, the firm was selected as contractors for the British Royal Air Force in Sharjah. In the early 1970s, CCC completed several projects in Sharjah including the police towers, Al Qassimi Hospital, and Arab Bank. When the Lebanese Civil War broke out in 1975, the company relocated to London before settling in Athens in 1976.

Contracting Marine Engineering was a multidisciplinary firm founded by Egyptian engineer Fikry El Gawly in the 1970s. The Sharjah-based company oversaw contracting for El Gawly's projects designed by architect Ramzi Shaker, including a housing complex in Sharjah and Hotel Aladin.

Contractors Group International was established in Sharjah in 1973 and completed several projects for Sharjah's government, including the Emiri Diwan and Al Seef Palace. The firm was renamed Globe Constructors by a special ruler's decree after its chairman and director died in a plane crash in September 1983. Globe Constructors was behind the construction of many Sharjah monuments including those at Rolla Square and Ittihad Park.

Costain Group was founded in Liverpool in 1865 as a building company, at first concentrating on suburban housing development and mining. It grew in size through overseas contracts, beginning with a railway in Iran in 1939. Costain's first projects in the Gulf included a water distillation plant in Kuwait followed by airports in Bahrain and Dubai in the 1960s.

Alexander Cvijanovic (1923–2019, Belgrade) studied architecture in Paris before continuing at Harvard Graduate School of Design. After graduating in 1954, he worked at The Architects Collaborative from 1956 to 1986. He was responsible for many of TAC's designs alongside Walter Gropius, including the Bauhaus Archive in Berlin, the Rosenthal am Rotbühl porcelain factory in Selb, Germany, and the Inter-Continental Hotel in Sharjah.

Vedat Dalokay (1927–1991, Elazıg) studied at Istanbul Technical University where he earned an architectural engineering degree in 1949. While working for French architect Auguste Perret, he pursued graduate studies at the Sorbonne in Paris from 1952 to 1954. In 1954, he established his own practice in Ankara which delivered such prominent buildings as King Faisal Mosque in Islamabad (1969) and the Islamic Development Bank in Riyadh (1981). In 1974, Dalokay was elected mayor of Ankara.

Dar Al-Handasah was founded by five American University of Beirut professors in November 1956. After securing the commission to design a Kuwait power station in 1958, the company expanded to other cities in the Gulf and greater region, becoming one of the region's largest consulting companies.

Mohamed Salah Darweesh (b. 1937, Cairo) earned a civil engineering degree in 1959 from Ain Shams University. He pursued post-graduate studies in engineering at Illinois Institute of Technology (US) and University of Manchester Institute of Science and Technology (UK) before returning to Cairo. He earned a PhD in structural engineering from Cairo University in 1969. While associate professor at Cairo University, he co-founded International Consultation Office for Developing & Construction.

Darwish Engineering has been in Dubai since as early as 1960, with projects for the airport and Dubai Municipality. In the late 1960s, the company built projects in Abu Dhabi including Mushrif Palace. After the firm built the Union House in Dubai in the 1970s, it established branches in Sharjah, Ajman, and Fujairah. In Sharjah, Darwish Engineering built some of the emirate's first modern architecture, including the BBME and Arab Bank Buildings.

DAFCO (Demas and Al Farhan Engineering & Contracting Co.) was founded by Rashed Demas and Mahmoud Al-Farhan in Sharjah in 1969. DAFCO oversaw the construction of many buildings for Sharjah Municipality, starting with a parking garage, followed by the traffic department building and later Africa Hall, the municipality building, the *musalla al eid*, and the fire department headquarters.

Design Construction Group was established in 1958 by British architects Anthony Irving and Gordon Jones in collaboration with ARKBuild of Beirut. The firm was an association of architects, planners, engineers, and industrial designers, based in Beirut with associated offices in several locations including Britain, Saudi Arabia, and Iran. The firm completed major bank buildings in Kuwait, several projects for Abu Dhabi Petroleum Company, and the First National City Bank building in Dubai.

Jean Dubuisson (1914–2011, Lille) graduated from the École des beaux-arts in Paris in 1939. In the 1940s, he won the Grand Prix de Rome twice. In 1950, he won a design competition with Marcel Lods for 800 dwellings in Strasbourg, with a proposal that defined his career as focused on mass housing and Le Corbusier's legacy. He ran his own practice until his retirement in 1983.

Kanwal Krishan Duggal (1938–1985, Amristar, Punjab, India) graduated from the School of Planning and Architecture in New Delhi in 1967. He practiced architecture in Kuwait, gaining experience in the office of Sabah Abi Hanna. In 1974, he co-founded Gulf Design Group in Sharjah with Karnail Singh Kler and Harbhajan Singh Vedi.

Eastern Contracting Company was established in 1974 by Emirati businessman Abdulrahman Bukhatir. It has been involved in many construction projects in the UAE and other Gulf cities, including the Inter-Continental Hotel and Marbella Club in Sharjah and Holiday Inns in Sharjah, Khor Fakkan, and Abu Dhabi.

Engineering Consultants Group was founded by Mahmoud Sami Abdelkawi and Ashraf Hassan Allouba in Cairo in 1969. In addition to infrastructural projects in Egypt, the firm also contributed to a man-made river project in Libya and other infrastructural and construction projects across the Middle East. In the early 1980s, the firm opened a branch office in Abu Dhabi.

Mohamed Essam Eldin Fahmy (1926–2005, Al Monofiya, Egypt) graduated in 1952 with an architecture degree from the Faculty of Fine Arts, Helwan University, Cairo. He opened Arab Engineering Bureau's branch office in Dubai, along with fellow Egyptian architects Gamal Abdul Haleem and Mahmoud Ali Khalifa. In 1975, Fahmy opened the Sharjah branch of the company.

Michael Fowler (b. 1939, US) graduated with a BS in civil engineering from University of Minnesota in 1965. He was a partner at Fowler Hanley Inc., a Minnesota-based engineering and architecture firm. New commissions in the UAE led the firm to open an office in Sharjah in 1976.

Fowler Hanley Inc. established its Sharjah office in 1976 in partnership with Al Habtoor Engineering Enterprise to facilitate design and construction of the Sharjah Beach Novotel. The office was led by Nick Ruehl, John Hanley, and Michael Fowler and managed by Brian Grimwade. After pursuing projects in Sharjah, Dubai, and Doha, it was forced to close in 1978 due to financial difficulties and lack of commissions.

Ibrahim Gaafar (1917–2006, Cairo) studied civil engineering at Cairo University and earned a PhD in structural engineering from University of Michigan in 1949. Upon returning to Cairo, he worked for the Egyptian National Railways until 1958. He taught at Ain Shams University and Cairo University, where he led the structural engineering department. He founded Gaafar Engineering Consultants in Cairo with Shafik Nasr and Mohamed Salah Darweesh. In the UAE, the company was known as International Consultation Office for Developing & Construction with offices in Sharjah, Dubai, Ajman, and Umm Al Quwain.

George Trew Dunn Beckles Willson Bowes began as a partnership founded by William Pite and R. S. Balfour in London in 1908. With an early reputation for hospital design, the practice earned more varying commissions during Great Britain's postwar rebuilding. In 1975, the office was commissioned by Spinney's Limited to design a supermarket and office building in Sharjah. In the same year, the practice opened a branch in Bahrain in a temporary partnership with Iraqi architect Hameed Abid that lasted until 1976. The firm secured projects including the Bankers Club and Chartered Bank in Bahrain, a Bank of Oman branch in Fujairah, and a supermarket in Amman, Jordan. From 1985, the practice was known as GTD until its dissolution in 2002.

Ahmed Al Ghroobti (b. 1946, Khor Fakkan, Sharjah) attended English-language courses in Washington, DC, and Chicago before enrolling in Portland State University's architecture program from which he graduated in 1970. With Ali Al Shamsi, he co-founded Gulf Consulting Office, the first architecture firm owned and operated by Emiratis. The firm closed six years later when the founders accepted federal government positions.

Gulf Design Group was founded by three Indian architects—Kanwal Krishan Duggal, Harbhajan Singh Vedi, and Karnail Singh Kler—when they moved to Sharjah in 1975. The firm designed projects in India, Sharjah, Bahrain, Iraq, and Kuwait until the partnership ended with the death of Duggal in 1985.

Gulf General Projects Co., also referred to as Gulf General Projects International Co., was founded by Sheikh Butti bin Suhail Al Maktoum in the 1970s. The Sharjah-based firm worked on the SNTTA Building and some of the Bank Street buildings. GGP also worked with Professional Group Australia on the Sharjah Sandgate projects.

Mohammad Ben Habib (1892–c. 1955, Dubai), was a builder and contractor who worked in Sharjah and Ajman. He built projects for Ajman's ruler Sheikh Rashid bin Humaid Al Nuaimi and for the assistant to the British resident agent Khansaheb Hussain bin Hassan, including his house on Sharjah Creek in 1935. He also built Dubai's Al Ahmadiya School.

Sir William Halcrow & Partners, also **Halcrow**, was founded in 1866 and grew in stature and size through large-scale British government contracts. The first project in the Gulf was commissioned in Kuwait in 1952. When work there dried up, British officials invited them to complete harbor studies in Dubai and Sharjah in 1954. Until its acquisition by the US-based conglomerate CH2M, the British firm Halcrow remained an omnipresent actor in the UAE's urban development. In 2017, CH2M was acquired by US-based Jacobs Engineering Group.

Gamal Abdul Haleem (1926–2002, Giza, Egypt) studied at the Faculty of Fine Arts of Helwan University and graduated with an architecture degree in 1953. He co-founded Arab Engineering Bureau in Qatar in 1966. The firm later opened branch offices in Dubai and Sharjah in partnership with Mohamed Essam Eldin Fahmy and Mahmoud Ali Khalifa.

Fred W. Hammond (1926–2012, Great Britain) obtained his architecture degree at Hull School of Architecture (UK) in 1952. Upon graduation, he worked two years in local government service before joining Cable & Wireless in March 1954, where he was appointed chief architect in 1971.

John (Jack) Hanley (1923–1985, US) taught civil engineering at University of Minnesota and was partner at Fowler Hanley Inc, a Minnesota-based engineering and architecture firm. Hanley was based in the US office where he handled Sharjah liaisons until accrued debts led to the office's closing.

Sabah Abi Hanna (b. 1938, Lebanon) studied architecture at American University of Beirut. In 1958, he interned at Kuwait's public works department where he also worked after his graduation in 1959. In 1961, he established his own office in Kuwait.

The J. Seymour Harris Partnership was formed in 1962 upon the British founder's retirement. In the 1970s, the firm designed projects in Damascus, Sharjah, and Manama, among other places. The firm still operates an office in Birmingham under the name Seymour Harris Architecture.

Mohamed El Mahdy Hegazy (1928–2016, Egypt) earned a degree in architectural engineering from Cairo University in 1952. He co-founded A. Moez & Moh. Hegazy Architects in Cairo with Abd El Moez Hussein in 1954. In 1978, he began work as a consulting architect. He was awarded the Certificate of Merit by the Egyptian Engineers Syndicate and by the Sixth Convention of Egyptian Architects, in 1986 and 1990 respectively.

Antoine Helal (1938–2006, Bekaa, Lebanon) obtained his civil engineering degree from Beirut's École des arts et métiers in 1958. He moved to Paris where he studied at the École spéciale d'architecture until 1963 and later obtained an urban planning degree from the Institut d'urbanisme de l'Université de Paris. In 1964, he co-founded Dar El-Emara in Lebanon with Antoine Elias Chamaa. In 1965, he founded Helal & Partners, carrying out works in both Lebanon and, as early as 1968, the Gulf region. While living in the UAE, he also co-founded the Lebanese Business Group.

Helal & Partners was founded by Lebanese architect Antoine Helal in 1965 and opened an office in Abu Dhabi in 1968. The firm opened branches in Sharjah and Al Ain. It designed the Coral Beach and Riviera Hotels in Sharjah. The firm still operates offices in Abu Dhabi and Lebanon.

Fayek Howeedy (b. 1935, Cairo, Egypt) graduated from Cairo University in 1959 with a bachelor's degree in civil engineering and completed his graduate studies at University of Illinois in 1968. In 1971, he founded Howeedy Consultant in Cairo a few years before launching Consulting Architecture & Civil Engineering Bureau (CAB Consulting) in Sharjah in 1972 in partnership with Mohamed Bahaei Aliyan.

Hugh Hubbard Ford (1906–1980, Eastbourne, UK) graduated from London's Bartlett School of Architecture and trained in the offices of British architects Albert Richardson and Aston Webb. He set up his practice in Eastbourne in 1929, eventually expanding with branch offices in London and Brighton and Hove. In the mid-1970s, the office produced low-rise, mixed-use developments along Sharjah's Al Meena Street.

Hubbard Ford & Partners was founded in Eastbourne, UK, in 1929 by architect Hugh Hubbard Ford. In the 1950s, the practice expanded to London, then Brighton and Hove. From April 1980, the practice became known as the Hubbard Ford Partnership, with a head office in London.

Peter Hudson (b. 1940) earned his civil engineering degree at Sheffield University (UK) in 1962, before working for Ove Arup & Partners. Later representing RMJM, Hudson moved to the Trucial States as the firm's local senior engineer to supervise construction of Dubai's new airport runway. In 1974, he established RMJM's UAE office and managed new roadway projects for the Ministry of Public Works & Housing. In 1975, he started his own consultancy firm. Upon his retirement, WSP, now WSP | Parsons Brinckerhoff, acquired his firm. During his time in Sharjah, Hudson served as chairman of several professional committees and as chairman of the Dubai International Arts Centre.

Peter Hudson & Partners, later **Peter Hudson Buckle & Partners**, was founded in 1975 in Sharjah, where the firm designed a number of projects including the Marbella Club in 1978. In 1985, the firm opened an office in Dubai that operated under the name Lootah Hudson Buckle and Partners. The Glasgow office oversaw all structural and civil engineering design work. In 2003, Peter Hudson retired, and the practice was taken over by WSP | Parsons Brinckerhoff, later known as WSP USA.

International Consultation Office for Developing & Construction was a subsidiary of Cairo-based Gaafar Engineering Consultants. It was founded in the UAE in the 1970s by Ibrahim Gaafar, Hassan Ismail, Shafik Nasr, and Mohamed Salah Darweesh with offices in Sharjah, Dubai, Ajman, and Umm Al Quwain.

Interplan 4 SA, a Lucerne-based consultancy and planning firm, was part of Swiss shareholding company IP4, founded in 1973. The firm had offices around the world, with projects in Bahrain, Alexandria, Riyadh, Kuwait, Sharjah, and Abu Dhabi.

Iraq Consult was founded in 1952 by Rifat Chadirji, Abdulla Ihsan Kamil, and Ihsan Sherzad. It is one of Iraq's most prominent twentieth-century architecture and engineering practices. Outside Iraq, the office also pursued projects in Kuwait, the UAE, Bahrain, and Lebanon.

Anthony Robert Irving (1925–2015) completed his architecture studies in 1951 at University of Durham and earned a subsequent postgraduate degree in town planning. In 1955, he began work in the Beirut offices of British architecture firm Farmer & Dark. In 1957, he co-founded Beirut-based Design Construction Group with Gordon Jones. He remained with the firm until 1978 and practiced as a design consultant in London until 1990.

Hosni Iskandar (b. 1931, Asyut, Egypt) graduated with a bachelor's degree in engineering from Cairo University in 1952. He then studied at Harvard University's Department of Urban Planning and Design from 1961 to 1965. From 1965 to 1972, he worked at the Department of Urban and Regional Planning, University of Minnesota. In 1973, Iskandar moved to Beirut where he worked at Dar Al-Handasah until 2010.

Naman Ameen Al Jalili (1922–1994, Mosul) graduated with a BS degree in architecture from Cairo University in 1946. He earned a master's degree in city planning from Harvard University in 1961 and a PhD in regional and town planning from University of Pennsylvania in 1965. In the 1940s, he worked as an architect at Baghdad Municipality and the Ministry of Public Works & Housing. In 1959, the Iraqi Ministry of Construction assigned him to oversee the University of Baghdad master plan being produced by The Architects Collaborative. He became head of the building design department of the Ministry of Public Works in 1965 and was later appointed director general of housing and urban planning and then director general of urban engineering and planning in 1971. In 1977, he was appointed United Nations consultant in the UAE until 1982. He represented the UN in Saudi Arabia from 1982 until 1985. Al Jalili also served as acting director and lecturer at the Institute for Urban and Regional Planning for Postgraduate Studies at University of Baghdad between 1971 and 1976.

Joannou & Paraskevaides was founded by Stelios Joannou and George Paraskevaides in Cyprus in 1961. Its first overseas construction projects were secured in the following years in Libya. In 1969, the company won contracts for the Dhahran Airport in Saudi Arabia, Seeb International Airport in Oman, and later the Abu Dhabi International Airport in the UAE (1981). The company's reach expanded to Greece, Egypt, Algeria, and Jordan. In 2018, J&P went bankrupt and was forced into liquidation.

Gordon Alfred Jones (1930–2000, Kent) completed his architecture studies, including coursework at Brixton School of Building and the Architectural Association, in 1957. After working at UK-based architecture firms, he co-founded Beirut-based Design Construction Group with fellow British architect Anthony Irving in 1957 and ran the firm until 1983. After closing the firm, Jones pursued residential development projects in Florida (US) and served as consultant for various restoration projects in Kuwait.

The Kalpataru Group was founded by Indian billionaire Mofatraj P. Munot in 1967. Today a major Indian real estate developer, the firm's early work in Bombay included residential complexes, towers, and a cultural center. In the early 1970s, the company expanded its operations overseas. In Yemen, Kalpataru built facilities for University of Sanaa and various private developers. In the UAE, the firm collaborated on many projects contracted to Abdulrahman Bukhatir's development companies, including the Bank Street buildings and 1000 Villas in Sharjah, the police headquarters complex in Abu Dhabi, and a mosque in Ajman.

Nabil Kanafani (b. 1937, Lebanon) earned his architecture degree from American University of Beirut in 1962 and an urban planning degree from the Royal Academy of Arts, Copenhagen, in 1964. He worked for several firms including Khatib & Alami where he designed the school prototype for the UAE Ministry of Public Works & Housing. He later worked at Dar Al-Handasah in Lebanon and as a planning consultant for the Riyadh Development Authority in Saudi Arabia. He taught architecture and urban planning at American University of Beirut, Lebanese University, and the Royal Academy, Copenhagen. Kanafani also served as a consultant to the UN Center for Human Settlements (UN-Habitat) in Libya and Yemen from 1990 to 1992.

Mahmoud Ali Khalifa (b. 1938, Egypt) earned his architectural engineering degree at Cairo University in 1956. He moved to Sharjah in 1968 and opened Arab Engineering Bureau with Mohamed Essam Eldin Fahmy and Gamal Abdul Haleem. In 1972, he established his own practice, Architectural Academic Office, which is still operating in Sharjah.

Afzal Ahmed Khan (b. 1945, Pakistan) earned his bachelor's degree in city and regional planning from West Pakistan University of Engineering & Technology in 1968. He worked as a town planner at firms such as Techno Consult Karachi, Engineering Consultants Karachi, and Akbar & Aleem Associates Karachi. In May 1974, he became chief town planner of Sharjah Municipality and, in 1987, chief engineer of the town planning department in Al Ain (Abu Dhabi). In 2005, he returned to Pakistan as chief town planner at Engineering Consultant International (Pvt) Limited Karachi.

Khansaheb Civil Engineering was founded in 1935 by Khansaheb Hussain bin Hassan to secure British government contracts in the Trucial States. Early projects included the Sharjah–Ras Al Khaimah road and Dubai's Al Maktoum Hospital in the 1950s. In Sharjah, Khansaheb built the British-funded trade school in 1959 and was the main contractor of Sharjah International Airport in 1975 through a partnership with India-based Gammon Construction.

Khatib & Alami, one of the Gulf's most prolific architecture and engineering firms, was originally Lebanon-based Consolidated Engineering Company, a merger of Mounir & Partners (Mounir Khatib) with Zuheir Alami's practice in 1964. The firm opened its first international office in Sharjah in 1968, followed by others in Dubai and Riyadh in 1969. It later expanded to other Gulf cities in the 1970s and 1980s.

Emile Khoury (b. 1946, Lebanon) graduated with a BArch from the Lebanese Academy of Fine Arts (ALBA) in 1975. Upon graduation, he worked for offices in Lebanon and Jordan. In 1977, he returned to Lebanon as an in-house architect for the National College of Choueifat. He currently lives in Beirut.

Milan Kovac (b. 1940, Celje, Slovenia) graduated from the architecture department of University of Ljubljana in 1964. Upon completing postgraduate studies in town planning and Japanese at the Royal Academy in Stockholm in 1968, he established his own architecture practice in Stockholm.

Milan Kovac Arkitektkontor was founded in Stockholm in 1968 by architect Milan Kovac. The firm kept offices in Kuwait and the UAE to oversee projects, including those in Muscat and Doha, until 1979. Thereafter, the practice focused on cultural heritage projects in Luxor, Egypt, until 1986 and later worked on projects in Italy and Sweden until 1992. The practice moved to Ljubljana, Slovenia, where it operated until 2005.

Ivor Lloyd (b. 1928, Australia) completed his architectural studies at Sydney Technical College in 1950. In 1972 and 1976, he accepted government invitations to represent Australia as part of a "five-man professional consultants trade mission" to the Middle East. He formed Professional Group Australia to oversee projects in the Middle East from 1968 until the late 1970s. In the mid-1970s, he established PGA Sharjah Ltd. to complete a number of projects in the UAE and elsewhere in the Gulf.

Michael Lyell (1924–2014, East Sussex, UK) graduated from London's Architectural Association in 1949. He worked for Canadian architect Wells Coates in London. In 1951, he established Michael Lyell Associates in London, which he ran until retirement in the 1990s.

Najeeb Maktari (b. 1941, Aden) earned a diploma in architecture from Brighton Polytechnic in Sussex. In 1973, he moved to the UAE to work in the architecture department of the Ministry of Public Works & Housing and to supervise Al Qassimi Hospital's construction. While at the ministry, Maktari supervised the design of several projects including facilities for Al Ain University and the police training school in Al Hamriyah. He also designed Sharjah's Al Riqqa Secondary School and several primary care clinics in the 1970s. In 2005, after thirty years with the ministry, Maktari became architectural advisor to the UAE Ministry of Justice.

Edward Mansfield (1925–2002, Scotland) studied at Southend College in Essex and Regent Street Polytechnic in London. As chief architect at Sir William Halcrow & Partners, he led various Sharjah projects including the 1969 town plan, Al Soor Building, and Al Majarrah Souk.

Carlos Marinas Rubio (b. 1944, Madrid) is a sculptor and designer who studied at the Higher Polytechnic Center in Madrid, Spain. He came to Sharjah in 1978 upon the advice of Egyptian architect Ramzi Shaker. He contributed many public monuments to Sharjah, including the Cultural Palace's Quran monument as well as the city's Majaz and Rolla Square monuments.

Marwan Engineering & Construction Enterprise was established in Dubai in 1976 by Sultan bin Khalifa Al Habtoor to build a residential tower in Sharjah. The firm also built residential and commercial buildings in Abu Dhabi and Dubai.

Al Masaood Engineering & Contracting Company was founded by Mohammad bin Masaood in Abu Dhabi in 1970 as part of Al Masaood Group. The contracting company has worked on several major projects in the UAE, including the Hotel Meridien Sharjah.

Gabriel Matta (b. 1933, Bhamdoun, Lebanon) has been an active engineer since 1969 with offices in Beirut, UAE, and France. He graduated in 1955 from Lebanon's French School of Engineering, later earning his PhD in engineering from Toulouse University in 1958. He taught at American University of Beirut from 1958 to 1966 and at the French School of Engineering from 1967 to 1970.

Alistair McCowan (1926–2020, Inverness, Scotland) was a British consultant engineer with an engineering degree from Glasgow University. After jobs with several engineering firms, he became senior engineer at J. G. L. Poulson in Pontefract, England. In 1970, he established Alistair McCowan & Associates, Consulting Engineers with offices in Pontefract, London, Bahrain, Nigeria, Malta, and the UAE.

Alistair McCowan & Associates was founded in Pontefract, West Yorkshire, UK. The firm housed three engineering divisions: civil and structural, mechanical, and electrical. Projects in the UAE include the Police Training Academy for the UAE Ministry of Public Works & Housing as well as private commissions for houses and residential blocks.

Alan F. Meldrum was Halcrow's resident architect for Sharjah International Airport.

MOBIC Contracting was founded in the early 1970s in Sharjah. Since its establishment, the firm has completed projects including the National College of Choueifat in Sharjah and residential blocks in Ajman and Abu Dhabi.

Ashok Mody (b. 1948, Rajkot, Gujarat, India) graduated in 1971 with a BArch from what is today known as University of Mumbai. His career started at the firm Karani & Sanghoi in Bombay. From 1975 to 1980, he lived in Sharjah where he co-founded Architectural Consultants. In 1981, he returned to Bombay and eventually re-established his design practice. He is currently a partner at Connect Four Design Studio in Mumbai.

Abd El Moez Hussein (1928–1998, Egypt) earned a degree in architectural engineering from Cairo University in 1952. He co-founded A. Moez & Moh. Hegazy Architects in Cairo with Mohamed El Mahdy Hegazy in 1954. In 1978, he began work a consultative architect. He was awarded the Certificate of Merit by the Egyptian Engineers Syndicate and by the Sixth Convention of Egyptian Architects, in 1986 and 1990 respectively.

A. Moez & Moh. Hegazy Architects was founded in Cairo in 1954 by Egyptian architects Abd El Moez Hussein and Mohamed El Mahdy Hegazy. The two founders studied at Cairo University where they earned their architecture degrees in 1952. In February 1968, they opened branches of their design practice in Abu Dhabi and Dubai. The firm established additional offices in Sharjah and Ajman in 1973. They completed several prototypes of schools and housing for the UAE Ministry of Public Works & Housing as well as residential and mixed-use blocks for private clients. The office still operates out of Cairo and the UAE.

Momen Architects & Consulting Engineers was founded in Cairo in 1945 by four siblings Fahmy Momen, Mostafa Momen, Galal Momen, and Atteya Momen. After several prominent government projects in Cairo, including the Maspero television building in 1960, the office expanded internationally in the 1970s with projects in Saudi Arabia and the UAE, where it secured projects for the governments of Sharjah and Abu Dhabi. The UAE projects were designed and supervised by Galal Momen and Mostafa Momen from offices in Sharjah and Abu Dhabi.

Galal Momen (1925–1995, Manfalut, Asyut, Egypt) studied architecture at the Faculty of Fine Arts, Zamalek. Upon graduation, he won a scholarship to study at Paris's École des beaux-arts, graduating with a PhD in 1953. In 1954, he received a degree in city planning from the Sorbonne in Paris. After returning to Cairo, he taught at his alma mater and later became head of the architecture department. He also worked alongside his brothers at the family firm, undertaking several regional and international projects, the most prominent of which is Cairo's Maspero television building.

Mostafa Momen (1922–2005, Qena, Egypt) graduated in 1945 from the engineering faculty of King Fuad I University, now Cairo University. In addition to other degrees, he completed a PhD in political and legal sciences in 1960. He began his architectural career working with his brother Fahmy Momen in 1945. He was the consultant engineer for London's Islamic Festival in 1976.

Robert Montague (b. 1942, Wellington, NZ) studied architecture in Wellington and Auckland from 1960 to 1966. He joined Alexander & Lloyd in 1968 and worked on projects in Oman in 1971 before he was appointed resident manager of Professional Group Australia in the UAE in 1973.

Contracting & Trading Company (CAT) was founded in 1937 by Lebanese entrepreneur and politician Emile Bustani, later with Shukri Shammas and Abdallah Khoury as business partners. CAT's earliest projects were mostly for the British army, including construction of a military base, and an oil pipeline project for Iraq Petroleum Company in 1947. In 1951, CAT merged with Scotland-based Motherwell Bridge Engineering to create the company eventually known as Mothercat. The new partnership won contracts in Kuwait, Syria, Iraq, and Qatar. In 1962, the firm completed its first project in the Trucial States, leading to various contracts to build cement plants across the UAE. In the 1970s, Mothercat opened an office in Sharjah, where it completed a number of projects including the Sharjah Sports Club.

Kamal Philippe Mujaes (b. 1936, Lebanon) studied architecture at American University of Beirut until 1963. Upon graduation, he worked for Conseil exécutif des grands projets de la ville de Beyrouth until he became partner at Code International in 1971.

Al Nahda Contracting & Trading was established in Doha in 1969. It later expanded operations to the UAE and opened an office in Sharjah in 1972. The company still operates from Sharjah.

Shafik Nasr. See International Consultation Office for Developing & Construction.

Ali Nassar (1919–1996, Egypt) earned his degree in architectural engineering from Cairo University in 1940. In addition to establishing a joint partnership in Cairo, he also worked for Egypt's Army Engineering Corps. In 1948, Nassar left Egypt to join armed forces in Palestine. Until 1956, he held several governmental positions in Egypt, overseeing planning and construction projects for the military. His private practice, International Company for Construction & Trade, which he established in Cairo in 1950, still operates under the management of his daughter, architect Hala Nassar.

Nitco-Miller Ltd was a British-UAE joint venture and a subsidiary of Miller Construction. The Sharjah-based entity was established in the early 1970s to oversee projects across the UAE, including the Sandgate low-rise buildings in Sharjah. The company was associated with Bukhatir Investments Ltd.

Pacific Consultants Co. Ltd has roots in a formerly US-based company later registered in Tokyo in 1954 under Fukujiro Hirayama. The practice cooperated with such architects as Kenzo Tange in Kuwait and Kisho Kurokawa in Saudi Arabia. By the late 1960s, it had secured many projects outside Japan including the Dubai Municipality building, completed in 1979, and the Kuwait University Science Annex, completed in the late 1960s.

Page & Broughton Architects. See Keith Page and Brian Broughton.

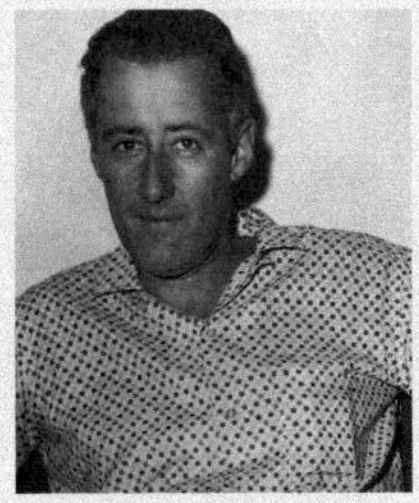

Keith Page (1928–2008, Sheffield, UK) trained as a draftsman with no formal education. He began his career in 1950 at the London-based firm Harrison, Barnes & Hubbard, where he worked on new buildings for University of Ghana, his first overseas projects. In Kuwait in the early 1960s, he co-founded Page & Broughton with Brian Broughton. The partnership completed proposals for an early hospital in Sharjah, the sultan of Oman's palace in Seeb, and Dubai International Airport.

Georges Philippe (1920–2016, Venette, France) graduated from l'atelier Tournon de l'ENSBA in 1941. He pursued graduate studies between 1947 and 1948 and taught at the ENSBA from 1953 to 1963. From 1947 to 1977, he ran an architectural practice with Henri Colboc based in Paris, Montpellier, and Abu Dhabi. After the partnership ended, he worked with Pierre Grégoire until 1985. From 1983 to 1988, he worked on town planning schemes for Morocco with Michel Pinseau, advisor to King Hassan II. He was secretary general and later curator of l'Académie d'architecture from 1993 to 2002.

Józef Zbigniew Polak (b. 1923, Lomza, Poland) graduated in 1949 with an architecture degree from Warsaw University of Technology. From the 1940s through the 1970s, he designed projects in Prague, Brussels, Paris, Kabul, and Chicago, the city where he lived between 1971 and 1974. In 1976, he spent one year in the UAE with short stays in Tripoli, Libya, and Karachi before returning to Poland.

Michael Prodanou (b. 1933, Canada) earned his bachelor's degree in architecture from University of Toronto. Following graduation, he traveled and worked in Europe and Africa before joining The Architects Collaborative. He worked there for ten years on projects in Saudi Arabia, the UAE, and Kuwait. In 1976, he established his own practice, Michael Prodanou Assoc Inc., with projects in the Middle East and North America. He sold his firm in 1999 to pursue painting.

Professional Group Australia (PGA), is a project management and consultancy firm wholly owned by architecture firm Alexander Lloyd Mitchell Gibb. Founded in 1967 as a consortium of professionals, PGA expanded beyond Australia to secure international projects, including those in the UAE. PGA's Sharjah office was located in the Arab Bank building on Al Arouba Street.

Rais & Tukan Architects was established in 1973 by George Rais and Jafar Tukan. Headquartered in Beirut, the firm had branch offices in Abu Dhabi, Dubai, Riyadh, and Amman until the partnership ended in 1976.

George Rais (1915–2002, Lebanon) earned degrees in architecture from Bartlett School of Architecture, the Architectural Association, and the Lebanese Academy of Fine Arts (ALBA). At the start of his career, he worked for the Palestine Mandate Government's public works agency and CAT from 1939 to 1941. He established his own practice in Palestine with operations in Lebanon, Jordan, Switzerland, and the Gulf until forming Rais & Tukan in 1973.

Regnault & Partners was established in Sharjah in 1976 by French architect Jean-Michel Regnault. As of 2020, the office is under new ownership.

Jean-Michel Regnault (b. 1944, Paris) earned his bachelor's degree in France in 1972. He established Regnault & Partners in Sharjah in 1976 after having worked for Henri Colboc & Partners on the design of Zayed Stadium in Abu Dhabi.

Riad Architecture was founded in Cairo by Egyptian architect Mahmoud Riad in 1934. The office designed some of Cairo's iconic buildings including the Arab

League Headquarters, Nile Hilton, Cairo Municipality Building, and the Soviet Union embassy. The practice's urban-scale work included plans for the districts of Mohandessin and Nasr City as well as the industrial city Kafr El Dawar. Upon the founder's death in 1979, his sons Ahmed Riad and Mohamed Riad took over operations until passing the firm on to grandson Mahmoud M. M. Riad.

Mohamed Riad (1942–2021, Cairo) earned his architectural engineering degree from Cairo University in 1967. His professional career began with an internship at AB Vattenbyggnadsbyrån in Sweden in 1965. After graduation, he worked at the Development & Popular Housing Office (DPHO) in Cairo and joined his brother Ahmed Riad at their father's architectural practice. During his time at DPHO, he worked on the master plan for Helwan University (Skidmore, Owings & Merrill) and on the Institute for the Blind in Benghazi, Libya. Riad left DPHO in 1981 and continued work at Riad Architecture, designing projects in Cairo, Oman, Abu Dhabi, and Sharjah, where he collaborated with Arab Engineering Bureau.

Nicolas Bou Rjaili (b. 1939, Lebanon) earned his architecture degree in 1968 from the École des beaux-arts, Paris. He started his own office in Lebanon before moving to the UAE to join his friend Antoine Helal's office in Abu Dhabi. In 1976, he moved to Sharjah to oversee construction of the Coral Beach Hotel. In 1982, he established New Form Consultants, still operating in Sharjah.

RMJM (Robert Matthew Johnson-Marshall) was formed in 1956 as a partnership between Robert Matthew and Stirrat Johnson-Marshall with offices in London and Edinburgh. In the 1960s, the firm expanded internationally. In Saudi Arabia, it worked on development projects in Makkah; its portfolio also included projects in Libya, Iraq, Egypt, and the UAE, where it designed Sharjah Sports Stadium.

Nick Ruehl (b. 1948, US) graduated with a BArch from University of Minnesota in 1971. He managed Fowler Hanley's Sharjah office after its establishment in 1976. He later founded Ruehl + Associates in 2005 and served as mayor of Excelsior, Minnesota, from 2002 to 2012.

Adnan Saffarini (1931–1993, Tulkarem, Palestine) completed his civil engineering studies in 1956 at Cairo University. He started his career at Kuwait's public works ministry before returning to Palestine as municipal engineer in Jenin, Yabad, and Tulkarem. He moved to Dubai in 1967 and worked two years for Al Mulla Group. He founded his Dubai-based firm in 1969, opening offices in Sharjah in 1975 and later in Oman, Jordan, Tajikistan, and Iraq.

Al Salaam Consultants was founded in 1974 by Khalil Khoury with offices in Abu Dhabi, Al Ain, and Beirut. In the 1980s, as the practice expanded, Fadi Assad and Hamdi Natsheh joined its board. In Sharjah, the company designed Corniche Plaza in the mid-1980s and later its twin tower on the neighboring plot.

Saudi Binladin Group (SBG) was founded in 1931 in Saudi Arabia. In the 1950s, the company worked on the expansion of the Prophet's Mosque in Madinah and the Holy Haram in Makkah. In the 1960s, SBG's work extended to road-building and infrastructural projects in Saudi Arabia and other Gulf states. In the late 1960s, the firm established a presence in the UAE and completed several housing and government projects, including Al Qassimi Hospital, the police headquarters, and the civil court in Sharjah.

Setec (Société d'études techniques et économiques) is an engineering and consulting firm founded by Henri Grimond and Guy Saias in 1957. In the 1960s, the Paris-based firm expanded its operations beyond France. The firm was present in Sharjah in the 1970s alongside French architect Jean Dubuisson, who was commissioned to design the unrealized Charles de Gaulle Center.

Adnan Abu Shaar (1926–1974, Damascus) earned his bachelor's degree in Syria and worked for the Damascus Governorate until 1960. He then moved to Berlin where he took courses at the Private Technical School until 1966. Upon graduation, he moved to Sharjah and established his own practice. In 1972, he traveled to Saudi Arabia to perform the hajj but was not permitted to re-enter the UAE. He remained in Saudi Arabia to work as a teacher and eventually returned to Syria to start an architectural practice with his brother.

Ramzi Shaker (b. 1930, Egypt) earned his BArch in Egypt in 1951. Between 1965 and 1966, he taught architecture at Mansura University in Egypt. He was awarded a scholarship and studied architecture at the Higher Technical School of Architecture of Madrid (ETSAM) until 1967. He then pursued further architectural studies in Seville from 1972 to 1974. He began his work in the Gulf in 1975 after practicing architecture in Egypt and Europe.

Ali Al Shamsi (b. 1940, Sharjah) earned his bachelor's degree in civil engineering in 1972 from Ain Shams University, Cairo. With Ahmed Al Ghroobti, he co-founded Gulf Consulting Office, the first architecture firm owned and operated by Emiratis. The firm closed six years later when the founders accepted UAE federal government positions. Al Shamsi began working with the Ministry of Public Works & Housing in the mid-1970s until he took leave to pursue studies at Northeastern University (Boston) and to earn a master's degree at Northwestern University (Chicago) in 1988. Upon graduation, he returned to the same government ministry.

Kanwar Ramesh Singh (b. 1939, Delhi) studied architecture at the School of Planning and Architecture in Delhi. Following graduation in 1968, he worked for India's public works department. In 1970, he moved to Dubai, where he worked several months for Adnan Saffarini and a year for Page & Broughton. In 1971, he opened Singh & Associates with Hassan Abdullah Al Noman. Singh left the UAE in 1987, and his firm closed in 2005.

Karnail Singh Kler (1938, Amritsar, Punjab, India) graduated in 1967 from the School of Planning and Architecture in New Delhi. He pursued a master's degree in architecture at University of Michigan before finding work in Kuwait. In 1974, he moved to Sharjah to co-found Gulf Design Group with Kanwal Krishan Duggal and Harbhajan Singh Vedi.

Harbhajan Singh Vedi (1937–2013, Lyallpur [Faisalabad, Punjab, Pakistan]) graduated in 1967 from the School of Planning and Architecture in New Delhi. In the early 1970s, he practiced architecture in Kuwait. In 1974, he moved to Sharjah to co-found Gulf Design Group with Kanwal Krishan Duggal and Karnail Singh Kler.

Six Construct is a subsidiary of Société Belge des Bétons (SBB Group) and was established to manage the Belgian company's work in the Middle East after securing the contract to build Abu Dhabi's corniche in 1965. In 1967, it started work on a deepwater harbor in Doha, and in 1968 it won the contract for a port in Dammam, Saudi Arabia. Its first project in Sharjah was the National Cement Factory.

Sogex Contracting & Trading Company was founded by Mustapha Rachad Dernaika and Samir Daher Hamzah in 1971. In 1984, it was acquired by the Bahwan Group and renamed Sogex Oman. The firm built several major projects in Oman, such as Al Ghubrah Power & Desalination Plant and the Hotel Inter-Continental Muscat. Sogex's work in the UAE included residential construction and maintenance of a water and power plant in Fujairah.

Instant Sprung Structures was founded as a Canada-based family business in 1887. In 1977, the company secured its first contract in Sharjah to produce tensile structures for Sharjah Expo. With Sharjah businessman Abdulrahman Bukhatir as its local agent, the company soon thereafter set up a warehouse and a sales office in Sharjah. Its domed structures became a familiar presence in both Sharjah and Dubai.

Mel Stewart (b. 1940, UK) earned his civil engineering degree from Sunderland Technical College in 1963. Upon graduation, he practiced in the UK in the 1960s before working overseas in Saudi Arabia and Oman in the early 1970s. He joined Sir William Halcrow & Partners as resident engineer in Sharjah in 1974. In 1983 he was appointed regional managing director of UAE projects. He worked for Halcrow until 1998, when he was appointed engineering advisor to the ruler of Sharjah, a post he served until 2008. He works in Sharjah as a consultant to Jacobs Engineering Group, which acquired Halcrow through CH2M.

Tecnica y Proyectos S.A. (TYPSA) is an architecture and engineering firm, once a subsidiary of a construction company. It signed its first contracts in the Gulf in 1976. Outside Sharjah, their work in the Gulf included the expansion of Kuwait's sewage system and a university campus in Riyadh.

Jafar Tukan (1938–2014, Jerusalem) graduated from American University of Beirut with a BS degree in architectural engineering. Upon graduation in 1960, he worked for Jordan's public works ministry before joining Dar Al-Handasah from 1961 to 1968. He established his own practice in Kuwait and the UAE before founding Rais & Tukan in 1973.

Jafar Tukan & Partners was established by Palestinian-Jordanian architect Jafar Tukan in 1968 with offices in Kuwait and the UAE. The practice remained in operation until the formation of Rais & Tukan in 1973.

Tunisia & United Arab Emirates Engineering Company was established in Abu Dhabi in the late 1970s after the Arab League's decision to move the Arab Academy for Science, Technology & Maritime Transport from Alexandria, Egypt, to Sharjah. The firm designed and supervised the construction of the new campus's planetarium for astronomy instruction.

Reinder de Vries, apparently born in the Dutch East Indies, arrived in Dubai via Mombasa in the late 1960s and established an architecture firm. In 1970, he co-founded De Vries Fairhurst & Partners with the Scottish engineering firm Fairhurst. The short-lived partnership saw the completion of a number of projects including Sharjah Cinema and the St. George Hotel for Galadari Brothers business group in Dubai. After the partnership ended, De Vries continued to practice under De Vries & Partners with offices in Dubai, Doha, Abu Dhabi, and Sharjah. The firm designed a housing project in Sharjah in 1974 and a residential tower in Dubai in 1979, likely operating in the UAE until the 1980s.

White Young & Partners was formed as a consulting and structural engineering firm in 1964 by Ron Young and Terence White. In the early 1970s, the firm was active in the Middle East with several projects including Abu Dhabi Sports Stadium, Doha Hotel, and Gulf Hotel in Bahrain. They completed Sharjah's Central Souk in 1978.

Tanweer Ahmad Zaidi (b. 1944, Uttar Pradesh, India) earned a BS from Karachi University in 1963 and an engineering degree from NED University of Engineering & Technology (Karachi) in 1967. He worked in Pakistan and Dubai with various consulting firms before joining Sharjah Municipality in 1970. He was chief engineer from 1974 until 1987. For two years, he ran his own firm for projects in Sharjah and Karachi. From 1989 to 2012, he worked for consulting firms until his return to Pakistan.

Al Zarooni General Contracting Company was established in the 1960s in Sharjah by Ismail Mohammad Ahmed Al Zarooni. The firm operates in Sharjah, Dubai, Ajman, and Umm Al Quwain. Projects include 103 social housing units in Sharjah's Dasman district and 140 social housing units in Al Rifa'a and Al Tala'a that were funded by Dubai's ruler Sheikh Rashid bin Saeed Al Maktoum in the early 1980s.

Index

Page references to illustrations are set in italics.

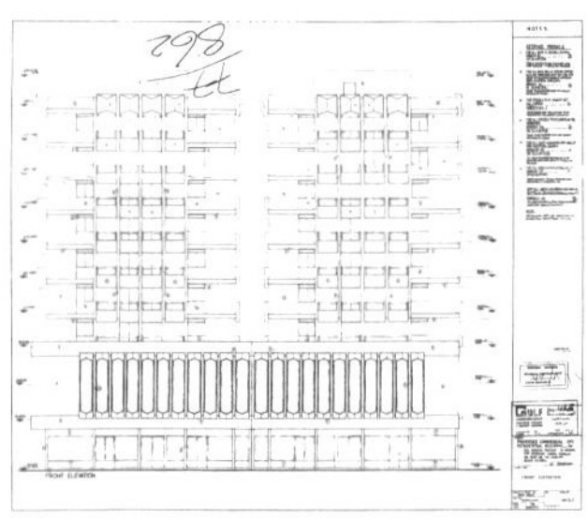